ORTHO'S *All About*

Floors
and Flooring

Written by
Martin Miller

Meredith® Books
Des Moines, Iowa

Ortho® Books
An imprint of Meredith® Books

All About Floors and Flooring
Editor: Larry Johnston
Senior Associate Design Director: Tom Wegner
Assistant Editor: Harijs Priekulis
Copy Chief: Terri Fredrickson
Managers, Book Production: Pam Kvitne,
    Marjorie J. Schenkelberg
Contributing Copy Editor: Steve Hallam
Technical Proofreader: Ray Kast
Contributing Proofreaders: Sara Henderson,
    Beth Lastine, Ron Lutz, Debra Morris Smith
Indexer: Barbara L. Klein
Editorial and Design Assistants: Renee E. McAtee,
    Karen McFadden
Edit and Design Production Coordinator: Mary Lee Gavin

Additional Editorial Contributions from
    Art Rep Services
Director: Chip Nadeau
Designer: lk Design
Illustrator: Dave Brandon

Meredith® Books
Editor in Chief: Linda Raglan Cunningham
Design Director: Matt Strelecki
Managing Editor: Gregory H. Kayko
Executive Editor: Benjamin W. Allen

Publisher: James D. Blume
Executive Director, Marketing: Jeffrey Myers
Executive Director, New Business Development:
    Todd M. Davis
Executive Director, Sales: Ken Zagor
Director, Operations: George A. Susral
Director, Production: Douglas M. Johnston
Business Director: Jim Leonard

Vice President and General Manager: Douglas J. Guendel

Meredith Publishing Group
President, Publishing Group: Stephen M. Lacy
Vice President-Publishing Director: Bob Mate

Meredith Corporation
Chairman and Chief Executive Officer: William T. Kerr

In Memoriam: E.T. Meredith III (1933-2003)

Photographers
    (Photographers credited may retain copyright ©
    to some photographs.)
Laurie Black
Carpet and Rug Institute
Grey Crawford
DeGennaro Associates
Colleen Duffley
Edward Golich
Bob Greenspan
Wm. Hopkins Sr.
InsideOut Studio
Jon Jensen
Mike Jensen
Jenifer Jordan
Lynn Karlin
Tom McWilliam
Mohawk Industries, Inc.
Pergo, Inc.
Ken Rice
Eric Roth
Rick Taylor
Philip Thompson

All of us at Ortho® Books are dedicated to providing you
with the information and ideas you need to enhance your
home and garden. We welcome your comments and
suggestions about this book. Write to us at:
    Meredith Corporation
    Ortho Books
    1716 Locust St.
    Des Moines, IA 50309–3023

If you would like to purchase any of our home improvement,
gardening, cooking, crafts, or home decorating and design
books, check wherever quality books are sold. Or visit us at:
meredithbooks.com

If you would like more information on other Ortho
products, call 800-225-2883 or visit us at: www.ortho.com

Copyright © 2004 The Scotts Company. First Edition.
Some text, photography, and artwork copyright © 2004
    Meredith Corporation. All rights reserved. Printed in the
    United States of America.
Library of Congress Control Number: 2004102048
ISBN: 0-89721-510-9

4

EXPLORING FLOORING

Perhaps more than any other aspect of home remodeling, new flooring sets the tone of a room. It can be a room's dominant feature or it can provide a neutral setting for furnishings and decorating elements.

The floor not only contributes to a room's appearance; it affects its comfort too. So select

Laminate floors such as this one make it easy for do-it-yourselfers to achieve professional looking results. The material comes in planks that snap together and realistically mimic a variety of natural materials, especially wood, stone, and tile.

flooring that looks good and is durable, practical, and appropriate to daily living. If you plan to install the flooring yourself, consider the time you have available and your skill level before choosing a material.

Today flooring comes in more materials, colors, patterns, and styles than ever before, with greater choices in every price range from low-budget to blow-the-budget. This book is packed with information to help you select and install a new floor.

This chapter starts with a comprehensive section on design to familiarize you with color, form, pattern, texture, and theme as it applies to flooring selection. A 10-page gallery of stunning and practical floors follows, to help you envision the look you want. The chapter concludes with other considerations—from cost to comfort to pet compatibility—that you'll want to keep in mind when choosing a floor.

Later chapters show you how to plan and prepare for the installation of your new floor. Illustrated step-by-step instructions show how to install traditional favorites, such as wood, resilient sheet and tiles, ceramic tile, and laminate products.

A dramatic sunburst tile mosaic in this powder room shows that a focal point floor can transform even small, utilitarian spaces into something special.

COLOR

A neutral floor acts as a background for the patterned furniture and draperies in this living room. The carpet's nubby texture keeps it from appearing bland.

Color is the most powerful design element. It's usually the first one we notice about a room and the one that most affects how we feel. To learn to use color effectively, familiarize yourself with these terms:

■ **HUE:** the pure color—red, blue, and yellow are the primary hues.

■ **VALUE:** the relative brightness of a color—the shade of gray it would appear in a black-and-white photo. Colors of lower value (darker ones) usually recede and make a room seem smaller. Those with high values (lighter colors) tend to stand out and make a room appear large and airy.

■ **SHADE AND TINT:** modified hues. A shade is darker than the original hue, as if by adding black. A tint is lighter, as if by adding white. Pink is a tint of red, for instance.

Color, pattern, scale, and texture work together to create a floor that either dominates the room or provides a background for other elements. For example, highly saturated colors complement and harmonize with other hues of the same value. (Examples are dark walnut with blue tile countertops or pastel carpeting with peach walls.) A color scheme with low contrasts lets other decorating elements stand out. Contrasting hues (white and black tile, for example) are forceful; they call attention to themselves. Black—the universal contrast—can make large rooms seem smaller.

Creating a pleasing color combination can require an exercise of restraint. Too much color harmony can be bland, and colors that are too dynamic can be unsettling.

When selecting a color, don't stop with the

first one that appeals to you. You may find another that will work better. For example, you might want a bright blue carpet, but after bringing home samples and looking at them on the floor, you may see that a gray carpet with a subtle blue grid goes with your flowered sofa better.

If you don't want one color to dominate, sprinkle it throughout your design. A dash of your favorite color on black or white or on a neutral tone will tame it. For example, set off pine or stained cherry planking with a light-colored parquet pattern or with one or more accent colors stenciled in a border.

CHOOSING A COLOR

Follow these guidelines when choosing a color for your new flooring:
■ Whether you're buying paint or another kind of floor covering, choose the color—
not the color's name. Fanciful color names can influence you more than you think.
■ Trust your instincts. They reflect the color preferences you'll be most happy with long-term.
■ Narrow your choices to three or four. Take samples of each color home.
■ If you're doing a complete makeover, cover the draperies, carpets, furniture, and fixtures so the colors you have now won't affect your new choices. Compare the flooring samples with paint chips of the new colors as well as new wallcovers and upholstery.
■ Check colors at different times of the day and under different lighting. Sunlight will give the truest hue. Incandescent light adds a pinkish tone. Fluorescence may change the hue completely.
■ Take your time. A couple of days' consideration can help to make sure you've chosen the right color.

Subtle variations in the shade of this floor complement the striped walls and prevent the color from becoming overpowering.

FORM AND PATTERN

Form is the physical shape of the flooring material itself: square tiles, for example, or rectangular planks.

Pattern is the decorative motif on the surface of the flooring: figures, shapes, and colors.

Form and pattern greatly affect a room's mood and style. Small or understated patterns generally soften the mood of a room, but they can also lend an air of informality. Bold, active patterns can be formal or informal; either way, they make the floor a design element in its own right.

Form and pattern are closely related in flooring materials. For example, the form of solid and manufactured wood (and many laminated materials) is linear and rectangular, and so is the pattern it creates. These board floorings can lend varying degrees of formality to a room, depending on the width of the pieces.

Solid wood strips (1½–3 inches wide) with an eased or square edge make a rich, formal looking floor. Plank flooring (3–8 inches wide) looks more informal and serves well in rooms that have a rustic atmosphere.

The subtle pattern of this bedroom carpet is calming and relaxing. The colors harmonize with the room's furnishings.

The wood grain of strip flooring also becomes part of the design. Oak's highly figured grain, for example, weaves a random, active pattern across the floor, which can look dramatic and distinguished. Douglas fir's straight, plain grain, conversely, is well-suited to contemporary or informal rooms. Knots and blemishes in lower-grade woods can enhance informality and reduce costs.

Parquet, which comes in square sections, forms geometric patterns on the floor. So does resilient (vinyl) tile. Parquet almost always creates a formal look, while the effect of resilient tile depends on the pattern of the tile itself and the arrangement in which you lay it.

Ceramic tile carries the concept of designing with form even further. Tile shapes range from small squares or octagons to large, elaborately shaped pieces that can be combined to establish any look imaginable.

Scale is the relative size of the pattern. These guidelines will help you make decisions concerning scale and pattern:

■ Large patterns make a room seem smaller.

■ Large areas generally call for large patterns; small areas usually benefit from small patterns. That's because small patterns can become lost in a large area and large patterns can overpower a small room.

■ The smaller the pattern and the more linear it is (stripes, for example), the more difficult it is to match flooring materials at the seams.

A combination of hardwood, ceramic tile, and stone tile give this custom floor a distinctive elegance. Laminate applied in strip and block patterns could provide a similar look at a more affordable price.

FORMAL OR INFORMAL?

Style generally falls into two broad categories: formal and informal. Symmetrical patterns, straight lines, right angles, and geometric figures characterize formal styles. Informal styles are based on curves, random motifs, or asymmetrical patterns, and natural forms. A formal room usually has an air of seriousness and propriety; an informal one might seem more hospitable or casual.

Within these general styles, you'll find design schemes that relate to eras, places, or architecture—French provincial, Art Deco, Southwestern, and contemporary are a few. Keep your favorite styles—and the predominant style of your home—in mind when shopping for flooring materials.

The geometric pattern created by wood parquet flooring in this foyer provides a striking and formal first impression.

A free-form tile layout in bold colors makes this hallway attractive and inviting.

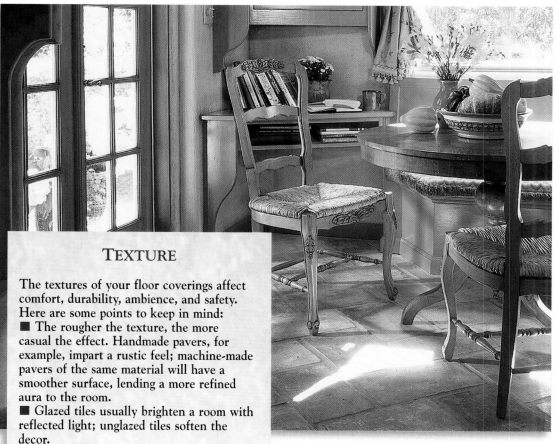

The tile's rough texture lends warmth and informality to this breakfast nook.

TEXTURE

The textures of your floor coverings affect comfort, durability, ambience, and safety. Here are some points to keep in mind:

■ The rougher the texture, the more casual the effect. Handmade pavers, for example, impart a rustic feel; machine-made pavers of the same material will have a smoother surface, lending a more refined aura to the room.

■ Glazed tiles usually brighten a room with reflected light; unglazed tiles soften the decor.

■ Carpet comes in a wide range of textures. Some manufacturers offer the same style, color, or pattern in a variety of textures—heavy-duty, low-loop pile for the playroom and luxurious plush for the living room, for instance.

■ Texture affects safety. Slick surfaces are dangerous at entryways, in kitchens, and near tubs and showers; a roughened surface helps prevent slipping on a wet surface.

■ It's harder to maintain some textures than others. Smooth-textured floors are easier to sweep and mop than rougher-textured ones. Wood, cork, and other materials may require periodic reapplications of protective coatings. Footprints, vacuum-cleaner trails, and lint may be more noticeable on uniform-pile carpeting than on carpeting with uneven pile. The exception is heavy-duty, low-loop pile carpeting.

■ Sound absorption varies with texture. Hard, slick surfaces such as ceramic and stone tile reflect sound; soft surfaces such as carpet absorb sound. Also, soft and textured surfaces tend to muffle footsteps—worth remembering when you consider what flooring to use on stairways and hallways near nurseries and home offices where quiet is precious.

The smooth surface of this wood flooring supports both formal and informal styles.

THE DESIGN THEME

Grain and color combine in this hardwood floor to create a dramatic border around the room's perimeter.

Creating formal and informal themes—or any style—depends on how you use the elements of design. Stripes, squares, and lines in carpet or resilient material can create a strong, formal look. A stenciled border on a plank floor can look cozy, even if it's in bright colors that command attention.

Floral or curved patterns will soften corners and unify floor spaces that might otherwise seem disrupted in a room with nooks and crannies. They will also look harmonious in rooms with curved spaces—under bay windows, for example. Muted greens or blues will enhance this effect.

Random geometric motifs are often employed to add interest to a room with regular dimensions, square corners, and straight walls. If the patterns are in reds and oranges, or in contrasting hues, the appearance can be even more dramatic.

Curves often work together to build a sense of motion. Angular elements oppose and hold each other in place. Geometric pattern elements interact with one another to form an integrated field. An embossed texture can highlight and punctuate a pattern.

Patterns also affect the perception of space within a room. If you extend a linear pattern along the length of a room, you'll make the room look longer and narrower. The same pattern arranged across the width of the room will make the space seem shorter and wider.

Two-foot-square carpet tiles provide a geometric counterpoint to landscape wallpaper in this basement family room. The carpet's beige and rust colors complement this room's earthy theme. The carpet tiles mimic ceramic, complete with faux grout lines, but they're softer underfoot and easier to install than real ceramic—just peel off the backing and stick them down on a smooth, clean floor. They're great for adding instant warmth to basements.

PRETTY IN PAINT

On the next ten pages, you'll see how creative use of flooring materials can enhance any room's appearance. Photos will show that floors can be bold, elegant, playful, or relaxed—and clever effects don't necessarily require a big budget.

Take paint, for example. As a floor finish, it's an often-overlooked alternative. Yet it can be just what the decorator ordered. It's inexpensive and easy to install, too.

This cottage by the sea always had painted pine floors. A high-gloss porch and deck enamel in bright yellow gives new vibrancy to this hallway's rustic boards—and keeps the confined space bright with reflected light. It's easy to clean, too. Cracks between boards and patterns of wear just add to the room's character.

A more muted and restful pastel hue in a softer, satin finish graces a guest bedroom.

A soothing sea green washes up the stairway of this waterfront cottage. The half-moon-shape painted "treads" are practical as well as artful, as they make the steps easier to see.

SPECIAL EFFECTS

An ordinary wood strip floor is given new life with paint. The checkerboard pattern is scaled to the size of the room and features a hand-painted, decorative border.

Paint allows you to execute a custom design quickly, with almost infinite flexibility. For example, a coat of glossy paint can transform a plain softwood floor into a colorful backdrop that imparts a cottage feel to a guest bedroom. Porch and floor enamel is not only inexpensive, it's fairly durable and easy to keep clean with just a broom and a mop. When worn, you can easily refinish it.

Take paint one step further with faux finishes. With a little practice, you can re-create the look of stone, brick, tile, and a host of other expensive flooring materials at a fraction of the cost of the real thing. And don't forget whitewashes, stains, aniline dyes, and wood bleaches, all of which allow you to change the color and tone of natural wood while allowing the beauty of the grain to show through.

If you own a Colonial-style home, you might try your hand at making your own painted-canvas "floor rugs" to add interest to a plain wood floor. If you have a concrete floor, consider dying the material with specially formulated concrete dye. It

penetrates the surface and will never fade, peel, or scratch off. Such dyes can also be sealed with a polyurethane or high-gloss wax.

A new generation of water-based, quick-dry, low-odor, easy-cleanup paints, stains, and clear and tinted polyurethanes make it easier than ever to achieve the results you seek. Such coatings allow you to apply several coats in just one day—without introducing toxic fumes into your home. Soap-and-water cleanup eliminates solvent odors and disposal problems. There's simply no greater decorative effect for the dollar than the creative application of liquid finishes.

For more information on these techniques, check out a book on decorative painting from your local library, or visit a well-stocked home center or paint store. There you'll find information and products that can help you achieve an exotic, custom look at low cost.

Paint in toned-down, antique colors with a pleasing satin finish adds charm to this entry. The treatment really enlivens an expanse of wooden floor.

A floor of whitewashed pine complements the barn-like look of this loft retreat. A compass motif adds bold pattern and a splash of color to the floor in this top-of-the-stairs hallway.

A concrete basement floor was transformed with faux "tiles" that fool everyone. Thanks to an acid stain, the surface is chemically etched with color that won't fade or scuff.

MIXING MATERIALS

The availability of a wide variety of flooring materials has led to the recent trend of mixing materials and finishes for greater impact and design flexibility. Careful measuring, planning, design, preparation, and installation are required to carry off a multimaterial floor, but the result can be well worth the effort.

Wood, tile, stone, laminate, carpet, cork, linoleum, vinyl, solid-surfacing—there's a wider array of flooring materials available now than ever before. You can use your design creativity to mix two, three, or more materials to create added interest underfoot.

Slate tiles inset into carpet with a subtle pattern complement the contemporary design of this entertaining room. The diagonal set of the tiles mimic the bottle racks that zigzag through the wine cellar.

INDUSTRIAL-STRENGTH SOLUTIONS

Heavy-duty materials and finishes developed for commercial and industrial use have obvious functional advantages—and their own aesthetic appeal. Some, like concrete, have been part of residential architecture for eons but are only now coming up from the basement or out from under cover. Others, such as rubber flooring, have just recently become available to homeowners.

Dot-textured rubber floors are a common sight in commercial kitchens. They're easy to clean, offer good traction when wet, and are soft enough to be easy on the feet. This tough material is gaining favor for use in mudrooms and laundry rooms such as this one.

Concrete is not for basement floors alone, nor is it necessarily cold, rough, and dusty. Concrete can be polished on installation to an almost mirror-gloss finish. It takes paints, stains, and waxes wonderfully. This warm, leathery-looking bathroom floor gets its look from a dry pigment that was troweled on after the concrete was poured. The floor was then waxed to a high luster. An added benefit: The sealed floor is impervious to moisture.

Concrete can be stamped with dyes before it cures to mimic other flooring materials—including tile, slate, and rough-hewn stone—at a lower cost. It can also be dyed while being mixed for integral color. Whatever the color or texture, concrete should be sealed after installation to prevent spills from staining the material, and to make it dust-free and easy to clean.

IT'S EASY BEING GREEN

An upsurge in interest in earth-friendly building materials is making some new products available—and rekindling interest in some old favorites. Most are just as durable, easy to apply, and user-friendly as more conventional alternatives. All are made from renewable, environmentally friendly materials that not only conserve resources for other uses but also offer the benefits of less outgassing of volatile organic compounds after installation, helping to preserve good indoor air quality in your home.

Baking each cork tile in a large commercial roaster before installation created the color variations, above, in this floor—the longer a piece is heated, the darker it becomes. Some of the tiles were coated in gloss polyurethane, some in a matte finish, providing a variation in gloss as well as color.

At first glance, you'd might think these tiles are natural stone. But a closer look reveals cork tile. Cork flooring is made from the bark of cork trees, a renewable resource that can be harvested without damaging the trees. Popular in the 1930s, cork is enjoying a resurgence. The natural material is warm and soft underfoot, yet extremely durable—it can be sanded and refinished like wood, and damaged pieces can easily be popped out and replaced.

Linoleum is back, and better than ever. Not to be confused with vinyl, linoleum is made of natural raw materials: Linseed oil, resin, cork, limestone, and wood flout are mixed with pigments, then rolled onto jute backing and dried. As the linseed oil oxidizes, the linoleum becomes harder and more durable than vinyl. Although old-style linoleum was noted for unstable colors that faded over time, today's linoleum offers bright, dependable color choices.

Although bamboo flooring looks much like hardwood, it's actually three layers of grass laminated under high pressure to form planks, then finished with a clear urethane sealer. A quick-growing, renewable resource, bamboo is harder and more stable than oak, so it's long-wearing and highly impact-resistant.

COMFORT, COST, AND COMPATIBILITY

Hard floors can be made more comfortable. The rugs on this wood-plank floor provide comfort and define separate areas of the room.

No matter how beautiful your new floor looks, it will satisfy you over the long run only if it proves to be practical. To pass the practicality test, flooring must meet these three criteria:

■ It must be comfortable.

■ It must be reasonably priced, including the cost of materials, installation, finishing (if applicable), and maintenance.

■ It must be able to stand up to the traffic and activities in the room.

COMFORT

Comfort, like style, usually is a matter of personal preference. Most flooring materials (except carpets and rugs) have hard surfaces. That's because they have to stand up to years of foot traffic.

Ceramic tile and dimensioned stone are the hardest. Wood floors are hard, too, although some softwood species give a little more underfoot than do oak or maple. Cushioned

Ceramic tile is an ideal, easy-care floor in a kitchen or any room where there is high traffic or moisture.

resilient flooring has even more give, but not as much as laminate flooring, which is installed over a foam underlayment. Carpet is softest of all.

Soft flooring offers another aspect of comfort: It helps control the level of noise in a room by absorbing sound. Hard materials reflect sound.

COST

Choose the best flooring you can afford. High-quality flooring usually reduces long-term maintenance and repair expenses and helps enhance the resale value of your home. Cheaper or lower-grade flooring materials are often less durable. Wood flooring, however, is graded primarily on appearance, not strength, so lower grades may wear as well as higher grades.

COMPATIBILITY

Technological improvements in materials, adhesives, and finishes have made almost all flooring materials suitable for any room and any use, but some continue to be considered better choices than others in particular rooms.

Entryways get a lot of use. Foot traffic brings in dampness and grit that will wear away a surface. Solid wood will provide a reasonably durable surface, but even polyurethane finishes for wood are not as hard and durable as ceramic tile.

Bathroom and kitchen floors must withstand moisture, so ceramic tile and

resilient flooring are among the best choices. Textured vinyl tile tends to hide dirt, which makes it an excellent material for kitchens and playrooms.

Manufactured wood, laminate flooring, ceramic tile, and resilient materials are good choices for below-grade floors.

Floor maintenance is not as complicated as it used to be. Most hard-surface materials require only periodic sweeping and damp mopping. Carpet usually stays clean with regular vacuuming.

Laminate flooring is easy to install and maintain, and offers a harder wearing surface than wood.

SAFETY

Consider safety when choosing your new floor. Resilient materials resist damage from moisture in bathrooms, for instance, but can be slick when wet. For safety, choose a resilient flooring material with a pebbled or embossed surface. Glazed ceramic tile is slippery when wet, so be cautious about using it on a bathroom or kitchen floor. If you do install it in wet areas, cover areas subject to spills or water with nonslip rugs. Lay nonslip rugs on hardwood floors, too.

FLOORS AND PETS

Floors are not created equal when it comes to their suitability for homes with pets.

Ceramic tile and stone are the most

Resilient flooring is popular for kitchens and bathrooms because of its water resistance. An embossed surface can improve traction and prevent slips when the floor does get wet.

impervious to claw scratches and damage from "accidents." Glazed tile cleans easily, but tile and stone may be cold and uncomfortable for pets to lie on unless the floor is equipped with a radiant heating system (*see below*).

Wood is not scratch- or stain-resistant, but a hard urethane finish can minimize the potential for damage. The finishes on most manufactured wood products are durable enough to fend off pet scratches.

Resilient sheets and tile—depending upon their composition—fall somewhere between ceramic tile and solid wood in resistance to pet damage. Laminates are very hard and hold up well to scratches and abrasion.

Carpet is the most comfortable flooring for pets and people, but it is also the easiest to stain. When you install carpet, you have to either really trust your pet or be able to respond quickly to remove any stains that occur—ideally, with a water-extraction carpet-cleaning machine.

If your pet sheds profusely, a neutral tone will camouflage hair between vacuuming sessions. Tight-piled carpet will reduce the chances that pet claws will catch in it.

Whatever flooring material you choose, minimize problems by clipping your pet's nails regularly, sweeping the floor at least weekly, wiping up stains and spills immediately, and choosing water bowls with wide bases.

Consider your household pets—their comfort and the potential damage they can do— when you make your flooring decisions.

RADIANT HEATING

In a radiant heating system, hot water flows through tubing in the subfloor, warming the floor, which, in turn, radiates heat into the room. The benefits are many: The systems are highly energy-efficient and virtually silent, heat is constant and evenly distributed, and the warm-underfoot floors are a pleasure to walk and sit on—your pets and young children will love them! Radiant flooring is ideal for mudrooms and baths, where it helps dry damp floors. You can add radiant heat to an existing slab by installing the tubing and pouring new concrete to cover it. Some new radiant heating systems can even be installed over wood floors using a special pourable material.

Although all flooring materials can be used with radiant heat, manufacturers' recommendations for installation of radiant systems vary. Check with your flooring distributor before choosing a material to cover a radiant-heating system. Here are some general guidelines:

■ Dry out concrete slabs by turning on the system about two weeks before laying the floor and gradually increasing temperature. Leave it at maximum for 72 hours, then turn it off for two days to allow the floor to cool before installing.

■ For any flooring materials that require adhesive, ensure that both the flooring material and the adhesive are compatible with the heating system.

■ When installing nail-down flooring, don't puncture the piping when you drive in the fasteners.

■ Repeated temperature changes can damage some flooring. Ask your heating contractor about installing an outside thermostat, which might help your floor maintain a more consistent temperature.

■ Carpet and pad may insulate the floor and keep the heat out of the room. Install carpet pads made specifically for radiant heat.

CHOOSING MATERIALS

Different flooring materials separate areas visually. The marble in this foyer makes an easy transition to the wood in the living room.

Combinations of standard materials can result in an attractive floor. Pine boards and Mexican tiles make up this kitchen floor.

Ceramic tile lends itself to creative designs. Here, the floor's blue mosaic tile and the border pattern repeat on the walls and tub surround.

Wander through any well-stocked retail flooring outlet and you'll discover a large selection of materials. At least one of them is bound to be ideal for each room in your home.

You'll find solid wood and manufactured wood flooring in different species. Some wood flooring comes prefinished so you can see exactly how it will look in the dining room.

The multitude of colors, sizes, and shapes of ceramic tile might inspire you to think about the geometric or free-form patterns you could lay out in a renovated bathroom or kitchen.

The display of carpet—a wide assortment of colors, textures, and sculpted patterns—might be where you find the perfect floor covering for the master suite, guest bedroom, or nursery.

And you're bound to see exciting colors and patterns in the resilients, either sheet flooring or tile, something that would go perfectly in the utility room or offer another choice for the kitchen or bath.

Recent innovations have improved the practicality, style, and affordability of all flooring materials. With few exceptions, most materials will work fine in most rooms today,

and installation has never been easier. Not long ago, a solid wood floor couldn't have been installed in a lower-level office. Manufactured strip or plank flooring makes it possible now—and you can install it yourself in one weekend. New technologies have made carpet longer lasting and more stain and moisture resistant. You may even consider carpet for the kitchen, and at a price you can afford.

All the new choices mean you have to be prepared when you shop for flooring. That's how this chapter will help. On the pages that follow are descriptions of each material, design ideas, and tips on which rooms the materials

and ideas are best suited for. You'll also find out how each one is installed so you can decide whether to hire a professional installer or do the job yourself.

Plush carpet lends an air of comfort and tranquility to this living room without lessening its casual feel.

FLOORING MATERIALS—COMPARISONS

Material	Design Qualities	Uses/Rooms	Skill Level Required	Relative Cost	Durability
Solid wood	Strips and planks create linear and wood grain patterns. Wood tones. Parquet creates geometric layouts.	Popular in—but not limited to—dining rooms, living rooms, and entryways.	Requires moderate skill. Can cover minor irregularities.	High; slightly less costly than ceramic tile.	Durable, but can stain, dent, and fade. Can be refinished. Lasts indefinitely.
Manufactured wood	Same as solid wood strips and planks.	Same as solid wood. Can be installed below grade.	Easy to install. Some forms can cover minor irregularities.	Moderate; much less than solid wood materials.	Same as solid wood.
Resilient materials	Extensive variety of colors and patterns.	Versatile enough for any room. Excellent for kitchens and baths.	Generally easier to install than other materials, but will show unrepaired irregularities in subfloor.	Moderate; similar to costs for carpet. Solid vinyl and complex patterns increase costs.	Can dent, scratch, stain, and fade. Easy to replace.
Laminates	Variety of colors and patterns, including wood grains and ceramic tile look-alikes.	Almost any room that doesn't get wet.	Easy to install. Adapts to some irregularities in floor.	Laminate products are slightly more expensive than vinyl.	Resists dents, warping, rips, and scratches. Won't fade.
Ceramic & stone	Extensive variety of colors, patterns, and textures.	Suited for high-traffic or damp areas.	Layout and installation must be precise. Requires special tools.	In general, the most expensive floor covering.	Properly installed tile and stone is virtually repair free.
Carpet	Diverse colors and patterns. Softer texture than other flooring materials.	Popular for adding comfort to bedrooms, family rooms, and hallways.	Fairly easy, but requires special tools.	Moderate; dense fibers and complex patterns are more expensive.	Least durable of flooring materials. Can stain and wear.

SOLID WOOD FLOORING

Strip flooring is made in- 1½-, 2¼-, and 3¼-inch widths and establishes a strong linear pattern.

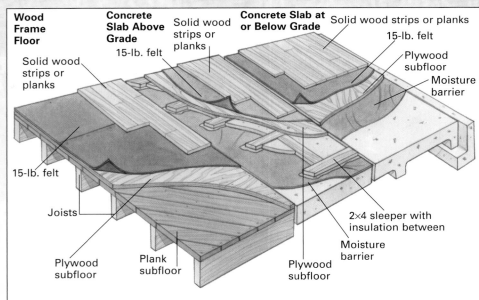

Parquet flooring in square tiles makes a geometric pattern.

The warmth, beauty, and durability of wood make it one of the most popular flooring materials.

Wood can add a feeling of quality, permanence, and livability to any room, and it will last the lifetime of the house if it is properly installed and cared for. The patina that comes with age only improves its appearance.

DESIGNING WITH WOOD

One of the first decisions about a wood floor is whether you want strips, planks, or parquet. Strips and planks make linear patterns. Parquet offers geometric options not possible with strips and planks. However, strip and plank flooring allows more flexibility than its linear form might first suggest. For example, boards lend

Planks are wider than strips—from 3 to 8 inches—and are often used in rooms with country themes.

themselves well to inlays and border designs. In addition, their directional nature can affect the apparent proportions of a room.

A long, narrow room will look more spacious if the strips or planks run across its width. A short room will appear longer if you lay the material parallel to the long walls. (Check the direction of the joists, however—strip and plank must run perpendicular to them unless you add additional underlayment and bridging.)

Although the color range of wood flooring is less than some other materials—ceramic tile, for instance—it is still broad enough to satisfy most design requirements. Colors run the spectrum from deep reds and browns through rich golden tones to almost white, and you can push these extremes by staining or bleaching. Or you can paint a wood floor in a solid color or pattern. Area rugs or larger carpets will add color and pattern to a wood floor. Rugs are also an effective way to set off areas in large rooms with wood flooring.

SOLID WOOD—INSTALLATION AT A GLANCE

Wood Frame Floor

Concrete Slab Above Grade

Solid wood strips or planks

Concrete Slab at or Below Grade

Solid wood strips or planks

15-lb. felt

Solid wood strips or planks

15-lb. felt

Plywood subfloor

Moisture barrier

Solid wood strips or planks

15-lb. felt

Joists

Plywood subfloor

Plank subfloor

2×4 sleeper with insulation between

Moisture barrier

Plywood subfloor

Solid wood flooring is milled in two forms: tongue-and-groove, in which nails are concealed in a strong interlocking joint; and square edged, which you must nail through its surface. Both types of flooring require a solid subfloor, plywood underlayment, and a layer of felt.

Installed over a concrete slab, solid wood usually requires a moisture barrier for either plywood or sleeper installation. Insulation laid between sleepers suppresses noise and helps keep the floor warm on an unheated slab.

Grain in wood products provides textures that range from almost imperceptible to the fully figured patterns of red oak. How the board is sawn also affects the grain pattern. Plain-sawn stock (the least expensive) displays flat patterns along the length of each board. Quarter-sawn boards bear distinguishing cross-grain markings and perpendicular accents. They are the most distinctive wood products and the most costly.

FINISHED OR UNFINISHED?

Both solid and manufactured wood products come either unfinished or with a finish already applied. Choosing one or the other means balancing design with convenience.

■ Unfinished flooring (most solid wood products) lets you color and finish the floor exactly as you want. But finishing on site creates noise, dust, and delays your use of the room.

■ Prefinished floors (most manufactured products) eliminate the mess, noise, and inconvenience of finishing the floor on-site. They come in a wide variety of finishes, but you are more limited in color options than if you finished your own.

SOLID WOOD EDGE PATTERNS

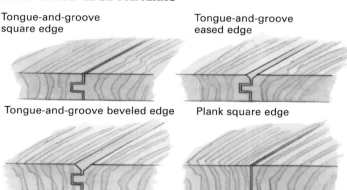

Tongue-and-groove square edge

Tongue-and-groove eased edge

Tongue-and-groove beveled edge

Plank square edge

Solid wood flooring is milled in thickness from ¼ to ¾ inch and widths from 1½ to 8 inches. Edge styles impart different design qualities to a room. A square edge is more formal and a beveled one more informal. Eased-edge flooring is somewhat less expensive and more usable over uneven floor surfaces.

WOOD FLOORING MATERIALS

Species	Color/Grain	Durability	Relative cost	Comments
HARDWOOD				
Red oak	Tan to light pink-red/ Highly figured	Very good	Moderate	Most popular species; stains, finishes well
White oak	Light tan to yellow/ Straight to highly figured	Excellent	Moderate	Works and finishes like red oak
Ash	Light tan to white/ Straight	Very good	Moderate	May be special-order species
Maple/Beech	Light honey to white/ Fine and close	Very good	Moderate	Beech may be special-order
Pecan/Hickory	Honey to light pink/ Open grain	Excellent	High	Hardest wood flooring; may be special order
Birch	Light tan to white/ Open grain	Very good	Moderate	May be special order
Walnut	Dark red to light brown/ Fine to figured	Very good	Expensive	Not a stock species, special order
Cherry	Red to pink/ Moderately figured	Very good	Expensive	Not a stock species, special order
Mahogany	Dark red to brown/ Finely figured	Moderate	High	Not a stock species, special order
SOFTWOOD				
Douglas fir	Golden orange/ Straight	Fair	Inexpensive	Not a stock species, special order
White pine	Pale white/Open grain	Poor	Inexpensive	Not a stock species, special order
Yellow pine	Golden/Open grain	Fair	Inexpensive	Special order

SOLID WOOD FLOORING
continued

Choose wood species based on your design needs, your budget, and your room's wear requirements. Although grading terms vary for different species, the higher grades are generally more attractive and more expensive.

WHAT ROOMS FOR WOOD?

Deciding where to install wood flooring requires balancing aesthetics and durability. In a kitchen, for example, the contrast between warm wood and colder steel and plastic appliances and surfaces enlivens the room and provides a comfortable setting for family gatherings. But kitchens can be wet places, and moisture can damage wood flooring. To resist damage from standing water and spills, a floor must have a waterproof finish—usually polyurethane. Even with this protection, wood floors in kitchens need special attention and immediate action when spills and splashes occur. Acrylic impregnated wood flooring provides even more protection.

On the other hand, living rooms, family rooms, bedrooms, and many multipurpose areas present less-demanding flooring environments. Rugs or carpets can protect wood from scratches and abrasion in places that get hard use. Rugs are also great for separating and delineating areas on a large expanse of floor.

Foyers and entryways cast first impressions, making them a perfect place for features, accents, and borders.

WHAT SPECIES IS BEST?

Flooring comes in more than 30 species, domestic and imported, hardwood and softwood. There really is no best species, but red oak is by far the most popular flooring. Other favorites are white oak, ash, cherry, and maple. Each species has its own specific color range, grain pattern, texture, and density, all of which contribute to the look and feel of the finished floor. Base your flooring choice on design qualities, costs, and durability.

The chart on page 31 compares the qualities of some of the most common species.

Don't be misled by the terms *hardwood* and *softwood* when assessing the durability of wood flooring. Those terms refer to botanical characteristics of the trees that yield the wood, not to the texture or density of the wood itself. Some softwoods are as dense and durable as other hardwoods. (Balsa, for example, is classified as a hardwood.) Some softwood flooring, such as pine, tends to dent easily. Most hardwoods will dent too. Fir or pine flooring develops a rich, warm patina with age.

GRADES

Grades differ by species. Oak and ash, for example, are graded as Clear, Select, Number 1 Common, and Number 2 Common. Maple, beech, and birch are identified as First Grade, Second Grade, Third Grade, or 2nd or 3rd and Better. For all species, grades are based on appearance; strength and serviceability are the same in all grades. Highest-grade flooring, which is nearly free of visual defects, costs the most. The number of blemishes allowed increases as the grade and cost decrease. Don't rule out the lower grades, however; knots, streaks, and spots in the boards can make a highly interesting floor.

BUYING AN OLD HOUSE WITH WOOD FLOORS

What could be more enticing than the patina of a well-maintained wood floor in an old home? Especially in a home you're planning to buy. But old wood can charm you out of your pocketbook after you move in. Investigate a bit before you sign the deal.

■ If the floor is carpeted, pull back a corner or two and check the condition of the floor.

■ If the seller doesn't want you snooping under the carpet, make sure your contract states who is liable for repairs or refinishing.

■ Look for pet stains (a smelly carpet is a sure sign of damage below it)—they almost always require replacement and refinishing.

■ Listen for squeaks, then look further. Squeaks might require only minor subfloor repair, but they could mean damage or structural problems you can't fix easily.

■ Determine what finish is on the floor (you may need a professional to do this). Some new finishes will not adhere to old coatings; most waxed woods will need to be sanded before refinishing.

PARQUET

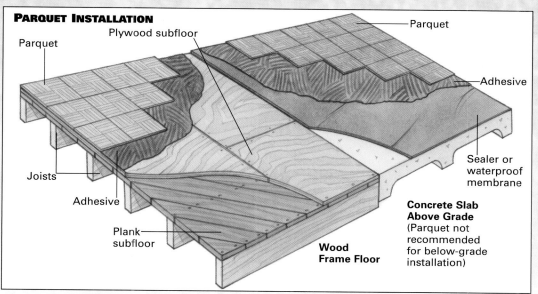

PARQUET INSTALLATION

Parquet
Plywood subfloor
Parquet
Parquet
Adhesive
Joists
Adhesive
Sealer or waterproof membrane
Plank subfloor
Wood Frame Floor
Concrete Slab Above Grade (Parquet not recommended for below-grade installation)

Parquet is usually wood tile manufactured for glue-down installations. It can be laid as shown here or in some cases, directly over solid wood flooring, resilient tile, or sheet flooring (but not on cushioned vinyl or no-wax surfaces).

Once beyond the means of the average homeowner—because the individual strips or *fillets* were cut and assembled by hand—parquet is now prefabricated, affordable, and easy to install.

DESIGNING WITH PARQUET

Parquet is manufactured in hundreds of patterns, each pattern determined by the arrangement and sizing of the fillets. It's a solid wood product, but unlike its strip and plank counterparts, it produces a nondirectional, geometric pattern. Because of this, and because it's made in almost as many species as solid wood strips and planks and in a number of shapes and sizes, parquet lends itself to fascinating design possibilities. You can even purchase individual fillets if you feel like creating your own design. You'll find parquet blocks available unfinished or in a number of prestained and finished styles.

ROOMS AND USES

Parquet does have its limitations. It's sensitive to moisture, so it doesn't work well in bathrooms or on below-grade floors. It must be laid over a completely dry subfloor. Parquet flooring fits into most decorating styles, though it tends to fit formal styles best. Properly sealed and finished, it will work in a kitchen. It makes a stylish surface for entryways and can bring elegance to living and dining rooms. Parquet would be a durable floor for a children's playroom too.

PARQUET CONSTRUCTION

Groove
Tongue
Tongue
Fabric mesh
Tongue
Spline
Groove

Parquet fillets are held together either by a fabric mesh, splines, or a lamination process. Some parquet blocks are cushioned and some are self-sticking. Parquet comes in both tongue-and-groove and square-edge styles, ranging from 5/16- to 3/4-inch thick and in squares, rectangles, octagons, and other shapes, from 4 to 12 inches wide.

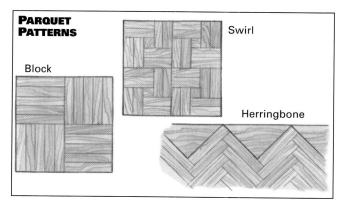

PARQUET PATTERNS

Block
Swirl
Herringbone

MANUFACTURED WOOD FLOORING

Manufactured flooring comes in two configurations— engineered and longstrip. Engineered flooring (above) is one board wide, no matter what its width. Longstrip materials (right) are usually three boards wide which allows you to cover more floor space in a shorter time.

Manufactured wood flooring has become one of the most popular products for do-it-yourself flooring. That's because it offers the rich appearance of solid wood in a form that can be installed by a homeowner over a weekend.

LAYERS OF WOOD

Solid wood throughout, manufactured wood flooring is constructed like plywood, as a sandwich of either three or five layers glued together with the grain of each layer running at 90 degrees to adjacent ones. The top layer, usually about $1/16$ inch thick, is the finish surface or *wearlayer*.

The layered construction results in flooring that is more dimensionally stable than solid wood strips and planks. This means it reacts less to moisture and humidity variations— it won't warp, cup, or buckle. This stability makes manufactured flooring a good choice for installation in damp areas or on below-grade slab floors.

LOWER COSTS, HIGHER WARRANTIES

Because only the top layer is visible, manufacturers can produce standard base layers of less expensive woods, changing only the top layer to meet the demands of their orders. That's why this flooring is more affordable than traditional strip and plank.

Manufactured flooring is graded for appearance based on the finish-surface species. Grades follow those for solid wood flooring of the same species. Manufactured flooring also has something that no unfinished solid-wood products do— a warranty. Warranties commonly cover the floor for from one to five years, but go up to 25 years for some materials. Some products can be sanded and refinished two or three times, depending on the thickness of the top layer. Although in most cases refinishing a manufactured floor is a job best left to the pros, some finishes require only light sanding to touch up a worn surface.

ENGINEERED OR LONGSTRIP?

New products bring with them new terminology. Manufactured flooring is made in two styles: single strips or planks, called *engineered* flooring, and planks with multiple strips (usually three) on their surface, called *longstrip* flooring.

Both styles are constructed with tongues and grooves and are cut to fixed or random lengths from 12 to 60 inches. Most manufactured materials come prestained and prefinished (which also shortens installation time), but some manufacturers produce unfinished products as well.

Not all suppliers and manufacturers use the same terms to describe their products, and the term *laminated* causes some confusion.

ANATOMY OF MANUFACTURED WOOD FLOORING

Manufactured wood flooring comes in thicknesses from 1/4 to 9/16 inch, widths from 2 to 7 inches, and lengths from 12 to 60 inches.

3–5 hardwood layers with grain running perpendicular to one another

Hardwood wearlayer

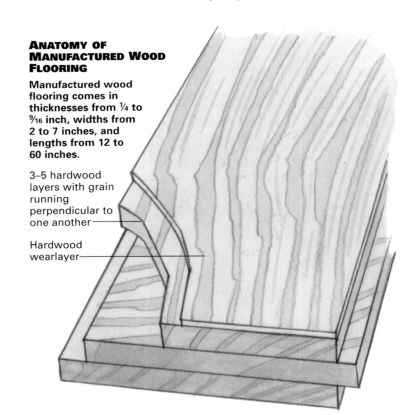

Manufactured flooring is a laminated product (layers glued together) but some suppliers also describe flooring made from synthetic materials, such as plastic laminates, as laminate flooring (see "Resilient and Laminate Flooring," page 36). Talk to the flooring dealer to make sure you get the material you want.

DESIGNING WITH MANUFACTURED WOOD

The pattern of both engineered and longstrip flooring is strips and planks, so they share the same linear design characteristics as solid wood flooring. However, their lower cost can make exotic hardwood surface layers more affordable. Homeowners who had not considered such species as santos mahogany, Brazilian cherry, or teak in a solid-wood tongue-and-grooved floor might find such woods within their financial reach as manufactured flooring.

WHERE CAN I INSTALL IT?

Versatility is a key characteristic of these materials—they can go almost anywhere. You can lay them in kitchens and baths where concern about moisture would rule out solid wood (but don't let spills and water pool on

them). And if you've been looking for a way to convert the basement spare room into an office, this is the flooring you want—even if the current floor is covered with ancient vinyl. Begin any installation over a concrete slab by laying down a moisture barrier.

FLOORING THAT'S A GRASS

While the words *bamboo flooring* might call up visions of the reedlike material used in fences, this is not flooring made like grass mats. It is, however, flooring made from a grass.

Bamboo is a grass, not a tree, and as a flooring material it's making rapid headway as a new and environmentally friendly product—after harvest it regrows to maturity in only 4 years.

Manufacturers cut strips from mature bamboo stems that grow in excess of 6 inches in diameter. Processing the stems removes starch and makes them insect and mildew resistant. The material is kiln dried and laminated in a process similar to other manufactured flooring materials.

Bamboo flooring is available unfinished or prefinished. It sands and finishes like oak (and of course can be refinished), and it can be glued down or nailed down for installation, depending on the manufacturer. Some products are slightly less hard than oak and others are as hard as maple.

MANUFACTURED WOOD FLOORING—INSTALLATION AT A GLANCE

Manufactured strips or planks

Manufactured strips or planks

Foam underlayment

Moisture barrier or waterproofing membrane (may not be required)

Joists

Plywood subfloor

Plank subfloor

Concrete Slab Floor (Floating installation)

Wood Frame Floor (Glue-down installation)

Although some manufactured flooring can be nailed or stapled down, most is designed to be glued to an adhesive bed or to float on a foam underlayment.

Subfloor preparation for both methods is similar to that for other materials, but installation on a concrete slab generally requires a moisture barrier.

In a floated floor, the edges of the material are glued together (but not to the underlayment), locking the entire surface in a single unit (see "Laminate Installation," page 39).

RESILIENT AND LAMINATE FLOORING

Resilients are made from a variety of materials. The most popular are vinyl sheet products and tiles. Their resistance to surface moisture and wide variety of designs make them ideal for kitchens and baths.

Resilient and laminate flooring combine appearance, durability, and ease of installation. Although no flooring is completely dentproof, resilients are able to withstand high compressive shock (dents from furniture, for example) without suffering long-term damage. Resilient flooring includes vinyl products, cork, and rubber.

VINYL SHEET AND TILE

Vinyl has long since replaced the old amalgam of linseed oil, cork, and wood that was called linoleum. (You can still special-order linoleum.) Likewise, vinyl has taken over the tile market from old vinyl asbestos tile (containing fibers that are a health hazard). The technological improvements have brought with them a number of different looks for flooring.

SHEET VINYL is manufactured in two forms—*rotogravure* and *inlaid*. The pattern is printed on the surface of a rotogravure sheet. A cushioned back helps hide imperfections in the underlying floor surface, and the sheet's flexibility makes it easy to install. Inlaid sheet goods are not printed; instead, vinyl chips are fused into the body material to make a pattern that goes completely through the

material. The solid pattern is less subject to wear than an imprinted pattern.

Both materials can be self-coved, curved, and extended up the wall for 4 to 6 inches to allow easy and effective cleaning in kitchens and baths.

VINYL COMPOSITION AND SOLID VINYL TILE differ in their manufacturing process and their vinyl content. Solid vinyl tile contains more vinyl, so it's more resilient—and costly. The pattern and color in both materials are integrated throughout, and both are available in no-wax finishes. Solid vinyl tile has more patterns to choose from, including some that look like hardwood, stone, and ceramic tile. Vinyl composition tile usually has self-stick backings.

CUSHIONED VINYL TILES are the thinnest (and least costly) vinyl tiles. They are made with a thin vinyl layer adhered to a foam backing. These tiles are soft underfoot, but dent very easily.

RESILIENT FLOORING MATERIALS

Inlaid Sheet Vinyl
Clear wearlayer
Inlaid vinyl chips and plasticizers
Backing

Rotogravure Sheet Vinyl
Printed layer
Gel coat
Backing

Vinyl Composition Tile
Vinyl chips and filler throughout

Solid Vinyl Tile
Vinyl chips and filler molded together by heat and pressure

RESILIENT AND LAMINATE FLOORING MATERIALS

	Solid Vinyl	Vinyl Composition	Rubber	Vinyl-Coated Cork	Laminates
Color, pattern, texture	Wide range of colors and patterns. Smooth or embossed surfaces.	Many colors and patterns. Solid and marbleized colors. Smooth or embossed surfaces.	Handful of solid and marbleized colors. Smooth, ribbed, or studded surfaces.	Limited range of natural cork colors. Smooth surfaces.	Wide range of colors and patterns. Surfaces are smooth.
Durability	Grease and oil resistant. Susceptible to heat. Medium- to heavy-duty gauges.	Good for damp areas, properly seamed. Good resistance to chemicals. Light-, medium- and heavy-duty gauges.	Good for damp areas. Resistant to most chemicals. Susceptible to grease and oil stains. Heavy-duty gauges.	Grease and oil resistant. Susceptible to heat. Cushioned, may dent. Medium- to heavy-duty gauges.	Very resistant to most kinds of damage, including stains and dents. Resists scratching.
Resilience	Good resiliency and sound insulation.	Not as resilient or sound insulating as solid vinyl.	Very comfortable underfoot. Good sound insulation.	Very comfortable underfoot. Good sound insulation.	Not resilient, but underlayment offers cushioning and sound insulation.
Maintenance requirements	Damp-mop or sponge-mop; avoid excess water.	Damp-mop or sponge-mop.	Damp-mop or sponge-mop.	Damp-mop or sponge-mop; avoid excess water.	Damp-mop.
Relative Cost	High.	Low to medium.	Medium to high.	Highest.	Moderate.

RESILIENT SHEET AND TILE—INSTALLATION AT A GLANCE

Resilient tile
Adhesive
Resilient sheet flooring
Adhesive
Sealer or waterproof membrane
Joists
Plank subfloor
Plywood subfloor
Concrete Slab Above, at, or Below Grade
Wood Frame Floor

Because resilients are soft, they will show the imperfections of the subfloor. Smooth and fill the surface before laying the flooring. Many resilient materials are ideal for below-grade slabs. All flooring installation on a slab should start with a moisture barrier that is firmly adhered to the surface. Certain wood frame floors may also require a moisture barrier and should be at least 18 inches above ground.

RESILIENT AND LAMINATE FLOORING
continued

RUBBER AND CORK

Rubber and cork are made from natural substances that are able to bounce back from being struck.

RUBBER TILE is limited to only a few colors and patterns, but it is used more these days in kitchens because it is soft underfoot and its studded surface helps prevent slipping. Extremely durable and long lasting, rubber tile can last up to 20 years.

CORK TILE is made with a cork layer sandwiched between a vinyl backing and a clear vinyl top layer. Each tile is unique in color and the pattern of its pores, so it's easy to create a singular design. It also insulates against noise effectively.

LAMINATE MATERIALS

Laminate materials have been used for floors in Europe for almost 20 years. In North America, they are a recent flooring innovation—one that's made to order for today's do-it-yourself market. They provide exceptional durability with moderate cost (somewhat higher than resilients) and easy installation. Like manufactured flooring, laminates are made in layers, with an extremely hard top layer, or *wearcoat*, usually made of melamine impregnated with hardening resins. The wearcoat, which borrows technology employed in the manufacture of laminate countertops, is tough enough to withstand the impact of high-heeled shoes. As on laminated countertops,

ANATOMY OF LAMINATE FLOORING

Clear melamine wearcoat

Print layer

Bonding layer

High density fiberboard core

Melamine backing

the surface resists damage from burns and stains. The flooring's pattern is printed on a film layer beneath the wearcoat. Laminates have tongue-and-groove edges. Some styles fit together with interlocking metal edges that can be unlocked later so you could move this flooring to a different room or take it with you to reinstall in a new home.

AN ARRAY OF DESIGN

Where a beautiful visual effect is the primary concern but practicality is still important, resilient flooring can meet both requirements while keeping the budget under control. Laminates are slightly more costly and come in slightly fewer styles.

You'll find classic resilient patterns reminiscent of the 1930s and 1940s, contemporary neutrals, and a rainbow of designer colors. Sheet materials come in many geometric patterns. Other patterns mimic other materials—ceramic tiles, pavers, cork, brick, and stone. Many laminate patterns look like solid wood, but you can find sandstone and marble patterns, abstract designs, ceramic patterns, and floral designs too. Many laminate products come in plank form. Planks that incorporate square-tile patterns are rapidly gaining in popularity.

Differences in form between resilients and laminates is another consideration when choosing either of them for your floor.

Sheet goods generally come in 6- and 12-foot widths. If the room is larger than the sheet width, you'll have to seam two pieces. Seam placement will affect the look and durability of the floor, so place seams in the least-used section of the room to make them less noticeable and less subject to wear. Joining sheets along a pattern line will make the seam less visible.

Seams don't pose problems with tile or laminate planks and boards. You can lay tile and laminate squares on a grid that's either square or diagonal to the walls. For added interest, set them in a border, a checkerboard pattern, or random designs.

Wood-strip and faux-stone laminate planks have a predominantly linear pattern.

ROOMS AND USES

Resilient and laminate materials can go in almost any room in the house and most are suited for below-, at-, and above-grade installations.

Resilients and laminates can create an expansive, elegant effect, whether they are glossy or matte surfaced, lightly mottled or highly textured, monochromatic or marbleized. The combination of elegance and practicality makes either kind of flooring a good choice for an entryway.

An entryway floor should make a good impression on guests, yet be able to withstand the wear and tear caused by tracked-in dirt and water. If you choose a laminate plank with a solid-wood strip pattern, it could be difficult to tell it from the real thing. Cork flooring makes a striking entryway, too.

Resilient vinyl and rubber flooring resist surface moisture. This makes them ideal for kitchens and other areas where heavy traffic or high activity can lead to soil and spills. Rubber is also an excellent choice in a photographic darkroom, because it is especially resistant to chemicals. Laminates, though tough on top, are susceptible to moisture, so most producers advise against kitchen or bath installations.

Many bathrooms need the softening effects of warm-colored floors to offset the cool look of fixtures. Resilient floors come in a variety of colors to fit any style. The textured surfaces available on resilient flooring help prevent slipping—another important consideration for rooms where moisture is unavoidable and the floor frequently may get wet.

Easy-to-maintain resilient and laminate floors are just right for rooms that are used for play—children's bedrooms and family rooms. Brightly colored tiles, sheet goods, and laminates in lively patterns can enliven a playroom design.

Although resilient flooring installs easily, proper preparation of the subfloor is essential to ensure long wear. The high surface gloss of

Laminate planks are all about the same size—4 inches wide and about ¼ inch thick. They look like wood plank, wood strip, and a variety of stone and ceramic patterns.

Laminate boards come in a variety of sizes, from roughly 7-inch to 2-foot squares, with either a single pattern in stone, abstracts, and florals, or one that mimics tile, complete with grout lines.

most resilient materials will call attention to subsurface defects and irregularities. Unless you prepare a smooth subsurface, sooner or later traffic moving through the room will wear off the finish over these irregularities and wear out the flooring. If you cannot make the subsurface smooth enough, you should choose a different type of material.

LAMINATE FLOORING—INSTALLATION AT A GLANCE

One decision you don't have to make with laminate flooring is how to install it. Laminates are laid over foam underlayment, with their tongue-and-groove edges glued together. The foam cushions the floor to make it feel more resilient underfoot, keeps the glue from adhering to the subfloor, and provides some thermal insulation.

Be sure to use the glue specified by the manufacturer or you may void the laminate warranty, which can be good for up to 25 years.

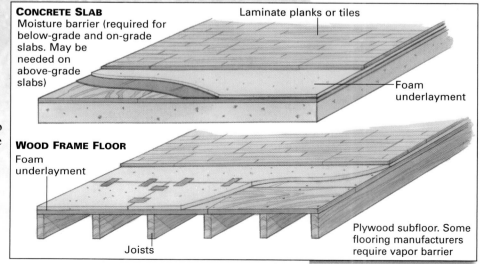

CONCRETE SLAB
Moisture barrier (required for below-grade and on-grade slabs. May be needed on above-grade slabs)

Laminate planks or tiles

Foam underlayment

WOOD FRAME FLOOR
Foam underlayment

Joists

Plywood subfloor. Some flooring manufacturers require vapor barrier

CERAMIC TILE AND DIMENSIONED STONE FLOORING

Ceramic tile and dimensioned stone have their origins in the earth, but their simple beginnings belie their versatility—and beauty—as flooring materials. The terms *ceramic tile* and *dimensioned stone* apply to a variety of products, some more suited to certain installations than others.

CERAMIC TILE

Ceramic tile refers to a clay product that has been baked in a kiln. As you search for the right tile for your floor, you will find these four types:

QUARRY TILE: These tiles are made from red clay and are about ½ to ¾ inch thick. They come in various sizes and shapes (4- to 12-inch squares and hexagons, and rectangles, usually 3×6 inches or 4×8 inches). Tiles can be either semivitreous or vitreous. (See "Water Absorption" on page 42.) The tile is made in natural earth tones—usually red—or can be tinted. Glazed tiles display a rainbow of colors and don't require sealing. Unglazed tiles must be sealed for protection against moisture and stains.

Ceramic tile and dimensioned stone are manufactured in a wide variety of sizes. Your choice of material size depends on the scale of the pattern you're designing, relative to the size of the room.

MORTAR BED

Installing tiles over a mortar bed is one of the oldest and most durable methods of tile installation. It's also the heaviest. If you want to set tile or brick in a mortar bed, make sure your floor can hold the weight.

If the original design of your home included plans for masonry flooring (which is unlikely) the building specifications would have allowed for the extra weight. In new wood frame construction, space the joists on 12-inch centers. If you're planning a tile or brick floor installation in an older home, you'll have to reinforce the floor to comply with your local building codes.

Once the floor is ready, anchor 1× float strips level with and parallel to each other in equal-size sections of the area. Trowel latex additive mortar (available premixed) between them, then drag a wood screed (a 2×4) across the float strips to level the bed. Fill depressions and rescreed, then let mortar cure for 24 hours before setting the tile or brick.

PAVERS: These handmade or machine-made tiles are generally ½ inch to ¾ inch thick. They may be made of any material from porcelain to nonvitreous terra-cotta. Machine-made pavers are made to precise dimensions in a range of colors and textures. Handmade pavers are usually earth toned and rough, which adds to their charm. Most pavers are square, but other shapes are available. Pavers come glazed or unglazed.

MOSAICS: Porcelain, clay, or glass tiles smaller than 2 inches, ranging from ³⁄₃₂ inch to ¼ inch thick, are called mosaic tiles. They are dense and vitreous, and almost always come mounted on a mesh backing.

PATIO TILES: These are thicker than other tiles—up to about 1 inch —and have irregular shapes and sizes. Most of these are unglazed and absorbent.

CEMENT-BODIED TILE

Cement-bodied tiles are made of mortar. Some are molded, others are cut or pressed from a sheet. The tiles are cured, not fired, which makes them less expensive than ceramic materials. Their appearance ranges from the rough appeal of unglazed Saltillo tiles to more costly faux-stone or ceramic surfaces and colorful decorative tile. They are not vitreous so you should not lay them in areas that might freeze.

CERAMIC AND DIMENSIONED STONE FLOORING MATERIALS

	Glazed (quarry, porcelain tile, mosaic)	Unglazed (quarry, porcelain, terra-cotta, pavers)	Cement-Bodied Tiles	Dimensioned Stone
Appearance	4- to 12-inch squares and hexagons (single tiles), 1- to 2-inch mosaics. Other geometric shapes. Rounded or squared edges.	4- to 12-inch squares and rectangles; other geometric shapes. Machine-made—uniform dimensions. Handmade—rustic appearance.	4- to 12-inch squares and rectangles. Often imitates quarry tile or stone, but appearance ranges from rough to sanded and colored.	12- to 24-inch squares and rectangles.
Colors and textures	Wide variety of brilliant and muted colors. Glossy, matte, or textured nonslip surface.	Natural earth tones, some blues, greens, and pastel hues. Matte or textured nonslip surface.	Earth tones to a wide variety of colors.	Unusual colors and veining, depending on origin. Glossy, matte, or honed (nonslip) texture.
Durability	Low to high, depending on method of glazing.	Machine made—high. Handmade—low.	Medium to high.	High.
Maintenance	Low.	Medium. Unglazed tiles require sealing and periodic resealing to resist stains. May be waxed.	Low to medium; depends on material density. Requires periodic sealing.	Most should be sealed for best wear. Sealing darkens slate. Waxing is unnecessary.
Relative Cost	Medium to very high.	Medium to high.	Low.	Medium to very high.

DIMENSIONED STONE TILE

Dimensioned stone tile may either be cut from solid stone and polished or molded from a mix of stone chips and resins. Cut stone can be honed to give it a rougher, slip-resistant surface. You can install both types of stone tile in any locations suitable for ceramic tiles, using the same methods.

Although many types of stone are used, the most popular are marble, granite, and slate. The vitreosity of stone varies—marble is porous, but granite is usually dense. Stone tile requires an absolutely flat subsurface and must be handled carefully to avoid breakage.

Twelve-inch squares are the most common size, but you'll find squares up to 24 inches as well as smaller cut tiles. (You can cut smaller tiles yourself from larger ones.) Stone weighs substantially more than a ceramic tile of the same size. A $\frac{3}{8}$-inch-thick stone tile can weigh close to 6 pounds per square foot. Stone is a classic flooring material, but it is expensive and—because it's heavy and can crack easily—difficult to install.

CERAMIC TILE AND DIMENSIONED STONE—INSTALLATION AT A GLANCE

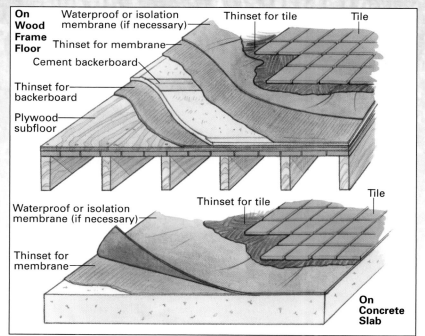

Most tile and stone floors can be installed with thinset mortar. Backerboard provides stability on wood frame floors, but is not required on concrete slabs. Some installations call for waterproof and isolation membranes—one keeps out moisture and the other allows materials to expand at different rates without cracking the tile.

CERAMIC TILE AND DIMENSIONED STONE
continued

IT LOOKS GOOD, BUT...

Tile might look beautiful but not be manufactured to high quality standards. Colorful or elaborately patterned tiles can be as inferior as plain tiles. Density and vitreosity make the difference between high-quality tiles and what the industry classifies as rubbish (tiles with a water absorption rate of 7 percent or more).

TILE GLAZES

Glazes made of lead silicates and pigments are brushed or sprayed onto the surface of the bisque (the tile body) to add color and protect the surface of the tile. Glaze can be applied to the raw bisque before it is fired, or it can be applied to fired tiles, which are then fired again. Glaze gives glazed tiles their color. Additives are sometimes mixed with the glaze to add texture as well. Unglazed tiles get their color solely from the clay.

Glazed ceramic tiles are water-resistant. The grout lines between them are not—unless they are carefully sealed. Unglazed surfaces are water permeable and should be sealed against water absorption.

GRADING SYSTEMS

Ceramic and natural stone are graded according to their quality. Familiarizing yourself with these grades will help when choosing the right tile for your room.

CERAMIC TILE GRADES:
■ **Group 1:** Tile suitable for bathrooms with little foot traffic.
■ **Group 2:** Suitable for residential use, but not in heavy-traffic areas, such as kitchens and entrance halls.
■ **Group 3:** Suitable for all residential areas.
■ **Group 4 & 5:** Tile suitable for various commercial applications.

DIMENSIONED STONE GRADES:
■ **Group A:** Uniform and consistent. You can work these tiles without much fear of breaking them.
■ **Group B:** Similar to Group A, but more prone to breakage and surface damage.
■ **Group C:** Natural variations may increase likelihood of breakage.
■ **Group D:** Often the most beautiful, but also the most likely to break or be damaged.

DESIGNING WITH TILE

No other material offers the design possibilities of tile. With tile, you can control color, form, pattern, scale, and texture.

Your design scheme can draw the eye to a focal point with vivid colors. Or you can rely on a monochromatic scheme to unify other colors in the room. You could repeat different shapes and colors to create an overall motif and rejuvenate a single-colored room or border a checkerboard pattern with contrasting colors, patterns, and shapes. Another option would be to make the checkerboard itself with three or more colors or different glazes.

Your floor can be dignified or bold, quiet or dramatic. Put a floral-and-fruit pattern in

Glazed tiles will brighten a room with their limitless hues and shades. Color is a versatile element, but it must be used with caution to keep it from overpowering the room.

WATER ABSORPTION

Tile varies in its vitreosity—its ability to resist water absorption.

Nonvitreous tile is absorbent. It can absorb more than 7 percent of its weight in water and is not suitable for installations where it will get wet or freeze.

Semivitreous tile has an absorption rate of 3 to 7 percent—not water resistant enough for outdoor use.

Vitreous tile absorbs only .5 to 3 percent of its weight in water, and is ideal for use in almost any location. It's also denser, which makes it stronger.

For most flooring installations, select a tile that resists water—an impervious or vitreous tile. In certain cases, nonvitreous and semivitreous tile will work. Ask your distributor about the vitreosity of a tile and its suitability for your proposed use before you purchase it.

Although the tiles seen most commonly are square, tiles are cut in octagons, hexagons, rectangles, and triangles. You can cut triangles yourself from squares or rectangles.

Texture plays an important role in tile installations. Rough textures provide traction and tend to mute colors. Glossy textures are slick and create or augment modern themes.

the kitchen to celebrate nature's bounty or use stark geometrics if efficiency is desired look.

Re-create a turn-of-the-century interior with 2-inch mosaics. Make the entry to your family room feel like a villa by weaving tiles in an offset pattern. Separate the entry from the living room with a ceramic tile grid. Or use dimensioned stone for a great first impression.

Small tile or small patterns will blend together in a large room to create a single pattern across the floor; large tiles will appear as distinct units. Large tiles will jump out in a small room; smaller tiles will look quiet.

WHERE TO USE TILE

Ceramic and dimensioned stone tile can be used in any room of the house. Tile is a traditional floor surface for kitchens and bathrooms, but be sure you choose a vitreous tile for these installations. Nonslip textures offer additional safety. Unglazed tile does not resist water or staining well enough for use in a kitchen unless you seal it. Use glazed tiles with a matte finish around showers and tubs. Coordinate the decor with the same tile on tub and shower surrounds and on vanities. A family room is another great place to put tile; messes caused by pets, children, or party guests clean up easily. Tiles installed around fireplaces and hearths unify the appearance of the room as well.

Ceramic and stone tiles feel cool to the touch, an advantage in hot weather but not in cold climates. Where the weather gets cold, you can install tile over radiant heating or let it collect solar heat.

WATCH YOUR WEIGHT

The weight of a tile installation—even one installed on a thinset bed—can overstress a wood frame floor enough so you may have to reinforce it to comply with local codes. If you are in doubt about your floor's capacity, consult an architect, builder, or engineer.

Tile thickness will raise the floor level. This may make a tile surface impractical where floor levels are established, where the raised level will interfere with cabinets and appliances, and where raised transitions to other rooms might be awkward. To ease the height difference between different materials, install transitions made especially for this purpose.

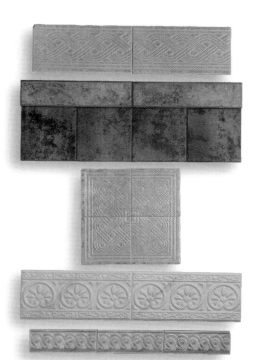

The pattern of a tile installation comes from both the individual tiles and the repeated figures (color, texture, shape, and size) throughout the design.

CARPET

Texture affects the look of a carpeted room. Here, the carpet's sculpted pattern adds dimension to the otherwise neutral background.

With its wide range of colors, fibers, and textures, carpet is the most luxurious of flooring materials. The higher and denser the pile and the thicker the pad, the warmer and quieter the floor is to walk on. Like other flooring materials, carpet comes in a number of grades and qualities and a wide variety of materials. Do your homework before making your final choice.

(see "Styles and Textures" on page 47)

CARPET HOMEWORK

Before you buy, obtain as much information as possible and compare claims and prices. These pages will tell you about different carpet fibers (see chart, opposite) and piles (see "Styles and Textures" on page 47). Some fibers age better than others. The best carpets are made of wool, but modern synthetic fibers combine quality with affordability.

Consider density—the number of yarns per square inch—when you shop for carpet. Generally the more yarn per square inch, the more durable the carpet. Ask friends whether they are pleased with their carpet. Is it wearing well? Is it easy to clean? Has it faded in the sunlight?

HOW IS IT MADE?

The variety of carpet can seem intimidating at first. A look at three of the most common manufacturing techniques will clarify things. **WOVEN CARPET** is similar to a hand-woven rug in that pile material is woven into an integrated backing. Woven carpet won't come apart at the layers and won't snag as easily as others. Woven carpet ranks highest in quality and cost.

TUFTED CARPET is made by sewing loops of pile material through a backing material (the primary backing), which then gets a coat of latex to keep the yarn in place. A secondary backing gives the carpet its stability. This process is extremely cost effective.

NEEDLE-PUNCHED manufacture uses barbed needles to punch the pile through a mesh backing. The pile is locked in and is difficult to unravel, making this kind of carpet ideal for outdoor installations.

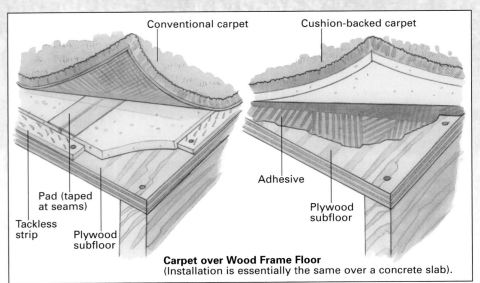

CARPET INSTALLATION AT A GLANCE

Conventional carpet

Cushion-backed carpet

Pad (taped at seams)

Tackless strip

Plywood subfloor

Adhesive

Plywood subfloor

Carpet over Wood Frame Floor
(Installation is essentially the same over a concrete slab).

Installation varies depending on whether the carpet is conventional (with a separate pad) or cushion-backed (with a pad attached to the backing). Conventional carpet requires tackless strips around the perimeter to keep it in place. The pad is laid loose on a wood floor or taped to a slab. Cushion-backed carpet is glued to the floor.

HOOKS AND LOOPS

Manufacturers have taken the hook-and-loop fasteners popular in children's and sports attire to a new level: They've put it on the floor. Hook-and-loop technology eliminates not only tackless strips, but also seaming irons and heat-sensitive tape. The beauty of this carpet is that if you make a mistake, you can lift up the carpet and start all over. And no adhesives means no fumes or odors.

To install this carpet, first press the hook-and-loop tape around the perimeter of the room, leaving its protective cover in place. Then cut the carpet to the exact dimensions of the room (no need for surpluses here), and mark seam locations on the floor.

Dry-lay the carpet in place and butt the seam edges together. Carefully run a pencil line down the center of the seam to mark its location on the floor. Fold both seam edges back and press the 4-inch seam tape to the floor, centered on your mark. Roll the tape to adhere it. Then remove the protective cover on the seam tape, press the seam edges into it and roll the seam. Fasten the edges the same way.

CARPETS AND ALLERGIES

Carpet materials—backings, fibers, dyes, and other products used in its construction—may contain substances that some people are allergic to. Here are some ways to minimize discomfort during installation of new carpet.

■ Purchase carpet and adhesives that meet industry standards for low total volatile organic compound emissions.

■ Increase the fresh air ventilation during installation and afterwards for 48–72 hours.

■ If possible, unroll carpet and let it air out for two to three days before installing it.

■ Vacuum your old carpet before you remove it. Then vacuum the floor or subfloor after taking up the carpet and pad.

■ Remove loose fibers with a vacuum.

■ Keep humidity below 65 percent and vacuum regularly to minimize mite allergens.

THE BACKING MAKES A DIFFERENCE

The quality of the backing will not affect the installation of your carpet, but it will make a difference in maintenance and longevity. Look for a tighter weave (top, at right). A tighter weave usually means that the carpet is denser, more durable, and will stand up better to soils than a carpet with a loose weave (bottom).

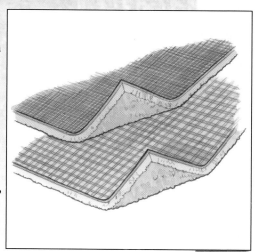

COMPARISON OF CARPET MATERIALS

Material	Resilience	Staining	Abrasion	Fading	Mildew	Cost
Wool	Excellent. Feels springy underfoot.	Very good, but may be difficult to clean.	Very good.	Damaged by long exposure to sunlight.	Requires treatment.	High.
Nylon	Very good. Resists crushing.	Very good. More easily cleaned than wool.	Very good.	Damaged by long exposure to sunlight.	Excellent.	Medium to high.
Polyester	Fair. Susceptible to crushing.	Fair. Cleans well.	Excellent.	Damaged by long exposure to sunlight.	Requires treatment.	Low to medium.
Acrylic	Good. Almost as good as wool.	Good, but must be treated after deep cleaning.	Poor.	Good.	Excellent.	Low to medium.
Polypropylene olefin	Varies with construction and type of pile.	Very good. Doesn't retain dirt.	Very good.	Treated to resist fading.	Excellent.	Low.

CARPET
continued

Carpet unifies this bedroom by incorporating the colors of its furnishings and wallcovering.

This traditional floral pattern will remain stylish for as long as the carpet lasts.

Most of the carpet installed today is tufted carpet made from synthetic material. Carpet also comes with a separate pad (conventional carpet) or with a pad adhered to its backing (cushion-backed carpet).

CARPETS IN DESIGN

A broad expanse of carpet pulls the room together and creates a simple sweep of color, pattern, and texture. Make these features work with—not against—each other. If bold color is important, choose an unsculpted texture and a simple pattern. If you want texture or pattern to be a dominant feature, choose a color that recedes. Soft, organic figures, plants, and leaves go well with other patterns. So do blues and water greens. Thick piles can soften geometric designs.

Textured carpet in a soothing green adds to the casual, relaxing atmosphere of this family room.

A bright, vivid color may be eye-catching on the swatch, but be careful! On a floor of any size, it might overwhelm you. Neutral colors, such as beige, taupe, cream, celadon, and gray provide a versatile background that does not conflict with the overall interior design scheme. They also adapt to changes in room decoration. You'll find them sprinkled throughout other neutral backgrounds in today's carpet designs.

PICKING PATTERNS

Patterned carpet is a textile, so it can have variations in the consistency of the pattern size, configuration, and match from one section to another. Fortunately, manufacturers have established tolerances and instructions that will result in an error-free installation. However, patterned carpet installation is best left to the pros. Here are some things to keep in mind when you contract the job.

■ Use the same criteria for choosing a carpet pattern as you would any other flooring material (see pages 22–27).

■ Installing patterned carpet requires more time and expertise than an unpatterned one—installation costs will be higher.

■ Exact pattern matches are seldom guaranteed, but the eye will not detect variations if the installer follows the manufacturer's instructions. Take your time in choosing a contractor—check references and certifications.

THE LABEL TELLS THE STORY

When you've narrowed your choices down to three or four, check the label on the back of the carpet sample. It tells what the carpet is made of, the width it comes in, warranty details, and its performance rating, based on industry standards.

The performance rating is based on a 5-point scale. A rating of 4 or 5 is best for high-traffic areas. A 2 to 3 will work fine in rooms with less traffic.

If you want a lively accent, look for carpet with bowed patterns or swirls, plaids, and dots. You can find them in cut-and-loop carpets or multilevel loops. The texture of these piles doesn't detract from the pattern, it adds to the feeling of quality.

Carpet pile—whether looped, cut, or sculptured—runs in a definite direction, or nap. To get the best visual effect of color and texture as you enter the room, install carpet with the pile leaning toward the doorway.

Always choose the highest quality carpet you can afford. High-density carpet like this will stand up to heavy traffic and look new for years. The pattern adds impact in this room.

A CARPET FOR EVERY ROOM

Be practical when choosing carpet. Think of the worst things that can happen in your home—muddy shoes, fireplace sparks, spilled cranberry juice—and plan accordingly.

Pattern can help disguise stains. A hard, high-density carpet with a small pattern wears well in heavy-traffic areas, such as kitchens and entrances. It helps camouflage inevitable stains, marks, and scuffs. Select fibers that resist moisture and mildew. For a family room, you'll want a carpet that resists stains and spills but feels soft enough to sit or lie on.

Carpet can make a bathroom cozier, taking the cold edge off of slick surfaces. You can install tile around the shower, washbasin, and tub, and moisture and mildew resistant carpet on the drier sections of the floor.

A single sweep of soft carpet makes the bedroom a more inviting place. It adds warmth on cold mornings and cuts down on noise. Carpet will also reduce noise of stairways and hallways too.

STYLES AND TEXTURES

The style of the pile affects both a carpet's durability and its looks. Here are profiles of some of the more popular styles.

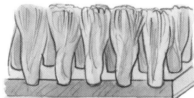

Saxony: smooth, formal, velvety; shows footprints.

Textured saxony: casual, hides footprints.

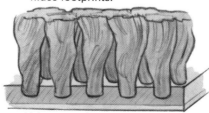

Velvet cut: elegant, shows footprints.

Cut and loop: multi-colored surface looks carved, hides stains.

Multilevel loop: casual, durable, hides footprints.

Level loop: casual and durable, ideal for basement family rooms.

GETTING READY

Preparation and planning are crucial to a successful floor installation. The new flooring will be only one of several layers that make up the floor, and a relatively thin one at that. The flooring's durability and appearance will depend greatly on the foundation under it.

This chapter will acquaint you with the basic steps in planning your project, estimating materials, and installing or preparing a subfloor that will properly support your new flooring. First, you'll find information to help you decide whether you want to contract some (or all) of the job out to a professional, or whether you want to do it yourself.

The first question you should ask is: "Do I really want to do this myself?" The answer is often not easy. Doing it yourself will almost always save money. But cost is only one factor in the decision.

D.I.Y. OR CONTRACT IT?

If you're accustomed to doing home-improvement projects, you'll probably want to tackle your new flooring too. Doing the job yourself will probably save money, although your savings might be less if a contractor includes labor costs in the price of materials. Generally, the less expensive the materials and the higher the labor cost, the more you will save doing the job yourself.

DEALING WITH THE PROS

If you can't decide how you want your room to look, get some help from an interior designer. Interior designers are trained to help you choose design ideas and materials. Even an hour or so with a designer can quickly get you over design hurdles that you might otherwise wrestle with for days. Many home centers and flooring dealers have designers on staff who can help you, often at no charge. Independent designers are listed in the phone directory.

Once you've chosen your materials, you can start planning the installation. Dealers and installers can help you make decisions about installation. But make a list of questions to ask before you contact them. Here are some things you might want to ask:

ASK THE DEALER:
■ Does the material have characteristics that will affect installation?
■ What does the warranty cover, and for how long? Does it specify installation techniques?
■ Do material costs include installation?
■ Can required special tools be borrowed or rented with purchase?

ASK THE INSTALLER:
■ Are costs for moving and replacing furnishings included in the bid?

- How long will the installation take?
- Are disposal costs included?
- What is guaranteed and for how long?

When consulting with a dealer or installer, take along a copy of your dimensioned drawing. Suppliers can accurately estimate costs from it, and an installer will need a copy if he or she is to give you an accurate bid. Once you've gotten information from all sources, plug them into a chart like the one below. But remember—savings represent only one side of the equation. Even if you have the skills to lay wood flooring or ceramic tile, you may want to contract the job out if you have only one weekend available to do the project.

A scale drawing of the room makes planning easier. Start by making a rough sketch, shown on the opposite page. Then take measurements of the room and add them to your sketch. Redraw the room layout on graph paper to create your planning drawing.

CONTRACTOR/D.I.Y. COST COMPARISON

If you decide to do the job yourself, you'll probably save money on materials and labor costs, but you'll take more time to do the job than a pro would. To compare contracted versus do-it-yourself costs, itemize each of the elements shown below. Then consider the D.I.Y. skill level required to do the work and the time you have available.

Contractor costs

1. Subfloor preparation:	
Materials	$
Labor	$
2. Installation:	
Materials	$
Labor	$
3. Additional costs:	
Moving furniture	$
Delivery	$
Finishing, trimming, disposal	$
Total contractor costs	$

Do-It-Yourself costs

1. Underlayment costs:	$
2. Flooring material costs:	$
3. Tools to buy (list):	$
4. Tools to rent (list):	$
5. Supplies:	
Adhesive	$
Grout or wood filler	$
Nails or screws	$
Sealers, stains, finishes	$
Tackless strip for carpet	$
Baseboards, thresholds	$
Other	$
Total D.I.Y. costs	$

PLANNING CHECKLIST

Use this checklist to keep your flooring project organized from start to finish.
- Measure all rooms carefully and calculate their areas.
- Create a scale drawing of the rooms where you plan to install new flooring. Include all dimensions.
- Estimate material quantities, starting with underlayment and other materials required for preparation—adhesives, grouts, tackless strips, and fasteners. Using the area of each room, estimate the amount of any finishing materials you will need.
- Make a list of the tools you'll need. Purchase or rent them.
- Estimate your total costs and do some comparison shopping for the best deals.
- Make a contingent living plan, including the temporary relocation of furniture and anything else you can do to keep disruptions in your life to a minimum.

REQUIRED SKILL LEVELS

Listed below are relative comparisons of the skill levels required for installation of various flooring materials. Consider your proficiency when deciding whether to contract a job or do it yourself.

Solid and manufactured wood	Basic woodworking.
Resilient and laminate flooring	Installing tiles is easy. Sheet goods require accurate measuring and cutting and help with handling.
Ceramic tile and stone	These require precise layout and placement and special tools for cutting.
Carpet	Requires special tools, accurate cutting and seaming, and help with handling.

PLANNING

Whether or not you install the flooring yourself, you'll want to do a certain amount of detailed planning to ensure that the finished job looks and lasts exactly as you expect it to. Planning starts with measuring the room and making a drawing showing the shape and dimensions of the floor. This drawing serves two purposes:

■ Dealers and installers can use it to estimate or bid materials and labor costs.

■ You can compute areas and plan the layout of your materials with the drawing. It will also remind you of any quirks in the room that you should plan for if you lay the flooring yourself. The drawing begins with a sketch.

SKETCHING THE ROOM

Rooms come in an infinite variety of shapes and sizes. Some consist of four straight walls, others have nooks, jogs, and crannies, built-in closets, cabinets, and appliances. When you make your dimensioned drawing, measure everything—exactly. First, make a rough sketch of the contours of the room, identifying appliances, closets, cabinets, doorways, and built-in furnishings.

Then start in a corner and measure the length of every surface to the point where it changes direction. Include the depth of toe-kicks under appliances, cabinets, and other built-in furnishings, and don't forget the area covered by things you will move out of the way, such as the refrigerator. Record the measurements on your sketch. The illustration on the opposite page shows how to check the room for square and curved or bowed walls. Don't be surprised if the room isn't square and regular—rooms seldom are. However, there are ways to accommodate irregularities.

Now transfer your sketch and all of its details to graph paper. Use a scale that is comfortable (¼ inch=1 foot is convenient). Be sure to transfer all of the measurements and irregularities noted on your sketch to the graph paper. If you're planning to install different materials in different rooms, note where each one starts and stops. When you're done, your drawing will look something like the one at left. Now you're ready to make material estimates and move on to some more detailed planning activities.

SCRAPS AND SURPLUS

Even if you plan carefully, you're bound to have material left over. Save it for later repairs.

Resilient and ceramic materials patch easily; repairs cost far less than installing new material. Besides, saved scrap will keep you from having to remember the name of the pattern when a repair is needed. Carpet patches are almost invisible if the materials match. Save some in a dark room and some in a lighted room so you can get the best match if light has changed the color of the carpet on your floor.

MAKING ESTIMATES

Somewhere on your dimensioned plan, compute the total area of each room that will have a new floor. Rooms with four walls and no built-in furnishings or appliances are easy. Simply multiply the length by the width.

Kitchen

Extend flooring under movable appliances and toe-kicks

Family room

Ceramic tile stops here

Parquet stops here

Seams

Reducer strip

Hardwood strip stops here

Carpet

Dining room

Living room

ROUGH MATERIAL ESTIMATES
LR: 18 × 17 = 306 sq ft ÷ 18 (strip or bundle coverage) + 10% = 19 Bundles
DR: 14 × 13 = 182 sq ft ÷ 25 (number of tiles/box) + 10% = 8 Boxes of parquet tile
Kitchen: 9 × 8 = 72 sq ft ÷ 1¹⁄₁₂ (area of 1 tile w/grout) = 67 (number of tiles) ÷ 28 (number of tiles/box) + 10% = 3 boxes of ceramic tile
Family room: 23 x 14 = 322 sq ft ÷ 9 = 35.7 sq yd = 36 sq yd +20% = 43.2 sq yd of carpet

In rooms with nooks, crannies, and closets, you will have to compute the area in smaller sections, then add the results to get the total. You may find it easiest in some rooms to multiply the largest dimensions, then subtract the area occupied by permanent features. Don't forget to include the areas under toe-kicks in your totals.

The information in the charts below and on the following page will help you find reliable estimates for costs of materials and supplies. It will also help you prepare preliminary sketches for laying out the materials. Charts on subsequent pages will help you estimate hardwood materials and grout quantities for tile.

CHANGING YOUR MIND

Now is the time to experiment with patterns and layouts. Pattern choices for solid and manufactured wood are fairly limited—they're almost always installed parallel to the long wall in a room. The same is true for

CHECKING THE ROOM FOR SQUARE

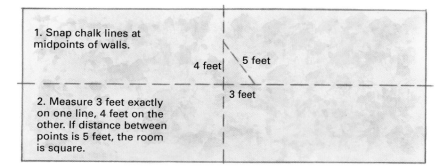

1. Snap chalk lines at midpoints of walls.

4 feet 5 feet 3 feet

2. Measure 3 feet exactly on one line, 4 feet on the other. If distance between points is 5 feet, the room is square.

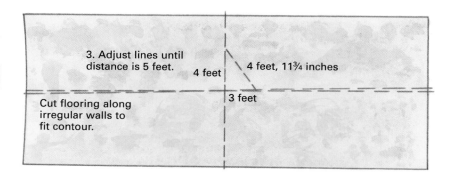

3. Adjust lines until distance is 5 feet.

4 feet   4 feet, 11¾ inches   3 feet

Cut flooring along irregular walls to fit contour.

HOW MATERIALS ARE SOLD

Estimating material quantities is not as exacting as people often assume. All you need to know is how materials are sold and the area of your floor. Then add an allowance for doorways, seams, errors, and waste. The information below will get you started.

Flooring material	Sold by:
Solid wood strips and planks	Sq. ft. in bundles. An 8-ft. nested bundle covers 18 sq. ft. Add 8 to 10 percent.
Manufactured flooring	Sq. ft. Packaging varies by manufacturer.
Tile (parquet, resilient ceramic and dimensioned stone)	Sq. ft. in boxes. Add 8 to 10 percent. The area a box will cover varies with material and style.
Resilient sheet and carpet	Sq. yd. in rolls, commonly 12 ft. wide. Add 4 ft. to each dimension for cutting, 8 to 10 percent for seams and 20 percent for pattern matching.
Laminates	Sq. ft. in cartons. Add 8 to 10 percent. The area of coverage varies with manufacturer and style.

unpatterned carpet, although with any carpet you want the seams to go where the traffic is least. Parquet, resilient, and ceramic tile offer many design possibilities. Experiment on tracing paper laid over your graph paper so you can make changes without erasing and starting over.

DESIGN TOOLS

Your home center may carry design kits that include graphic representations of furniture, appliances, and other decorating features. These kits have stick-on or magnetic profiles of furnishings to help you plan everything to scale. Design programs for home computers are also available from software outlets.

IT'S THE LAST THING YOU DO

Installing a new floor is actually one of the last steps in remodeling a room. If you're planning to paint or wallpaper, do it before tackling any of the floor work. It's a lot easier to clean up the old floor than it is to try to protect your new floor from potential damages from other remodeling projects.

PLANNING
continued

LAYOUT METHODS

SOLID WOOD, MANUFACTURED, AND LAMINATE FLOORING

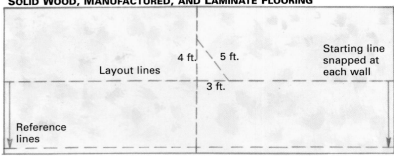

Chalk line adjusted for square

TILE (PARQUET, RESILIENT, AND CERAMIC)

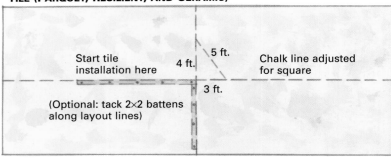

PERIMETER ALTERNATE FOR TILE OR BORDERS

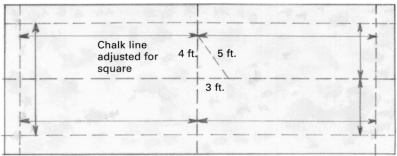

Width of parquet or resilient tile, or width of ceramic tile including grout

ESTIMATING HARDWOOD STRIP FLOORING
(Board feet, assuming 5 percent waste)

Area sq. ft.	Flooring size, inches						
	¾×1½	¾×2¼	¾×3¼	½×1½	½×2	⅜×1½	⅜×2
5	8	7	6	7	7	7	7
10	16	14	13	14	13	14	13
20	31	28	26	28	26	28	26
30	47	42	39	42	39	42	39
40	62	55	52	55	52	55	52
50	78	69	65	69	65	69	65
60	93	83	77	83	78	83	78
70	109	97	90	97	91	97	91
80	124	111	103	111	104	111	104
90	140	125	116	125	117	125	117
100	155	138	129	138	130	138	130

GETTING IT RIGHT

Your new floor will look just right if you align patterns, grout lines, wood grain, carpet pile, and other repetitive features of the material. In other words, the layout of the materials can make or break your design. You'll physically lay out the materials after you have prepared the subfloor, but using layout techniques in the planning stages will keep any mistakes on paper, where they are easy to correct.

LAYOUT METHODS

There are three general methods for laying out a floor. Which one you use depends largely on the flooring material you've chosen. Wood strips and planks almost always begin along or close to one wall. So does carpet. Parquet and other tiles generally start in the center so the materials along the edges can be cut evenly.

All layout methods, however, begin with reference lines at a true right angle at or near the center of the room. Use the 3-4-5 triangle (see page 51) to establish reference lines, and adjust one or both of them until the angle is exactly 90 degrees. Then follow the directions below and in the illustration above left when establishing layout lines. Transfer them to your dimensioned drawing when necessary.

STARTER LINE METHOD: This works for wood strip and plank floors without a border. Establish a starter line at one end of the room by marking the floor an equal distance at each end of your reference line. Tack or chalk a line between your marks and align the first course of flooring on it.

QUADRANT METHOD: Parquet and tile can be laid out this way. The quadrant method makes it possible to create a symmetrical layout in any room (no matter how out-of-square it is) and to finish the installation at opposite walls with cut tiles of equal size.

You begin using this method by establishing the center point. Mark the midpoints of all four walls. Snap a chalk line between each pair of opposite midpoints. If the two chalk lines are not exactly perpendicular to each other, adjust one or the other until they are (use the 3-4-5 triangle). Lay down a trial run of tile in both directions and adjust tiles until borders are even. Begin the installation of each quadrant at the intersection.

PERIMETER METHOD: Lay out bordered floors and some tiled installations this way. Measure from both reference lines toward the wall a distance that equals the full tile (or board) width, plus any allowance for expansion space, grout lines, or irregularities in the wall.

Whatever method you use, test it on paper to see what the final layout will look like before you install the flooring. Consider especially the placement of cut material when installing piece goods, such as tile. Don't lay small pieces of flooring at the edges of the room or across high-traffic areas because they do not look as good or wear as well there as larger pieces.

ESTIMATING ERRORS

Estimating tile quantities isn't always a straightforward mathematical problem. For some materials and styles, the mathematical method of computing room area and dividing it by the amount of coverage in a package of tile will work just fine. In other cases, it will deceive you. For an example, take a look at the layout at top right.

The area of this floor is 79 square feet (182×62 = 11,284÷144 = 78.36). You might believe from that calculation that you would need only seventy-nine 12-inch-square tiles to cover it.

If you purchased cartons of 25 tiles, each of which covered 26.5 square feet (allowing for spacing between tiles), you could assume that 3 boxes, totalling 79.5 sq. ft., would do the job. However, these computations do not take appearance into account.

Edge tiles in a layout should not be less than half the width of a full tile. The layout shows tiles 2 inches wide along two edges.

To fix that, on the graph paper layout remove the 2-inch edge tiles plus one full adjacent tile along the edges. That leaves an uncovered area 14 inches wide along the edges, shown in the middle drawing. Next, shift the remaining full tiles to the center of the layout so the borders will be an even 7 inches all around. Draw in the new edge tiles. You'll find that you need 56 full tiles plus 40 more for the edges—a total of 96 tiles, or four boxes (which will give you four spare tiles).

ESTIMATING GROUT SQ. FT. PER LB.

Tile Size	Joint width, inches					
	1/16	1/8	1/4	3/8	1/2	3/4
1"×1"×1/4"	5.0	2.5	1.0	–	–	–
2"×2"×1/4"	10.0	5.0	2.0	–	–	–
4 1/4"×4 1/4"×5/16"	14.5	7.0	3.0	–	–	–
6"×6"×1/4"	25.0	12.0	5.0	3.5	2.4	–
6"×6"×1/2"	12.5	6.0	2.5	1.7	1.2	–
4"×8"×1/2"	11.0	5.5	2.2	1.5	1.0	–
8"×8"×1/4"	33.0	17.0	6.6	4.5	3.0	2.4
8"×8"×3/8"	22.5	11.5	4.5	3.0	2.0	1.6
8"×8"×3/4"	11.0	5.5	2.7	1.5	1.0	0.8
12"×12"×3/8"	28.0	14.0	7.0	4.5	–	2.0
12"×12"×3/4"	14.0	17.0	7.0	–	–	1.0
16"×16"×3/8"	45.0	22.5	9.0	5.7	3.7	3,0
24"×24"×3/8"	65.0	32.5	13.0	9.0	6.0	4.8

ESTIMATING TILE

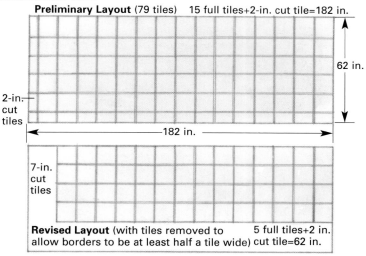

Preliminary Layout (79 tiles) 15 full tiles+2-in. cut tile=182 in.

2-in. cut tiles

62 in.

182 in.

7-in. cut tiles

Revised Layout (with tiles removed to allow borders to be at least half a tile wide) 5 full tiles+2 in. cut tile=62 in.

Final Layout (with more than half tiles on all borders= 96 tiles)

8 1/2 in.

8 3/4 in.

8 1/2 in.

9 in.

When working with tile layouts and estimates, always be sure to include the grout size as part of the area covered by the tile.

GROUT WIDTH

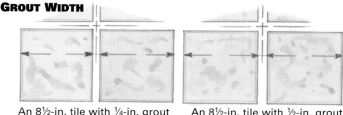

An 8 1/2-in. tile with 1/4-in. grout line covers an 8 3/4-in. square.

An 8 1/2-in. tile with 1/2-in. grout line covers a 9-in. square.

UNDER THE FLOORING

Before you decide on the covering for your finished floor, take a look at what's underneath it. The flooring material you're going to install is essentially a skin over the structural floor that holds up everything (the walls, furnishings, and occupants) and keeps out moisture and drafts.

Familiarizing yourself with the construction of your floor system can keep you from covering up problems that will affect both the materials you've chosen and their installation. It will also save you from undoing mistakes.

Most houses are built with either a wood frame or a concrete slab structural floor, and, in one way or another, both rest on a foundation wall or footings.

WOOD FRAME FLOORS

The primary structure of a wood frame floor is a system of *joists,* generally 2× stock set on edge on 16-inch centers and supported by either foundation walls, bearing walls, or piers, posts, and girders. At the perimeter, a girder or rim joist ties them together. Perpendicular or angled *bridging* adds strength along the joists and prevents them from twisting or bowing under the load above.

The joists are covered with a *subfloor* (generally plywood, structural composition

board, dimensional lumber, or tongue-and-groove planks) that distributes weight evenly over the joists and provides a stable surface for the finished flooring.

Next comes the *underlayment,* which adds rigidity to the finished floor, increases its resilience, provides a smooth surface for the flooring material, and protects it from moisture, drafts, and dust below. Although some materials can be laid directly over a subfloor, most materials require some kind of underlayment sandwiched between the subfloor and the finished materials.

The kind of underlayment depends on the type of finished floor materials (see illustration below). Padded carpet may not require an underlayment at all, but other materials call for plywood (from ¼ inch to ¾ inch thick, either sanded or unsanded). Floating floors need a foam underlayment made specifically for this kind of installation. Ceramic tile requires cement backerboard.

SLAB FLOORS

A slab floor is a continuous thickness of concrete spanning foundation walls or footings (often poured as one unit). The thickness of the slab depends on the structural requirements of the building. From the ground up, slab construction starts with a moisture barrier that covers the soil and keeps ground moisture from migrating up into the

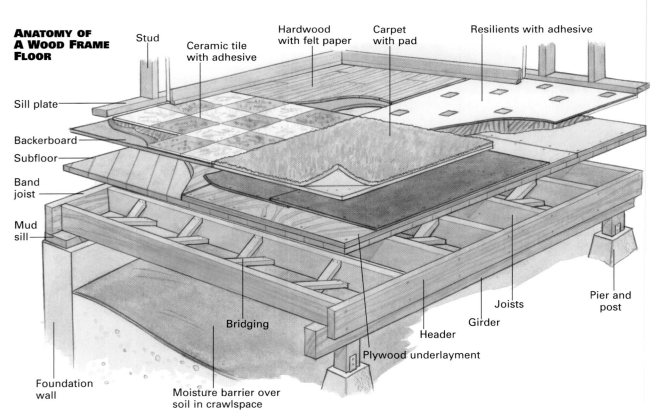

ANATOMY OF A WOOD FRAME FLOOR

Stud

Ceramic tile with adhesive

Hardwood with felt paper

Carpet with pad

Resilients with adhesive

Sill plate

Backerboard

Subfloor

Band joist

Mud sill

Bridging

Foundation wall

Moisture barrier over soil in crawlspace

Plywood underlayment

Header

Girder

Joists

Pier and post

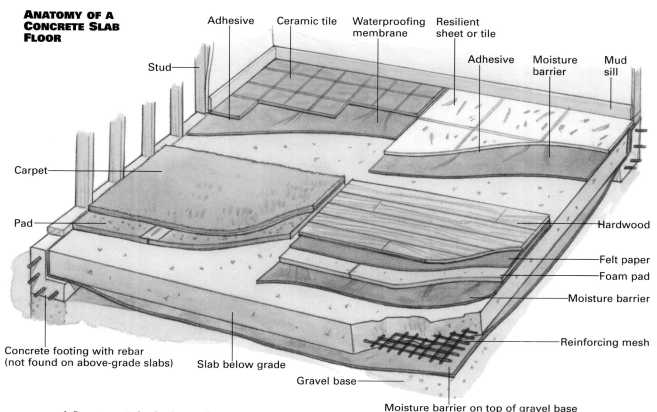

ANATOMY OF A CONCRETE SLAB FLOOR

Adhesive — Ceramic tile — Waterproofing membrane — Resilient sheet or tile

Stud

Adhesive — Moisture barrier — Mud sill

Carpet

Pad

Concrete footing with rebar (not found on above-grade slabs)

Slab below grade

Gravel base

Hardwood

Felt paper

Foam pad

Moisture barrier

Reinforcing mesh

Moisture barrier on top of gravel base

concrete and flooring. A bed of gravel (or sand and gravel) supports the slab and minimizes cracking. The slab is reinforced with wire mesh. Underlayments are required for nailed materials and floating floors installed over concrete slabs, but are not always needed for glued-down materials.

TROUBLE UNDERNEATH?

A knowledge of your flooring construction will allow you to troubleshoot it before you install your finished floor. The essential question is: Is the existing subfloor in good enough condition for new flooring?

You can get a pretty good idea of the condition of your floor by removing a floor vent. At a minimum, you can see the number of flooring layers already installed. If you have several, it's best to remove them. Here are some other clues to look for:

WOOD FRAME FLOOR:
■ **SAGGING/SPLIT JOISTS** will cause uneven flooring surfaces and can even crack your new flooring. (See pages 60 and 103 for remedies.)
■ **SQUEAKS AND NOISES** are an indication of subfloor problems. (See page 103 for solutions.)
■ **SETTLING FOUNDATIONS** make floors uneven and can result in severe damage. The only adequate repair is to jack up the house and reinforce or reinstall the foundation.
■ **MOISTURE** in a crawlspace can ruin the floor above it. (See page 103 for solutions to moisture problems.)

CONCRETE SLAB:
■ **MOISTURE** is the worst enemy of floors on slabs, and it's one that comes with the territory. Concrete retains a certain amount of moisture for months after it's poured and it's not waterproof. It will wick moisture from the ground and the surrounding air. Check for moisture and eliminate it before laying your new floor. (See pages 62–63.)
■ **CRACKS** can mean serious structural problems (sinking floor, footings, or foundation walls) or may require only minor repairs. Consult an engineer or contractor if you don't know what's causing the problem. At worst, you may have to pull up the old slab and pour a new one (or sections of it). If the situation is less serious, you may be able to treat it as a surface problem. (See pages 62–63.)
■ **CHIPS AND SURFACE BLEMISHES** aren't a major problem, but they need to be patched before installing the finished floor. (See pages 62–63 for solutions.)

UNDERLAYMENT

Underlayment has more than one meaning. It usually refers to nonstructural material (plywood, foam, or oriented strand board) that is added just before the finish floor is installed.

However, it also describes any layer immediately below the finished floor—even the subfloor itself or an existing floor that will function as a base for your new flooring. When ordering materials or discussing your floor with a professional, make sure you are talking about the same thing.

GETTING THE ROOM READY

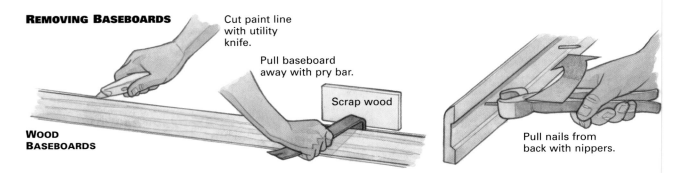

REMOVING BASEBOARDS

Cut paint line with utility knife.

Pull baseboard away with pry bar.

Scrap wood

WOOD BASEBOARDS

Pull nails from back with nippers.

Preparing your floor for its new covering means removing things—baseboards, moldings, and the existing flooring. Of course, not all new flooring will require removal of the existing floor—some can be laid over the old floor. Charts at the beginning of each of the next chapters will tell you whether you need to take up the old flooring for your installation; if you do, follow the steps below.

Leave the doors hanging for the time being, unless you need to remove them to take up the old flooring. With the doors in place and the subfloor exposed, you can easily trim the doors so they will clear the new underlayment and flooring. Remove the doors if you're sure they will swing over the new flooring.

EDGES FIRST

Take off the shoe moldings and baseboards or the cove moldings first. Before you start to remove them, cut along the paint line at the top of the base molding with a knife. This will keep you from pulling the paint off the wall when you remove the molding.

SHOE MOLDINGS: Start removing shoe moldings in one corner. Some corners are coped, with one piece cut to fit against the face of the other. For those, slide a thin putty knife behind the corner of the cut piece, and work it out until you can get a pry bar behind it. Pry against a piece of scrap wood so you don't dent the baseboard.

Work the nail out carefully—you may have to partly remove the next nail to avoid splitting the wood. Repeat the process for all the nails in that section. Number the pieces if you're going to reuse the shoe molding; they won't go back in a different order.

BASEBOARDS: After you've cut the paint line, use the same procedures you employed to remove the shoe molding—

PREPARATION SEQUENCE

Regardless of whether the floor is wood frame or slab, your preparation will be more efficient if you organize your efforts.
- Remove appliances and floor-mounted fixtures.
- Remove baseboards and shoe moldings.
- Put an exhaust fan in a window to increase ventilation.
- Paint or put up new wallcoverings.
- Cover openings with plastic sheets.
- Cover heat and return air ducts.

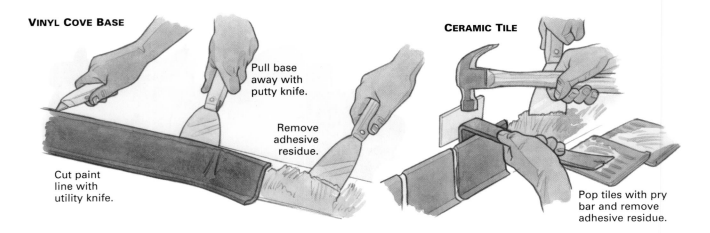

VINYL COVE BASE

Pull base away with putty knife.

Remove adhesive residue.

Cut paint line with utility knife.

CERAMIC TILE

Pop tiles with pry bar and remove adhesive residue.

SAFETY FIRST

Preparing an old floor is demolition work—
and it's not without its dangers. Always:

■ Wear boots and work gloves.

■ Wear a dust mask or respirator.

■ Wear knee pads—kneeling on nails,
splinters, and broken ceramic tile can
cause serious injuries.

■ Don't remove any existing resilient
flooring without determining whether it
contains asbestos. Asbestos fibers (usually
found in resilient floors laid before 1986)
are dangerous when inhaled. It's safer to
cover an asbestos-containing floor with
underlayment than it is to remove it.

REMOVE THE THRESHOLDS

Thresholds generally come up easily. If a
threshold fits under the door trim, cut it in
half with a backsaw first. If it is nailed in
place, pry it up with a pry bar,
protecting the adjoining
floor with a wide-blade
putty knife under the bar.
If it's fastened with
screws, remove them
and slide out the
threshold.

REMOVING SOLID WOOD FLOORING

You can pry up
nailed-down solid
wood flooring (both strip
and plank) with a pry bar,
but you will probably have to
cut pieces out to give yourself some
working room. Refer to the illustration
at right, and cut the flooring as shown.
Then, along the length of the board and at
each nail, insert your pry bar under the
body of the flooring—not under
the tongue—and force it up. If
you are removing plugged planks,
first bore out the plugs, then take
out the screws and proceed as
above. Pry up boards that are
face-nailed.

To remove parquet, force a
wide chisel under each piece
and tap it loose. Scrape up the
adhesive residue.

REMOVING SOLID WOOD FLOORING

TONGUE AND GROOVE FLOORING

1. Make several
plunge cuts in one
board to the depth of
the flooring. Chisel
out the cut wood.

2. Use a pry
bar to lift
the board
where it is
blind-nailed.

slide a putty knife behind the board and pull
it away with a pry bar. Protect the wall with
thin scrap wood and number the pieces if
you're going to reuse them. To avoid
damaging the face of the baseboard, pull the
nails from the back with nippers.

VINYL COVE MOLDING: After scoring
the paint line, slide a putty knife behind the
molding and strip it off, working as much as
possible with the putty knife handle parallel
to the floor. Scrape adhesive from the wall.

CERAMIC TILE: Score the joint between
the tiles and the wall as described above, then
gently tap the end of a pry bar into the joint.
When the pry bar can grip the rear of the tile,
pop it loose. Protect the wall with a piece of
scrap wood.

REMOVING WOOD THRESHOLDS

Cut
threshold
with a
backsaw.

Chisel out
each piece.

PLUGGED PLANK FLOORING

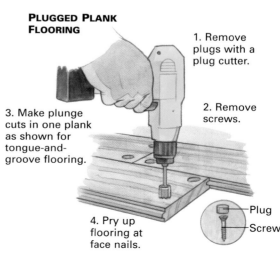

1. Remove
plugs with a
plug cutter.

2. Remove
screws.

3. Make plunge
cuts in one plank
as shown for
tongue-and-
groove flooring.

4. Pry up
flooring at
face nails.

Plug

Screw

GETTING THE ROOM READY
continued

REMOVING RESILIENT SHEET AND TILE FLOORING

1. Cut sheet flooring into 6- to 12-inch strips with a utility knife.

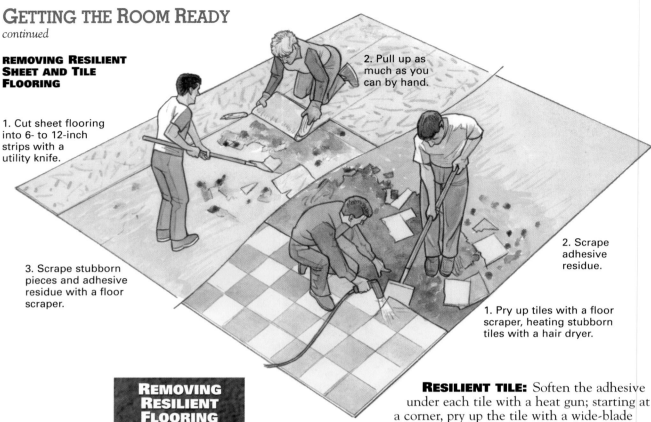

2. Pull up as much as you can by hand.

3. Scrape stubborn pieces and adhesive residue with a floor scraper.

2. Scrape adhesive residue.

1. Pry up tiles with a floor scraper, heating stubborn tiles with a hair dryer.

REMOVING RESILIENT FLOORING

Before removing resilient flooring, check with a professional to make sure it doesn't contain asbestos. Used as a binder in resilient materials installed before 1986, asbestos fibers are harmful when inhaled, and cutting or breaking the flooring will release the fibers into the air.

If your floor contains asbestos, cover it with underlayment and install the new material over it. If it doesn't contain asbestos, use the techniques below to remove it. To make the job easier, rent a floor-stripping machine.

PERIMETER-BONDED SHEET FLOORING: Sheet material stapled or bonded to the floor only at its perimeter pries up easily. Just lift the staples or loosen the bond with a wide-blade putty knife. Then roll the sheet up and take it out of the room. If the piece is large and unwieldy, cut it into strips of manageable sizes. Scrape off the remaining adhesive with a floor scraper.

SURFACE-BONDED SHEET FLOORING: First, use a utility knife to cut the flooring into 8- to 12-inch strips. Then roll the strips off the floor, working the adhesive loose behind the roll with a wide-blade putty knife.

If the flooring has a felt backing, spray it with a water/dish-soap solution to loosen it.

If the flooring is unbacked, have a helper work ahead of you, softening the adhesive with a heat gun (not a torch) as you go. Scrape off the remaining adhesive.

RESILIENT TILE: Soften the adhesive under each tile with a heat gun; starting at a corner, pry up the tile with a wide-blade putty knife. Scrape off the remaining adhesive.

STUBBORN STUFF: If the flooring does not come up easily, you still have another option—remove it along with the underlayment. Set your circular saw to the depth of the underlayment (don't cut into the subfloor) and cut in 4×4-foot sections. Use an old or carbide-tipped flooring blade—sawing through nails will be unavoidable. Pry up each section with a pry bar.

REMOVING CERAMIC TILE

The method you use for taking up ceramic tile will depend on whether it has been set with a thinset mortar or in a mortar bed. Be especially careful next to floor drains. Wear safety goggles when breaking and removing ceramic tile.

THINSET INSTALLATIONS: To remove thinset tile, chip out the grout around one tile with a hand maul and cold chisel. Then break the tile with the maul and take out the pieces. Hold the cold chisel under the edge of each tile and pop them loose with a sharp tap of the maul.

MORTAR-BED INSTALLATIONS: It's often easier to remove the mortar bed in sections rather than trying to remove individual tiles. First, break the bed into manageable sections by striking the corners of the tiles with a large sledge hammer. Work from the center of the bed to the perimeter. Then insert a large wrecking bar under one corner of the mortar bed (you may have to take up a tile or two to give yourself more working room). Pry up the sections until you can get a wire snips into the joint to cut the reinforcing mesh. Remove each section and haul it out of your way.

REMOVING CARPET

Conventional and cushion-backed carpet are installed differently and require different removal methods.

CONVENTIONAL CARPET: First, remove all the metal edgings. Then cut the carpet into 12- to 18-inch sections with a utility knife. Pry up one corner with a screwdriver and pull it away from the tackless strip on adjacent walls. Roll up each strip and dispose of it. If the carpet is tacked, remove a few tacks and pull the carpet up. If that doesn't work, you'll have to pry up each tack individually.

Tear up as much of the pad as you can by hand and pull the staples with a cat's paw. Then pry up the tackless strips with a pry bar.

CUSHION-BACKED CARPET: Cut the carpet into 12-inch strips with a utility knife. Pull up each strip, working it free as you roll

REMOVING CERAMIC TILE

1. Score the first tile with a chisel and small sledge, then break out pieces.

3. Chip out grout as you go.

2. Tap a masonry chisel under an adjacent tile and pop it free.

it back. Drive a wide-blade putty knife between the backing and the floor to break the adhesive bond. Scrape up the remaining adhesive and chunks of cushion backing with a floor scraper or wide chisel.

REMOVING CARPET

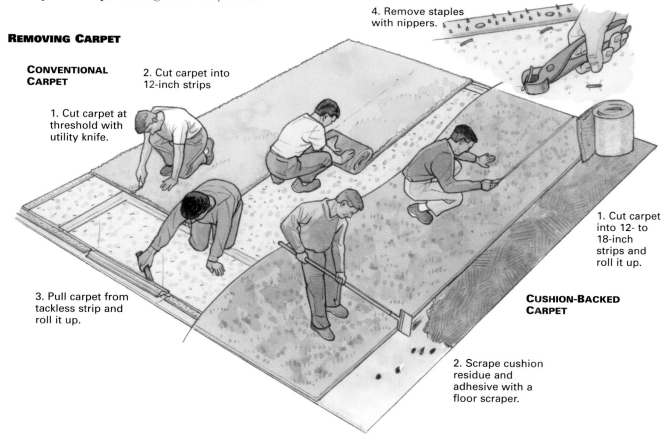

4. Remove staples with nippers.

CONVENTIONAL CARPET

2. Cut carpet into 12-inch strips

1. Cut carpet at threshold with utility knife.

3. Pull carpet from tackless strip and roll it up.

1. Cut carpet into 12- to 18-inch strips and roll it up.

CUSHION-BACKED CARPET

2. Scrape cushion residue and adhesive with a floor scraper.

PREPARING A WOOD SUBFLOOR

Most of the preparation for wood subfloors consists of making surface repairs and installing underlayments. Subfloor defects will be magnified by the layers you put on top, so be sure to make all surface repairs to the subfloor before you lay down underlayment or new flooring.

First, inventory the problems. Look for high spots, low spots, protruding nails, gaps, chipped-out areas, and other defects.

MARKING THE DEFECTS

Divide the floor into imaginary 6-foot sections and, within each section, rotate a 6-foot level. Mark all defects with a carpenter's pencil. Drive in any protruding nails, then turn to the remaining problems in the following order:

CHECKING THE SURFACE

Rotate a 6-foot level across sections of the floor. Mark areas that need repair.

Low area, chip

High spot

PREPARING THE SURFACE

Level high spots with a belt sander, fill dents and low spots with filler and smooth, and reset protruding nails.

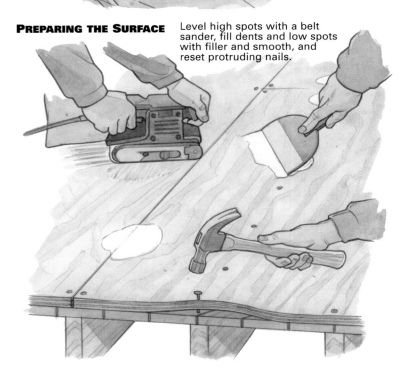

FIXING SAGS AND QUIETING SQUEAKS

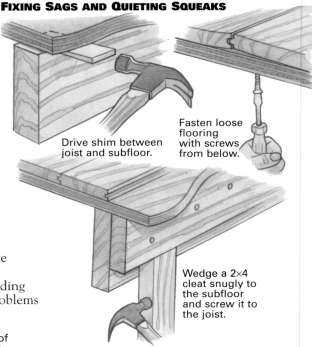

Drive shim between joist and subfloor.

Fasten loose flooring with screws from below.

Wedge a 2×4 cleat snugly to the subfloor and screw it to the joist.

SAGS AND SQUEAKS

A sagging floor means that a joist is sagging, either due to failure of its support or because of warpage. Floor squeaks occur when something moves or rubs—the finish floor moving against the subfloor, for instance.

FIXING SAGS: Refer to the illustration above. There are two ways to stabilize the subfloor—you can either attach a cleat to an existing joist, or drive shims between the joist and the subfloor. Choose the method that best fits the situation, and follow the directions in the illustration.

QUIETING SQUEAKS: Squeaks may be caused by nails that have worked loose or boards that have shrunk or cupped. Anchor the loose flooring with 6d or 8d ringshank nails driven at an angle. If the squeak persists, drill pilot holes and countersink wood screws through the floor into the joists.

CRACKS, CHIPS, AND DENTS

If your new flooring calls for plywood underlayment, you can skip some subfloor repairs. However, if your new flooring requires an absolutely smooth surface—cushion-backed carpet or resilient materials, for example—you may have to repair chips and dents in the underlayment itself.

To fill depressions, choose a filler that is compatible with any sealers or adhesives you plan to use later. Most fillers are water- or latex-based. First vacuum the area, then mix the filler just before you use it—fillers set up quickly. Trowel it into the depression and feather the edges with a wide-blade putty knife while it's still pliable. After it's dry, sand it flush with the surrounding floor.

HIGH SPOTS AND SLICK SURFACES

Use a belt sander to level out any high spots and warped boards you have marked. If a board is badly warped, remove that section from joist to joist. If your new flooring requires adhesive and the subfloor is slick, roughen the surface with a medium-grit sandpaper attached to a long-handled block.

UNDERLAYMENTS

Different flooring materials call for different kinds of underlayment. Refer to the illustration on page 54, and install the underlayment best suited to your new flooring. For more information, refer to the chapter in this book that covers your particular type of new flooring.

PLYWOOD: This sheet material is made of an odd number of thin wood layers glued under pressure with the grains of each layer at right angles to the others. Plywood won't warp, buckle, twist, cup, or split. Install underlayment-grade plywood. Sold in a range of grades, thicknesses, and sheet sizes, its smooth outer face satisfies the general subsurface requirements of most finished floors.

TILE BACKING UNITS: Fiberglass-and-concrete backerboard is designed to underlay ceramic and dimensioned stone tile. Unlike plywood, it provides no structural strength and must be installed over a subfloor. It can be used in both dry and moisture-prone areas.

LIQUIDS: Liquid underlayments are used to smooth, level, fill, patch, and even moisture-proof subfloors. Most should be applied by professionals.

TRIMMING DOORS AND CASINGS

To trim a door so it clears your new flooring, lay a piece of the flooring material on the underlayment and mark the door at a point ⅛ to ⅜ inch higher. Remove the door as shown in the

INSTALLING PLYWOOD UNDERLAYMENT

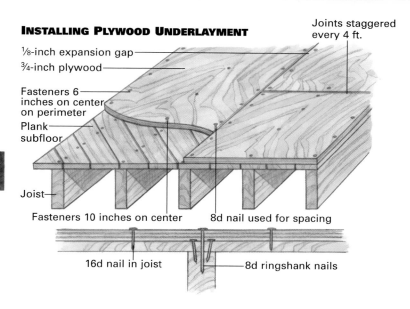

Joints staggered every 4 ft.

⅛-inch expansion gap

¾-inch plywood

Fasteners 6 inches on center on perimeter

Plank subfloor

Joist

Fasteners 10 inches on center   8d nail used for spacing

16d nail in joist   8d ringshank nails

TRIMMING A DOOR

Mark door ⅛ to ⅜ in. higher than the new flooring.

Remove bottom hinge pin first, then others, and pull door away.

Mask cut line on both sides to prevent door from splintering.

Score trim line with a utility knife and cut with a circular saw.

illustration, center right. If a nail won't work, try tapping a screwdriver blade under the edge of the hinge pin or remove the hinges from the door. Trim the door as shown. Cut the door trim to the thickness of the new flooring with a trim saw.

TRIMMING THE DOOR CASING

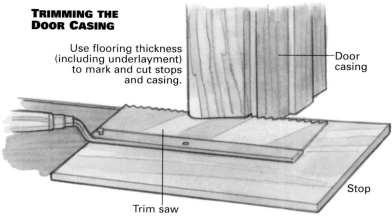

Use flooring thickness (including underlayment) to mark and cut stops and casing.

Door casing

Stop

Trim saw

PREPARING A SLAB

All flooring materials must be installed over a dry surface. Although preparing a concrete slab for new flooring involves many of the same steps required for a wood frame floor, concrete brings with it additional concerns because of its ability to absorb moisture. Correct the moisture problems first.

will collect in the surrounding soil and migrate into the slab. These and several other problems are fairly easy to correct. The illustration below shows typical solutions.

Moisture wicking up from the soil is more difficult to correct. Unless a moisture barrier was laid over the soil before a below-grade or on-grade slab was poured, the slab may wick up moisture from the ground. Tracking down and correcting moisture problems caused by wicking may require professional help.

WET SLABS— CAUSES AND CURES

Several factors contribute to moisture problems in slabs. Missing or inadequate gutters and downspouts or soil that drains toward the foundation will let water in. Without a subsurface drainage system, water

SURFACE REPAIRS

After correcting moisture problems, check your slab's surface with a 6-foot level, and mark any defects.

CRACKS AND HOLES: Key minor cracks or holes with a chisel, clean them out, and fill them with a quick-setting hydraulic cement. Major cracks may be a sign of structural failure. Consult a pro for recommendations.

LOWS AND HIGHS: Fill depressions with patching compound, feathering it to the surrounding floor. Grind high spots down with a rented concrete grinder. If extensive leveling and smoothing are both required, consider using a liquid underlayment.

ALKALINE SALT DEPOSITS: Alkaline deposits will interfere with adhesive bonding on glued-down floors. Remove them by mopping the surface with a solution of 4 parts water and 1 part muriatic acid. Then rinse the slab with clean water. Muriatic acid is hazardous; follow directions carefully.

CHECKING FOR MOISTURE

Alkali deposits on the slab, or damp, puffy-looking, or buckled flooring, are danger signals. To check for moisture, tape 2×2-foot clear plastic squares to the floor every 2 feet. After a couple of days, lift them. If droplets have formed under the plastic, or the plastic looks cloudy, you probably have a moisture problem.

SOLVING MOISTURE PROBLEMS

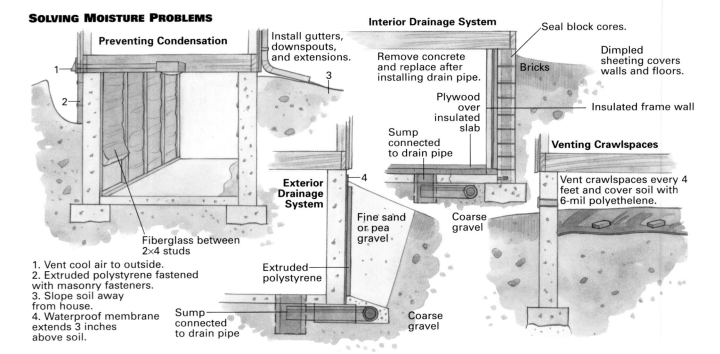

Preventing Condensation

Install gutters, downspouts, and extensions.

Interior Drainage System

Seal block cores.

Remove concrete and replace after installing drain pipe.

Dimpled sheeting covers walls and floors.

Bricks

Plywood over insulated slab

Insulated frame wall

Sump connected to drain pipe

Venting Crawlspaces

Vent crawlspaces every 4 feet and cover soil with 6-mil polyethelene.

Fiberglass between 2×4 studs

Exterior Drainage System

Fine sand or pea gravel

Coarse gravel

Extruded polystyrene

Coarse gravel

Sump connected to drain pipe

1. Vent cool air to outside.
2. Extruded polystyrene fastened with masonry fasteners.
3. Slope soil away from house.
4. Waterproof membrane extends 3 inches above soil.

MAKING SURFACE REPAIRS

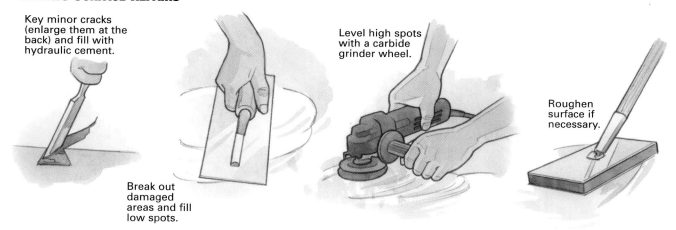

Key minor cracks (enlarge them at the back) and fill with hydraulic cement.

Break out damaged areas and fill low spots.

Level high spots with a carbide grinder wheel.

Roughen surface if necessary.

ROUGH AND CLEAN IT

Adhesives will not bond to slick or dirty surfaces. Break the sheen caused by sealers (if water sprinkled on the slab beads, the slab has been sealed), paint, or a steel-trowel finish by sanding the concrete lightly with a medium-grit abrasive on a long-handled wood block. Scarify hard surfaces with a rented scarifier. Then scrub the slab with a degreasing agent or a trisodium phosphate solution and hot water. Rinse with clean water and let dry.

INSTALLING SLEEPERS

Solid wood floors and other nail-down flooring require a wood surface to drive nails into. You can fasten plywood underlayment directly to a slab or you can install it over wooden sleepers, as shown at right.

Either installation will support any material that can be laid on plywood underlayment. Even though you can install most glue-down and floating floors directly on a slab, sleepers will insulate the flooring from the cold concrete and help make the finished surface more comfortable.

To install sleepers, first vacuum the slab and seal it with asphalt primer. Then spread a

⅛- to ¼-inch layer of asphalt mastic over the entire floor. Lay a moisture barrier over that. On 16-inch chalk lines, embed pressure-treated 2×4s in a mastic bed and anchor them with concrete nails. Leave a gap between the sleepers for circulation. Cover the sleepers with ⅝ or ¾-inch plywood. Cut out 2×8-inch holes every 6 feet along the walls perpendicular to the sleepers, to allow air to circulate under the floor. Insert floor grilles after you have installed the finished floor.

INSTALLING A SLEEPER SUBFLOOR

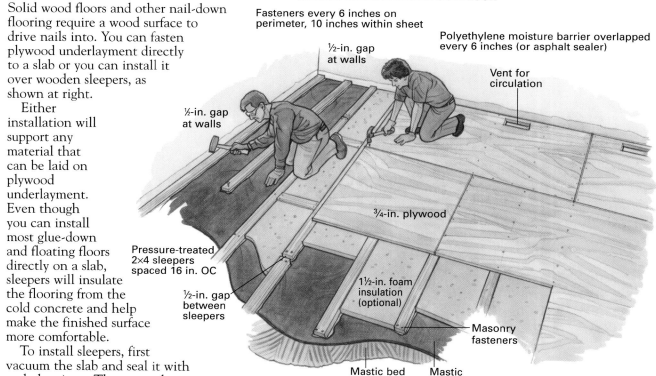

Fasteners every 6 inches on perimeter, 10 inches within sheet

½-in. gap at walls

Polyethylene moisture barrier overlapped every 6 inches (or asphalt sealer)

Vent for circulation

½-in. gap at walls

¾-in. plywood

Pressure-treated 2×4 sleepers spaced 16 in. OC

½-in. gap between sleepers

1½-in. foam insulation (optional)

Masonry fasteners

Mastic bed   Mastic

INSTALLING WOOD FLOORS

Wood flooring will give years of service when installed over a subfloor that is structurally sound, dry, relatively level, smooth, and free of dust and foreign matter. The chart on the opposite page shows how to prepare a floor for new wood flooring.

Installation of all solid wood products is fairly straightforward, once you have established your layout on paper and transferred it to the floor. The illustration on page 66 will help you plan the installation if your project involves more than one room.

When you're satisfied that the subfloor is ready and the layout is just the way you want it, you're ready to bring in the materials.

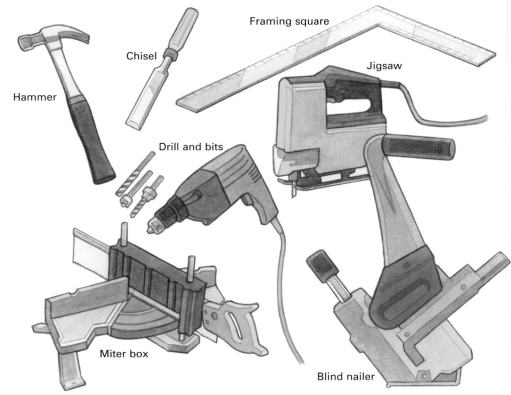

Hammer

Chisel

Framing square

Jigsaw

Drill and bits

Miter box

Blind nailer

Because damp air makes wood swell and dry air makes it shrink, you'll have to protect your materials from extremes of temperature and humidity.

To keep the wood dry and ready for installation, don't have it delivered during rain or snow. For new construction, don't deliver the flooring until after the building is enclosed and all the concrete work, plaster work, and painting are finished and completely dried.

Acclimate the wood in the room where it will be installed, at a temperature of 65 to 70 degrees. Stack the material log-cabin style—or just spread it around the room—for at least five days before you install it.

ORIENTATION

Strip, plank, and manufactured flooring are normally laid perpendicular to the floor joists and parallel to the long wall in the room. If you run the flooring parallel to the joists, you must install at least two layers of ¾-inch plywood and strengthen the floor with additional bridging (every 2 feet) between the joists. Parquet pieces are usually square, so joist direction is not relevant.

To determine the joist direction and position, look at the nails on the subfloor (or look from below if the subfloor is covered). Mark the center of each joist on the walls, so you can see the marks when you're nailing.

PREPARING A FLOOR FOR WOOD FLOORING

Find your existing floor in the left column below, then prepare the floor as shown.

Existing Floor	T&G or Square-Edge	Parquet or Glue-Down	Floating Floor
Exposed joists	1. Install ¾-inch plywood. 2. Lay felt paper.	Install ¾-inch plywood.	1. Install ¾-inch plywood. 2. Install foam underlayment.
Bare concrete	1. Install sleepers or ¾-inch plywood subfloor. 2. Lay felt paper.	1. Remove sealer/finishes. 2. Repair and roughen surface.	1. Repair surface. 2. Install foam underlayment.
Wood subfloor or finish floor over wood frame or concrete slab	1. Repair surface, install ¾-inch plywood as needed. 2. Lay felt paper.	Remove finish, repair surface. On rough surface or planks wider than 4 inches, install ⅜- or ½-inch underlayment.	1. Repair surface. 2. Install foam underlayment.
Resilient sheet/tile	If existing resilient is cushioned or loose, remove and repair surface. Otherwise, repair surface.	If existing resilient is cushioned or loose, remove and repair surface. Otherwise, repair surface.	If existing resilient is cushioned or loose, remove and repair surface. Otherwise, repair surface.
over wood frame	1. Install ¾-inch underlayment-grade plywood. 2. Lay felt paper.	Install ⅜-inch underlayment.	Install foam underlayment as needed.
over concrete slab	1. Install sleepers or ¾-inch plywood subfloor. 2. Lay felt paper.	1. Remove wax or finish and roughen surface. 2. Lay felt paper.	Install foam underlayment.
Ceramic tile	Remove tile and repair surface.	If tile is bonded, remove finish, level, and roughen surface. Otherwise, same as below.	
over wood frame	1. Install ¾-inch plywood as needed. 2. Lay felt paper.	Remove tile, repair surface, and install ⅜-inch underlayment.	1. If tile is bonded, remove finish and level surface. 2. Install foam underlayment.
over concrete slab	1. Install sleepers or ¾-in. plywood. 2. Lay felt paper.	Repair surface as needed.	Same as above.
Carpet over wood frame	1. Remove carpet and pad. 2. Repair subfloor as necessary. 3. Install ¾-inch plywood as needed. 4. Lay felt paper.	1. Remove carpet and pad. 2. Repair subfloor.	1. Remove carpet and pad. 2. Repair subfloor. 3. Install foam underlayment.
over concrete slab	1. Remove carpet and pad. 2. Install sleepers or ¾-inch plywood. 3. Lay felt paper.	1. Remove carpet and pad. 2. Repair surface. 3. Remove sealer/finish and roughen surface.	1. Remove carpet and pad. 2. Repair surface. 3. Install foam underlayment.

INSTALLING TONGUE-AND-GROOVE FLOORING

PLANNING THE LAYOUT FOR MULTIPLE ROOMS

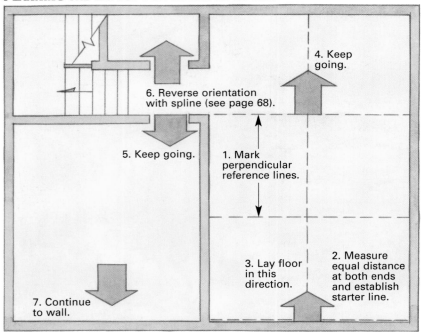

Strong, interlocking tongue-and-groove joints create a surface that functions as a single unit. Before laying tongue-and-groove flooring, install felt paper as an underlayment. This will cushion the flooring and keep noise down by preventing the wooden surfaces from touching when they flex.

LAYING THE FELT

Follow these steps to install the felt underlayment.
■ Mark the joist locations. Make the marks on the wall.
■ Lay down strips of 15-pound asphalt felt paper perpendicular to the new flooring. Overlap all edges 4 inches and trim the ends so they lie flat.
■ Staple or tack the felt paper across its surface and at the edges; countersink the fasteners slightly. Then, from one wall to the other, snap chalk lines on the felt paper at the joist marks.
■ Establish the starting wall. It's usually best for your starting wall to be opposite a doorway. At each end of the starting wall and ¾ inch out from it (to allow for expansion), measure from your reference line and tack a nail at both points. Stretch a line between the nails—this is your layout line. If the starting wall is not square with the rest of the room, use the quadrant layout method (see page 52). This will ensure that the floor looks square, because the flooring will be in line with the centerline of the room.

THE STARTER COURSE

The starter board should always be your longest, straightest board.
■ Lay the starter board—tongue toward the center of the room—against the starter line with its end ½ inch from the side wall. Mark joist locations on the face of the board closest to the wall and predrill at the marks at the proper interval for your flooring (see "Nailing Schedule" at left).
■ Lay the board exactly on the starter line, then face-nail and countersink the board with the fasteners specified in the nailing schedule.
■ At the same locations on the tongue, predrill holes at a 45-degree angle and blind-nail the tongue by hand. Drive nails partway and countersink the heads with a nail set, being careful not to mar the face or tongue.
■ Cut a board to fit the remainder of the wall and install it in the same fashion.

TONGUE-AND-GROOVE NAILING SCHEDULE

This chart shows the nail sizes and spacing for blind-nailed T&G flooring.

Flooring in Inches	Barbed Fastener Size	Spacing
⅜×1½	1¼-in. machine-driven fastener; 4d screw, cut steel, or wire casing nail	8 in.
½×1½	1½-in. machine-driven fastener; 5d bright wire casing nail	10 in.
¾×1½	2-in. machine-driven fastener; 7d or 8d screw or cut nail	10–12 in.
¾×2¼	2-in. machine-driven fastener; 7d or 8d screw or cut nail	10–12 in.
¾×3¼	2-in. machine-driven fastener; 7d or 8d screw or cut nail	10–12 in.
¾×3 to 8	2-in. machine-driven fastener; plank 7d or 8d screw or cut nail into and between joists	7-8 in.

For ½-in. plywood subfloor, fasten at and between each joist.
On slab with ¾-in. plywood, use 1½-in. fasteners.

RACKING THE FIELD

To ensure a random joint pattern, loosely arrange the next seven or eight courses, mixing long and short lengths from different bundles. Overlap the joints by at least 6 inches. If you're laying planks of various widths, make piles of each width and rack from each pile so you won't run out of a width before finishing the room. Plan each course to start with the piece left over from the previous one if it's at least 2 feet long.

LAYING FELT PAPER

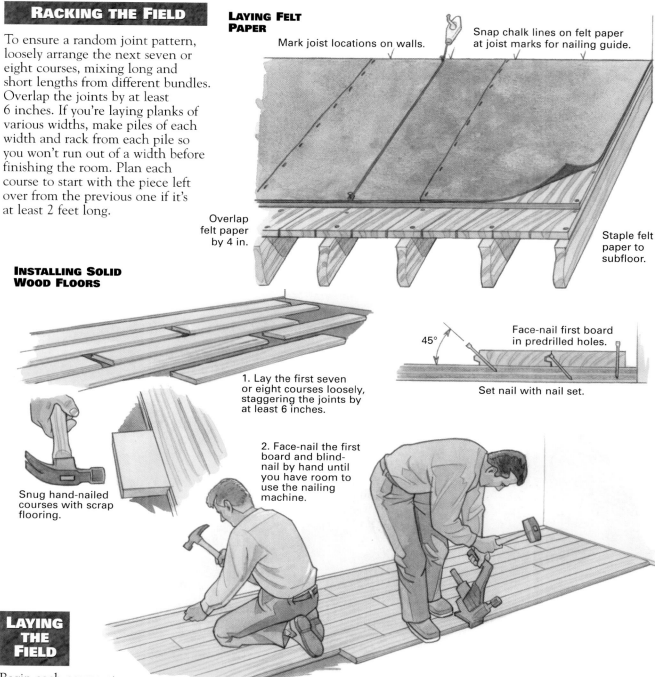

Mark joist locations on walls.

Snap chalk lines on felt paper at joist marks for nailing guide.

Overlap felt paper by 4 in.

Staple felt paper to subfloor.

INSTALLING SOLID WOOD FLOORS

1. Lay the first seven or eight courses loosely, staggering the joints by at least 6 inches.

Snug hand-nailed courses with scrap flooring.

45°   Face-nail first board in predrilled holes.

Set nail with nail set.

2. Face-nail the first board and blind-nail by hand until you have room to use the nailing machine.

LAYING THE FIELD

Begin each course at the same side wall, and leave ½ inch at the ends. Snug each board into place with scrap flooring and blind-nail the tongues by hand. When you have enough room to get behind a power nailer, finish the remainder of the floor, keeping your toes on the previous strip or plank. Rack several courses and start nailing 2 inches from the end of each board. Drive at least 2 nails in each board, no matter what its length. When you come across a bent board, refer to the illustration at right.

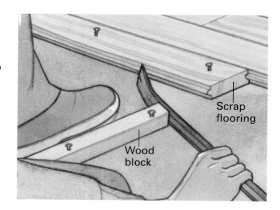

Scrap flooring

Wood block

USING BENT BOARDS

1. Tack a wood block to the floor with duplex nails.

2. Force the warped board in place with a crowbar.

3. Keeping pressure on, drive duplex nails into scrap to hold flooring until you can nail it.

TONGUE-AND-GROOVE FLOORING
continued

MEETING OBSTACLES

If the starting wall has a doorway, you will need to change the direction of the tongue edge so you can continue blind-nailing the boards through the doorway. Glue a spline into the groove of the nearest board. Then install the reversed courses.

If the floor has furnace vent holes or other obstructions, cut and fit the flooring around them, mitering corners where possible. Rip off the exposed tongue on a table saw.

REVERSING DIRECTIONS

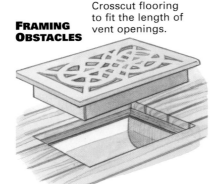

Spline glued to both grooves.

FRAMING OBSTACLES

Crosscut flooring to fit the length of vent openings.

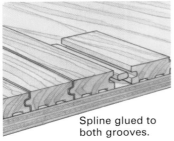

THE LAST COURSES

As you approach the opposite wall and run out of room for the power nailer, blind-nail the tongues by hand. When you don't have room to swing the hammer for blind-nailing, face-nail the boards. Scribe the final course to the contour of the wall if necessary (leave a ¾-inch gap). Pull it into place with a pry bar leveraged against scrap on the wall, as shown below. Face-nail the final board.

INSTALLING TRANSITIONS

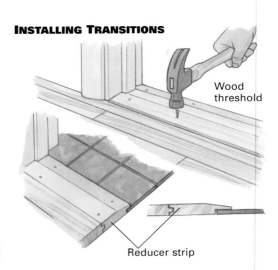

Wood threshold

Reducer strip

FINISHING UP

Where the two floors are of different heights, a reducer strip will ease the transition. Where the heights are the same, install a tapered threshold. Nail the baseboards at the studs and angle-nail the shoe molding to the baseboard, not to the flooring, so the flooring can expand and contract freely.

Fill unfinished face-nailed flooring with a wood filler, or prefinished flooring with a color-matched putty stick. Next, sand and seal unfinished floors (see page 105). Clean and buff prefinished flooring.

THE LAST COURSE

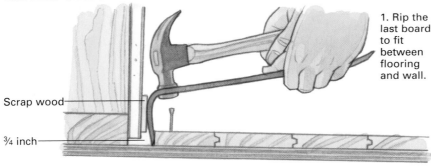

Scrap wood

¾ inch

1. Rip the last board to fit between flooring and wall.

Outside corner (miter cut)

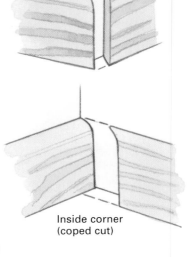

Inside corner (coped cut)

INSTALLING BASEBOARDS

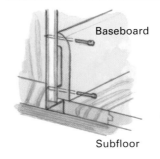

Baseboard

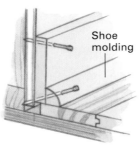

Shoe molding

Stud

Molding

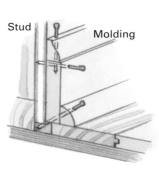

Subfloor

INSTALLING SQUARE-EDGE FLOORING

Installation of square-edged flooring begins with felt paper underlayment (see page 66) and calls for the same basic techniques as tongue-and-groove flooring. Instead of blind-nailing, however, each board is fastened with face-nails. The work will go faster if you rent a nail gun that countersinks the nails when it drives them.

BORDERING A FLOOR

If you plan to install a border, refer to page 53 for information about perimeter layouts. Establish a starter line on each wall, each line ¾ inch away from the wall and square with the other lines. Then select your first board and predrill holes 1 inch from each end and at 7-inch intervals along the board, as shown below right.

Keeping the edge of the plank on the line, face-nail it as shown in the nailing schedule at right. Finish the first course to the end of the wall. Follow the sequence shown and complete the border, measuring each course exactly so it butts tightly. Snug each board along its length with a chisel leveraged into the floor. Then lay the field.

THE SQUARE-EDGED FIELD

Dry-lay the field, rack it (see page 67), and face-nail the field. Predrill the holes if necessary and keep each board snugly against the previous one.

PLUGGING PLANKS

Plugged fastener holes lend a rustic touch to planked flooring, but they require a little forethought. First, measure and mark each plug location—about 1 inch from each end. A 3-inch plank gets 1 plug, a 5-inch plank gets 2, and a 7-inch plank, 3. If you're using preplugged planks, duplicate and mark the plug pattern on the ends of any boards you've cut. Predrill holes at the marks and follow the directions in the illustration below to set them.

SEQUENCE FOR INSTALLING A BORDER

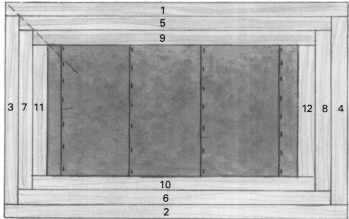

NAILING SCHEDULE FOR SQUARE-EDGE FLOORING

This chart shows the nail sizes and spacing for square-edged flooring.

Flooring in Inches	Barbed Fastener Size	Spacing
$5/16 \times 1\frac{1}{4}$	1-in. 15-gauge fully barbed flooring brad	5 in. on alternate sides
$5/16 \times 1\frac{1}{2}$	1-in. 15-gauge fully barbed flooring brad	2 nails every 7 in.
$5/16 \times 2$	1-in. 15-gauge fully barbed flooring brad	2 nails every 7 in.

7 in.   7 in.   1 in.

1. Predrill holes 1 inch from ends, then every 7 inches along the board.

2. Using techniques for tongue-and-groove flooring, rack the floor, lay the first plank on the starter line, and face-nail it with floor brads.

3. Lever the boards in place by digging a chisel into the subfloor.

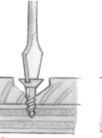

SETTING PLUGS IN PLANKS

With random-width planks, use cut-off pieces to begin rows of the same width.

Counterbore holes.   Tighten screws.   Chisel and sand level with floor.

INSTALLING MANUFACTURED WOOD FLOORING

Manufactured flooring is made for today's do-it-yourself consumers. While installation of solid wood requires some carpentry skills and is time-consuming, manufactured flooring can be installed relatively quickly and doesn't call for special skills.

Most products are designed for either glue-down or floating installations, but a few are made for nailing. (Some products are made for installation by any of the three methods.) Be sure to follow the manufacturer's installation recommendations.

If your flooring is designed for nailing, employ the procedure described on pages 66–68 for tongue-and-groove flooring. If your material is designed to be glued or floated, follow the instructions on these two pages. Regardless of the method, when you cut the material, refer to the illustrations on the opposite page so the pieces will fit and won't have frayed edges.

TROWELS AND ADHESIVES

Manufactured wood flooring is made to precise tolerances and specifications, and each product will carry with it specific recommendations for fasteners or adhesives and spreading trowels.

Be sure to follow the recommendations. Don't assume that an adhesive that worked well for your parquet or resilient tile will suit your new wood floor. Using products or tools not recommended by the maker could result in a voided warranty.

LET IT ACCLIMATE

Manufactured flooring is a wood product, and like solid wood flooring, it must be acclimated to your house before you install it. If you're laying the floor in a newly constructed or remodeled room, give any plaster, drywall compound, concrete, or latex-based paints plenty of time to dry to make sure the room is dry. After you prepare the subfloor, unpack the flooring in the room and let it sit in its new environment for at least five days.

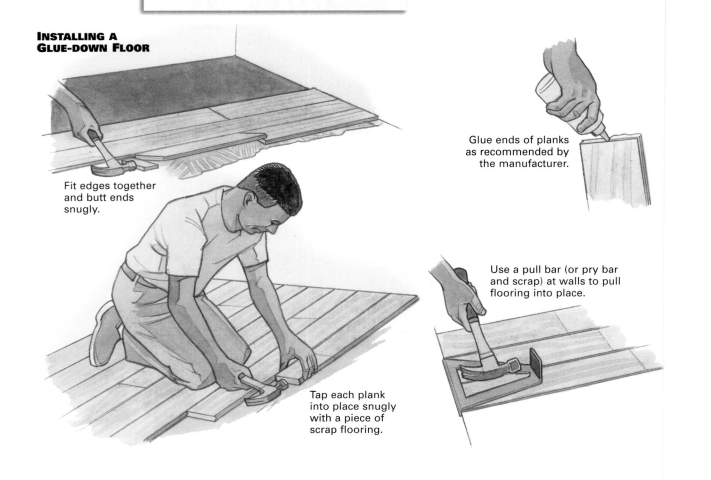

INSTALLING A GLUE-DOWN FLOOR

Fit edges together and butt ends snugly.

Glue ends of planks as recommended by the manufacturer.

Tap each plank into place snugly with a piece of scrap flooring.

Use a pull bar (or pry bar and scrap) at walls to pull flooring into place.

INSTALLING A FLOATING FLOOR

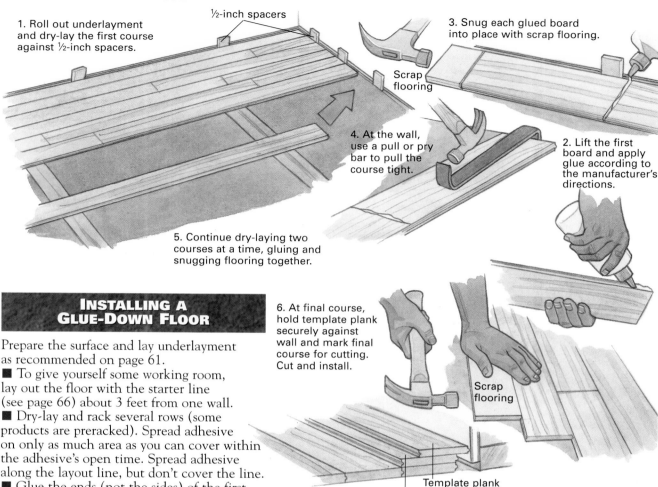

1. Roll out underlayment and dry-lay the first course against ½-inch spacers.

½-inch spacers

3. Snug each glued board into place with scrap flooring.

Scrap flooring

4. At the wall, use a pull or pry bar to pull the course tight.

2. Lift the first board and apply glue according to the manufacturer's directions.

5. Continue dry-laying two courses at a time, gluing and snugging flooring together.

6. At final course, hold template plank securely against wall and mark final course for cutting. Cut and install.

Scrap flooring

Template plank
Mark cut line on this board.

INSTALLING A GLUE-DOWN FLOOR

Prepare the surface and lay underlayment as recommended on page 61.

■ To give yourself some working room, lay out the floor with the starter line (see page 66) about 3 feet from one wall.

■ Dry-lay and rack several rows (some products are preracked). Spread adhesive on only as much area as you can cover within the adhesive's open time. Spread adhesive along the layout line, but don't cover the line.

■ Glue the ends (not the sides) of the first board and install it with the tongue to the wall, leaving a ½-inch expansion gap at the end. Angle the tongues of successive courses into the grooves of the preceding ones and slide the end joints together immediately.

■ Cinch the flooring tight every several courses by tapping boards with a hammer and scrap piece. Pull the ends tight at the wall with a pry bar or flooring tool as shown above.

■ When you reach the wall, go back and lay in the bare floor that was your working room when you started the installation.

■ Roll the entire floor with a roller.

FLOATING A FLOOR

Lay a floated floor over a foam underlayment recommended by the manufacturer. Prepare the floor, then:

■ Snap a starter line ½ inch from the wall or dry-lay the first boards against spacers. Trim the board as needed, and apply glue according to the manufacturer's recommendations. (Some recommend putting it on the tongue, some in the groove, some on both.)

■ Dry-lay several courses to establish the recommended pattern. Follow the procedures shown above to lay the rest of the floor.

CUTTING MANUFACTURED WOOD FLOORING

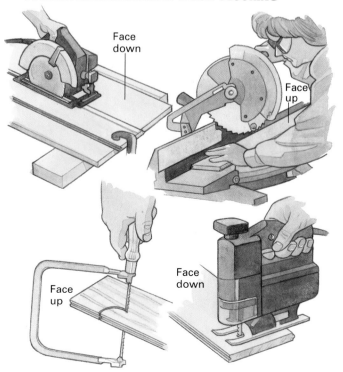

Face down

Face up

Face up

Face down

INSTALLING WOODBLOCK AND PARQUET FLOORING

PARQUET AND WOODBLOCK LAYOUT

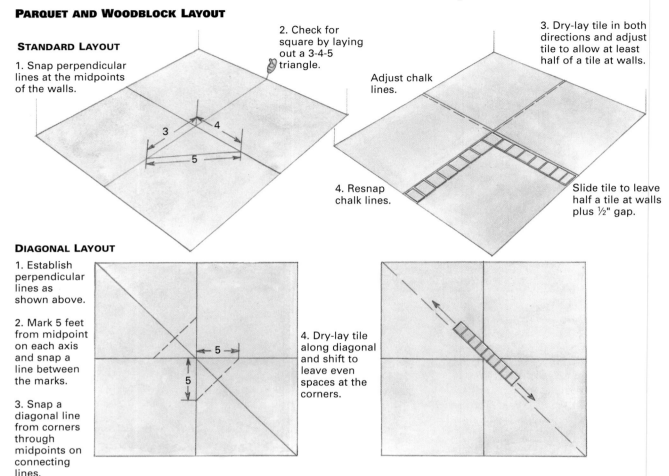

STANDARD LAYOUT

1. Snap perpendicular lines at the midpoints of the walls.

2. Check for square by laying out a 3-4-5 triangle.

3. Dry-lay tile in both directions and adjust tile to allow at least half of a tile at walls.

Adjust chalk lines.

4. Resnap chalk lines.

Slide tile to leave half a tile at walls plus ½" gap.

DIAGONAL LAYOUT

1. Establish perpendicular lines as shown above.

2. Mark 5 feet from midpoint on each axis and snap a line between the marks.

3. Snap a diagonal line from corners through midpoints on connecting lines.

4. Dry-lay tile along diagonal and shift to leave even spaces at the corners.

Parquet flooring comes in the form of square tiles, so the floor usually looks best if you lay it out to make the borders even on all walls—except those with doorways. As with other tile installations, the quadrant layout method works well (see page 52 and the illustrations above). Prepare the floor, then vacuum it before snapping layout lines. If you clean it after you lay it out, you'll remove the chalk lines.

LAYING OUT THE FLOOR

Using the information on page 52 and the illustration above, snap a chalk line at the center of the room. Snap a second line at the middle of the first one and perpendicular to it. Establish a 3-4-5 triangle to adjust the line square with the first.

Diagonal patterns require another set of squared lines, as shown above. Establish one diagonal using the method shown. Make the second diagonal perpendicular to the first so the lines are square to each other.

THE TEST RUN

Lay a dry run along both layout lines until you get the pattern centered in the room. Begin the test layout at the quadrant with a doorway. Lay a row of blocks from the center point toward the doorway wall and slide the row back and forth until you have a full block at the doorway, less ¼ inch for expansion. Snap a new line where the center-most block now falls; repeat the process on the other axis, sliding the tiles until the borders on both ends are equal. Then bring the parquet cartons into the room and put them around the room so you can reach them easily.

SETTING THE FIRST QUADRANT

Pros say applying adhesive is "all in the wrist" (and, of course, to some extent in the manufacturer's recommendations).

■ Dump or scoop a small amount of adhesive on the floor and—holding a toothed trowel at a 35- to 45-degree angle—spread enough adhesive for six to eight blocks. Don't cover the chalk lines. If you do, snap lines over the adhesive.

■ Set the first tile in the adhesive exactly at the intersection of the layout lines. If this tile is positioned incorrectly, everything else will be —and the error will be compounded across the room. Insert the tongue of each tile into the groove of the previous tile, and press each one tightly into place by hand. (Refer to the illustration at right.) Don't slide the tiles into place—adhesive will ooze through the joint. Clean adhesive off the surface immediately.

■ Fill the quadrant according to the pattern sequence you have chosen, working toward the walls.

■ At the walls, use the process illustrated below right for marking and cutting border tiles to fit. For complex shapes, cut an exact template from cardboard and trace it onto the wood block to serve as a guide. Cut the blocks with a fine-toothed backsaw or saber saw when you need to fit them around obstacles.

■ As you run out of room to work freely and need to walk or kneel on the tile, lay down plywood to distribute your weight and to avoid displacing or scuffing your new floor.

■ Fill the expansion gap with cork to keep the tiles from shifting.

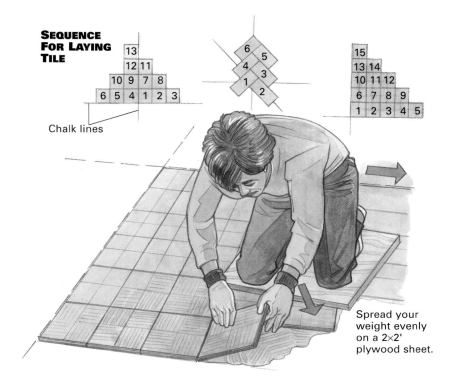

SEQUENCE FOR LAYING TILE

Chalk lines

Spread your weight evenly on a 2×2' plywood sheet.

■ Follow the same process to install the other quadrants. When you're done, don't walk on the floor yet. Let it stand as long as the adhesive manufacturer specifies. Then finish it if necessary, and trim and rehang the doors. If the parquet is prefinished, clean and buff it.

INSTALLING PARQUET TILE

1. Apply adhesive with a notched trowel up to but not covering the layout line.

Layout line

2. Lay the first tile exactly on the layout line.

3. Engage tongues and grooves of succeeding tiles and lower into place. Don't slide them.

4. At walls, lay the tile to be cut squarely on the last full tile and use an extra tile to mark the cut.

Tile to be cut

Spare tile used as marking guide

½- to ¾-in. spacer

PAINTING A FLOOR

Painted floors, whether they are wood or concrete, bring a special touch to any room. Paint is durable, attractive, and reasonably priced. It's an easy project for the do-it-yourselfer and offers endless opportunities for artistic expression.

The range of styles and techniques is limitless. The four techniques shown here are within the skills of any homeowner.

WHAT TO PAINT ON?

Any stripped wood floor, wood subfloor, or concrete slab can be painted. Paint may not stick well to resilient tile, resilient sheet, or ceramic tile, so it's better to remove those materials. The surface must be smooth and clean, so prepare it as you would for installing resilient flooring. Vacuum the floor and wipe it with a tack rag. Then seal it and paint it with one coat of high-quality, oil-based, exterior-grade primer.

WHAT KIND OF PAINT?

There are two basic paint choices—oil-base or latex. Special floor paints are available.
■ Oil-base paints create a hard film and cover a poorly prepared surface better.
■ Latex paints will give you a more resilient film and, because they breathe, are more suitable in damp environments such as basements or concrete slabs.

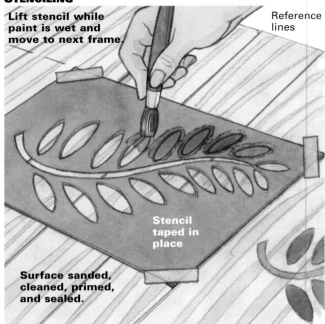

STENCILING

Lift stencil while paint is wet and move to next frame.

Reference lines

Stencil taped in place

Surface sanded, cleaned, primed, and sealed.

■ Alkyd or modified epoxy latex porch and floor paints dry to a durable surface, but color selection is limited.
■ Industrial enamels are tough, but their high gloss tends to make them slippery.
■ Porcelain-epoxy paints are excellent. Some lighter colors come in a satin finish.

SEAL THE FLOOR

Sealer closes pores in the wood and leaves a smooth base for the remaining coats. Test the drying time on scrap wood, then apply the sealer as recommended by the manufacturer. Wipe the excess after 10 minutes, and buff it with steel wool when dry. Then dust with a tack rag.

STENCILING

If you want wood tones and grains to show through your pattern, stencil right over the sealed floor. Otherwise, prime and paint the surface with two coats of oil or latex paint. Map out your design layout and snap perpendicular lines at both the center of the room and at locations that will keep the pattern regular and square. Tape the stencil into place and apply paint with a stencil brush. Lift the stencil before the paint dries. Wait 24 hours and apply a polyurethane finish.

COMB PAINTING

Comb painting is a repeated pattern of swirled lines made with a window squeegee you've cut notches into or other notched tool.

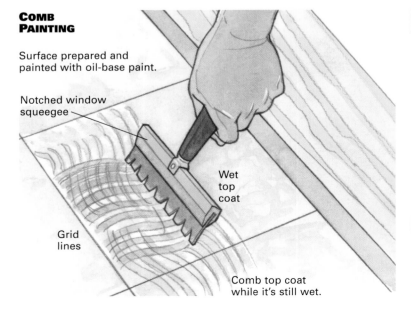

COMB PAINTING

Surface prepared and painted with oil-base paint.

Notched window squeegee

Wet top coat

Grid lines

Comb top coat while it's still wet.

Prime and paint the floor with two coats of light-colored oil-base paint. Then tape a grid on the floor in 12- to 24-inch sections. Thin a contrasting color with one part thinner to three parts paint and paint a section with this mixture. While this coat is still wet, run your comb through it to create patterns. When the design coat is dry, pull the tape up to reveal the colored borders.

MARBLEIZING

Marbleizing requires patience and practice. Experiment on a piece of plywood first.
■ Prime and paint the floor with two coats of semigloss latex. Then set out three pie tins—these will be your palettes.
■ In tin No. 1, thin some white latex paint and tint it with another color to a light neutral tone. In tin No. 2 put thinned white paint and at each edge dab different, brightly colored acrylics. Create veins in this tin by dragging the acrylics into the white paint

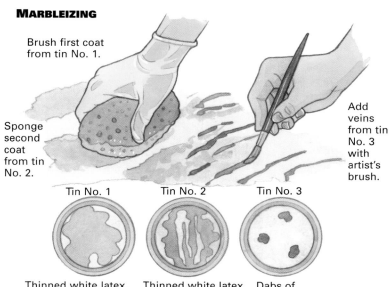

MARBLEIZING

Brush first coat from tin No. 1.

Sponge second coat from tin No. 2.

Add veins from tin No. 3 with artist's brush.

Tin No. 1 — Thinned white latex, tinted to neutral tone.

Tin No. 2 — Thinned white latex veined with acrylics.

Tin No. 3 — Dabs of unthinned acrylics.

with a sponge applicator. In tin No. 3 put dabs of unthinned acrylic colors.
■ Brush paint from tin No. 1 on the floor to create a neutral base. Immediately sponge with a paint pad containing the veining from tin No. 2. Add more veins from tin No. 3 with an artist's brush.

SPATTER PAINTING

Prime and paint the floor with two coats of floor enamel. When it's dry, spatter on another color. To spatter, load the brush with paint, then flick the brush to fling paint spots onto the floor. Repeat with a third color.

SPATTER PAINTING

Spatter succeeding colors after each coat has dried.

Surface prepared, primed, then painted with a solid color.

PAINTING A SLAB

You can dress up a drab slab with paint by using the same techniques used on wood floors. But concrete takes a little more preparation. Here's what you should do:
■ Make sure the slab is clean and dry. If it's new, cure it for at least 30 days before painting. If it's old, test for moisture (see page 62) and correct any problems.
■ Patch cracks and uneven joints with an expansive mortar designed for such applications. Allow it to cure, following the manufacturer's instructions.
■ Scrape off loose or flaking paint, and if the entire old paint job is rough, remove all of it by scraping or stripping it.
■ Scrub the floor with trisodium phosphate (TSP) mixed with water, according to instructions.
■ Etch the concrete with a solution of 1 part muriatic acid in 10 parts water. If you'll be using water-based paint, use phosphoric acid in the same ratio. Be careful; acids are corrosive. Mix them in a plastic pail. Wear rubber gloves and goggles, and follow all precautions on the container.
■ When the floor is dry, vacuum up the dusty residue.
■ Seal the floor (not necessary with an acrylic latex paint or an alkyd porch and floor enamel). Once the concrete is prepared, apply the paint with the same methods used on wood.

INSTALLING
RESILIENT AND
LAMINATE FLOORS

Sheet vinyl is easy to install, but calls for careful measuring and cutting.

TOOLS FOR INSTALLING RESILIENT FLOORING

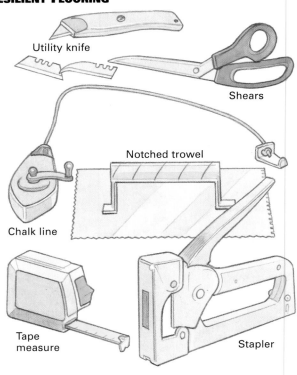

Utility knife

Shears

Notched trowel

Chalk line

Tape measure

Stapler

Both resilient and laminate flooring need to be acclimated before you install them. Store materials away from freezing or fluctuating temperatures. Let sheet flooring relax to remove the curl. Unroll it in a room at 70 degrees for 24 to 48 hours before installation. Let resilient tile and laminate boards and planks adjust to their new conditions for at least 48 hours in their unopened containers.

Resilient flooring is the thinnest of all flooring materials, so it will conform to almost every defect in the surface under it—cracks, voids,

dips—even small depressions from nailheads will show. If the subfloor or the existing floor is not smooth, cover it with underlayment-grade plywood to make it smooth.

The subsurface must be absolutely dry too. Unlike wood or carpet, through which small amounts of subsurface moisture can evaporate harmlessly, a resilient floor will trap moisture underneath it. Trapped moisture can weaken the adhesive bond. In humid climates, add a waterproof underlayment material.

PREPARING A FLOOR FOR RESILIENTS AND LAMINATES

CAUTION: Old resilient tile may contain asbestos fibers, which are harmful if inhaled. Covering this old tile with new flooring minimizes its potential hazard. If tile must be removed, consult an asbestos abatement professional.

Existing Floor	Preparation for Resilients	Preparation for Laminates
Exposed joists	1. Install ¼-inch T&G plywood or OSB subfloor.	1. Install ¾-inch plywood.
	2. Install lauan plywood or ¼- to ½-inch rated underlayment.	2. Install foam underlayment.
	3. Fill all nail holes and joints and sand smooth.	
Bare concrete	Level and smooth slab as necessary.	1. Repair surface.
		2. Install foam underlayment.
Wood floor or subfloor		
Over wood frame	1. Replace broken floor or subfloor boards.	1. Repair surface.
	2. Install lauan plywood or ¼- to ½-inch rated underlayment.	2. Install foam underlayment.
	3. Fill all nail holes and joints and sand smooth.	
Over concrete slab	1. Remove all wood materials.	1. Repair surface.
	2. Level and smooth slab as necessary.	2. Install foam underlayment.
Resilient sheet or tile		
Over wood frame	1. If existing resilient is cushioned, remove and repair surface.	If loose, remove and repair surface.
	If existing resilient is loose, has wax/gloss surface, or is embossed, install lauan or ¼- to ½-inch rated underlayment.	Otherwise, repair surface. Install foam underlayment.
	2. Fill all nail holes and joints and sand smooth.	
Over concrete slab	If existing resilient is cushioned or loose, remove and level slab as necessary.	Install foam underlayment.
	If existing resilient is embossed, smooth the surface with a liquid leveler; otherwise, remove wax and sand smooth.	
Ceramic tile		
Over wood frame	Remove tile or smooth with liquid leveler.	
	1. If tile is removed, repair subfloor as necessary.	1. If tile is bonded, level surface.
	2. Install lauan plywood or ¼- to ½-inch rated underlayment.	2. Install foam underlayment.
	3. Fill all nail holes and joints and sand smooth.	
Over concrete slab	1. Remove tile; otherwise, smooth with liquid leveler.	Same as over wood frame.
	2. If removing tile, repair slab as necessary; if slab is uneven, smooth with liquid leveler.	
Carpet		
Over wood frame	1. Remove carpet.	1. Remove carpet and pad.
	2. Repair subfloor as necessary.	2. Repair subfloor.
	3. Install lauan plywood or ¼- to ½-inch rated underlayment.	3. Install foam underlayment.
	4. Fill all nail holes and joints and sand smooth.	
Over concrete slab	1. Remove carpet and pad.	1. Remove carpet and pad.
	2. After removing carpet, repair slab as necessary; if slab is uneven, smooth with liquid leveler.	2. Repair surface.
		3. Install foam underlayment.

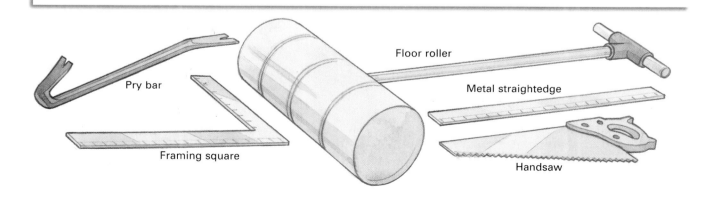

Pry bar

Floor roller

Metal straightedge

Framing square

Handsaw

INSTALLING RESILIENT SHEET FLOORING

Next to proper surface preparation, measuring and cutting are the keys to success when installing resilient sheet flooring. Careful work will save you from wasting the entire sheet.

There are two kinds of sheet flooring: one kind is installed by spreading adhesive only on the edges, the other kind requires spreading adhesive on the entire floor. Cutting both kinds to size and seaming them call for the same techniques.

No matter which style you have, the first thing to do is prepare the surface as outlined in the chart on page 77. Then follow the steps below to make a paper template, a room-sized form that will allow you to fit the sheet exactly to the walls and fixtures of your room.

MAKING A TEMPLATE

Making a template may seem like more trouble than simply bringing the sheet into the room and cutting it. Properly prepared, however, a template will give you a guide for cutting the flooring to fit exactly—without waste or risk of ruining the material.

To make the template, cover the perimeter of the floor with 15-pound felt, other building paper, or heavy butcher's paper, as shown on the opposite page. The heavier felt or building paper is less likely to move around.

■ Position the paper within ¼ inch of the walls, cabinet bases, and other obstacles. The template doesn't have to fit precisely; baseboards and shoe moldings will cover up the difference.

■ To keep the paper from shifting, cut out small triangles every 2 or 3 feet and tape the sheet to the floor underlayment through the holes. Overlap all edges at least 2 inches, and tape them together with a heavy tape such as duct tape.

■ Now that the template is in place, mark a line on the underlayment around the perimeter of the template, using a marker and steel straightedge. When you cut the resilient sheet and bring it into the room, this line will place it exactly where the template was. Then carefully roll up the template and take it to the room where you'll cut the sheet.

TRIMMING THE SHEET

Unroll the sheet flooring face up, if you haven't already done so. If the sheet will be seamed, make sure the pieces overlap by 3 inches at the seam and that pattern lines run unbroken along the length of the seam. Tape the seam securely—don't let it move.

■ Orient the sheet the same way it will be installed in the room, then unroll the paper

TIPS FOR SEAMS

Find the best location for seams before you get the resilient sheet in the room. Pick an inconspicuous, low-traffic area and mark the location of the seam on both sections of the sheet.

RESILIENT FLOORING ADHESIVES

What kind of adhesive should you use for your new resilient floor? It depends on the flooring material and the subfloor. Here are various adhesives and their applications. Always work in a well-ventilated room and follow manufacturer's instructions.

Flooring Material	Subfloor	Adhesive	Comments
Vinyl materials with rubber backing, cork, vinyl cork (not solid vinyl, asphalt, vinyl-composition)	Concrete or wood above grade	Water-soluble paste	Must be rolled.
Asphalt, vinyl-composition	Concrete or wood above, on, or below grade	Asphalt emulsion, cut-back asphalt	Do not thin with water for on- or below-grade floors.
Solid vinyl, vinyl-composition, rubber, cork, linoleum	Concrete or wood above, on, or below grade	Latex adhesive	Good for moist locations; dries quickly. Keep from freezing.
Vinyl, rubber, cork, linoleum	Concrete or wood above grade	Alcohol-resin	Flammable. Not entirely waterproof.
Solid vinyl, rubber tiles	Concrete or wood above, on, or below grade	Epoxy cement	Good for perimeter and seam sealing; high strength; two parts must be mixed.
Vinyl and rubber cove base	Above grade	Cove base cement (solvent based)	Flammable; wear gloves.
Vinyl cove base, metal nosings (not asphalt, vinyl-composition)	Any wall and edges	Synthetic rubber cement	Flammable.
Vinyl and rubber stair treads, nosings, corner guards	Any wall	Neoprene adhesive	Water resistant. Flammable.

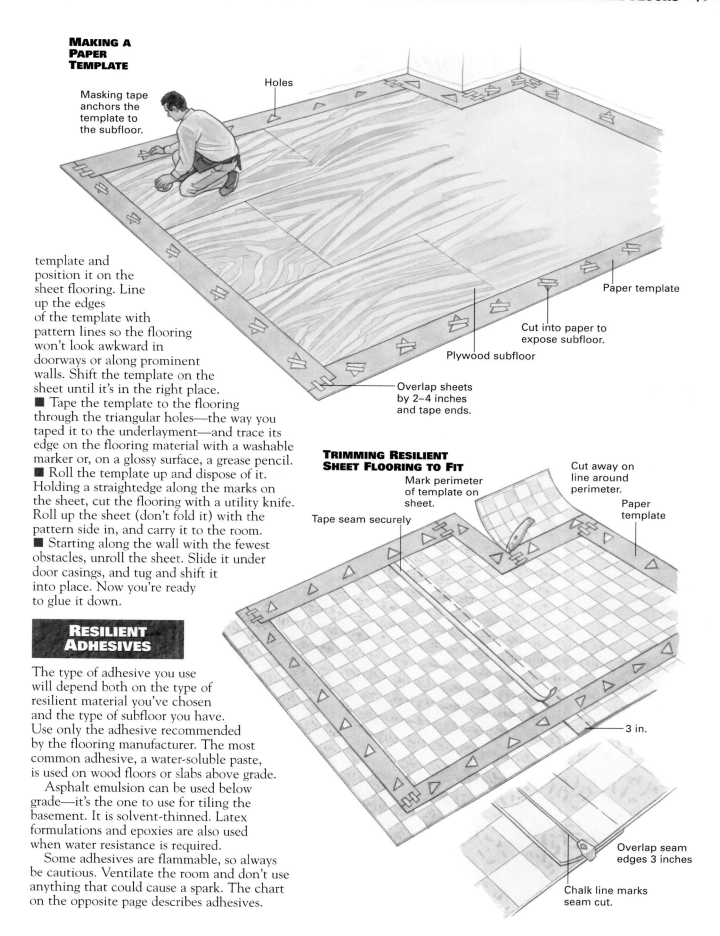

MAKING A PAPER TEMPLATE

Masking tape anchors the template to the subfloor.

Holes

Paper template

Cut into paper to expose subfloor.

Plywood subfloor

Overlap sheets by 2–4 inches and tape ends.

template and position it on the sheet flooring. Line up the edges of the template with pattern lines so the flooring won't look awkward in doorways or along prominent walls. Shift the template on the sheet until it's in the right place.

■ Tape the template to the flooring through the triangular holes—the way you taped it to the underlayment—and trace its edge on the flooring material with a washable marker or, on a glossy surface, a grease pencil.

■ Roll the template up and dispose of it. Holding a straightedge along the marks on the sheet, cut the flooring with a utility knife. Roll up the sheet (don't fold it) with the pattern side in, and carry it to the room.

■ Starting along the wall with the fewest obstacles, unroll the sheet. Slide it under door casings, and tug and shift it into place. Now you're ready to glue it down.

RESILIENT ADHESIVES

The type of adhesive you use will depend both on the type of resilient material you've chosen and the type of subfloor you have. Use only the adhesive recommended by the flooring manufacturer. The most common adhesive, a water-soluble paste, is used on wood floors or slabs above grade.

Asphalt emulsion can be used below grade—it's the one to use for tiling the basement. It is solvent-thinned. Latex formulations and epoxies are also used when water resistance is required.

Some adhesives are flammable, so always be cautious. Ventilate the room and don't use anything that could cause a spark. The chart on the opposite page describes adhesives.

TRIMMING RESILIENT SHEET FLOORING TO FIT

Mark perimeter of template on sheet.

Cut away on line around perimeter.

Paper template

Tape seam securely

3 in.

Overlap seam edges 3 inches

Chalk line marks seam cut.

INSTALLING RESILIENT SHEET FLOORING
continued

ADHERING PERIMETER-BOND VINYL

Perimeter-bond vinyl is glued only around the edges. After you have positioned the sheet in the room, start at a corner and carefully pull back the edge along one wall. Expose about 8 inches of underlayment or subfloor— or as much as the manufacturer recommends.

■ Using a ¼-inch notched trowel, spread a band of adhesive all along the edge of the floor. If the sheet will have a seam in it, stop the adhesive about 18 inches from where the seam edges will meet.

■ Ease the edge of the sheet back onto the adhesive and roll it with a floor roller to ensure good contact. Then move on to the other edges of the floor and finish gluing and rolling each edge in turn.

■ Seam the sheet, following the procedures described on page 81 and illustrated below.

Some products require edge stapling to further secure the sheet to the plywood underlayment. Follow the manufacturer's instructions. Make sure the base trim will cover the staples.

GLUING FULL-SPREAD VINYL

To apply full-spread adhesive, carefully lift up one half of the sheet and fold it back (don't crease it) onto the other half. (See the illustration on the opposite page.)

■ Working from the corners to the center on each length of wall, spread the adhesive on the floor with a ¼-inch notched trowel. Applicators are available for hard-to-reach spots. If the sheet will be seamed, stop the

PERIMETER-BOND VINYL: INSTALLING AND SEAMING

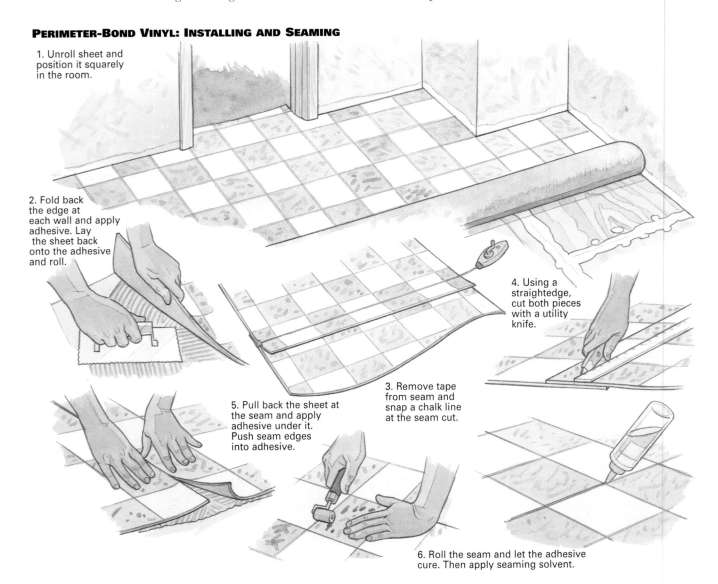

1. Unroll sheet and position it squarely in the room.

2. Fold back the edge at each wall and apply adhesive. Lay the sheet back onto the adhesive and roll.

3. Remove tape from seam and snap a chalk line at the seam cut.

4. Using a straightedge, cut both pieces with a utility knife.

5. Pull back the sheet at the seam and apply adhesive under it. Push seam edges into adhesive.

6. Roll the seam and let the adhesive cure. Then apply seaming solvent.

adhesive about 18 inches short of the seam.

■ Refold the sheet back into place and roll it from the center to the corners. Adhere the second sheet (or the other half if not seaming).

SEAMING SHEET VINYL

Make seams in sheet flooring after the sheets have been adhered.

■ On the face of the seam overlap, snap a chalk line down the center of the seam.

■ Cut with a sharp utility knife against a steel straightedge, with enough pressure to cut through both layers of flooring. Don't cut twice— you'll leave gaps.

■ Remove the scrap overlaps and clean the floor under the seam.

■ Pull back both edges of flooring and spread a band of adhesive along the floor. Join the two edges and press them into the adhesive.

■ Immediately wipe off any adhesive that oozes up between the pieces, and clean the seam with a solvent for the adhesive.

■ After the adhesive has set for the time specified by the manufacturer, seal the seam with seaming solvent, which melts the edges and fuses them to make the seam waterproof. The solvent bottle comes with a special applicator spout which you run along the seam, following the directions on the label. Apply the sealer only to the seam, not to the flooring. To finish the job, replace the trim, install baseboards and shoe molding or vinyl cove base (see illustration below). Install thresholds and rehang the doors.

INSTALLING FULL-SPREAD SHEET VINYL

1. Unroll sheet and position it squarely in the room.

2. Pull back one half of the sheet and apply adhesive to within 18 inches of the seam.

3. Pull back the other half and apply adhesive.

4. Seam the sheet, following the procedures illustrated on the opposite page.

5. Roll the entire surface with a floor roller.

IMMEDIATELY AFTER INSTALLATION

After you've laid your new resilient floor, take these steps to protect it until both adhesive and seams have set.

■ Protect the seams for at least 8 hours. If possible, don't walk on them.

■ Keep the room at 65 degrees or above for 48 hours to let the adhesive cure properly.

■ Don't scrub or wash the floor for 5 days.

INSTALLING VINYL COVE BASE

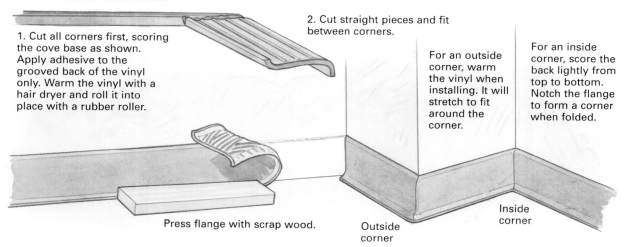

1. Cut all corners first, scoring the cove base as shown. Apply adhesive to the grooved back of the vinyl only. Warm the vinyl with a hair dryer and roll it into place with a rubber roller.

2. Cut straight pieces and fit between corners.

For an outside corner, warm the vinyl when installing. It will stretch to fit around the corner.

For an inside corner, score the back lightly from top to bottom. Notch the flange to form a corner when folded.

Press flange with scrap wood.

Outside corner

Inside corner

INSTALLING RESILIENT TILE

STANDARD LAYOUT

Snap perpendicular lines at the midpoints of the walls and square them to each other. Dry-lay tile in both directions to center layout. Snap new chalk lines.

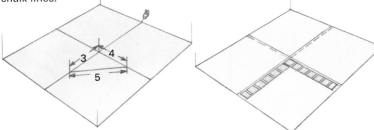

DIAGONAL LAYOUT

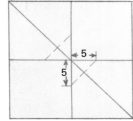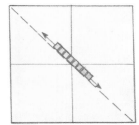

Lay out perpendicular lines as shown below and snap diagonal lines (see page 72). Dry-lay tile along a diagonal and shift the tiles to leave even spaces at the corners. Snap a perpendicular line at the center of the tile layout.

Just about anyone can install resilient tile. It requires few special tools and the materials are not particularly expensive. If you do make a mistake, you've only lost one tile—and you might be able to use it along an edge.

Prepare the floor using the information on page 77, then sweep and clean it.

LAYOUT

The quadrant layout method (see page 72 and the illustration at left) works best for most tile installations. It allows you to center the pattern with equal-width cut tiles along the edges. For durability and appearance, borders that extend into an opening or a doorway should have full tiles. If the room is irregular or contains many built-in protrusions, mark the reference lines—either square or diagonal—on the largest rectangular portion of the floor.

Next, test the layout. Dry-lay tiles along both axes, starting at the center and working toward the walls. If you end up with less than half a tile at the wall, adjust the test run on that axis until the edge tile is at least a half tile. Continue testing layouts with dry runs until you're satisfied with the way the borders look. Then mark your layout lines again.

SETTING THE FIRST QUADRANT

Before opening the can of adhesive, read the label to find out its open time—how many minutes you have before the adhesive becomes too dry to make a good bond. Some adhesives will allow you enough time to set only six or seven tiles; with others you'll be able to set most of a quadrant.

■ With the smooth side of a notched trowel (use the size recommended by the adhesive

INSTALLING RESILIENT TILE

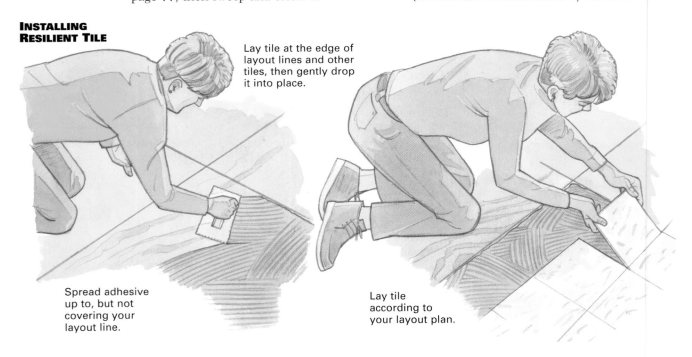

Lay tile at the edge of layout lines and other tiles, then gently drop it into place.

Spread adhesive up to, but not covering your layout line.

Lay tile according to your layout plan.

manufacturer), spread a small amount of adhesive at the intersection of your layout lines. Don't cover the lines. Avoid spreading it too thick, which will cause it to ooze between the tiles; or too thin, which will not produce a good bond. Then use the notched side of the trowel to comb the adhesive. Allow the adhesive to become slightly tacky before setting the tiles.

■ Carefully position the first tile so it's perfectly aligned on the intersection of both layout lines. Set the next few tiles along each axis. Then fill the area between the axes, working toward the walls.

■ Snap the tiles into place; don't slide them. Work very carefully. Minor errors early can build to major alignment problems later.

■ Continue laying tiles along each axis and filling in the area between them.

■ Cut tiles at the borders and to fit around obstacles as shown in the illustration below. Resilient tiles can be brittle when cold. Warm them briefly with a hair dryer to make the cuts easier.

FINISHING UP

Finish the other three quadrants in the same manner as the first, starting in the center of the room and working out along both axes. To prevent displacement of newly laid tiles, lay a 2×2-foot piece of plywood over tiles before walking or kneeling on them.

INSTALLING SELF-STICK TILE

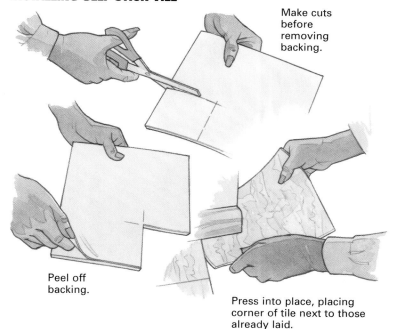

Make cuts before removing backing.

Peel off backing.

Press into place, placing corner of tile next to those already laid.

Watch for adhesive oozing out of the joints. Wipe it up immediately with a rag and a compatible solvent.

Don't walk on the floor until the adhesive has set. Check the manufacturer's instructions for set-up time. When the floor can safely be walked on, install the finish details.

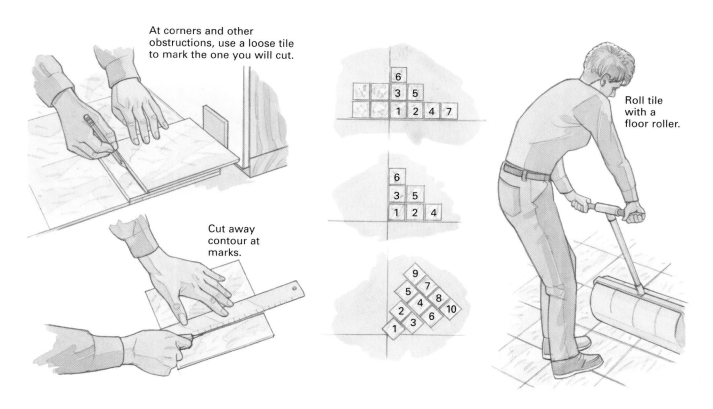

At corners and other obstructions, use a loose tile to mark the one you will cut.

Cut away contour at marks.

Roll tile with a floor roller.

INSTALLING LAMINATE FLOORING

Although laminate flooring needs a smooth and level subfloor, its foam underlayment makes it somewhat forgiving of subfloor imperfections. Manufacturers specify ventilation requirements, so if your floor will be over a crawlspace, make sure it meets the specifications.

Prepare the floor as shown in the chart on page 77, making surface repairs to wood frame floors and slabs as discussed on pages 60–64.

UNDERLAYMENT FIRST

After you have properly prepared the subfloor—including laying a vapor barrier over a slab—lay down the underlayment. Start in a corner; butt the end of the underlayment against one wall. Unroll the underlayment to the other wall and

GLUING TIPS

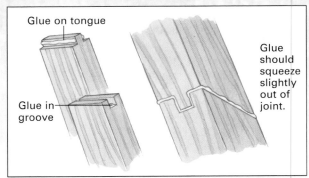

Glue on tongue

Glue in groove

Glue should squeeze slightly out of joint.

Not all brands of laminate flooring are glued the same way. Some manufacturers recommend gluing the tongue of the board, others the groove, and still others, both the tongue and groove. Follow the directions and use only the glue specified by the manufacturer.

One requirement that is consistent among products is the amount of glue to apply—and getting this right might take some experimenting. Properly applied glue should just barely seep from between fully closed joints. If you're applying too little, the boards won't stay together; too much, and you won't get the boards together tightly or you'll have excess glue to clean up.

FLOATING A LAMINATE FLOOR

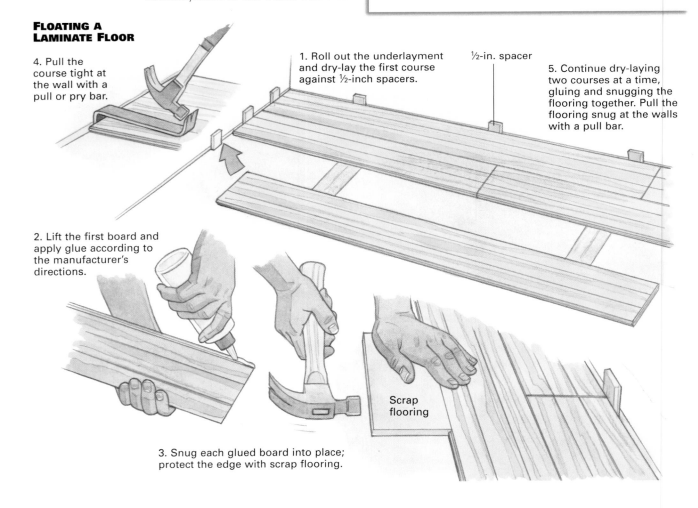

4. Pull the course tight at the wall with a pull or pry bar.

1. Roll out the underlayment and dry-lay the first course against ½-inch spacers.

½-in. spacer

5. Continue dry-laying two courses at a time, gluing and snugging the flooring together. Pull the flooring snug at the walls with a pull bar.

2. Lift the first board and apply glue according to the manufacturer's directions.

Scrap flooring

3. Snug each glued board into place; protect the edge with scrap flooring.

cut it to fit. If the manufacturer recommends laying a section of flooring at this point, start the next step and rotate through the steps for underlayment and installation. Otherwise, stick with unrolling the underlayment, butting each strip against the previous one (don't overlap them). Tape the seams (unless the manufacturer recommends otherwise). If you're using solid-panel underlayment, use the same methods, but leave a ¼-inch expansion gap between the panels.

THE FIRST PLANK

If your starting wall is square to the room, dry-lay the first row against ½-inch spacers, as shown in the illustration on the opposite page. Or you can use the starter-line layout method shown on page 52. When you get to the side wall, lay a plank next to the first one and mark a cut line. Transfer the line to the back of the plank. Cut the plank with a carbide-tipped blade in your circular saw (turn the plank facedown when cutting). Set the cut board in place and pull it snug with a pull bar or pry bar.

At each end of the first plank and in the middle, measure from the edge to the opposite wall. If the measurement will divide by the plank width and leave more than 2 inches, dry-lay two more rows. If you won't have at least a 2-inch plank on the far wall, split the difference between the first and last rows and trim the first row accordingly. Then continue dry-laying the next two rows, racking the ends if necessary.

Manufacturers' recommendations for the amount of joint overlap differ. Refer to the illustration at right if your flooring does not come with specific instructions.

GLUING THINGS DOWN

Once three courses are laid, you can start gluing. Make sure the courses are running straight in the room. Take up all the planks except the first one—number them or keep them in order—and apply glue to the planks as specified by the manufacturer.

Set the planks back in place, press them together, and wipe off excess glue. Tap the blocks together and clamp them as specified by the manufacturer. Continue to dry-lay, glue, and clamp, starting each row with the piece left over from the previous one, if the piece is a foot long or longer.

WHAT GOES UNDER THE FLOORING?

Laminate flooring materials require a foam underlayment, which cushions the floor underfoot. Underlayment also deadens sound and allows the entire floor to function as a single unit held down by the base moldings.

Installation on a concrete slab requires a moisture barrier. Some floating-floor manufacturers build a moisture barrier into underlayment. Others require a two-step application. Be sure to use only the materials recommended by the manufacturer of your flooring. Some choices are:

■ **6-MIL POLYETHELYENE:** Keeps moisture out of the laminate flooring, but requires a separate foam underlayment.

■ **2-IN-1 FOAM:** A more expensive product than separate moisture barriers and underlayments, but it allows you to cover the floor in one application. Install the film side down (facing the slab).

■ **FOAM UNDERLAYMENT:** This companion to polyethylene moisture barriers is made of closed-cell poly.

■ **RUBBER-BACKED AND SOLID POLY:** A more expensive product, but worth it if you want the most comfortable floor and the highest degree of sound absorption.

THE FINAL PLANK

Mark the width of the last row and apply glue to the plank. Set it in place with a pull bar, or lever it with a pry bar and a piece of scrap. Remove excess glue, and let the floor set overnight before you walk on it.

Some laminate planks have a soft, almost clear grain with no strip or plank division. Use these layout methods with them.

LAMINATE PLANK PATTERNS

Joints fall on midpoint of previous plank.

Minimum 12-inch stagger

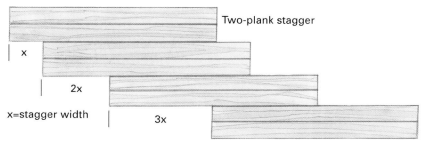

Two-plank stagger

x

2x

x=stagger width

3x

Laminate planks are also manufactured in two-plank or three-strip configurations, each with racked or staggered joint lines.

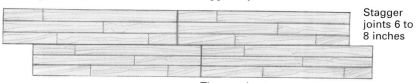

Stagger joints 6 to 8 inches

Three-strip stagger

CERAMIC TILE
& DIMENSIONED STONE

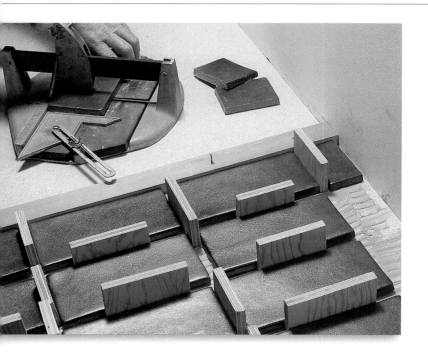

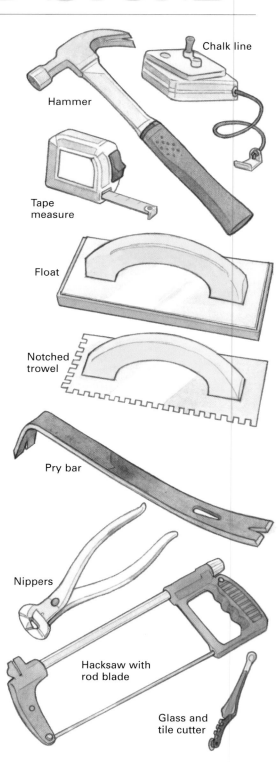

Chalk line

Hammer

Tape measure

Float

Notched trowel

Pry bar

Nippers

Hacksaw with rod blade

Glass and tile cutter

Ceramic and dimensioned stone tile are the heaviest of flooring materials, so they require a floor structure that has been designed or reinforced to carry the weight. If you plan to lay tile over an existing tile floor, remove the existing tile first to reduce the weight.

Ceramic and dimensioned stone tile are the most stable of flooring materials, but like other materials it's better to let them sit in the room before you install them. Bring the materials in one day before installation to equalize the temperature of the tile and the subfloor. Arrange the cartons so you can reach them easily but still keep them out of your way. Store the tiles in a separate room if the subfloor isn't prepared yet.

Cement backer board provides a smooth surface that makes installation of ceramic tile and stone over a wood frame floor easier.

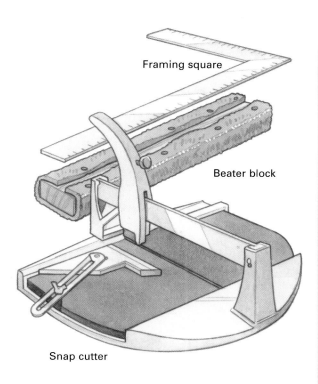

Framing square

Beater block

Snap cutter

Installation on a concrete slab usually requires only surface repairs. The chart at right shows how to prepare your subfloor. Your local rental outlet has special tools that are not normally part of your do-it-yourself tool box.

Procedures for installing either ceramic tile or dimensioned stone tile are similar, but stone tiles come with some of their own peculiarities. You must cut them with a tile-cutting saw; trying to cut stone with nippers or by scoring and snapping usually fractures it. Joints between stone tiles must be tighter than joints for ceramic tiles (usually not more than ⅛ inch), which reduces layout flexibility. The natural grain of the stones that makes cutting difficult also gives each piece a distinctive look.

PREPARING A FLOOR FOR CERAMIC TILE

Exposed Joist	Install a double-wood subfloor—¾-in. T&G CDX plywood on the joists and underlayment-grade plywood or tile-backing units over the subfloor.
Bare Concrete	Make surface repairs to slab as needed. Roughen the surface for best adhesion.
Wood Subfloor	
Over wood frame	Make surface repairs as needed. Install underlayment-grade plywood or tile-backing units over subfloor.
Over concrete slab	Remove all wood materials to expose the slab. Make surface repairs to slab as needed. Roughen the surface for best adhesion.
Wood Finish Floor	
Over wood frame	Remove finish flooring to expose the subfloor. Install underlayment-grade plywood.
Over concrete slab	Remove all wood materials to expose the slab. Make surface repairs to slab as needed. Roughen the surface for best adhesion.
Resilient Sheet or Tile	
Over wood frame	If the resilient flooring is installed over particleboard underlayment, remove both. If the resilient flooring is installed over plywood, is dense (neither cushioned nor springy), and is sound, remove wax or finish. Otherwise remove the flooring to subfloor. Install underlayment-grade plywood or tile-backing units.
Over concrete slab	If the resilient flooring is cushioned, springy, or unsound, remove it and make surface repairs to the slab as needed. Otherwise remove wax or finish and use an adhesive compatible with the resilient flooring.
Ceramic Tile	
Over wood frame	If possible, remove existing tile, then install underlayment-grade plywood or tile-backing units over the subfloor. Otherwise secure loose tiles and roughen the surface. Smooth uneven surfaces with liquid underlayment. Reinforce floor if necessary.
Over concrete slab	Remove tile, if possible. Repair slab as necessary. Otherwise secure loose tiles and roughen the surface. Smooth uneven surfaces with liquid underlayment.
Carpet	
Over wood frame	Remove existing carpet and pad, then install underlayment-grade plywood or tile-backing units.
Over concrete slab	Remove existing carpet and pad, then repair slab surface as necessary.

INSTALLATION TECHNIQUES

WATERPROOFING MEMBRANE

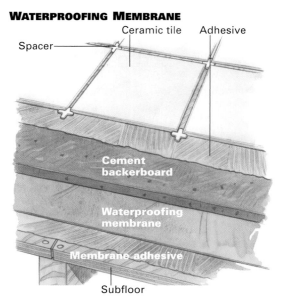

Spacer
Ceramic tile
Adhesive
Cement backerboard
Waterproofing membrane
Membrane adhesive
Subfloor

ISOLATION MEMBRANE

Ceramic tile
Thinset adhesive
Isolation membrane
Membrane adhesive
Wood floor
Concrete slab

Ceramic and stone tiles are not flexible, so they require a more rigid subsurface than other materials. Cement backerboard—a laminated sheet of concrete and fiberglass made specifically to support tile—is the best material to use. Many installations are made with plywood under tile, however. In addition, some situations require extra layers of protection beneath the tiles.

WATERPROOF MEMBRANE: A waterproof membrane stops moisture from seeping up through or down through floors. In wet areas, such as shower floors, install a waterproof membrane over the subfloor and under the cement backerboard. See the illustration at left.

ISOLATION MEMBRANE: An isolation membrane protects tile from excessive movement or different rates of movement in underlying surfaces caused by temperature and humidity changes. If you're tiling over different materials, install an isolation membrane as illustrated at left.

LAYING CEMENT BACKERBOARD

Backerboard comes in a number of sizes, and installing it is much like installing drywall. Purchase the size that will result in the

SIZING THE JOINTS

Here are guidelines to help you decide how wide the joint should be for the particular tile you're setting. You can vary the size to suit your installation, but larger joints are more likely to crack. Irregular tiles usually need large joints.
Glazed tiles—3/16 to 3/8 in.
Porcelain tiles—1/8 to 1/4 in.
Terra-cotta tiles—3/4 in.
Cement-bodied tiles—3/8 to 1/2 in.
Stone tiles—Up to 1/8 in.

ADHESIVES FOR TILE AND STONE

The type of adhesive you use for your tile or stone floor depends in part on the conditions in which it will be installed. The chart below shows appropriate adhesives for several installation conditions. Consult with your tile dealer to make the selection that best fits your project.

Conditions	Type/Composition	Comments
Adhesives		
Damp areas	Type I mastic (solvent based)	Flammable. Possible lung and skin irritant. Thinset. Ready to use.
Dry areas	Type II mastic (latex based)	Easy cleanup, nonflammable.
Wet areas or over plywood or resilient materials	Epoxy adhesive (2-part epoxy)	Expensive, toxic to skin. Works best at 70 to 85 degrees.
Mortars		
Wet areas or uneven subfloors	Portland cement (portland, sand, water)	For reinforced thick-bed installations. Long-lasting, waterproof, strong.
Over cement backerboard, not over wood or resilient floors	Dry-set mortar (portland, sand, additives, water)	Not water-resistant. Nonflammable, easy cleanup, rigid, impact resistant.
	Latex-portland (portland, sand, liquid latex, water).	More water-resistant than dry-set mortar, easier to work.
Wet areas over concrete or ceramic tile	Epoxy mortar (epoxy resin, hardener, sand, portland cement)	More body and water-resistance than epoxy adhesive. Levels uneven surfaces.

LAYING CEMENT BACKERBOARD

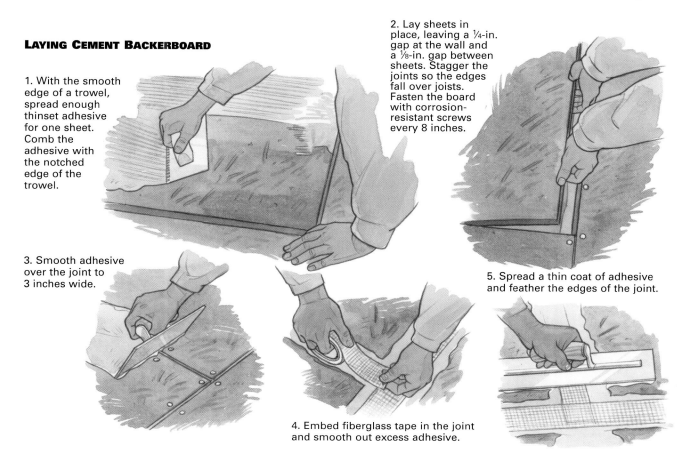

1. With the smooth edge of a trowel, spread enough thinset adhesive for one sheet. Comb the adhesive with the notched edge of the trowel.

2. Lay sheets in place, leaving a 1/4-in. gap at the wall and a 1/8-in. gap between sheets. Stagger the joints so the edges fall over joists. Fasten the board with corrosion-resistant screws every 8 inches.

3. Smooth adhesive over the joint to 3 inches wide.

4. Embed fiberglass tape in the joint and smooth out excess adhesive.

5. Spread a thin coat of adhesive and feather the edges of the joint.

least waste and follow the procedures in the illustration above. Once the backerboard is in place, you're ready to lay out the room.

LAYOUT

To lay out your installation, use either the perimeter layout method or the quadrant method. We've shown the quadrant method here, because it will result in evenly spaced borders and cut tiles.

Snap chalk lines in the center of the room and square them with the 3-4-5 triangle method. Then lay tiles and spacers along both axes until you get full tiles at doorways and equal tiles on the borders. If the pattern doesn't fit exactly, you may be able to adjust it by changing the width of your grout lines slightly.

Resnap chalk lines at the new locations, then make a jury stick, as shown in the illustration at right. Lay the jury stick along the walls and use it to mark and snap additional layout lines. Additional layout lines keep the pattern from wandering as you lay the tile.

LAYING OUT A TRIAL RUN

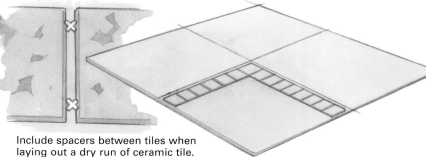

Include spacers between tiles when laying out a dry run of ceramic tile.

MAKING A JURY STICK

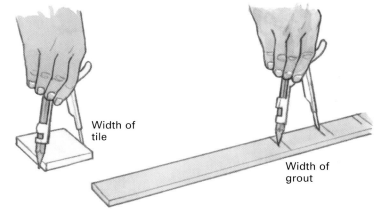

Width of tile

Width of grout

INSTALLATION TECHNIQUES
continued

SPREADING TILE ADHESIVE

1. Dump just enough adhesive to cover the area and spread it with the smooth edge of the trowel held at a 30-degree angle

2. Comb adhesive with notched edge at a 45- to 75-degree angle.

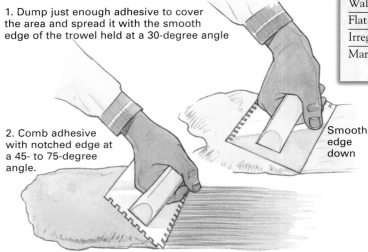

Smooth edge down

Notched edge down

WHAT TROWEL TO USE?

Type of Tile	Notch Size and Shape
Mosaics and smaller tiles	$\frac{3}{16} \times \frac{5}{32}$ in. or $\frac{1}{4} \times \frac{1}{16}$ in., V
Wall tiles	$\frac{1}{4} \times \frac{1}{4}$ in., square
Flat-backed floor tiles	$\frac{1}{4} \times \frac{1}{4}$ in., square
Irregular or lug-backed tiles	$\frac{1}{4} \times \frac{3}{8}$ in. or $\frac{1}{2} \times \frac{1}{2}$ in., square
Marble and granite	$\frac{1}{4} \times \frac{1}{4}$ in. or $\frac{1}{4} \times \frac{3}{8}$ in., square

■ Use the adhesive and trowel size recommended by the manufacturer.
■ Keep your layout lines visible; put adhesive up to them, but not over them.
■ Place tiles in the adhesive with a gentle twisting motion—do not slide them.
■ Immediately clean adhesive from surfaces.
■ To level the tiles, press them into the adhesive with a handmade beater block—a carpet-covered length of 2×4.
■ In tight places, back-butter the tile by applying a small amount of adhesive on the back of the tile and spreading it with the notched side of the trowel.
■ Lay down plywood to walk on set tiles.

SETTING THE FIRST TILES

Setting tiles is a series of repetitive steps. Go slowly at first—you'll pick up speed and expertise as you work. The illustration below will take you through the steps, but here are some things to keep in mind.

CUTTING TILES

Cutting tiles is usually a snap—although sometimes it may be slightly more difficult.

LAYING CERAMIC TILE

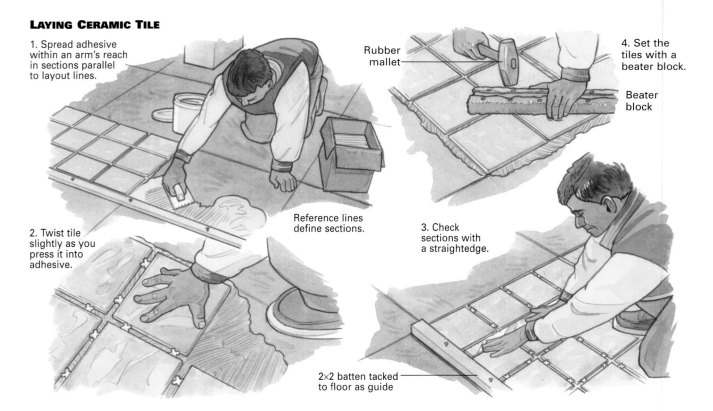

1. Spread adhesive within an arm's reach in sections parallel to layout lines.

2. Twist tile slightly as you press it into adhesive.

Reference lines define sections.

Rubber mallet

3. Check sections with a straightedge.

4. Set the tiles with a beater block.

Beater block

2×2 batten tacked to floor as guide

The illustration below right shows the steps in making a cut. Allow yourself to make some mistakes—that's one of the reasons you should buy extra tile. If the layout is regular and perfectly square, cut several tiles ahead of time. Rent a tile saw if you'll have a lot of cuts. The cost will be worth the time saved.

IN DOUBT ABOUT GROUT?

When you shop for grout, you'll find they all do pretty much the same thing and there's not much difference in the way they look.

Most grouts will work with any residential tile installation, but the most common are cement-based grout (a mixture of portland cement and sand or additives) or latex-portland cement grout (like cement grout, but with latex additives).

Look for hardened polymer-modified grouts. They are more flexible, hold color longer, and are more water-resistant than regular grouts. Colored sealant and caulk make expansion joints that match your grout. Sealants last somewhat longer than caulk, but caulk is easier to apply.

GROUTING

When the adhesive has set for 24 hours, remove the spacers between the tiles and mix the grout to about the consistency of mayonnaise. Mix only as much grout as you can apply during the open, or working, time. Apply the grout as shown below. Here are some other points to keep in mind:
■ Grout that has set cannot be remoistened.
■ Pack the joints tightly.
■ Work the float diagonally across— not parallel to—the tiles.
■ After 10–15 minutes, remove the surplus.
■ After another 30 minutes, wipe away the grout haze with a nearly dry sponge. Let the grout cure, then install a tile base border.

INSTALLING A TILE BASE BORDER

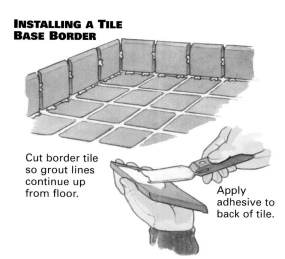

Cut border tile so grout lines continue up from floor.

Apply adhesive to back of tile.

CUTTING CERAMIC TILE

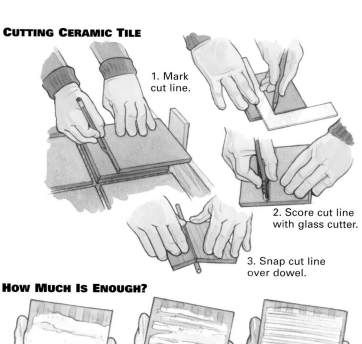

1. Mark cut line.

2. Score cut line with glass cutter.

3. Snap cut line over dowel.

HOW MUCH IS ENOUGH?

Too thick

Too thin

Proper application

GROUTING TILE

Force grout into joints with a grout float.

Sweep grout across tile to ensure complete coverage and to remove excess.

Sponge off haze.

INSTALLING CARPET

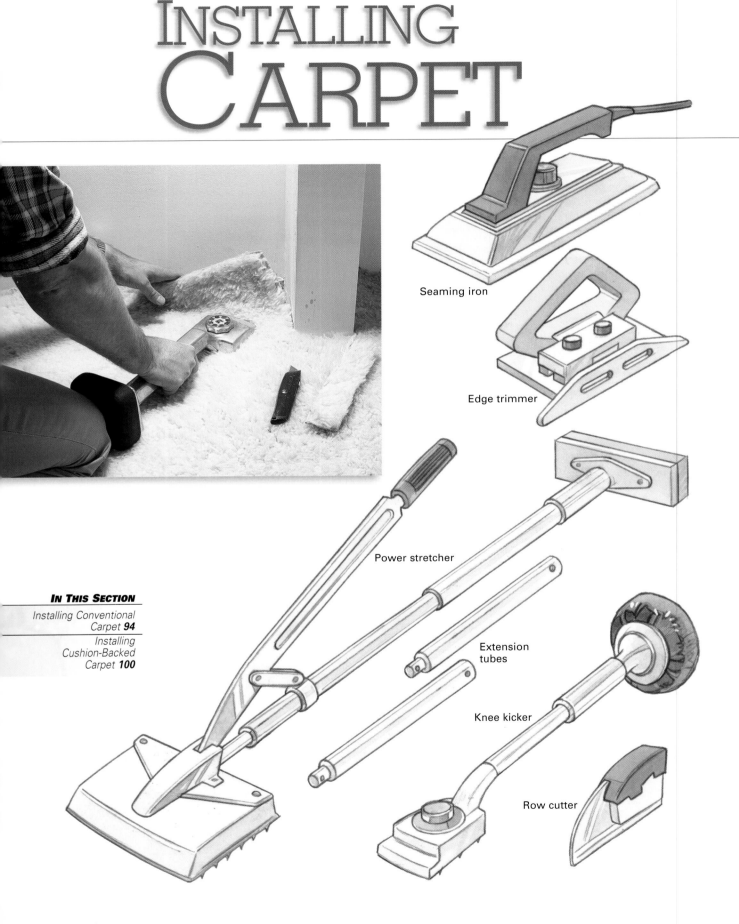

Seaming iron

Edge trimmer

Power stretcher

Extension tubes

Knee kicker

Row cutter

Carpet generally requires less preparation for installation than do other flooring materials. The subfloor must be dry, free of debris, and relatively smooth. If you're replacing existing carpet, replace the pad. Carpet pad is relatively inexpensive, and the old one may harbor mildew, mold, and odors. You might be able to reuse tackless strip that's in good condition.

If you have radiant heating, be careful when nailing down tackless strip—you might puncture a pipe. Locate the pipes first by spraying water on the surface along the edge of the wall where the tackless strip will go. Then turn up the heat. Mark the areas that dry first; that's where your radiant heating pipes are. Transfer the marks to the wall or make a precise diagram of the pattern of the piping so you can avoid nailing there.

When you bring the carpet home, store it on a clean surface in a dry area. If the surface is damp, lay a sheet of plastic underneath the carpet roll. Cut the carpet to rough size on a large, clean, dry surface, such as the floor of a large, empty room, a garage floor, or even the driveway that's been swept clean. Then carry the pieces separately into the rooms where they will be installed. Roll and unroll carpet in the direction of the pile.

Weight and bulk make carpet awkward to handle—you may need a helper. One good way to carry a large unrolled piece of carpet is to fold both long sides toward the center and then loosely roll it up. The shorter roll is bulky but easier to maneuver.

PREPARING A FLOOR FOR CARPET

Preparation for conventional and cushion-backed carpet is much the same. This chart notes where additional smoothing is needed for cushion-backed carpet.

Existing Floor	Preparation
Exposed joists	Install ¾-in. T&G CDX/PTS plywood subfloor. Fill nail holes and joints and sand smooth.
Bare concrete	Level and smooth surface.
Wood subfloor	
Over wood frame	Repair surface as needed. If subfloor is rough or gapped, install ⅜- or ½-in. underlayment. For cushion-backed carpet, fill and sand.
Over concrete slab	Remove all wood materials to expose slab, then level and smooth slab.
Wood finish floor	
Over wood frame	Repair surface as needed. For cushion-backed carpet on rough floor, remove floor and install underlayment. Fill and sand.
Over concrete slab	Remove all wood materials to expose slab. Level and smooth slab.
Resilient sheet or tile	
Over wood frame	If existing material is cushioned and loose, remove it. Repair surface or install ⅜- or ½-in. underlayment. For cushion-backed carpet, fill and sand. If existing material is not cushioned but is loose, install ⅜- or ½-in. underlayment. For cushion-backed carpet, fill and sand. If resilient flooring is smooth and tightly bonded, repair surface as needed. For cushion-backed carpet, remove wax and roughen surface.
Over concrete	Repair surface as needed.
Ceramic tile	
Over wood frame	Remove existing tile, if possible. Repair surface and level it with liquid underlayment. If tile is smooth and tightly bonded, level the surface with a liquid underlayment. Otherwise remove tile and repair surface.
Over concrete slab	For cushion-backed carpet, liquid underlayment must be compatible with carpet adhesive.
Carpet	
Over wood frame	Remove existing carpet and pad. Repair surface as needed. If subfloor is rough, uneven, or gapped, install ⅜- or ½-in. underlayment.
Over concrete slab	Remove existing carpet and pad. Repair surface as needed.

INSTALLING CONVENTIONAL CARPET

Carpet installation requires a number of steps, but the job is straightforward. You don't have to draw layout lines on the floor, but doing some planning on paper helps, especially in deciding where to locate seams. (See the illustration on the opposite page.) See page 93 for information on preparing the subfloor.

TACKLESS STRIP

Start the job by laying tackless strip—thin pieces of wood with tack points embedded in them. The sharp points grip the carpet, but they will also easily prick your hands and fingers; wear leather gloves for this job.

Starting in one corner, nail the strips around the perimeter of the room with the points angled toward the wall. Leave a gap between the strip and wall that is two-thirds the carpet thickness. Cut strip sections with tin snips and fasten each section with at least two nails. Follow all the angles around door casings or trim.

At doorways in a slab room, nail down a gripper edge with concrete nails. When the flange is hammered down over the carpet, it will bind the carpet edge and makes a clean-looking transition. If you do not want a visible strip, use a Z-bar binding. Nail it under a length of tackless strip installed in the door opening. The carpet wraps over the Z, which then clinches it. (See "Transitions," page 97.)

Staple carpet pad to the floor after you install tackless strip around the edge of the room.

INSTALLING THE PAD

Cut a piece of pad long enough to cover the room from one end to the other. (A utility knife cuts pad easily.) Butt one end of the pad and its edge against the edge of the tackless strip. At the other end, overlap the strip slightly. Staple the pad every 6 to 12 inches around its edges on a wood floor. On a slab, tape the edges down with double-faced carpet tape. Butt the next piece against the first.

Tape the seams with duct tape. Trim the pad back ¼ inch from the tackless strips to keep it from riding on top of the strips when you stretch the carpet. Snap a chalk line on the pad at any seam locations.

CHOOSING A CARPET PAD

Carpet pad is one of the keys to carpeting success. It adds to the resilience of the carpet itself, insulates the floor from temperature changes and noise, provides additional comfort, and can add to the life of the carpet when chosen to match the characteristics of the carpet. Because the pad is the foundation for your carpet, you want one that is firm and resilient.

THE FOUR CARPET PAD MATERIALS:

■ **POLYURETHANE FOAM:** prime foam, like that used in car seats and mattresses.

■ **BONDED POLYURETHANE:** chopped and shredded pieces of scrap polyurethane bonded into a solid piece, often with a reinforcing netting for a backing.

■ **RUBBER:** made from a blend of natural and synthetic rubber, either flat or waffled.

■ **FIBER:** fiber pads may be natural (animal hair and jute) or synthetic (polypropylene, nylon, and acrylics).

Be sure to check with your distributor so you get the pad that matches your carpet style, fibers, and uses. The thickness of the pad you need depends in part on the traffic the carpet will bear. In light traffic areas such as bedrooms and dens, use thicker and softer pads; use a thinner one in high-traffic areas such as living rooms and hallways.

CUTTING THE RUG

■ Cut loop-pile carpet from the front. Clear a cutting path on the pile side using a screwdriver, then cut it with the face side up, using a row cutter or a utility knife.

■ Cut other carpets from the back. Measure the length along both edges on the face side. Mark the cutting points. Roll back the carpet, and snap a chalk line across the back between the marks. Using a straightedge, cut with a utility knife just deep enough to sever the backing. Cut the pile yarn as you separate the pieces.

ROUGH-CUT THE CARPET

Fold the end of the carpet back 3 or 4 feet with the sides lined up to square the end. Measure from the corners to the fold at both sides. If the measurements are not equal, mark the long side at a point equal to the short side. Cut at the mark.

Cut sections for the room with a 4- to 6-inch surplus on each wall. If you have multiple sections, make sure the pile runs the same way. Overlap the seams 3 inches.

Square the carpet in the room and cut vertical slits at corners and obstructions so it lies flat. Seam and stretch the carpet next.

TACKLESS TIPS

Nail tackless strip to wood subfloors. Use masonry nails on concrete, but first drive a few test nails around the perimeter to make sure the concrete will hold them. If the nails don't hold, glue the strip to the slab. Use glue on ceramic tiles too, but roughen the tile surface first. Double-strip where you think one strip won't hold.

If the carpet is going over resilient materials that are laid on concrete, use long nails to get a good bite into the slab. Or remove a 2-inch strip of the flooring at the edges and nail a thicker strip to the slab.

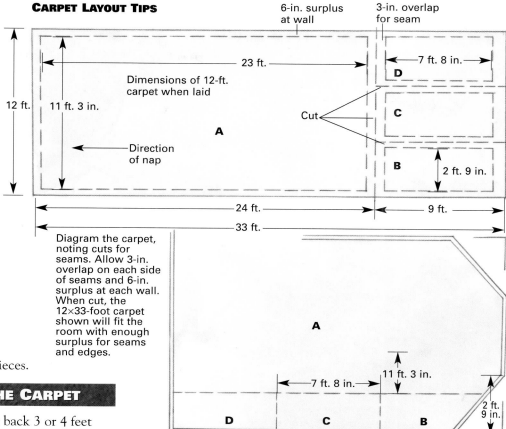

CARPET LAYOUT TIPS

6-in. surplus at wall

3-in. overlap for seam

23 ft.

7 ft. 8 in. — D

Dimensions of 12-ft. carpet when laid

12 ft.

11 ft. 3 in.

Cut — C

A

Direction of nap

B

2 ft. 9 in.

24 ft.

9 ft.

33 ft.

Diagram the carpet, noting cuts for seams. Allow 3-in. overlap on each side of seams and 6-in. surplus at each wall. When cut, the 12×33-foot carpet shown will fit the room with enough surplus for seams and edges.

A

7 ft. 8 in.

11 ft. 3 in.

2 ft. 9 in.

D   C   B

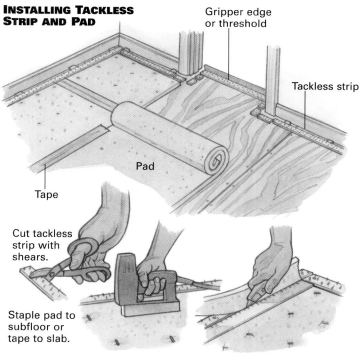

INSTALLING TACKLESS STRIP AND PAD

Gripper edge or threshold

Tackless strip

Pad

Tape

Cut tackless strip with shears.

Staple pad to subfloor or tape to slab.

Cut pad along straightedge ¼ in. from tackless strip.

INSTALLING CONVENTIONAL CARPET
continued

SEAMING THE CARPET

To cut seams for any carpet, first align the pieces with their edges parallel and the pile of both pieces running in the same direction. Overlap the edge at least 3 inches.

■ To cut loop-pile carpet, use the edge of the top piece as a guide and cut the bottom piece with a row cutter. Finish the cut with a utility knife at the edges where the carpet laps up the wall.

■ For other carpets, fold back the overlap at the seams. Snap a chalk line at equal distances on both edges and cut the seam line with a utility knife and straightedge. Cut the seam edges on both pieces perfectly straight and parallel. If the seam is in a doorway or other location where exact placement is necessary, stretch the first piece of carpet into place before trimming and seaming.

■ Cut hot-melt seaming tape to the exact length of the seam. Lift one of the seam edges and slide the tape into place, centering it on the floor under the seam—adhesive side up. Now warm up the seaming iron.

■ Slip the seaming iron onto the tape at one end of the carpet and let both pieces of carpet flop on top of the iron. Glide the iron along the tape, going about 1 foot every 30 seconds. Press the carpet edges tightly together along each just-heated section.

■ Move the iron with one hand while holding the edges together with the other. Keep the pile out of the adhesive and check to make sure that the backings butt tightly together. As you move away from each heated section, place books or other flat heavy objects on the seam to press it.

■ Continue seaming until you get as close as possible to the far wall. Then stop and let the seamed carpet cool for 5 or 10 minutes so you won't undo your work when seaming at the wall. Roll the edge back to expose the tape. Heat it and finish the seam. Groom the seam by cutting off stray backing threads and loose pile.

SEAMING CONVENTIONAL CARPET

1. Fold back overlapped edges of seams on both sides of largest carpet section. Snap a chalk line on the reverse of both pieces at seam edge.

2. Cut the seam edge on both pieces with a straightedge and utility knife or row cutter.

3. Pull back short edges of small sections, mark seam lines, then cut. Don't cut the long seam until the pieces are joined.

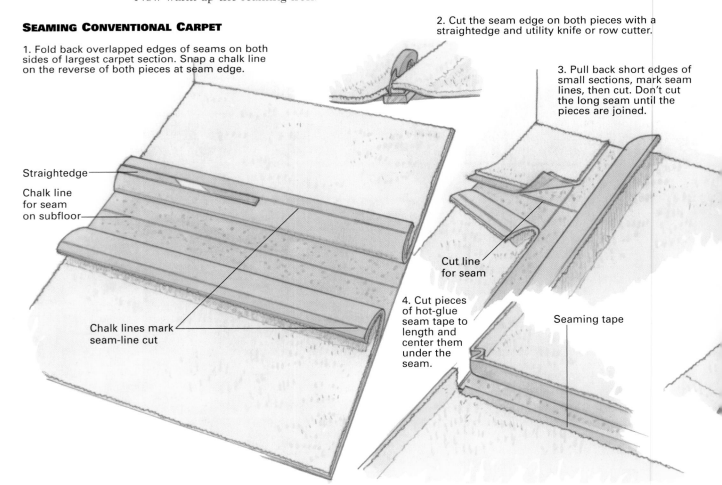

Straightedge

Chalk line for seam on subfloor

Chalk lines mark seam-line cut

Cut line for seam

4. Cut pieces of hot-glue seam tape to length and center them under the seam.

Seaming tape

ROUGH CUTTING CARPET TO FIT THE ROOM

1. Unroll the carpet in the room, orienting the pile in each section in the same direction. Notch the corners so it lays flat.

2. Measure carpet for seam cuts and notch the edges at the measurements.

Notch corners to lay material flat.

3. Fold back the carpet to the notches, snap a chalk line between them, then cut with a utility knife or row cutter.

6-in. surplus at walls

Seam overlap

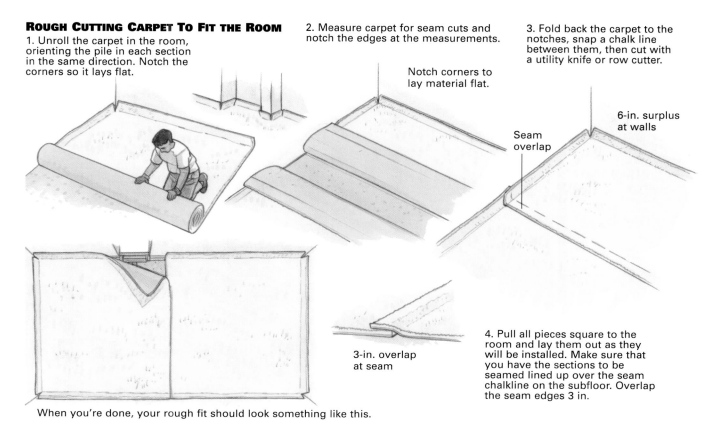

3-in. overlap at seam

4. Pull all pieces square to the room and lay them out as they will be installed. Make sure that you have the sections to be seamed lined up over the seam chalkline on the subfloor. Overlap the seam edges 3 in.

When you're done, your rough fit should look something like this.

5. Seam the smaller pieces first. Set the seaming iron under the carpet, and when the glue liquifies, draw the iron slowly toward you. Press down on the carpet behind the seaming iron. Weight the seam down until the glue sets.

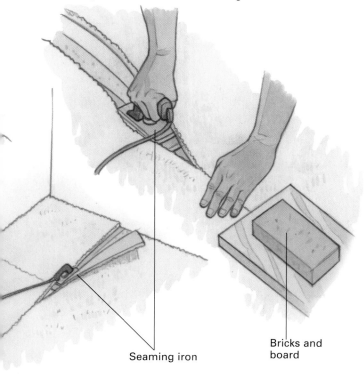

Seaming iron

Bricks and board

6. When smaller pieces are joined, repeat steps to cut and seam them to the larger piece.

TRANSITIONS

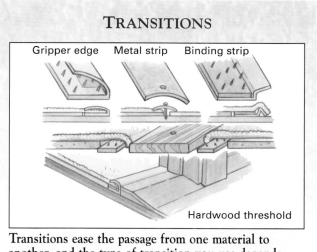

Gripper edge   Metal strip   Binding strip

Hardwood threshold

Transitions ease the passage from one material to another, and the type of transition you use depends on the adjoining materials.

Install a gripper edge on concrete slabs where the adjoining floor is at the same height or lower than the carpet. A reducer strip provides a slightly more stylish transition to a lower floor. For a hidden edge, install a Z-bar binding strip. It becomes invisible when you fasten the carpet to it. Join carpets on the same plane with hot-melt tape or a narrow hardwood threshold.

INSTALLING CONVENTIONAL CARPET
continued

STRETCHING

Before you bring out the stretching tools, decide which wall you're going to start with. It's usually best to start in a corner where an entrance is. Adjust the bite of the knee kicker and power stretcher so the teeth grab the carpet backing; the teeth should not go through the backing.

STRETCHING CONVENTIONAL CARPET

Tail block

Teeth grab carpet backing.

Knee kicker

2×4 spanning 2 or 3 studs

Pad   Subfloor

Push down handle to set stretcher.

Power stretcher

Kick swiftly with knee.

1 to 3 in. from wall

6 in. from wall, 24 in. from corners

Tuck carpet at edge with stair tool.

Head piece

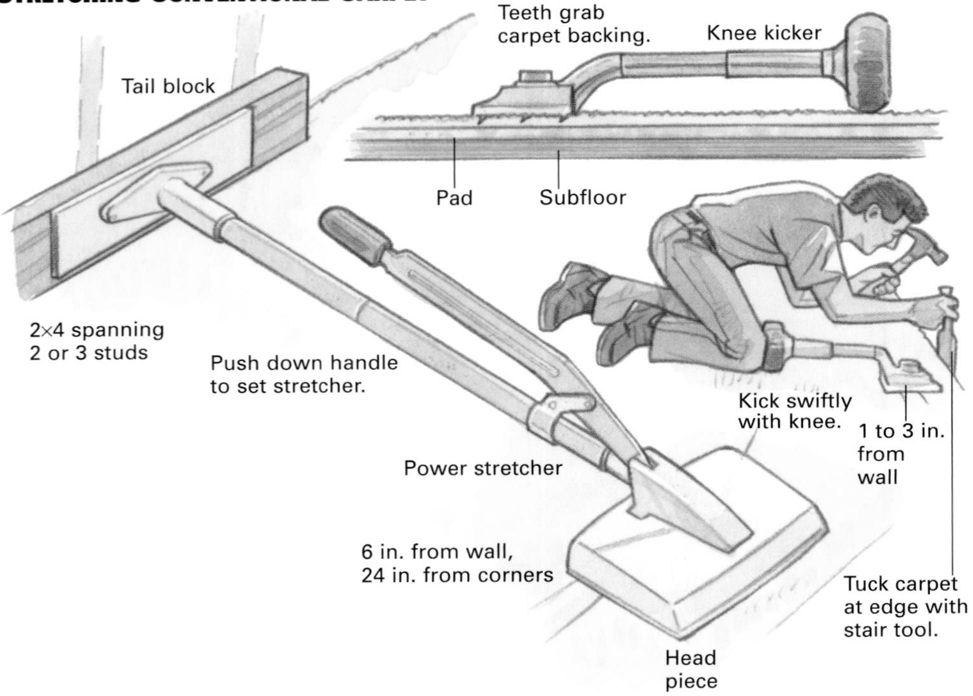

To secure the carpet onto the tackless strip, bite the head of the kicker into the carpet about 1 inch from the wall. Push down on the handle and swiftly kick the cushion with your knee. Proceed kick by kick, holding the secured carpet down on the strip with your hand or with a stair tool so it won't unhook.

Follow the kicking and stretching sequence illustrated in the diagram on the opposite page. For short distances (across hallways or small bedrooms, for example), use the knee kicker. In larger rooms, use a power stretcher.

Set the head of the power stretcher 6 inches from the wall and adjust the extension tubes so that the foot presses against the opposite wall (support the foot with a carpet-covered 2×4 that spans 2 or

3 studs). Then press down on the lever to stretch the carpet toward the wall. The lever should lock down with a gentle push.

If the carpet does not move easily, lift the head and lower the handle a bit before biting into the carpet again. With the handle locked and the carpet stretched, fasten the edge of the carpet to the tackless strip with the side of a hammer or the trowel-like paddle that comes with the stretcher. Push the carpet down onto the pins. Then release the stretcher head, move it over 18 inches, and repeat the process. Move the foot of the stretcher along the opposite wall as you go.

TRIMMING

Trim the carpet edges with a wall trimmer. Adjust the trimmer to the thickness of the carpet. Start at the lapped end of the carpet and slice downward at an angle until the trimmer is flat against the floor. Then hold the trimmer against both the wall and the floor and plow it along the edge of the carpet.

Carefully trim the last few inches with a utility knife. Using a stair tool, tuck the trimmed carpet edge down between the tackless strip and the baseboard. Position the tool on the surplus carpet that laps over the gap, rather than out on the edge of the carpet itself. That keeps the carpet from bulging back and lifting off the pins. Hit the stair tool with a rubber mallet if the carpet is stiff.

At doorways, trim the edge of the carpet to the center of the closed door. If you installed a gripper edge on a concrete floor, flatten the metal flange over the carpet with a rubber mallet or a wood block and hammer. If the edge of the carpet will be covered with a metal flat bar, nail it down first with tacks or 1-inch lath nails.

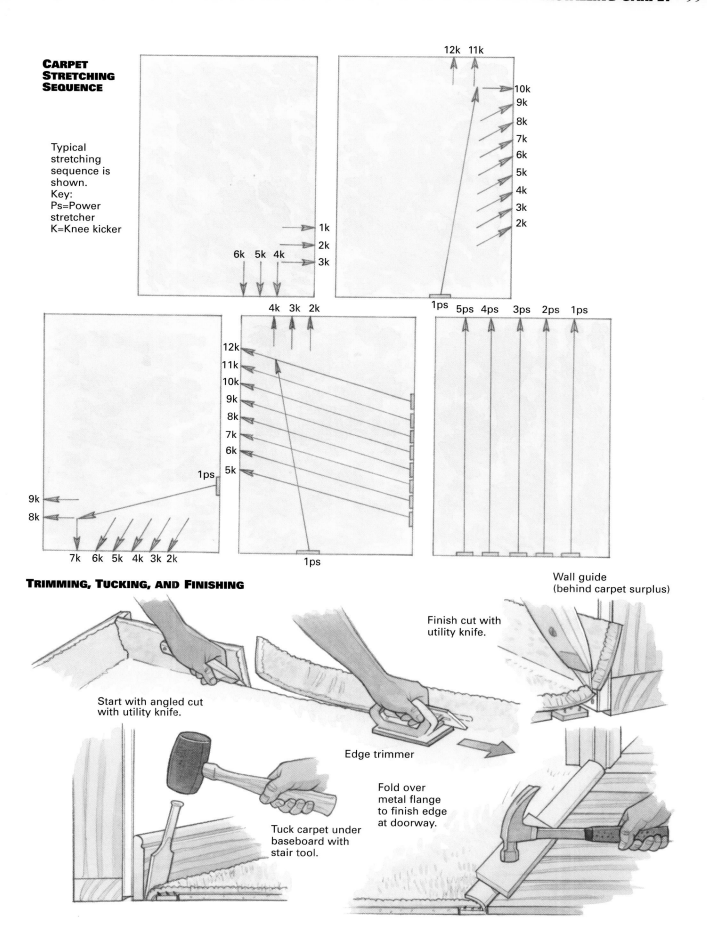

CARPET STRETCHING SEQUENCE

Typical stretching sequence is shown.
Key:
Ps=Power stretcher
K=Knee kicker

12k 11k

10k
9k
8k
7k
6k
5k
4k
3k
2k

1k
2k
3k
6k 5k 4k

1ps 5ps 4ps 3ps 2ps 1ps

4k 3k 2k

12k
11k
10k
9k
8k
7k
6k
5k

1ps

9k
8k

7k 6k 5k 4k 3k 2k

1ps

TRIMMING, TUCKING, AND FINISHING

Wall guide
(behind carpet surplus)

Finish cut with utility knife.

Start with angled cut with utility knife.

Edge trimmer

Tuck carpet under baseboard with stair tool.

Fold over metal flange to finish edge at doorway.

INSTALLING CUSHION-BACKED CARPET

Cushion-backed carpet has its own bonded foam backing, but since it's thin, it will show the smallest imperfection. You won't need to stretch this carpet; just glue it to the floor. First make sure the floor is properly prepared according to the information on pages 60–63.

Don't remove the baseboards before installing cushion-backed carpet. The carpet edges will be tucked under them during trimming. At doorways, install a toothless binder bar with a flange that clamps down over the carpet to finish the edge.

VENTILATE THE ROOM

Some carpet adhesives are noxious or even flammable. Read the manufacturer's instructions carefully, and make sure the room is well ventilated. Extinguish nearby pilot lights and other open flames before using adhesives.

Carpeting adds warmth and comfort to this cheery sitting room. The deep blue color complements the pale yellow walls.

ROUGHING IT IN

If your carpet will be seamed, snap a chalk line on the floor where a seam will fall. Then, whether seamed or not, rough-cut (face side up) the carpet with a 6-inch excess at the walls. If you're seaming, carefully align one edge of the piece on the chalk line. Place the second piece so that its edge overlaps the bottom one by ¼ inch. Be sure that the pattern, if any, lines up and that the pile of both pieces runs in the same direction.

SEAMING THE CARPET

At the seam, fold both edges back 2 or 3 feet and trowel a thin, even coat of adhesive onto the exposed floor. Roll one edge back down so it's exactly on the chalk line. Work the carpet with your hands to force air bubbles out to the edge.

Notch the seaming-fluid nozzle so it will apply a bead of adhesive at the height of the primary backing, not onto the pile or pad. Lay a bead of seaming fluid along the edge of the primary backing material on the piece of carpet that's glued to the floor.

Fold the second piece of carpet so that its edge tightly abuts the edge of the adhered piece. The edges should press tightly together because you allowed a ¼-inch overlap. Work the bulge produced by the ¼-inch allowance gently away from the seam. Where there are gaps, carefully rejoin both edges with your fingers until the entire seam is tight. Let the adhesive dry thoroughly, then snip off loose pile or backing threads.

GLUING

Pull the carpet from the side walls and fold in the corners. Then pull the whole piece back to the seam area. (If the carpet didn't require a seam, pull the single piece back until half the floor is exposed.) Trowel adhesive onto the floor and roll the carpet from the center to the wall. Work out wrinkles or bumps with your hands as you go. Repeat the process for the other half of the carpet. If you have to deflate a bubble, pierce it with an awl. Use a plastic syringe (available from carpet dealers) to inject contact adhesive into the hole. Press the carpet firmly onto the adhesive.

TRIMMING

Trim the carpet with a utility knife. Leave a margin equal to the thickness of the carpet and tuck it down against the wall with a stair tool. Flatten down any metal doorway flanges with a hammer and a block of wood.

INSTALLING CUSHION-BACKED CARPET

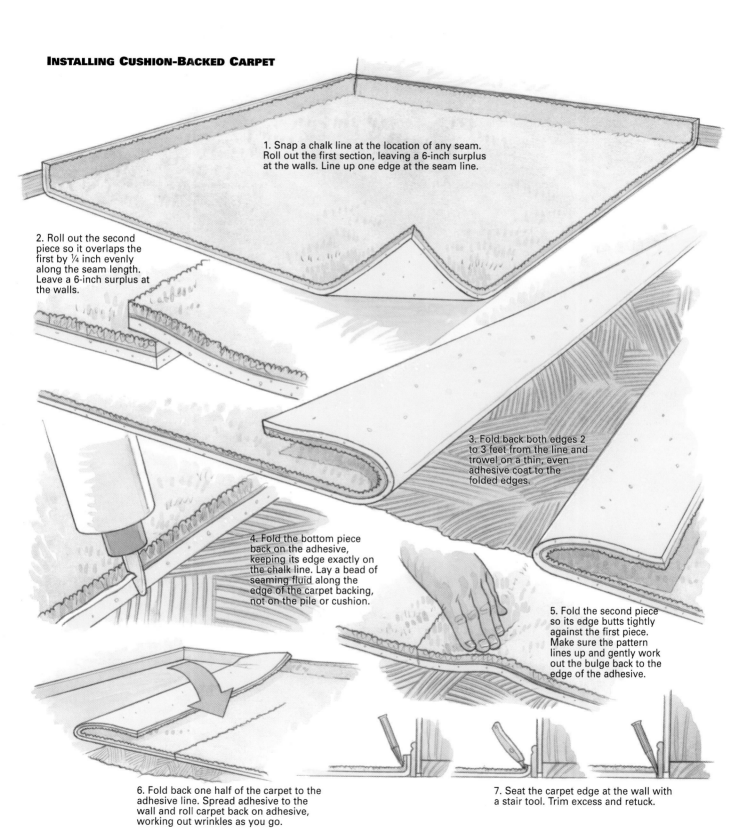

1. Snap a chalk line at the location of any seam. Roll out the first section, leaving a 6-inch surplus at the walls. Line up one edge at the seam line.

2. Roll out the second piece so it overlaps the first by ¼ inch evenly along the seam length. Leave a 6-inch surplus at the walls.

3. Fold back both edges 2 to 3 feet from the line and trowel on a thin, even adhesive coat to the folded edges.

4. Fold the bottom piece back on the adhesive, keeping its edge exactly on the chalk line. Lay a bead of seaming fluid along the edge of the carpet backing, not on the pile or cushion.

5. Fold the second piece so its edge butts tightly against the first piece. Make sure the pattern lines up and gently work out the bulge back to the edge of the adhesive.

6. Fold back one half of the carpet to the adhesive line. Spread adhesive to the wall and roll carpet back on adhesive, working out wrinkles as you go.

7. Seat the carpet edge at the wall with a stair tool. Trim excess and retuck.

CLEANING, MAINTENANCE, AND REPAIR

REPLACING DAMAGED STRIP OR PLANK FLOORING

1. Using a square, mark the damaged section.

2. Drill the damaged section with a ⅝-in. spade bit just to the inside edges of the marks.

3. Plunge-cut the section with a saw set to the depth of the flooring.

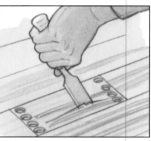

4. Chisel out the cut section.

5. Square drilled edge with a sharp chisel, bevel facing the edge.

6. Cut replacement board, removing bottom edge of groove.

7. Tap replacements into place, toenailing where possible and gluing if necessary. Remove bottom of groove.

MAINTAINING WOOD FLOORS

Modern wood finishes can stand up to more abuse than could finishes of 50 years ago. But, just as was true 50 years ago, floors still need to be cleaned regularly.

Cleaning techniques for floors with surface finishes and waxed floors are slightly different. To tell if your floor is waxed, drop a little water in an out-of-the-way corner. If white spots appear after about 10 minutes, the floor is waxed. Remove the white spots by buffing with #0000 steel wool and a little wax.

SURFACE FINISHES: Dust or vacuum the floor regularly. Clean spills immediately, using a dampened—not saturated—cloth. Clean the floor with a general-purpose floor cleaner or a product recommended by the finish manufacturer. Urethane-finished floors don't need wax—it will just make the floor slippery. A dulled urethane finish may need sanding and a recoat. Some urethanes can be recoated without sanding.

WAXED FLOORS: Dust or vacuum regularly. After taking up spills with a dampened—but not saturated—cloth, buff with a soft, dry cloth to return the shine. Buff only the dull areas of the floor. Clean the floor once a year with a solvent-based cleaner (water-based cleaners will fog the finish). Then wax and buff the floor.

BASIC WOOD-FLOOR REPAIRS

Wood floors may become damaged occasionally. A split, crack, or moisture damage in one area can usually be repaired without tearing up the floor. Some damage may be confined to the surface or finish; refer to the chart on the opposite page for advice about repairing surface damage to solid-wood floors. Replacing damaged sections of wood flooring is fairly straightforward; the illustrations on these two pages will lead you through the steps.

REPLACING DAMAGED PARQUET TILE

1. Plunge-cut the damaged tile with a circular saw set to the thickness of the parquet.

2. Place the bevel of a butt chisel toward the edge of the cuts and remove the cut pieces. Scrape up the remaining adhesive with a putty knife.

3. Cut bottom edges of the groove, spread adhesive on the subfloor, set the new tile into place, and tap it down.

FIXING WARPED BOARDS

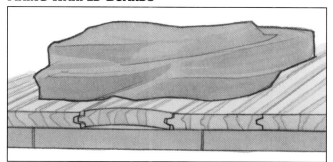

1. Remove wax or finish with appropriate solvent. Cover warped boards with damp rags for 48 hours.

2. Predrill and countersink holes, then screw the warped boards to subfloor. Keeping the flooring damp, tighten the screws a little each day until the board is flat.

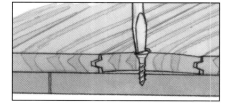

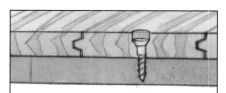

3. Let the flooring dry completely, then fill the holes and refinish to match original finish.

WOOD SURFACE REPAIRS

Problem	Remedy
Bubbles in finish	May be caused by incompatible finishes. For light damage, sand lightly and recoat. If heavy, sand, stain, and refinish.
Chewing gum, crayon, candle wax	Pop off with ice in a bag, scrape with plastic scraper. Seep cleaning fluid under chewing gum.
Cigarette burns	Burnish with fine steel wool or scrape charred area. Wax, or sand, stain, and refinish.
Dents	Cover with dampened cloth and press with an electric iron.
Scratches	Wax the area or hide the scratch with a thin coat of dusting spray rubbed into scratch.
Seasonal cracks	Increase humidity in dry season—install humidifier, boil water, open dishwasher after rinse.
Surface stains	Remove with sandpaper or steel wool, feathering edges; or clean with one of these solutions:
Heel marks	Wood cleaner or wax.
Ink	Wood cleaner, followed by mild bleach or household vinegar for up to an hour. A remaining spot is not likely to sand out. Cover damage with rug or remove, replace, and refinish.
Mold, mildew	Floor cleaner. If wood fibers are stained, remove and refinish.
Oil and grease	Try wood cleaner first. Then, on waxed floor, use TSP or soap with high lye content. On surface finish, use TSP.
Pet stains	Use same procedure as for ink.
Water spots	Buff lightly with #0000 steel wool, then wax. If necessary, sand with fine paper, stain, and recoat.

REFINISHING WOOD FLOORS

Refinishing a solid-wood floor is a time-consuming and exacting process. Before you start sanding your floor, first determine if the floor needs refinishing; you might just need to recondition it. Then pull off a floor vent to make sure you have sufficient wood left to sand. Standard ¾-inch flooring can be sanded a number of times, but if yours has only slightly more than ½ inch left, you should consult a floor contractor. The same applies to manufactured flooring; it's even thinner, so sanding it is definitely a job for the pros.

TIP-TOP REFINISHING

When you are refinishing a solid wood floor, you're going to have your hands full (of heavy equipment, for one thing). Here are a few tips that will make the job go smoothly.
- Sanding should remove less than ½₂ inch. Because the surface of manufactured flooring is relatively thin, refinishing a manufactured floor should be done by a professional.
- Grits—Very coarse (20 to 30), coarse (36 to 40), medium (50 to 80), fine (100, 120), very fine (150). Use coarse grits only on rough floors. If medium grit will level the floor on the first cut, don't use coarse grit.
- Immediately mark nails, hollows, and depressions as you sand.
- Don't skip more than one grade between grits (you can skip from 30 to 40, but not from 30 to 50).

SANDING A WOOD FLOOR

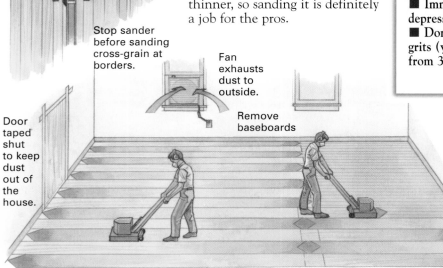

Pad sander

Stop sander before sanding cross-grain at borders.

Fan exhausts dust to outside.

Remove baseboards

Door taped shut to keep dust out of the house.

1. Start sanding about two-thirds of the way along the length of the room on the right side. Sand with the grain.

2. Push sander forward; at wall, move it left a few inches and pull it back to the starting point.

3. After sanding to the side wall, turn sander in the opposite direction and repeat the process, overlapping the starting point by the width of the sanding pad.

Use an edge sander along the walls and in other areas the pad sander won't reach. Sand with a circular motion along the wall, overlapping into the area removed by the pad sander.

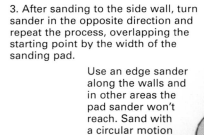

RECONDITIONING A WOOD FLOOR

If you don't change the color of your floor or if damage is superficial, you may only need to recondition it.

Reconditioning a wood floor means removing or lightly sanding only the finish of the floor. First, find out if you have a surface finish or not—scrape lightly in a corner. Flakes tell you it's a surface finish. No flakes mean it's a penetrant. In either case, check for wax by dropping a little water on the floor. If the beads turn white after 10 minutes, it's waxed and will have to be sanded and refinished. No wax means you can coat over it.

Clean the floor with a cleaner that won't leave a residue, dull the sheen with steel wool or a sanding screen, then coat with a compatible finish. Don't finish a floor with shellac or lacquer—the first is not durable, and the second is extremely flammable.

CHOOSING FINISHES

Wood finishes fall into two categories—penetrating and surface finishes.

■ Penetrants go into the wood pores. They don't wear off unless the wood does; you can retouch them and the floor won't look patched. There are two types of penetrants:

Stains—if you want a color in your wood other than its natural color, start with stain. Protect stain with a penetrating sealer or surface finish.

Sealers—these come either clear or tinted (making staining and sealing a one-step process). Protect sealers with a wax or surface finish.

■ Surface finishes set up on the surface of the wood, providing a harder and more durable coating than sealers. Here's a summary of their characteristics:

Urethane (oil-modified)—Easy to apply, dries slowly, amber color, very durable.

Urethane (water-based)—Easy to apply, dries fast, clear. More durable than oil-modified urethanes.

Urethane (moisture-cured)—Difficult to apply, dries quickly in presence of moisture, clear to amber. Most durable of the urethanes.

Almost all finishes will discolor over time, and some need protection from UV light (drape the windows). If you use area rugs, wait until the finish has cured—about two weeks for water-based urethane, a month for solvent-based finishes. Purchase rugs with backing that will let the floor breathe and won't react with the finish.

APPLYING FINISH TO A WOOD FLOOR

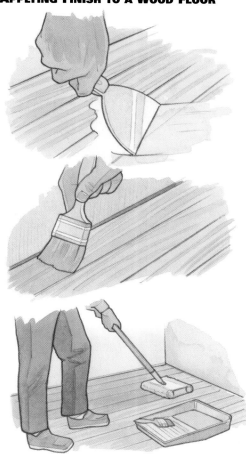

Using a wide-blade putty knife, fill cracks with a paste filler. Push the filler into the wood at an angle to the grain. Sand the filler with medium- and fine-grit paper.

Following the manufacturer's directions and using a lamb's wool applicator or brush, start in one corner of the room and work in the direction of the flooring. Apply a liberal amount of finish with the grain and work from unfinished areas to the edge that is still wet. Always leave a wet edge, feathering new finish into it on the next pass.

FINISHING STEPS

To refinish (or finish an unfinished floor), refer to the illustrations at top right and follow the steps below. Use an orbital pad sander instead of a drum sander—the pad sander takes off less wood, is less likely to make gouges, and is more forgiving of error.

■ Remove furniture, shoe moldings, vents, and protruding nails. Vacuum thoroughly.

■ Load the sander with coarse or medium paper; coarse if removing a surface or waxed finish or if the floor is rough.

■ To make the first pass, start at the right-hand wall, about two-thirds of the way from the end wall. Walk the sander toward the end wall, then walk it back on the same path. At the starting point, move the sander over 3 to 4 inches and repeat the process. Continue sanding, overlapping paths until you've sanded two-thirds of the room. Then face the other end wall and repeat the process; overlap the starting edge 2 to 3 feet.

■ Sand the edges with an edge sander (with the same or next finer grit) parallel to the

wall, moving in a quarter-circle pattern and overlapping the sanded area 4 to 6 inches.

■ Make the second pass. Repeat sanding and edging with the next finer grit.

■ Make the third pass. Fill nail holes and repeat sanding with fine paper.

■ Smooth corners with a scraper and sand with a small power orbital sander.

■ Vacuum thoroughly and remove fine dust by going over the entire floor carefully with a tack cloth.

■ Apply stain and finish of your choice.

REFINISHING PARQUET

Parquet refinishing follows the same procedures outlined above, with one exception—the sanding pattern. Make the first two passes along opposite diagonals and the third one parallel to the long wall in the room.

MAINTAINING RESILIENT AND LAMINATE FLOORS

REPAIRING RESILIENT SHEET FLOORING

 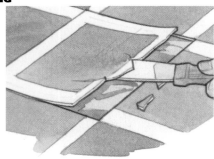 

1. Cut a piece of sheet material larger than the damaged area. Tape it over the damaged area with its pattern matching the rest of the floor exactly.

2. Using a utility knife and straightedge, cut through both pieces.

3. Pull off the patch and tape, then warm the area with a hair dryer. Remove the damaged area and adhesive with a putty knife. Apply adhesive to the floor and replace with new material. Weight it until the adhesive cures.

Caring for your resilient or laminate floor mostly involves keeping it clean. Regular sweeping or vacuuming will take care of most of the grit, but should be accompanied by periodic sponge-mopping with a mild solution of ammonia. Don't flood the surface.

Avoid abrasive cleaners or applicators that might scratch the floor. If you're in doubt about what cleaner is compatible with your resilient or laminate surface, contact the dealer; most flooring manufacturers market cleaning agents that are compatible with their floor materials.

The no-wax surface on resilient sheet and tiles makes cleaning easier, but be sure to use cleaners that are compatible with the material; many are not. One-step cleaners can scratch resilient or laminate flooring. Although the cleaner is supposed to remove dirt, some particles get caught in the applicator and are spread across the floor, where they can continue to abrade its surface.

REMOVING STAINS FROM RESILIENT FLOORING

Stain	Remove with
Asphalt, shoe polish	Citrus-based cleaner or mineral spirits.
Candle wax	Scrape carefully with plastic spatula.
Crayon	Mineral spirits or manufacturer's cleaner.
Grape juice, wine, mustard	Full-strength bleach or manufacturer's cleaner.
Heel marks	Nonabrasive household cleaner. If stain remains, use rubbing alcohol.
Lipstick	Rubbing alcohol or mineral spirits.
Nail polish	Nail polish remover.
Paint or varnish	Water or mineral spirits while still wet. If dry, scrape carefully with a thin plastic spatula. If stain still shows, rub with rubbing alcohol.
Pen ink	Citrus-based cleaner, rubbing alcohol, or mineral spirits.
Permanent marker	Mineral spirits, nail polish remover, or rubbing alcohol.
Rust	Oxalic acid and water (1 part acid to 10 parts water). Extremely caustic; follow all directions.

After removing the stain, rinse the area with a damp cloth to remove residue.

PREVENTING DENTS AND SCRATCHES

Resilient flooring is more prone to dents, scuffs, and scratches than other flooring. Unlike spots, you can't remove them. Here are some ways to prevent dents:
■ Protect the floor when moving appliances. Lay plywood panels on the floor and "walk" the appliance across the panels.
■ Use floor protectors to keep furniture legs from denting the floors; the heavier the furniture, the wider the protector should be.
■ Avoid furniture with rolling casters. If you must have casters, use double rollers.
■ Keep dust and dirt outside the house—use mats or rugs at entrances, but avoid rubber-backed rugs. They can discolor resilient flooring.
■ Keep the floor clean with regular sweeping or vacuuming, but don't use vacuums with beater bars—or any abrasive scrubbing aids. They can scratch the floor.

REFINISHING

The finish needs to be renewed periodically on resilient floors that don't have a no-wax surface. Clear acrylic products are suitable for this purpose. Periodic removal and restoration of the finish will probably also be necessary.

Laminate floors won't need refinishing, but if the shine begins to dull, renew it with the product specified by the manufacturer.

STAIN REMOVAL TECHNIQUES

If your flooring becomes stained, first attempt to clean it with soap and water on a soft cloth or a nylon nonabrasive pad. Never use abrasive applicators. For more stubborn stains, work up to liquid floor cleaner, rubbing (isopropyl) alcohol, diluted chlorine bleach, or mineral spirits. Use the cleaner recommended on the charts on these pages, if the stain is shown.

Regardless of the cleaner, work at the edges of the stain first, and change the surface of the cloth so you're not spreading the stain into unstained areas.

MAKING REPAIRS

From time to time, the inevitable happens—your floor becomes damaged to the point that repairs are necessary. Although you can repair laminate dents, chips, and scratches with a repair kit available from your dealer (see the illustration at right), leave substantial repairs and those that require removal and replacement of a plank to a professional.

Resilient materials are easier to repair. Repairing sheet flooring involves cutting out the damaged section and gluing in a patch of the same size and pattern. A damaged resilient tile can be removed, then replaced with a new tile, as shown at right. Both processes are well within the skill level of the average homeowner.

Although the wearlayer of laminate floors is extremely hard, small dents are bound to occur eventually. Flooring dealers sell a dent repair kit with a filler that hardens to a resistant surface and matches the color of the flooring. The illustration above shows a typical repair procedure. Replace damaged resilient tiles as shown at right.

LAMINATE FLOORING STAIN REMOVAL GUIDE

Stain	Remove with
Candle wax	Scrape carefully with plastic spatula.
Crayon, rubber heel marks	Rub out with a dry cloth or acetone if needed.
Grape juice or wine	Rub with a dry cloth or concentrated cleaner.
Lipstick	Paint thinner or acetone.
Nail polish	Acetone-based nail polish remover.
Paint or varnish	Wipe with water or mineral spirits while still wet. If dry, scrape carefully with a thin plastic spatula. If the stain still shows, rub with rubbing alcohol.
Pen ink	Acetone or paint thinner.
Shoe polish	Acetone or paint thinner.
Tar	Acetone.
Others	Start with concentrated cleaner, then acetone.

After removing the stain, rinse the area with a damp cloth to remove residue.

REPAIRING LAMINATE FLOORING

1. Clean the area; when dry, protect the surrounding surfaces with clear plastic tape.

2. Fill the dent with putty from flooring repair kit. Wipe up the excess with a cloth dampened with the recommended solvent. Remove tape.

REPAIRING RESILIENT TILE

1. Remove damaged tile and adhesive with a putty knife, softening tiles with a hair dryer.

2. Spread adhesive and lay in new tile.

MAINTAINING CERAMIC TILE

REPLACING GROUT

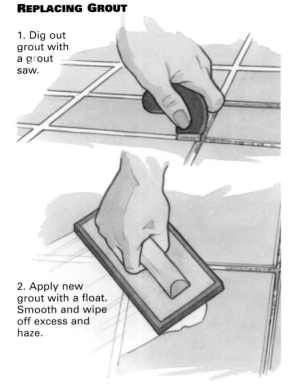

1. Dig out grout with a grout saw.

2. Apply new grout with a float. Smooth and wipe off excess and haze.

REPLACING BROKEN TILE

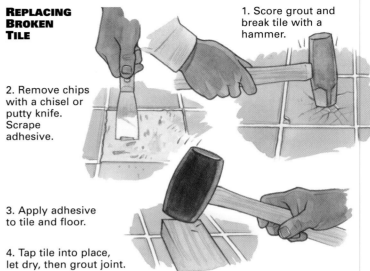

1. Score grout and break tile with a hammer.

2. Remove chips with a chisel or putty knife. Scrape adhesive.

3. Apply adhesive to tile and floor.

4. Tap tile into place, let dry, then grout joint.

Ceramic tile requires less maintenance than most other home flooring materials. Regular mopping and vacuuming are musts, of course. Glazed tiles resist stains better than stone and unglazed tile. Grout shows stains.

REMOVING STAINS FROM TILE

Stains	Cleaner and Method
Grease, fats	Clean with a commercial spot lifter.
Ink, coffee, blood, mustard, fruit juice, and some dyes	Start with a 3-percent hydrogen peroxide solution; if that doesn't work, try a nonbleach cleaner.
Nail polish	Use nail polish remover.
Oil-base products	Mild solvent, such as charcoal lighter or mineral spirits, then household cleaner in a poultice. For dried paint, scrape with a plastic (not metal) scraper.
Rust	Use commercial rust removers made for fabric, then household cleaner.

Rinse the area with a damp cloth to remove residue.

SEALING TILE

Unglazed tile usually requires sealing. Although many come from the factory presealed, periodic resealing may be necessary. Sealers come in two varieties:
■ Sealers penetrate tile to preserve its natural color and keep stains out of the pores.
■ Topical sealers lay on top of the tile. Depending on the sealer, they can lighten, darken, or change the sheen of an unsealed tile. Topical sealers wear faster and require more frequent application.

CLEANING TIPS

In addition to regular sweeping or vacuuming, periodic damp-mopping with a neutral-pH cleaner will keep both glazed and sealed, unglazed tiles looking good.

If you need to scrub something stubborn, don't use steel wool or metal tools. Metal will leave residue behind and there's almost nothing that will remove these marks. Use nylon scrubbers or brushes with plastic or natural bristles—a toothbrush for grout. Check the chart above for stain-removing tips.

STAINS ON STONE

A poultice—a mixture of plaster of Paris and hydrogen peroxide wrapped in a soft cloth— or one of the cleaners listed in the chart above can pull stains out of the pores of stone tile. This is a slow process. Spread the poultice mixture over the stain and tape plastic over it. Let it sit for a couple of days, then brush it off. Ask your dealer what cleaning products to use for your stone.

CARPET MAINTENANCE

Carpet—unlike other flooring materials—can look clean when it isn't. That's because dirt particles work their way down from the surface and into the fabric. They do more damage there than when they're visible on top; they abrade the fabric fibers when you walk on the carpet.

Vacuum once or twice a week. Use a quality vacuum cleaner that's in good repair—and empty the bag. The vacuum is less efficient with a full bag.

Even if you stick to a rigorous vacuuming schedule, clean your carpet periodically to restore it to brand-new condition.

CLEANING METHODS

There are a number of effective cleaning methods that you can hire done or do yourself with rented equipment. Some methods use brushes, some don't. Brushes can distort the pile of some carpets.

DRY EXTRACTION: An absorbent compound with detergents is brushed into the fabric with specially designed machines. The compound attaches to the dirt, and both are picked up by the vacuum.

DRY FOAM: Detergent foam is worked into the fibers by machine brushes and either wet-vacuumed or allowed to dry before being vacuumed up.

HOT WATER EXTRACTION (STEAM CLEANING): Cleaning solution is injected into the carpet under pressure and immediately taken out. This method doesn't use brushes, so it's good for pile that can be untwisted by brushes. Be careful; it's easy to over-wet the carpet, which can cause the backing to shrink or mildew to grow.

ROTARY SHAMPOO: Cleaning solution is injected into the carpet, worked by machine brushes, then vacuumed out when dry. This is the kind of machine you can usually rent at grocery stores and other outlets. Use the least amount of detergent possible to keep residue

STAIN REMOVAL GUIDE FOR CARPETS

When removing stains with any of the following methods, act quickly and blot the area. Do not scrub—it can distort the carpet pile and spread the stain. Formulas for ammonia, detergent, and vinegar solutions are at the bottom right of page 110.

Stain	Removal
Alcoholic beverages and soft drinks	Detergent solution, ammonia solution, or white vinegar solution.
Blood	Always use spot removing solutions cold to avoid setting the stain. Start with an ammonia solution, then try detergent solution, white vinegar solution, and warm water rinse.
Burns	Reweaving or resectioning are about the only cures for burn damage. Clipping the fabric just below the burn can improve its appearance.
Candle wax	Nail polish remover or dry-cleaning fluid.
Chocolate	Dry-cleaning fluid, detergent solution, ammonia solution, or white vinegar solution.
Coffee	Detergent solution or warm white vinegar solution.
Crayon	Dry-cleaning fluid or detergent solution.
Fingernail polish	Nail polish remover or detergent solution.
Gum	Soften the gum slightly with a hair dryer (don't melt the carpet). Lift the gum away with a plastic bag (the softened gum will stick to it). Finish with dry-cleaning fluid.
Ink	Nail polish remover, dry-cleaning fluid, detergent solution, or ammonia solution.
Latex paint	Detergent solution or ammonia solution.
Lipstick	Nail polish remover, dry-cleaning fluid, detergent solution, ammonia solution, or white vinegar solution.
Pet stains	Detergent solution, white vinegar solution or ammonia solution.
Rust	White vinegar solution or detergent solution.
Shoe polish	Nail polish remover, dry-cleaning fluid or detergent solution.

CARPET MAINTENANCE
continued

to a minimum. Dirt sticks to detergent residue, causing the carpet to wear more quickly. Don't use a counter-rotating floor-polishing machine to scrub carpet—you will untwist your carpet pile.

You can use all these cleaning methods on wool, cotton, rayon, and other synthetic carpets, but use only the manufacturer's recommended cleaning solutions.

FOOTPRINTS AND OTHER DEPRESSIONS

Carpet is a soft material, and it will show indentations that hard-surfaced flooring will not. How well a carpet resists these blemishes is determined partly by its density and partly by the method used to make it. Denser carpets usually bounce back more quickly. Here's an overview of some of the more common carpet problems and what (if anything) you can do about them.

CORNROWING is a condition you'll recognize if some of the rows of your carpet begin to stand out and others don't. High-density carpet is less prone to cornrowing because fiber tufts that are packed together tightly tend to support each other, even when stretched apart during installation. Vacuuming generally won't help. Special carpet rakes might help, but not permanently.

CRUSHING is the loss of pile thickness due to normal traffic. Vacuuming will lift the pile, but it can't replace worn fiber.

FADING can be caused by furnace fumes and sunlight. Have your furnace serviced regularly and close the drapes when the room is not in use to minimize fading.

SHEDDING is natural, caused by loose fibers left over from the manufacturing process rising to the surface. It will disappear within a year if you vacuum regularly.

RIPPLES are usually caused by improper stretching or a failed cushion. They can also appear where humidity is high. Have a professional installer remove them by restretching the carpet.

SPROUTING is the sudden appearance of one or two yarns for no apparent reason. Don't pull out carpet sprouts; snip them off at the level of the rest of the tufts.

DENTS caused by furniture can be minimized with wide furniture glides. You can sometimes work them out with your fingers. If that doesn't work, moisten the area, warm it slightly with a hair dryer, and ease the fibers into position with the back of a spoon.

STAIN REMOVAL SOLUTIONS

Modern carpets are manufactured with finishes that resist stains, but that still doesn't make them stainproof. Stain-resistant finishes hold the stain on the carpet's surface so you can remove it before it penetrates deeper.

Respond quickly when something stains your carpet; remove the spot as soon as possible. Blot stains; don't scrub them or you might damage the carpet pile and probably spread the stain.

Using a clean, white, absorbent cloth, gently work in the cleaner from the edges of the spot toward the center. Keep blotting until you can't see the stain on the cloth. Then use clean, warm water to take up the cleaner residue. Blot the excess water from the fibers. Let the carpet dry, then vacuum. If your cleaning efforts aren't successful, you'll have to call a professional cleaner.

Most carpet manufacturers offer a cleaning kit with ingredients that are compatible with their carpet fibers. If you use the manufacturer's kit, you won't have to worry about whether the cleaner will take the color out of the carpet. You can also brew your own cleaners for use with the methods shown in the chart on page 109. Try the methods in the order shown on the chart. Some of the cleaners listed are over-the-counter products like dry-cleaning fluid and nail polish remover. Others are home-brew mixtures. Here are the formulas for those:

■ Mild detergent solution (¼ teaspoon mild liquid detergent to a cup of lukewarm water).

■ Vinegar solution (1 cup white vinegar to 2 cups water).

■ Ammonia solution (2 tablespoons household ammonia to 1 cup water).

VACUUM CLEANER CHECKLIST

If you're shopping for a vacuum cleaner, purchase a model with adjustable and rotating brushes. Make sure it has a strong enough airflow to lift dirt up from the backing and a high-filtration bag to keep the dust contained.

Take these simple steps to help keep your vacuum efficient:
■ Replace worn brushes.
■ Don't vacuum with clogged hoses.
■ Keep a spare belt on hand and change it before it breaks.
■ Change the bag when it's just over half full—as it fills, the vacuum's efficiency decreases.

INDEX

METRIC CONVERSIONS

U.S. Units to Metric Equivalents			Metric Units to U.S. Equivalents		
To Convert From	Multiply By	To Get	To Convert From	Multiply By	To Get
Inches	25.4	Millimeters	Millimeters	0.0394	Inches
Inches	2.54	Centimeters	Centimeters	0.3937	Inches
Feet	30.48	Centimeters	Centimeters	0.0328	Feet
Feet	0.3048	Meters	Meters	3.2808	Feet
Yards	0.9144	Meters	Meters	1.0936	Yards
Square inches	6.4516	Square centimeters	Square centimeters	0.1550	Square inches
Square feet	0.0929	Square meters	Square meters	10.764	Square feet
Square yards	0.8361	Square meters	Square meters	1.1960	Square yards
Acres	0.4047	Hectares	Hectares	2.4711	Acres
Cubic inches	16.387	Cubic centimeters	Cubic centimeters	0.0610	Cubic inches
Cubic feet	0.0283	Cubic meters	Cubic meters	35.315	Cubic feet
Cubic feet	28.316	Liters	Liters	0.0353	Cubic feet
Cubic yards	0.7646	Cubic meters	Cubic meters	1.308	Cubic yards
Cubic yards	764.55	Liters	Liters	0.0013	Cubic yards

To convert from degrees Fahrenheit (F) to degrees Celsius (C), first subtract 32, then multiply by 5/9.

To convert from degrees Celsius to degrees Fahrenheit, multiply by 9/5, then add 32.

AT HOME WITH
crochet

A LEISURE ARTS PUBLICATION
PRESENTED BY OXMOOR HOUSE

EDITORIAL STAFF

Vice President and Editor-in-Chief:
   Anne Van Wagner Childs
Executive Director: Sandra Graham Case
Executive Editor: Susan Frantz Wiles
Publications Director: Carla Bentley
Creative Art Director: Gloria Bearden
Production Art Director: Melinda Stout

PRODUCTION
Managing Editor: Cathy Hardy
Senior Editor: Teri Sargent
Editorial Assistant: Sarah J. Green

EDITORIAL
Associate Editor: Linda L. Trimble
Senior Editorial Writer: Tammi Williamson Bradley
Editorial Associates: Terri Leming Davidson and
   Robyn Sheffield-Edwards
Copy Editor: Laura Lee Weland

ART
Book/Magazine Art Director: Diane M. Ghegan
Senior Production Artist: M. Katherine Yancey
Photography Stylists: Laura Bushmiaer, Sondra Daniel,
   Karen Smart Hall, Aurora Huston, Emily Minnick,
   and Christina Tiano Myers

BUSINESS STAFF

Publisher: Bruce Akin
Vice President, Finance: Tom Siebenmorgen
Vice President, Retail Sales: Thomas L. Carlisle
Retail Sales Director: Richard Tignor
Vice President, Retail Marketing: Pam Stebbins
Retail Customer Services Director: Margaret Sweetin
Marketing Manager: Russ Barnett
Executive Director of Marketing and Circulation:
   Guy A. Crossley
Circulation Manager: Byron L. Taylor
Print Production Manager: Laura Lockhart
Print Production Coordinator: Nancy Reddick Lister

CROCHET COLLECTION SERIES

Library of Congress Catalog Number: 94-74357
Hardcover ISBN 0-942237-58-7
Softcover ISBN 0-942237-59-5

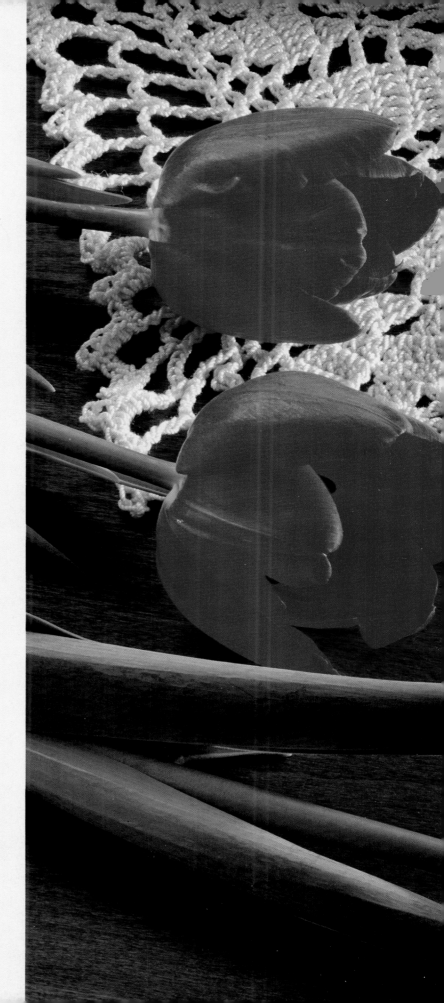

AT HOME WITH
crochet

Now's the time to get hooked on crochet! This fun, relaxing pastime provides the double pleasure of expressing your personal style and crafting projects to make your home more inviting. Cozy and familiar, crocheted pieces look great wherever they're displayed — whether you choose to create a showpiece afghan or a simple edging for a towel. Such heartwarming accents make At Home with Crochet *a treasury of handmade hospitality. In addition to traditional styles, it's filled with innovative designs that will spark your creativity and give you fresh ideas for enhancing your life with crochet.*

Pillows, place mats, and ensembles for the bedroom and bath are just a few of the imaginative accessories that will brighten rooms all through the house. If you're wrapped up in afghans, you'll be dazzled by our rainbow of colors, textures, and patterns. And when the celebration calls for a really special surprise, turn to our unique gift section. Just for the fun of it, we included a collection of whimsical projects, like a kid-pleasing stuffed dinosaur and a bath mat stitched with plastic bags! You'll find stylish wearables for men, women, and children as you browse through our fashion corner, and you'll adore the soft, cuddly creations to rock-a-bye baby with love. For stitchers who are hooked on holiday decorating, we have a fun mix of projects that reflects the special joys of each season.

Simple-to-follow instructions, helpful diagrams, and handy stitching tips make these designs easy to crochet — even if you're a beginner. And we labeled the "quick" projects to help you get the most out of your stitching time. With this indispensable volume by your side, you'll enjoy making yourself at home with crochet!

Anne Childs

LEISURE ARTS, INC.
LITTLE ROCK, ARKANSAS

table of contents

wrapped up in afghans

Cozy afghans — especially ones made by hand — are warmers for the body as well as the soul. A snuggly wrap draped across a chair offers an unspoken invitation to "come on in and make yourself at home." The variety of styles in this collection lets you extend the appealing comfort of afghans throughout your home. Whether you prefer traditional elegance, country charm, or bold, innovative looks, these creations will surround you with beauty.

PATCHWORK SAMPLER

The charm of patchwork quilts inspired this colorful sampler, which features four different textured blocks. The squares are individually edged with single crochets and whipstitched together to form the "quilt top." Leaf and vine embroidery enhance the afghan, and a placement diagram makes assembly easy.

Finished Size: Approximately 50" x 64"

MATERIALS

Worsted Weight Yarn, approximately:

Color A (Teal) - 14 ounces, (400 grams, 880 yards)
Color B (Gold) - 12 ounces, (340 grams, 755 yards)
Color C (Maroon) - 15 ounces, (430 grams, 945 yards)
Color D (Purple) - 12 ounces, (340 grams, 755 yards)
Color E (Green) - 8 ounces, (230 grams, 505 yards)

Crochet hook, size H (5.00 mm) **or** size needed for gauge
Yarn needle

PATTERN STITCHES

CLUSTER PUFF

YO, insert hook in same st, YO and pull up a loop, YO and draw through 2 loops on hook, skip next sc, YO, insert hook in next sc, YO and pull up a loop even with loop on hook, YO, insert hook in same st, YO and pull up a loop even with loop on hook, YO and draw through all 6 loops on hook.

DECREASE

Pull up a loop in next 2 sc, YO and draw through all 3 loops on hook **(counts as one sc)**.

GAUGE: One Square = 7" x 7"

SQUARE A (Make 16)

With Color A, ch 26 **loosely**.

Row 1 (Right side): Dc in fourth ch from hook and in each ch across: 24 sts.

Row 2: Ch 1, turn; sc in Back Loop Only of each st across **(Fig. 22, page 138)**.

Row 3: Ch 1, turn; working in free loops on previous dc row **(Fig. 23a, page 138)**, slip st in first st, ch 3 **(counts as first dc, now and throughout)**, dc in next dc and in each dc across: 24 dc.

Repeat Rows 2 and 3 until Square measures approximately 6½", ending by working Row 3; do **not** finish off.

Edging: Ch 1, work 22 sc evenly spaced across end of rows; working in free loops of beginning ch **(Fig. 23b, page 138)**, 3 sc in first ch, sc in each ch across to last ch, 3 sc in last ch; work 22 sc evenly spaced across end of rows; working across last row, 3 sc in first dc, sc in each dc across to last dc, 3 sc in last dc; join with slip st to first sc; finish off: 100 sc.

SQUARE B (Make 16)

With Color B, ch 24 **loosely**.

Row 1 (Right side): Sc in second ch from hook and in each ch across: 23 sc.

Note: Loop a short piece of yarn around any stitch to mark last row as **right** side.

Row 2: Ch 2 **(counts as first hdc, now and throughout)**, turn; work Cluster Puff, (ch 1, work Cluster Puff) across, hdc in same st as last st: 11 Cluster Puffs.

Row 3: Ch 1, turn; sc in each st across: 23 sc.

Repeat Rows 2 and 3 until Square measures approximately 6¹/₂", ending by working Row 3; do **not** finish off.

Edging: Ch 1, work 22 sc evenly spaced across end of rows; working in free loops of beginning ch, 3 sc in first ch, work 22 sc evenly spaced across to last ch, 3 sc in last ch; work 22 sc evenly spaced across end of rows; working across last row, 3 sc in first sc, work 22 sc evenly spaced across to last sc, 3 sc in last sc; join with slip st to first sc, finish off: 100 sc.

SQUARE C (Make 16)

With Color C, ch 26 **loosely**.

Row 1: Sc in second ch from hook and in next 7 chs, (ch 10, sc) 3 times in same ch as last sc, sc in next 10 chs, (ch 10, sc) 3 times in same ch as last sc, sc in each ch across: 31 sc.

Row 2 (Right side): Ch 1, turn; sc in first 7 sc, skip next sc, decrease working **behind** ch-10 loops, skip next sc, sc in next 9 sts, skip next sc, decrease working **behind** ch-10 loops, skip next sc, sc in each sc across: 25 sc.

Row 3: Ch 1, turn; sc in each sc across.

Row 4: Ch 1, turn; sc in first 4 sc, † holding next loop in front of next sc, sc in both loop **and** in next sc, sc in next 5 sc, skip next loop, holding next loop in front of next sc, sc in both loop **and** in next sc †, sc in next 3 sc, repeat from † to † once, sc in each sc across: 25 sc.

Row 5: Ch 1, turn; sc in each sc across.

Row 6: Ch 1, turn; sc in first 7 sc, holding center loop in front of next sc, 6 dc in both loop **and** in next sc, sc in next 9 sc, holding center loop in front of next sc, 6 dc in both loop **and** in next sc, sc in each sc across.

Row 7: Ch 1, turn; sc in first 7 sc, ch 1, skip next 6 dc, pushing dc to right side, sc in next 5 sc, (ch 10, sc) 3 times in same st as last sc, sc in next 4 sc, ch 1, skip next 6 dc, pushing dc to right side, sc in each sc across: 28 sts.

Row 8: Ch 1, turn; sc in first 12 sts, skip next sc, decrease working **behind** ch-10 loops, skip next sc, sc in each st across: 25 sc.

Row 9: Ch 1, turn; sc in each sc across.

Row 10: Ch 1, turn; sc in first 9 sc, holding next loop in front of next sc, sc in both loop **and** in next sc, sc in next 5 sc, skip next loop, holding next loop in front of next sc, sc in both loop **and** in next sc, sc in each sc across.

Row 11: Ch 1, turn; sc in each sc across.

Row 12: Ch 1, turn; sc in first 12 sc, holding center loop in front of next sc, 6 dc in both loop **and** in next sc, sc in each sc across.

Row 13: Ch 1, turn; sc in first 8 sc, (ch 10, sc) 3 times in same st as last sc, sc in next 4 sc, ch 1, skip next 6 dc, pushing dc to right side, sc in next 5 sc, (ch 10, sc) 3 times in same st as last sc, sc in each sc across.

Rows 14-24: Repeat Rows 2-12 once.

Row 25: Ch 1, turn; sc in first 12 sc, ch 1, skip next 6 dc, pushing dc to right side, sc in each sc across.

Row 26: Ch 1, turn; sc in each sc across; do **not** finish off.

Edging: Work same as Square B.

SQUARE D (Make 15)

With Color D, ch 24 **loosely**.

Row 1 (Right side): Sc in second ch from hook and in each ch across: 23 sc.

Note: Loop a short piece of yarn around any stitch to mark last row as **right** side.

Row 2: Ch 1, turn; sc in first sc, tr in next sc, sc in next sc pushing tr to right side, tr in next sc, (sc in next 4 sc, tr in next sc, sc in next sc, tr in next sc) twice, sc in last 5 sc.

Row 3 AND ALL RIGHT SIDE ROWS: Ch 1, turn; sc in each st across.

Row 4: Ch 1, turn; sc in first 2 sc, (tr in next sc, sc in next sc, tr in next sc, sc in next 4 sc) 3 times.

Row 6: Ch 1, turn; sc in first 3 sc, tr in next sc, sc in next sc, tr in next sc, (sc in next 4 sc, tr in next sc, sc in next sc, tr in next sc) twice, sc in last 3 sc.

Row 8: Ch 1, turn; sc in first 4 sc, tr in next sc, sc in next sc, tr in next sc, (sc in next 4 sc, tr in next sc, sc in next sc, tr in next sc) twice, sc in last 2 sc.

Row 10: Ch 1, turn; sc in first 5 sc, tr in next sc, sc in next sc, tr in next sc, (sc in next 4 sc, tr in next sc, sc in next sc, tr in next sc) twice, sc in last sc.

Row 12: Ch 1, turn; sc in first sc, tr in next sc, sc in next 4 sc, tr in next sc, (sc in next sc, tr in next sc, sc in next 4 sc, tr in next sc) twice, sc in last 2 sc.

Row 14: Ch 1, turn; sc in first 2 sc, (tr in next sc, sc in next 4 sc, tr in next sc, sc in next sc) 3 times.

Rows 16-24: Repeat Rows 2-10 once; do **not** finish off.

Edging: Work same as Square B.

FINISHING

ASSEMBLY

Following Placement Diagram and using matching colors as desired, whipstitch Squares together forming 7 vertical strips of 9 Squares each *(Fig. 28a, page 140)*; then whipstitch strips together.

BORDER

Rnd 1: With **right** side facing, join Color E with slip st in any corner sc; ch 1, sc in each sc around to last sc working 3 sc in each corner sc, skip last sc; join with slip st to first sc: 771 sc.

Rnd 2: Ch 1, sc in same st and in next 2 sc, ch 3, slip st in last sc worked, ★ sc in next 3 sc, ch 3, slip st in last sc worked; repeat from ★ around; join with slip st to first sc, finish off.

LEAVES AND VINES

Using Placement Diagram as a guide and Color E, embroider Leaves and Vines over seams, using Lazy Daisy St *(Fig. 38, page 142)* and Outline St *(Figs. 32a & b, page 141)*.

PLACEMENT DIAGRAM

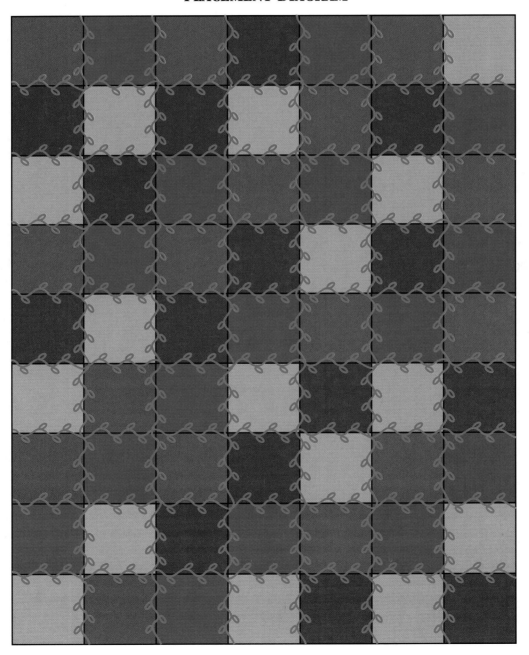

BUILDING BLOCKS QUILT

Diamonds in three shades of blue create the illusion of building blocks on this quilt-inspired afghan. Triangles fill in along the sides. The toasty wrap is easy to stitch in single crochet, and a color diagram makes assembly a breeze!

Finished Size: Approximately 47" x 71"

MATERIALS
Worsted Weight Yarn, approximately:
Color A (Light Blue) - 16 ounces, (450 grams, 1,190 yards)
Color B (Blue) - 16 ounces, (450 grams, 1,190 yards)
Color C (Dark Blue) - 18 ounces, (510 grams, 1,335 yards)
Crochet hook, size H (5.00 mm) **or** size needed for gauge
Yarn needle

GAUGE: 7 sc and 8 rows = 2"
One Diamond = 4½" wide and 7½" tall

PATTERN STITCH
DECREASE
Pull up a loop in next 2 sts, YO and draw through all 3 loops on hook **(counts as one sc)**.

DIAMOND A (Make 55)
Row 1 (Right side)**:** With Color A, ch 2; 2 sc in second ch from hook.
Note: Loop a short piece of yarn around any stitch to mark last row as **right** side and bottom.
Row 2: Ch 1, turn; sc in first sc, 2 sc in next sc: 3 sc.
Row 3: Ch 1, turn; sc in first 2 sc, 2 sc in last sc: 4 sc.
Rows 4-15: Ch 1, turn; sc in each sc across to last sc, 2 sc in last sc: 16 sc.
Rows 16-29: Ch 1, turn; skip first sc, sc in next sc and in each sc across: 2 sc.
Row 30: Ch 1, turn; skip first sc, sc in next sc; finish off.

DIAMOND B (Make 60)
With Color B, work same as Diamond A.

DIAMOND C (Make 60)
With Color C, work same as Diamond A.

TRIANGLE (Make 10)
Rows 1-15: Work same as Diamond A.
Finish off.

ASSEMBLY
Following Placement Diagram, using matching colors as desired and working in end of rows, whipstitch Diamonds together placing bottom of each Diamond A towards the right edge of afghan and bottom of each Diamond B & C towards bottom edge of afghan *(Fig. 28a, page 140)*.
Whipstitch Triangles to each long side, with Row 15 along outer edge.

PLACEMENT DIAGRAM

EDGING
Rnd 1: With **right** side facing, join Color C with slip st in any st; ch 1, sc evenly around working 3 sc in each outer corner and decreasing at each inner corner; join with slip st to first sc.
Rnds 2 and 3: Ch 1, turn; sc in each sc around working 3 sc in each outer corner and decreasing at each inner corner; join with slip st to first sc.
Rnd 4: Ch 1, do **not** turn; working from **left** to **right**, work reverse sc in each sc around *(Figs. 19a-d, page 136)*; join with slip st to first st, finish off.

SNUGGLY WRAPS

Worked in strips that are joined as you go, these two snuggly afghans use front post cross stitches to create their textured ridges. Each afghan, whether fashioned in a single color or stripes, is enhanced with a lovely scalloped effect.

Finished Size: Approximately 47" x 60"

MATERIALS

Worsted Weight Yarn, approximately:

Solid

37 ounces, (1,050 grams, 2,430 yards)

Striped

Color A (Blue) - 18 ounces, (510 grams, 1,185 yards)

Color B (Ecru) - 10 ounces, (280 grams, 655 yards)

Color C (Yellow) - 9 ounces, (260 grams, 590 yards)

Crochet hook, size I (5.50 mm) **or** size needed for gauge

GAUGE: (2 dc, ch 1) 5 times = 4¹/₄"

One Strip = 4¹/₄" wide

PATTERN STITCHES

FRONT POST DOUBLE CROCHET *(abbreviated FPdc)*
YO, insert hook from **front** to **back** around post of dc indicated *(Fig. 13, page 135)*, YO and pull up a loop **even** with loop on hook, (YO and draw through 2 loops on hook) twice.

FRONT POST CROSS STITCH *(abbreviated FP Cross St)*
Skip next dc, work FPdc around next dc, working in **front** of FPdc just worked, work FPdc around skipped dc *(Fig. 1)*.

Fig. 1

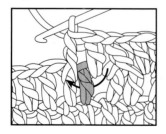

BACK POST DOUBLE CROCHET *(abbreviated BPdc)*
YO, insert hook from **back** to **front** around post of dc indicated, YO and pull up a loop **even** with loop on hook, (YO and draw through 2 loops on hook) twice.

DECREASE *(uses next 2 sts)*
★ YO, insert hook in Back Loop Only of **next** FPdc *(Fig. 22, page 138)*, YO and pull up a loop, YO and draw through 2 loops on hook; repeat from ★ once **more**, YO and draw through all 3 loops on hook.

FIRST STRIP

Note: For Striped Afghan, work in the following Color Sequence: 1 Rnd each Color C *(Fig. 24b, page 138)*, Color A, Color B, Color A.

Ch 198 **loosely**.

Rnd 1 (Right side)**:** (Dc, ch 1, 2 dc) in fourth ch from hook **(3 skipped chs count as first dc)**, ch 1, (skip next ch, dc in next 2 chs, ch 1) across to last 2 chs, skip next ch, (2 dc, ch 1) 3 times in last ch; working in free loops of beginning ch *(Fig. 23b, page 138)*, (skip next ch, dc in next 2 chs, ch 1) 64 times, skip next ch, 2 dc in same ch as first dc, ch 1; join with slip st to first dc: 134 ch-1 sps.

Note: Loop a short piece of yarn around any stitch to mark last round as **right** side.

Rnd 2: Slip st in next dc and in first ch-1 sp, ch 3, 2 dc in same sp, work FP Cross St, (dc in next ch-1 sp, work FP Cross St) 65 times, (3 dc in next ch-1 sp, work FP Cross St) twice, (dc in next ch-1 sp, work FP Cross St) 65 times, 3 dc in next ch-1 sp, work FP Cross St; join with slip st to top of beginning ch-3: 134 FP Cross Sts.

Rnd 3: Ch 4, † work BPdc around next 2 dc, ch 1, decrease, ch 1, (work BPdc around next dc, ch 1, decrease, ch 1) 65 times, work BPdc around next 2 dc, ch 1 †, (dc in Back Loop Only of next st, ch 1) 4 times, repeat from † to † once, (dc in Back Loop Only of next st, ch 1) 3 times; join with slip st to third ch of beginning ch-4: 274 ch-1 sps.

Rnd 4: Slip st in first ch-1 sp, ch 3, (slip st in next ch-1 sp, ch 1, slip st in next ch-1 sp, ch 3) 67 times, (slip st, ch 1, slip st) in next ch-1 sp, ch 3, (slip st in next ch-1 sp, ch 1, slip st in next ch-1 sp, ch 3) 68 times, (slip st, ch 1, slip st) in next ch-1 sp, ch 3, slip st in next ch-1 sp, ch 1; join with slip st to first slip st, finish off.

REMAINING 10 STRIPS

Work same as First Strip through Rnd 3.

Rnd 4: Slip st in first ch-1 sp, ch 3, (slip st in next ch-1 sp, ch 1, slip st in next ch-1 sp, ch 3) 67 times, (slip st, ch 1, slip st) in next ch-1 sp, (ch 3, slip st in next ch-1 sp, ch 1, slip st in next ch-1 sp) twice; holding Strips with **wrong** sides together, ★ ch 1, slip st in corresponding ch-3 sp on **previous Strip**, (ch 1, slip st in next ch-1 sp on **new Strip**) twice; repeat from ★ 64 times **more**, ch 3, slip st in next ch-1 sp, ch 1, slip st in next ch-1 sp, ch 3, (slip st, ch 1, slip st) in next ch-1 sp, ch 3, slip st in next ch-1 sp, ch 1; join with slip st to first slip st, finish off.

Quick LACY HEXAGONS

Because it's worked with two strands of worsted weight yarn, this airy wrap is less fragile than it looks! The hexagon motifs are worked separately and then whipstitched together. The afghan is edged with reverse half double crochets.

Finished Size: Approximately 56" x 64"

MATERIALS
Worsted Weight Yarn, approximately:
   57 ounces, (1,620 grams, 3,745 yards)
Crochet hook, size N (9.00 mm) **or** size needed for gauge
Yarn needle

Note: Entire Afghan is worked holding 2 strands of yarn together.

GAUGE: One Motif = 9" (from straight edge to straight edge)

MOTIF (Make 45)
Ch 5; join with slip st to form a ring.
Rnd 1 (Right side): Ch 3 **(counts as first dc, now and throughout)**, 11 dc in ring; join with slip st to first dc: 12 dc.
Note: Loop a short piece of yarn around any stitch to mark last round as **right** side.
Rnd 2: Ch 3, dc in same st, 2 dc in next dc, ch 1, (2 dc in each of next 2 dc, ch 1) around; join with slip st to first dc: 24 dc.
Rnd 3: Ch 3, dc in same st and in next 2 dc, 2 dc in next dc, ch 2, ★ 2 dc in next dc, dc in next 2 dc, 2 dc in next dc, ch 2; repeat from ★ around; join with slip st to first dc: 36 dc.
Rnd 4: Ch 3, dc in same st and in next 4 dc, 2 dc in next dc, ch 3, ★ 2 dc in next dc, dc in next 4 dc, 2 dc in next dc, ch 3; repeat from ★ around; join with slip st to first dc: 48 dc.
Rnd 5: Ch 3, dc in same st and in next 6 dc, 2 dc in next dc, ch 4, ★ 2 dc in next dc, dc in next 6 dc, 2 dc in next dc, ch 4; repeat from ★ around; join with slip st to first dc, finish off: 60 dc.

ASSEMBLY
Following Placement Diagram and leaving corner ch-4 sps free, whipstitch Motifs together forming strips *(Fig. 28b, page 140)*; then whipstitch strips together.

PLACEMENT DIAGRAM

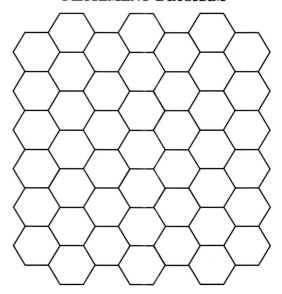

EDGING
Rnd 1: With **right** side facing, join yarn with slip st in any dc; ch 1, sc in each dc around working 4 sc in each corner ch-4 sp and 2 sc in each sp at joinings; join with slip st to first sc.
Rnd 2: Ch 1, hdc in same st, ch 1, working from **left** to **right**, ★ skip next sc, work reverse hdc in next sc *(Figs. 20a-d, page 136)*, ch 1; repeat from ★ around; join with slip st to first hdc, finish off.

BOLD APPEAL

Irresistibly soft, this luxurious fringed afghan is fashioned with cuddly brushed mohair blend and durable worsted weight yarns. The textured teal and purple panels are worked in bold graduated stripes and accented with vertical rows of navy slip stitches.

Finished Size: Approximately 49" x 65"

MATERIALS
Worsted Weight Brushed Mohair Blend, approximately:
　　Color A (Purple) - 14 ounces, (400 grams, 940 yards)
Worsted Weight Yarn, approximately:
　　Color B (Teal) - 32 ounces, (910 grams, 2,835 yards)
　　Color C (Navy) - 4 ounces, (110 grams, 270 yards)
Crochet hooks, sizes J (6.00 mm) **and** N (9.00 mm) **or** sizes needed for gauge

GAUGE: With smaller size hook and Color B,
　　　　13 dc and 7 rows = 4"
　　　　With larger size hook and Color A, 13 hdc = 4"

Note: Each row is worked across length of afghan.

PATTERN STITCH
SLANT ST
Skip next 3 sts, tr in next st, working **behind** tr just made, dc in 3 skipped sts.

BODY

With larger size hook and Color A, ch 213 **loosely**.
Row 1: Hdc in third ch from hook **(2 skipped chs count as first hdc)** and in each ch across: 212 hdc.
Row 2 (Right side): Ch 3 **(counts as first dc, now and throughout)**, turn; working in Back Loops Only *(Fig. 22, page 138)*, dc in next st, work Slant Sts across to last 2 sts, dc in last 2 sts: 52 Slant Sts.
Note: Loop a short piece of yarn around last dc to mark last row as **right** side and bottom.
Row 3: Ch 2 **(counts as first hdc, now and throughout)**, turn; hdc in Front Loop Only of next st and in each st across: 212 hdc.
Rows 4-16: Repeat Rows 2 and 3, 6 times, then repeat Row 2 once **more** changing to Color B at end of Row 16 *(Fig. 24a, page 138)*.
Row 17: Using smaller size hook, ch 3, turn; dc in Front Loop Only of next st and in each st across.

Row 18: Ch 3, turn; dc in Back Loop Only of next st and in each st across.
Row 19: Ch 3, turn; dc in both loops of next dc and in each dc across.
Rows 20-24: Repeat Rows 18 and 19 twice, then repeat Row 18 once **more** changing to Color A at end of Row 24.
Row 25: Using larger size hook, ch 2, turn; hdc in both loops of next dc and in each dc across.
Rows 26-33: Repeat Rows 2 and 3, 4 times changing to Color B at end of Row 33.
Rows 34-39: Using smaller size hook, repeat Rows 18 and 19, 3 times changing to Color A at end of Row 39.
Rows 40-43: With larger size hook, repeat Rows 2 and 3, twice changing to Color B at end of Row 43.
Rows 44-48: With smaller size hook, repeat Rows 18 and 19 twice, then repeat Row 18 once **more** changing to Color A at end of Row 48.
Row 49: Repeat Row 25.
Rows 50 and 51: Repeat Rows 2 and 3 changing to Color B at end of Row 51.
Rows 52-54: Using smaller size hook, repeat Rows 18 and 19 once, then repeat Row 18 once **more** changing to Color A at end of Row 54.
Rows 55-60: Repeat Rows 49-54.
Row 61: Repeat Row 25.
Row 62: Repeat Row 2 changing to Color B in last dc.
Rows 63 and 64: Repeat Rows 17 and 18; at end of Row 64 finish off.
Row 65: With **right** side facing, larger size hook, and working in both loops, join Color A with slip st in first dc; ch 3, dc in next dc, work Slant Sts across to last 2 dc, dc in last 2 dc changing to Color B in last dc.
Row 66: Repeat Row 17; finish off.
Row 67: With **wrong** side facing, larger size hook, and working in both loops, join Color A with slip st in first dc; ch 2, hdc in next dc and in each dc across changing to Color B in last hdc.
Rows 68-94: Using smaller size hook, repeat Rows 18 and 19, 13 times, then repeat Row 18 once **more**.
Finish off.

STRIPES

With **right** side facing, larger size hook, and working from bottom to top on Row 17, hold Color C at back, insert hook from **front** to **back** in sp **between** first and second dc, YO and pull up a loop, ★ skip next sp, insert hook in next sp, YO and **loosely** draw through loop on hook; repeat from ★ across to last dc, slip st around post of last dc, ch 1, **turn**; slip st **loosely** in each slip st across inserting hook from top to bottom; finish off.

Repeat Stripe on Rows 34, 44, 52, 58, 63, 66, and 68.

Add fringe using 6 strands each of Color A and Color B, and 3 strands of Color C, each 19" long *(Figs. 30a & b, page 140)*; attach matching color evenly spaced across end of rows on both ends of afghan.

Quick FILET RIPPLES

Using two strands of yarn and a jumbo hook makes it quick — and easy — to finish this pretty filet afghan. Worked in double crochets, a traditional ripple pattern gives the throw its lacy appeal. A simple scalloped edging borders the cozy coverlet.

Finished Size: Approximately 48" x 62"

MATERIALS

Worsted Weight Yarn, approximately:

MC (Off-White) - 36 ounces, (1,020 grams, 2,100 yards)

Color A (Green) - 12 ounces, (340 grams, 700 yards)

Color B (Rose) - 10 ounces, (280 grams, 585 yards)

Crochet hook, size P (10.00 mm) **or** size needed for gauge

Note: Entire Afghan is worked holding 2 strands of yarn together.

GAUGE: 7 dc = 3"

In pattern, 1 repeat = 6" and 6 rows = 7"

Gauge Swatch (12" x 7")

Ch 37 **loosely**.

Rows 1-6: Work same as Body.

Finish off.

PATTERN STITCHES

BEGINNING DECREASE

Ch 2, turn; skip next st, dc in next dc **(counts as one dc)**.

DECREASE

† YO, insert hook in **next** st, YO and pull up a loop, YO and draw through 2 loops on hook †, skip next 3 sts, repeat from † to † once, YO and draw through all 3 loops on hook **(counts as one dc)**.

ENDING DECREASE

† YO, insert hook in **next** st, YO and pull up a loop, YO and draw through 2 loops on hook †, skip next st, repeat from † to † once, YO and draw through all 3 loops on hook **(counts as one dc)**.

BODY

COLOR SEQUENCE

4 Rows MC *(Fig. 24a, page 138)*, ★ 1 row Color A, 1 row Color B, 4 rows MC; repeat from ★ throughout.

With MC, ch 157 **loosely**.

Row 1: Dc in fifth ch from hook **(4 skipped chs count as first dc plus ch 1)**, ch 1, (skip next ch, dc in next ch, ch 1) twice, skip next ch, (dc, ch 3, dc) in next ch, ★ ch 1, (skip next ch, dc in next ch, ch 1) 3 times, skip next ch, decrease,

ch 1, (skip next ch, dc in next ch, ch 1) 3 times, skip next ch, (dc, ch 3, dc) in next ch; repeat from ★ across to last 6 chs, ch 1, (skip next ch, dc in next ch, ch 1) twice, skip next ch, (dc, ch 1, dc) in last ch: 73 dc.

Row 2 (Right side): Work beginning decrease, (dc in next ch-1 sp, dc in next dc) 3 times, (2 dc, ch 3, 2 dc) in next ch-3 sp, (dc in next dc, dc in next ch-1 sp) 3 times, ★ decrease, (dc in next ch-1 sp, dc in next dc) 3 times, (2 dc, ch 3, 2 dc) in next ch-3 sp, (dc in next dc, dc in next ch-1 sp) 3 times; repeat from ★ across to last 2 dc, work ending decrease: 137 dc.

Note: Loop a short piece of yarn around any stitch to mark last row as **right** side.

Row 3: Work beginning decrease, ch 1, (skip next dc, dc in next dc, ch 1) 3 times, (dc, ch 3, dc) in next ch-3 sp, ch 1, (dc in next dc, ch 1, skip next dc) 3 times, ★ decrease, ch 1, (skip next dc, dc in next dc, ch 1) 3 times, (dc, ch 3, dc) in next ch-3 sp, ch 1, (dc in next dc, ch 1, skip next dc) 3 times; repeat from ★ across to last 3 dc, work ending decrease: 73 dc.

Rows 4-52: Repeat Rows 2 and 3, 24 times, then repeat Row 2 once **more**.

Finish off.

EDGING

With **right** side facing, join Color A with slip st in first dc; ch 1, sc in same st, skip next 2 dc, 5 dc in next dc, skip next 2 dc, sc in next dc, skip next 2 dc, 7 dc in next ch-3 sp, skip next 2 dc, sc in next dc, † (skip next 2 dc, 5 dc in next dc, skip next 2 dc, sc in next dc) twice, skip next 2 dc, 7 dc in next ch-3 sp, skip next 2 dc, sc in next dc †, repeat from † to † across to last 6 dc, skip next 2 dc, 5 dc in next dc, skip next 2 dc, sc in last dc; working in end of rows, (5 dc, sc) in first row, (5 dc in next row, sc in next row) across to last row, 7 dc in last row; working in unworked chs and in free loops of beginning ch *(Fig. 23b, page 138)* and in ch-3 sps, sc in first ch, (skip next 2 chs, 5 dc in next ch, skip next 2 chs, sc in next ch) twice, ★ skip next 2 chs, 7 dc in next ch-3 sp, skip next 2 chs, sc in next ch, (skip next 2 chs, 5 dc in next ch, skip next 2 chs, sc in next ch) twice; repeat from ★ 6 times **more**; working in end of rows, 7 dc in first row, (sc in next row, 5 dc in next row) across to last row, (sc, 5 dc) in last row; join with slip st to first sc, finish off.

BROWN-EYED SUSANS

Blooming against a field of green, rows of brown-eyed Susans pay tribute to a favorite wildflower. Our lacy throw is worked in squares that are joined as you stitch, and it's finished with a simple ruffled border.

Finished Size: Approximately 49" x 63"

MATERIALS
Worsted Weight Yarn, approximately:
MC (Green) - 16 ounces, (450 grams, 1,100 yards)
Color A (Brown) - 4 ounces, (110 grams, 275 yards)
Color B (Gold) - 21 ounces, (600 grams, 1,440 yards)
Crochet hook, size H (5.00 mm) **or** size needed for gauge

GAUGE: One Square = 4¹/₂"

PATTERN STITCHES

TR CLUSTER
★ YO twice, insert hook in same sp, YO and pull up a loop, (YO and draw through 2 loops on hook) twice; repeat from ★ once **more**, YO and draw through all 3 loops on hook **(Figs. 10a & b, page 134)**.

DC CLUSTER
★ YO, insert hook in st indicated, YO and pull up a loop, YO and draw through 2 loops on hook; repeat from ★ 2 times **more**, YO and draw through all 4 loops on hook.

FIRST SQUARE

With Color A, ch 3; join with slip st to form a ring.
Rnd 1 (Right side): Ch 1, 6 sc in ring; join with slip st to Front Loop Only of first sc **(Fig. 22, page 138)**.
Note: Loop a short piece of yarn around any stitch to mark last round as **right** side.
Rnd 2: Working in Front Loops Only, (dc, slip st) in same st, (slip st, dc, slip st) in next sc and in each sc around pushing dc to **wrong** side; join with slip st to first slip st, finish off.
Rnd 3: With **right** side facing and working in free loops on Rnd 1 **(Fig. 23a, page 138)**, join Color B with slip st in any sc; ch 1, 2 sc in each sc around; join with slip st to first sc: 12 sc.
Rnd 4: Ch 1, sc in same st, ch 3, (sc in next sc, ch 3) around; join with slip st to first sc: 12 ch-3 sps.
Rnd 5: Slip st in first ch-3 sp, ch 1, work (sc, ch 3, tr Cluster, ch 3, sc) in same sp and in each ch-3 sp around; join with slip st to first sc, finish off: 12 Petals.
Rnd 6: With **right** side facing, join MC with slip st in top of any Petal; ch 1, sc in same st, ch 5, sc in top of next Petal, ch 5,

(work dc Cluster, ch 5) twice in top of next Petal, ★ (sc in top of next Petal, ch 5) twice, (work dc Cluster, ch 5) twice in top of next Petal; repeat from ★ around; join with slip st to first sc, finish off.

ADDITIONAL SQUARES (Make 129)

Work same as First Square through Rnd 5.
Work One-Sided or Two-Sided Joining to form 10 vertical strips of 13 Squares each.

ONE-SIDED JOINING

Rnd 6: With **right** side facing, join MC with slip st in top of any Petal; ch 1, sc in same st, ch 5, sc in top of next Petal, ch 5, † (work dc Cluster, ch 5) twice in top of next Petal, (sc in top of next Petal, ch 5) twice †, repeat from † to † once **more**, work dc Cluster in top of next Petal, ch 2, with **right** side facing, slip st in any corner loop on **previous Square**, ch 2, work dc Cluster in same st on **new Square**, ch 2, slip st in next loop on **previous Square**, ch 2, (sc in top of next Petal on **new Square**, ch 2, slip st in next loop on **previous Square**, ch 2) twice, work dc Cluster in top of next Petal on **new Square**, ch 2, slip st in next corner loop on **previous Square**, ch 2, work dc Cluster in same st on **new Square**, ch 5; join with slip st to first sc, finish off.

TWO-SIDED JOINING

Rnd 6: With **right** side facing, join MC with slip st in top of any Petal; ch 1, sc in same st, ch 5, sc in top of next Petal, ch 5, (work dc Cluster, ch 5) twice in top of next Petal, (sc in top of next Petal, ch 5) twice, ★ † work dc Cluster in top of next Petal, ch 2, with **right** side facing, slip st in corner loop on **previous Square**, ch 2, work dc Cluster in same st on **new Square** †, ch 2, slip st in next loop on **previous Square**, ch 2, (sc in top of next Petal on **new Square**, ch 2, slip st in next loop on **previous Square**, ch 2) twice; repeat from ★ once **more**, then repeat from † to † once, ch 5; join with slip st to first sc, finish off.

BORDER

Rnd 1: With **right** side facing, join MC with slip st in any corner ch-5 loop; ch 1, ★ (sc, ch 3) twice in corner loop, (sc in next loop, ch 3) across to next corner loop; repeat from ★ around; join with slip st to first sc.

Rnd 2: Ch 1, sc in same st, 3 sc in next ch-3 sp, (sc in next sc, 3 sc in next ch-3 sp) around; join with slip st to first sc, finish off.

Rnd 3: With **wrong** side facing, join Color B with slip st in same st as joining; ch 1, sc in same st, tr in next sc, (sc in next sc pushing tr to **right** side, tr in next sc) around; join with slip st to first sc, finish off.

Rnd 4: With **right** side facing, join MC with slip st in second sc to **left** of joining; ch 1, sc in same st, ch 1, skip next tr,

★ (sc in next sc, ch 1, skip next tr) across to next corner sc, (sc, ch 1) twice in corner sc, skip next tr; repeat from ★ around; join with slip st to first sc: 928 sts.

Rnd 5: Ch 1, sc in same st, (ch 5, skip next 3 sts, sc in next st) around to last 3 sts, ch 2, skip last 3 sts, dc in first sc to form last loop.

Rnd 6: Ch 1, (sc, ch 5, sc) in same loop and in each loop around; join with slip st to first sc, finish off.

HANDSOME STRIPES

Warm, rustic colors give this textured throw a strong masculine appeal. Worked in a single piece, it features stripes of ecru openwork and a blue chain that's woven through the black double crochet stripes. The coordinating border is finished with an ample fringe.

Finished Size: Approximately 48" x 63"

MATERIALS

Worsted Weight Yarn, approximately:
- MC (Beige) - 26 ounces, (740 grams, 1,635 yards)
- Color A (Rust) - 18 ounces, (510 grams, 1,130 yards)
- Color B (Black) - 10 ounces, (280 grams, 630 yards)
- Color C (Blue) - 3 ounces, (90 grams, 190 yards)

Crochet hook, size I (5.50 mm) **or** size needed for gauge
Yarn needle

GAUGE: In pattern, 16 dc = 4" and Rows 1-9 = 3"

Note: Each row is worked across length of afghan.

PATTERN STITCH

CROSS ST

Skip next 2 sc, dc in next sc, ch 1, working in **front** of last dc made, dc in first skipped sc *(Fig. 1)*.

Fig. 1

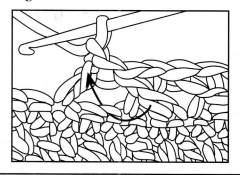

BODY

With Color A, ch 234 **loosely**.

Row 1 (Right side): Sc in second ch from hook and in each ch across: 233 sc.

Note: Loop a short piece of yarn around any stitch to mark last row as **right** side.

Row 2: Ch 1, turn; sc in first sc, (tr in next sc, sc in next sc pushing tr to **right** side) across changing to Color B in last sc *(Fig. 24a, page 138)*.

Row 3: Ch 1, turn; sc in each st across.

Row 4: Ch 3 **(counts as first dc, now and throughout)**, turn; dc in next sc and in each sc across changing to Color A in last sc.

Row 5: Ch 1, turn; sc in each dc across.

Row 6: Ch 1, turn; sc in first sc, (tr in next sc, sc in next sc) across changing to MC in last sc.

Row 7: Ch 1, turn; sc in each st across.

Row 8: Ch 3, turn; work Cross St across to last sc, dc in last sc: 77 Cross Sts.

Row 9: Ch 1, turn; sc in each dc and in each ch-1 sp across; finish off: 233 sc.

Row 10: With **right** side facing, join Color A with slip st in first sc; ch 1, sc in same st and in each sc across.

Rows 11-16: Repeat Rows 2-7.

Row 17: Ch 3, turn; dc in next sc and in each sc across.

Row 18: Ch 8 **(counts as first dc plus ch 5, now and throughout)**, turn; (skip next 3 dc, dc in next 3 dc, ch 5) across to last 4 dc, skip next 3 dc, dc in last dc: 39 loops.

Rows 19 and 20: Ch 8, turn; (dc in next 3 dc, ch 5) across to last dc, dc in last dc.

Row 21: Ch 6 **(counts as first dc plus ch 3, now and throughout)**, turn; sc **around** ch-5 loops of previous 3 rows, ch 3, ★ dc in next 3 dc, ch 3, sc **around** ch-5 loops of previous 3 rows, ch 3; repeat from ★ across to last dc, dc in last dc.

Row 22: Ch 6, turn; (dc in next 3 dc, ch 3) across to last dc, dc in last dc.

Row 23: Ch 3, turn; dc in next ch and in each ch and dc across changing to Color A in last dc: 233 dc.

Row 24: Ch 1, turn; sc in each dc across.

Rows 25-125: Repeat Rows 2-24, 4 times, then repeat Rows 2-10 once **more**.

Rows 126-129: Repeat Rows 2-5.

Row 130: Ch 1, turn; sc in first sc, (tr in next sc, sc in next sc) across; finish off.

BORDER

Row 1: With **right** side facing and working in end of rows, join Color A with slip st in first row; ch 1, work 187 sc evenly spaced across.

Rows 2-7: Repeat Rows 2-7 of Body.

Row 8: Ch 1, turn; sc in first sc, (ch 3, skip next 2 sc, sc in next sc) across; finish off: 62 ch-3 sps.

Repeat on other end.

TRIM

With Color C, chain a length long enough to weave through dc of Color B stripe. With **right** side facing, weave end of chain through stripe, adjusting chs as necessary; finish off. Secure ends on wrong side.

Repeat Trim for each Color B stripe across Body and Borders.

Add fringe using 6 strands of MC, each 17" long *(Figs. 30a & b, page 140)*; attach in each ch-3 sp across both ends of afghan.

PRETTY IN PEACH

*P*retty as a peach, this cozy afghan uses double crochets and simple shell stitches to create a pattern of alternating columns and vertical arches. The throw is finished with a lattice edging of single crochets and chains and enhanced with a tasseled fringe.

Finished Size: Approximately 48" x 64"

MATERIALS
Worsted Weight Yarn, approximately:
44 ounces, (1,250 grams, 2,565 yards)
Crochet hook, size K (6.50 mm) **or** size needed for gauge

GAUGE: 12 dc and 7 rows = 4"

BODY

Ch 146 **loosely**.
Row 1: Dc in fourth ch from hook and in next 3 chs, (ch 2, skip next 2 chs, dc in next 10 chs) across to last 7 chs, ch 2, skip next 2 chs, dc in last 5 chs: 12 ch-2 sps.
Row 2 (Right side): Ch 3 **(counts as first dc, now and throughout)**, turn; dc in next 2 dc, skip next 2 dc, (tr, 4 dc, tr) in next ch-2 sp, ★ skip next 2 dc, dc in next 6 dc, skip next 2 dc, (tr, 4 dc, tr) in next ch-2 sp; repeat from ★ across to last 5 sts, skip next 2 dc, dc in last 3 sts.
Note: Loop a short piece of yarn around any stitch to mark last row as **right** side.
Row 3: Ch 3, turn; dc in next dc, skip next dc, 2 dc in sp **before** next tr, skip next 2 sts, dc in next dc, ch 2, dc in next dc, skip next 2 sts, 2 dc in sp **before** next dc, ★ skip next dc, dc in next 4 dc, skip next dc, 2 dc in sp **before** next tr, skip next 2 sts, dc in next dc, ch 2, dc in next dc, skip next 2 sts, 2 dc in sp **before** next dc; repeat from ★ across to last 3 dc, skip next dc, dc in last 2 dc.
Repeat Rows 2 and 3 until Afghan measures approximately 61½", ending by working Row 2.

Last Row: Ch 3, turn; dc in next 2 dc, hdc in next tr, sc in next 4 dc, hdc in next tr, ★ dc in next 6 dc, hdc in next tr, sc in next 4 dc, hdc in next tr; repeat from ★ across to last 3 dc, dc in last 3 dc; do **not** finish off: 144 sts.

EDGING
TOP
Row 1: Ch 5, turn; skip next dc, sc in next dc, (ch 5, skip next 2 sts, sc in next st) across to last 3 sts, ch 2, skip next 2 sts, dc in last dc to form last loop: 48 loops.
Row 2: Ch 1, turn; sc in same loop, (ch 5, sc in next loop) across; finish off.

BOTTOM
Row 1: With **right** side facing and working in free loops of beginning ch *(Fig. 23b, page 138)*, join yarn with slip st in first ch; ch 5, skip next ch, sc in next ch, (ch 5, skip next 2 chs, sc in next ch) across to last 3 chs, ch 2, skip next 2 chs, dc in last ch to form last loop: 48 loops.
Row 2: Ch 1, turn; sc in same loop, (ch 5, sc in next loop) across; finish off.

Add fringe using 6 strands, each 11" long *(Figs. 30a & b, page 140)*; attach in each loop across both ends of afghan.

all through the house

Displayed throughout your home, handmade accents are more than just decorative pieces, they're expressions of your individual style. The unique designs we've included here are sure to inspire lots of new ideas for adding warm personal touches all through the house — from a flower-strewn boudoir to a beachside bath. So go ahead, brighten your decor with crochet!

THE LIVING ROOM

*A*dd old-fashioned elegance to the living room with these lacy accessories. (Below) A cozy chair is especially inviting when cushioned with plump pillows. These pretty throw pillows are crocheted with two strands of bedspread weight cotton thread. Coordinating coasters are quick-to-stitch projects that help unify your decor. (Opposite) Draped over a round accent table, our beautiful topper features the ever-popular pineapple pattern.

26

PINEAPPLE TABLE TOPPER

Finished Size: Approximately 36" in diameter

MATERIALS
Bedspread Weight Cotton Thread (size 10),
   approximately 540 yards
Steel crochet hook, size 6 (1.80 mm) **or** size needed
   for gauge

GAUGE: Rnds 1-4 = 2½"

PATTERN STITCHES

BEGINNING SHELL

Ch 3 **(counts as first dc, now and throughout)**,
(dc, ch 2, 2 dc) in same sp.

SHELL

(2 Dc, ch 2, 2 dc) in sp indicated.

DECREASE (uses next 2 dc)

★ YO, insert hook in **next** dc, YO and pull up a loop, YO
and draw through 2 loops on hook; repeat from ★ once
more, YO and draw through all 3 loops on hook **(counts
as one dc)**.

BEGINNING TR CLUSTER (uses first 4 dc)

Ch 3, ★ YO twice, insert hook in **next** dc, YO and pull up a
loop, (YO and draw through 2 loops on hook) twice; repeat
from ★ 2 times **more**, YO and draw through all 4 loops on
hook **(Figs. 11a & b, page 134)**.

TR CLUSTER (uses next 4 dc)

★ YO twice, insert hook in **next** dc, YO and pull up a loop,
(YO and draw through 2 loops on hook) twice; repeat from
★ 3 times **more**, YO and draw through all 5 loops on hook.

DC CLUSTER (uses next 4 dc)

★ YO, insert hook in **next** dc, YO and pull up a loop, YO
and draw through 2 loops on hook; repeat from ★ 3 times
more, YO and draw through all 5 loops on hook.

BODY

Ch 3; join with slip st to form a ring.

Rnd 1 (Right side): Ch 1, 10 sc in ring; join with slip st to
first sc.

Rnd 2: Ch 1, sc in same st, (ch 3, sc in next sc) around, ch 1,
hdc in first sc to form last sp: 10 sps.

Rnd 3: Ch 1, sc in same sp, ch 3, (sc in next ch-3 sp, ch 3)
around; join with slip st to first sc.

Rnd 4: Slip st in first ch-3 sp, work beginning Shell, ch 3, sc in
next ch-3 sp, ch 3, (work Shell in next ch-3 sp, ch 3, sc in next
ch-3 sp, ch 3) around; join with slip st to first dc: 5 Shells.

Rnd 5: Slip st in next dc and in next ch-2 sp, work beginning
Shell, ch 3, (sc in next ch-3 sp, ch 3) twice, ★ work Shell in
next Shell (ch-2 sp), ch 3, (sc in next ch-3 sp, ch 3) twice;
repeat from ★ around; join with slip st to first dc.

Rnd 6: Slip st in next dc and in next ch-2 sp, work beginning
Shell, ch 3, (sc in next ch-3 sp, ch 3) 3 times, ★ work Shell in
next Shell, ch 3, (sc in next ch-3 sp, ch 3) 3 times; repeat from
★ around; join with slip st to first dc.

Rnd 7: Ch 3, dc in same st, 2 dc in next dc, ch 3, (dc, ch 3)
twice in next ch-2 sp, 2 dc in each of next 2 dc, ch 3, skip next
ch-3 sp, (sc in next ch-3 sp, ch 3) twice, ★ 2 dc in each of
next 2 dc, ch 3, (dc, ch 3) twice in next ch-2 sp, 2 dc in each
of next 2 dc, ch 3, skip next ch-3 sp, (sc in next ch-3 sp, ch 3)
twice; repeat from ★ around; join with slip st to first dc.

Rnd 8: Ch 3, dc in next 3 dc, ★ † ch 3, skip next ch-3 sp, dc
in next ch-3 sp, (ch 1, dc) 9 times in same sp, ch 3, skip next
ch-3 sp, dc in next 4 dc, ch 3, skip next ch-3 sp, sc in next
ch-3 sp, ch 3 †, dc in next 4 dc; repeat from ★ 3 times **more**,
then repeat from † to † once; join with slip st to first dc.

Rnd 9: Ch 3, 2 dc in each of next 2 dc, dc in next dc, ch 3,
(sc in next ch-1 sp, ch 3) 9 times, skip next ch-3 sp, dc in next
dc, 2 dc in each of next 2 dc, ★ dc in next 2 dc, 2 dc in each of
next 2 dc, dc in next dc, ch 3, (sc in next ch-1 sp, ch 3) 9
times, skip next ch-3 sp, dc in next dc, 2 dc in each of next
2 dc; repeat from ★ around to last dc, dc in last dc; join with
slip st to first dc.

Rnd 10: Ch 3, dc in next 5 dc, ch 3, skip next ch-3 sp, (sc in
next ch-3 sp, ch 3) 8 times, ★ (dc in next 6 dc, ch 3) twice,
skip next ch-3 sp, (sc in next ch-3 sp, ch 3) 8 times; repeat
from ★ around to last 6 dc, dc in last 6 dc, ch 3; join with
slip st to first dc.

Rnd 11: Ch 3, dc in next 5 dc, ch 3, skip next ch-3 sp, (sc in
next ch-3 sp, ch 3) 7 times, dc in next 6 dc, ch 3, sc in next
ch-3 sp, ch 3, ★ dc in next 6 dc, ch 3, skip next ch-3 sp, (sc in
next ch-3 sp, ch 3) 7 times, dc in next 6 dc, ch 3, sc in next
ch-3 sp, ch 3; repeat from ★ around; join with slip st to first dc.

Rnd 12: Ch 3, dc in next 5 dc, ch 3, skip next ch-3 sp, (sc in
next ch-3 sp, ch 3) 6 times, dc in next 6 dc, ch 3, (sc in next
ch-3 sp, ch 3) twice, ★ dc in next 6 dc, ch 3, skip next ch-3 sp,
(sc in next ch-3 sp, ch 3) 6 times, dc in next 6 dc, ch 3, (sc in
next ch-3 sp, ch 3) twice; repeat from ★ around; join with
slip st to first dc.

Rnd 13: Ch 3, dc in next 5 dc, ch 3, skip next ch-3 sp, (sc in
next ch-3 sp, ch 3) 5 times, dc in next 6 dc, ch 3, (sc in next
ch-3 sp, ch 3) 3 times, ★ dc in next 6 dc, ch 3, skip next
ch-3 sp, (sc in next ch-3 sp, ch 3) 5 times, dc in next 6 dc,
ch 3, (sc in next ch-3 sp, ch 3) 3 times; repeat from ★ around;
join with slip st to first dc.

Rnd 14: Ch 3, ★ † decrease twice, dc in next dc, ch 3, skip
next ch-3 sp, (sc in next ch-3 sp, ch 3) 4 times, dc in next dc,

decrease twice, dc in next dc, ch 3, (sc in next ch-3 sp, ch 3) 4 times †, dc in next dc; repeat from ★ 3 times **more**, then repeat from † to † once; join with slip st to first dc.

Rnd 15: Ch 3, dc in next 3 dc, ★ † ch 3, skip next ch-3 sp, (sc in next ch-3 sp, ch 3) 3 times, dc in next 4 dc, ch 3, (sc in next ch-3 sp, ch 3) twice, work Shell in next ch-3 sp, ch 3, (sc in next ch-3 sp, ch 3) twice †, dc in next 4 dc; repeat from ★ 3 times **more**, then repeat from † to † once; join with slip st to first dc.

Rnd 16: Ch 3, dc in next 3 dc, ★ † ch 3, skip next ch-3 sp, (sc in next ch-3 sp, ch 3) twice, dc in next 4 dc, ch 3, (sc in next ch-3 sp, ch 3) twice, skip next ch-3 sp, dc in next 2 dc, ch 3, (dc, ch 3) twice in next ch-2 sp, dc in next 2 dc, ch 3, skip next ch-3 sp, (sc in next ch-3 sp, ch 3) twice †, dc in next 4 dc; repeat from ★ 3 times **more**, then repeat from † to † once; join with slip st to first dc.

Rnd 17: Ch 2, dc in next dc, decrease, ★ † ch 3, skip next ch-3 sp, sc in next ch-3 sp, ch 3, decrease twice, ch 3, (sc in next ch-3 sp, ch 3) twice, dc in next 2 dc, ch 3, skip next ch-3 sp, dc in next ch-3 sp, (ch 1, dc) 4 times in same sp, ch 3, skip next ch-3 sp, dc in next 2 dc, ch 3, skip next ch-3 sp, (sc in next ch-3 sp, ch 3) twice †, decrease twice; repeat from ★ 3 times **more**, then repeat from † to † once; skip beginning ch-2 and join with slip st to first dc.

Rnd 18: Work beginning tr Cluster, ★ † ch 5, (sc in next ch-3 sp, ch 5) twice, dc in next 2 dc, ch 3, (sc in next ch-1 sp, ch 3) 4 times, skip next ch-3 sp, dc in next 2 dc, ch 5, skip next ch-3 sp †, (sc in next ch-3 sp, ch 5) twice, work tr Cluster; repeat from ★ 3 times **more**, then repeat from † to † once, sc in next ch-3 sp, ch 5, sc in next ch-3 sp, ch 2, dc in top of beginning tr Cluster to form last loop.

Rnd 19: Ch 1, sc in same loop, ch 10, (sc in next loop, ch 10) twice, dc in next 2 dc, ch 3, skip next ch-3 sp, (sc in next ch-3 sp, ch 3) 3 times, dc in next 2 dc, ch 10, ★ skip next loop, (sc in next loop, ch 10) 4 times, dc in next 2 dc, ch 3, skip next ch-3 sp, (sc in next ch-3 sp, ch 3) 3 times, dc in next 2 dc, ch 10; repeat from ★ around to last 2 loops, skip next loop, sc in last loop, ch 5, dtr in first sc to form last loop.

Rnd 20: Ch 1, sc in same loop, ch 10, (sc in next loop, ch 10) 3 times, dc in next 2 dc, ch 3, skip next ch-3 sp, (sc in next ch-3 sp, ch 3) twice, dc in next 2 dc, ch 10, ★ (sc in next loop, ch 10) 5 times, dc in next 2 dc, ch 3, skip next ch-3 sp, (sc in next ch-3 sp, ch 3) twice, dc in next 2 dc, ch 10; repeat from ★ around to last loop, sc in last loop, ch 5, dtr in first sc to form last loop.

Rnd 21: Ch 1, sc in same loop, ch 10, (sc in next loop, ch 10) 4 times, dc in next 2 dc, ch 3, skip next ch-3 sp, sc in next ch-3 sp, ch 3, dc in next 2 dc, ch 10, ★ (sc in next loop, ch 10) 6 times, dc in next 2 dc, ch 3, skip next ch-3 sp, sc in next ch-3 sp, ch 3, dc in next 2 dc, ch 10; repeat from ★ around to last loop, sc in last loop, ch 5, dtr in first sc to form last loop.

Rnd 22: Ch 1, sc in same loop, ch 10, (sc in next loop, ch 10) 5 times, work dc Cluster, ch 10, ★ (sc in next loop, ch 10) 7 times, work dc Cluster, ch 10; repeat from ★ around to last loop, sc in last loop, ch 5, dtr in first sc to form last loop: 40 loops.

Rnd 23: Ch 1, sc in same loop, (ch 10, sc in next loop) around, ch 8, hdc in first sc to form last loop.

Rnd 24: Ch 1, sc in same loop and in next loop, ★ (ch 3, sc) 5 times in same loop, sc in next loop; repeat from ★ around, (ch 3, sc) 4 times in same loop, ch 1, hdc in first sc to form last sp: 200 sps.

Rnd 25: Ch 1, sc in same sp, ch 3, (sc in next ch-3 sp, ch 3) around; join with slip st to first sc.

Rnds 26-30: Slip st in first ch-3 sp, ch 1, sc in same sp, ch 3, (sc in next ch-3 sp, ch 3) around; join with slip st to first sc.

Rnd 31: Slip st in first ch-3 sp, work beginning Shell, ch 3, (sc in next ch-3 sp, ch 3) 9 times, ★ work Shell in next ch-3 sp, ch 3, (sc in next ch-3 sp, ch 3) 9 times; repeat from ★ around; join with slip st to first dc: 20 Shells.

Rnd 32: Slip st in next dc and in next ch-2 sp, work beginning Shell, ch 3, (sc in next ch-3 sp, ch 3) 10 times, ★ work Shell in next Shell, ch 3, (sc in next ch-3 sp, ch 3) 10 times; repeat from ★ around; join with slip st to first dc.

Rnd 33: Ch 3, dc in same st, 2 dc in next dc, ★ † ch 3, (dc, ch 3) twice in next ch-2 sp, 2 dc in each of next 2 dc, ch 3, skip next ch-3 sp, (sc in next ch-3 sp, ch 3) 9 times †, 2 dc in each of next 2 dc; repeat from ★ 18 times **more**, then repeat from † to † once; join with slip st to first dc.

Rnd 34: Ch 3, dc in next 3 dc, ★ † ch 3, skip next ch-3 sp, dc in next ch-3 sp, (ch 1, dc) 9 times in same sp, ch 3, skip next ch-3 sp, dc in next 4 dc, ch 3, skip next ch-3 sp, (sc in next ch-3 sp, ch 3) 8 times †, dc in next 4 dc; repeat from ★ 18 times **more**, then repeat from † to † once; join with slip st to first dc.

Rnd 35: Ch 3, ★ † 2 dc in each of next 2 dc, dc in next dc, ch 3, (sc in next ch-1 sp, ch 3) 9 times, skip next ch-3 sp, dc in next dc, 2 dc in each of next 2 dc, dc in next dc, ch 3, skip next ch-3 sp, (sc in next ch-3 sp, ch 3) 7 times †, dc in next dc; repeat from ★ 18 times **more**, then repeat from † to † once; join with slip st to first dc.

Rnd 36: Ch 3, dc in next 5 dc, ★ † ch 3, skip next ch-3 sp, (sc in next ch-3 sp, ch 3) 8 times, dc in next 6 dc, ch 3, skip next ch-3 sp, (sc in next ch-3 sp, ch 3) 6 times †, dc in next 6 dc; repeat from ★ 18 times **more**, then repeat from † to † once; join with slip st to first dc.

Rnd 37: Ch 3, dc in next 5 dc, ★ † ch 3, skip next ch-3 sp, (sc in next ch-3 sp, ch 3) 7 times, dc in next 6 dc, ch 3, skip next ch-3 sp, (sc in next ch-3 sp, ch 3) 5 times †, dc in next 6 dc; repeat from ★ 18 times **more**, then repeat from † to † once; join with slip st to first dc.

Continued on page 44.

FOR THE BATH

Create a relaxing haven from the cares of the day by decorating your bathroom in seaside splendor. (Below) Comb every beach, and you still won't find a treasure as lovely as our shell-shaped rug! This fast-to-finish floor covering is stitched with three strands of long-wearing worsted weight yarn. (Opposite) Crocheted using fabric strips, a scallop-edged basket is perfect for holding bath-time essentials. Satin ribbons woven through the eyelet rounds are sweet finishing touches for our jar toppers. The delicate covers are worked using bedspread weight cotton thread. A coordinating edging turns a plain linen hand towel into a pretty accessory.

Quick SHELL JAR TOPPER

MATERIALS

Bedspread Weight Cotton Thread (size 10),
   approximately 65 yards **each**
Steel crochet hook, size 6 (1.80 mm) **or** size needed for gauge
3¹/₂" Jar lid ring
³/₄ yard of ¹/₄" ribbon for **each**

GAUGE: Rnds 1-4 = 1³/₄"

Ch 5; join with slip st to form a ring.

Rnd 1 (Right side): Ch 1, 6 sc in ring; join with slip st to first sc.

Rnd 2: Ch 4, dc in same st, ch 1, (dc, ch 1) twice in next sc and in each sc around; join with slip st to third ch of beginning ch-4: 12 ch-1 sps.

Rnd 3: Ch 1, sc in same st, ch 3, (sc in next dc, ch 3) around; join with slip st to first sc: 12 ch-3 sps.

Rnd 4: Slip st in first ch-3 sp, ch 3 **(counts as first dc, now and throughout)**, 4 dc in same sp, ch 2, sc in next ch-3 sp, ch 2, ★ 5 dc in next ch-3 sp, ch 2, sc in next ch-3 sp, ch 2; repeat from ★ around; join with slip st to first dc: 30 dc.

Rnd 5: Ch 3, 2 dc in each of next 4 dc, ch 1, (dc in next dc, 2 dc in each of next 4 dc, ch 1) around; join with slip st to first dc: 54 dc.

Rnd 6: Ch 3, dc in same st and in next 7 dc, 2 dc in next dc, ch 1, (2 dc in next dc, dc in next 7 dc, 2 dc in next dc, ch 1) around; join with slip st to first dc: 66 dc.

Rnd 7: Ch 1, sc in same st, ch 3, (skip next dc, sc in next dc, ch 3) 4 times, ★ skip next dc, sc in next 2 dc, ch 3, (skip next dc, sc in next dc, ch 3) 4 times; repeat from ★ around to last 2 dc, skip next dc, sc in last dc; join with slip st to first sc: 30 ch-3 sps.

Rnd 8: Slip st in first ch-3 sp, ch 1, sc in same sp, ch 3, (sc in next ch-3 sp, ch 3) around; join with slip st to first sc.

Rnd 9: Slip st in first ch-3 sp, ch 3, 2 dc in same sp, 3 dc in next ch-3 sp and in each ch-3 sp around; join with slip st to first dc: 90 dc.

Rnds 10 and 11: Ch 3, dc in next dc and in each dc around; join with slip st to first dc.

Rnd 12 (Eyelet rnd): Ch 5 **(counts as first dc plus ch 2, now and throughout)**, skip next 2 dc, (dc in next dc, ch 2, skip next 2 dc) around; join with slip st to first dc: 30 dc.

Rnd 13: Ch 5, dc in next dc, ch 2, (dc, ch 2) twice in next dc, ★ (dc in next dc, ch 2) twice, (dc, ch 2) twice in next dc; repeat from ★ around; join with slip st to first dc: 40 dc.

Rnd 14: Ch 3, 4 dc in same st, ch 3, skip next dc, (sc in next dc, ch 3) 5 times, skip next dc, ★ 5 dc in next dc, ch 3, skip next dc, (sc in next dc, ch 3) 5 times, skip next dc; repeat from ★ around; join with slip st to first dc: 5 5-dc groups.

Rnd 15: Ch 3, dc in same st, 2 dc in each of next 4 dc, ch 3, skip next ch-3 sp, (sc in next ch-3 sp, ch 3) 4 times, ★ 2 dc in each of next 5 dc, ch 3, skip next ch-3 sp, (sc in next ch-3 sp, ch 3) 4 times; repeat from ★ around; join with slip st to first dc: 50 dc.

Rnd 16: Ch 3, 2 dc in next dc, (dc in next dc, 2 dc in next dc) 4 times, ch 3, skip next ch-3 sp, (sc in next ch-3 sp, ch 3) 3 times, ★ (dc in next dc, 2 dc in next dc) 5 times, ch 3, skip next ch-3 sp, (sc in next ch-3 sp, ch 3) 3 times; repeat from ★ around; join with slip st to first dc: 75 dc.

Rnd 17: Ch 3, dc in same st and in next 3 dc, 2 dc in next dc, (dc in next 4 dc, 2 dc in next dc) twice, ch 1, skip next ch-3 sp, sc in next ch-3 sp, ch 3, sc in next ch-3 sp, ch 1, ★ 2 dc in next dc, dc in next 3 dc, 2 dc in next dc, (dc in next 4 dc, 2 dc in next dc) twice, ch 1, skip next ch-3 sp, sc in next ch-3 sp, ch 3, sc in next ch-3 sp, ch 1; repeat from ★ around; join with slip st to first dc: 95 dc.

Rnd 18: Ch 1, sc in same st, (ch 3, skip next dc, sc in next dc) 9 times, ch 1, (sc, ch 3, sc) in next ch-3 sp, ch 1, ★ sc in next dc, (ch 3, skip next dc, sc in next dc) 9 times, ch 1, (sc, ch 3, sc) in next ch-3 sp, ch 1; repeat from ★ around; join with slip st to first sc, finish off.

See Washing and Blocking, page 140.

Weave ribbon through Eyelet rnd; place Topper over jar lid ring and tie ends in a bow to secure.

Quick SHELL BASKET

Finished Size: Approximately 10" long x 5" wide x 4" high

MATERIALS

100% Cotton Fabric, 44/45" wide, approximately 3 yards
Crochet hook, size N (9.00 mm) **or** size needed for gauge

Prepare fabric and tear into 1¹/₂" strips *(see Preparing Fabric Strips and Joining Fabric Strips, page 139)*.

GAUGE: 6 dc = 3"

Ch 13 **loosely**.

Rnd 1 (Right side): 6 Dc in fourth ch from hook, dc in next 8 chs, 7 dc in last ch; working in free loops of beginning ch *(Fig. 23b, page 138)*, dc in next 8 chs; join with slip st to top of beginning ch: 30 sts.

Rnd 2: Ch 3 **(counts as first dc, now and throughout)**, dc in same st, 2 dc in each of next 7 dc, dc in next 6 dc, 2 dc in each of next 9 dc, dc in next 6 dc, 2 dc in last dc; join with slip st to first dc: 48 dc.

Rnd 3: Ch 1, sc in Back Loop Only of each dc around *(Fig. 22, page 138)*; join with slip st to first sc.

Rnd 4: Ch 3, dc in both loops of next sc and in each sc around; join with slip st to first dc.

Rnd 5: Ch 1, sc in each dc around; join with slip st to first sc.

Rnd 6: Ch 3, 4 dc in same st, ch 1, skip next 2 sc, slip st in next sc, ch 1, skip next 2 sc, ★ 5 dc in next sc, ch 1, skip next 2 sc, slip st in next sc, ch 1, skip next 2 sc; repeat from ★ around; join with slip st to first dc, finish off.

Lower Edging: With **right** side facing, top of Basket toward you, and working in free loops on Rnd 2 *(Fig. 23a, page 138)*, join fabric with slip st in any st; slip st in each st around; join with slip st to first slip st, finish off.

SHELL TOWEL EDGING

Finished Size: Approximately 1³⁄₄" wide

MATERIALS
Bedspread Weight Cotton Thread (size 10), approximately 40 yards
Steel crochet hook, size 6 (1.80 mm) **or** size needed for gauge
Linen - 14" x 18¹⁄₂"
Straight pins
Sewing needle and thread

GAUGE: Dc, (ch 1, dc) 12 times = 4"

Ch 149 **loosely.**

Row 1 (Right side): Dc in eighth ch from hook **(7 skipped chs count as first dc plus ch 2)**, (ch 2, skip next 2 chs, dc in next ch) across: 48 sps.

Row 2: Ch 1, turn; sc in first dc, ch 3, (sc in next dc, ch 3) twice, skip next dc, 5 dc in next dc, ch 3, ★ skip next dc, (sc in next dc, ch 3) 5 times, skip next dc, 5 dc in next dc, ch 3; repeat from ★ across to last 4 dc, skip next dc, sc in next dc, (ch 3, sc in next dc) twice: 6 5-dc groups.

Row 3: Ch 6, turn; skip first ch-3 sp, sc in next ch-3 sp, ch 3, 2 dc in each of next 5 dc, ch 3, ★ skip next ch-3 sp, (sc in next ch-3 sp, ch 3) 4 times, 2 dc in each of next 5 dc, ch 3; repeat from ★ across to last 3 ch-3 sps, skip next ch-3 sp, sc in next ch-3 sp, ch 3, dc in last sc.

Row 4: Ch 1, turn; sc in first dc, ch 3, (dc in next dc, 2 dc in next dc) 5 times, ch 3, ★ skip next ch-3 sp, (sc in next ch-3 sp, ch 3) 3 times, (dc in next dc, 2 dc in next dc) 5 times, ch 3; repeat from ★ across to last 2 sps, skip next sp, sc in third ch of beginning ch-6.

Row 5: Ch 1, turn; sc in first sc, ch 3, 2 dc in next dc, dc in next 3 dc, 2 dc in next dc, (dc in next 4 dc, 2 dc in next dc) twice, ch 3, ★ skip next ch-3 sp, sc in next ch-3 sp, ch 1, sc in next ch-3 sp, ch 3, 2 dc in next dc, dc in next 3 dc, 2 dc in next dc, (dc in next 4 dc, 2 dc in next dc) twice, ch 3; repeat from ★ across to last ch-3 sp, skip last ch-3 sp, sc in last sc.

Row 6: Ch 1, turn; sc in first sc, ch 1, sc in next dc, (ch 3, skip next dc, sc in next dc) 9 times, ch 1, ★ sc in next ch-1 sp, ch 1, sc in next dc, (ch 3, skip next dc, sc in next dc) 9 times, ch 1; repeat from ★ across to last ch-3 sp, skip last ch-3 sp, sc in last sc; finish off.

Lower Edging: With **right** side facing and working over beginning ch, join thread with slip st in first ch-2 sp; ch 1, (sc, ch 3, sc) in same sp and in each ch-2 sp across; finish off.

FINISHING
See Washing and Blocking, page 140.
Make a ¹⁄₄" hem on each side of linen.
Using photo as a guide for placement, pin Edging along hem line on right side of linen and sew in place.

SHELL RUG

Finished Size: Approximately 22" x 27"

MATERIALS
Worsted Weight Yarn, approximately:
MC (Clay) - 9 ounces, (260 grams, 615 yards)
CC (Ecru) - 5 ounces, (140 grams, 345 yards)
Crochet hook, size N (9.00 mm) **or** size needed for gauge

Note: Rug is worked holding 2 strands of MC and 1 strand of CC together.

GAUGE: In pattern, 7 sts and 6 rows = 4"

PATTERN STITCHES

FRONT POST TREBLE CROCHET (abbreviated FPtr)
YO twice, insert hook from **front** to **back** around post of st indicated, YO and pull up a loop **even** with last st worked, (YO and draw through 2 loops on hook) 3 times *(Fig. 13, page 135)*. Skip st behind FPtr.

FRONT POST SINGLE CROCHET (abbreviated FPsc)
Insert hook from **front** to **back** around post of st indicated, YO and pull up a loop **even** with last st worked, YO and draw through both loops on hook. Skip st behind FPsc.

Ch 13 **loosely.**

Row 1 (Right side): 2 Dc in fourth ch from hook and in each of next 3 chs, dc in next 2 chs, 2 dc in each of last 4 chs: 19 sts.
Note: Loop a short piece of yarn around any stitch to mark last row as **right** side.

Continued on page 43.

FOR THE BEDROOM

A garden retreat awaits with these pretty pansy accents for the bedroom. (Below) Our floral fantasy afghan is enhanced with three-dimensional flowers. Stitched with worsted weight yarn, the snuggly throw is worked in motifs and then crocheted together. (Opposite) Featuring the charm of a woven basket, our boutique tissue box cover is abloom with pansies. The dainty sachet, worked in bedspread weight cotton thread, offers a lovely way to sweeten the air.

PANSY GARDEN AFGHAN

Finished Size: Approximately 48" x 74"

MATERIALS
Worsted Weight Yarn, approximately:
- MC (White) - 45 ounces, (1,280 grams, 2,545 yards)
- Color A (Lilac) - 22 ounces, (620 grams, 1,245 yards)
- Color B (Green) - 1¾ ounces, (50 grams, 100 yards)
- Color C (Black) - 1 ounce, (30 grams, 55 yards)
- Color D (Yellow) - 15 yards

Crochet hook, size G (4.00 mm) **or** size needed for gauge

GAUGE: One Motif = 7" (from straight edge to straight edge)

PATTERN STITCHES
BEGINNING CLUSTER
Ch 2, ★ YO, insert hook in st or sp indicated, YO and pull up a loop, YO and draw through 2 loops on hook; repeat from ★ once **more**, YO and draw through all 3 loops on hook *(Figs. 10a & b, page 134)*.

CLUSTER
★ YO, insert hook in st or sp indicated, YO and pull up a loop, YO and draw through 2 loops on hook; repeat from ★ 2 times **more**, YO and draw through all 4 loops on hook.

PICOT
Ch 4, sc in fourth ch from hook.

MOTIF A (Make 25)
With Color C, ch 4; join with slip st to form a ring.

Rnd 1 (Right side)**:** Ch 3 **(counts as first dc, now and throughout)**, 2 dc in ring, (ch 3, 3 dc in ring) 3 times changing to Color D in last dc worked *(Fig. 24a, page 138)*, ch 5, sc **around** ring in sp **between** second and third dc groups *(Fig. 1)*, ch 5; join with slip st to first dc, finish off.

Fig. 1

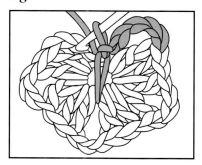

Note: Loop a short piece of yarn around any stitch to mark last round as **right** side.

Rnd 2: With **right** side facing, join Color A with slip st in first ch-5 loop; ch 1, in same loop work [sc, ch 4, dc, ch 1, (tr, ch 1) 7 times, dc, ch 4, sc], sc in next sc, in next loop work [sc, ch 4, dc, ch 1, (tr, ch 1) 7 times, dc, ch 4, sc], skip next dc, sc in next dc, skip next dc, ★ (5 dc, ch 1, 5 dc) in next ch-3 sp, skip next dc, sc in next dc, skip next dc; repeat from ★ 2 times **more**; join with slip st to first sc: 5 Petals.

Rnd 3: Ch 3, (sc in next sp, ch 3) 10 times, skip next sc, sc in next sc, ch 3, (sc in next sp, ch 3) 10 times, slip st in next sc, sc in next sc, ch 4, keeping Petals to front, (sc in next sc, ch 4) 3 times, working in sts of Rnd 2, (slip st in center tr of next Petal, ch 4) twice; join with slip st to sc between Petals, finish off: 6 ch-4 sps.

Rnd 4: With **right** side facing, join Color B with slip st in same st as joining; [ch 8 **loosely**, sc in third ch from hook, dc in next ch, tr in last 4 chs **(Leaf made)**], slip st in next ch-4 sp, ch 3, slip st in next ch-4 sp, (work Leaf, slip st in next ch-4 sp) twice; finish off: 3 Leaves.

Rnd 5: With **right** side facing and keeping Leaves to front, join MC with slip st in same ch-4 sp as last slip st; ch 1, 8 sc in same sp and in next 3 ch-4 sps, (working in next ch-4 sp, 4 sc on each side of slip st) twice **(Fig. 2)**; join with slip st to first sc: 48 sc.

Fig. 2

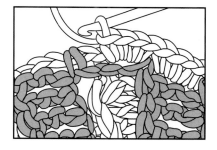

Rnd 6: Ch 5 **(counts as first dc plus ch 2, now and throughout)**, dc in same st, ch 1, (skip next sc, dc in next sc, ch 1) 3 times, skip next sc, ★ (dc, ch 2, dc) in next sc, ch 1, skip next sc, (dc in next sc, ch 1, skip next sc) 3 times; repeat from ★ around; join with slip st to first dc: 30 dc.

Rnd 7: Slip st in first ch-2 sp, ch 5, dc in same sp and in next dc, (dc in next ch-1 sp and in next dc) 4 times, ★ (dc, ch 2, dc) in next ch-2 sp, dc in next dc, (dc in next ch-1 sp and in next dc) 4 times; repeat from ★ around; join with slip st to first dc: 66 dc.

Rnd 8: Slip st in first ch-2 sp, work (beginning Cluster, ch 2, Cluster) in same sp, ch 2, (skip next 2 dc, work Cluster in next dc, ch 2) 3 times, skip next 2 dc, ★ (work Cluster, ch 2) twice in next ch-2 sp, (skip next 2 dc, work Cluster in next dc, ch 2) 3 times, skip next 2 dc; repeat from ★ around; join with slip st to top of beginning Cluster, finish off: 30 Clusters.

Rnd 9: With **right** side facing, join Color A with slip st in first ch-2 sp; ch 1, 3 sc in same sp, sc in next Cluster, (2 sc in next ch-2 sp, sc in next Cluster) 4 times, ★ 3 sc in next ch-2 sp, sc in next Cluster, (2 sc in next ch-2 sp, sc in next Cluster) 4 times; repeat from ★ around; join with slip st to first sc, finish off: 96 sc.

MOTIF B (Make 42)

With MC, ch 5; join with slip st to form a ring.

Rnd 1 (Right side)**:** Ch 3, 17 dc in ring; join with slip st to first dc: 18 dc.

Note: Mark last round as **right** side.

Rnd 2: Work (beginning Cluster, ch 2, Cluster) in same st, ch 2, skip next 2 dc, ★ (work Cluster, ch 2) twice in next dc, skip next 2 dc; repeat from ★ around; join with slip st to top of beginning Cluster: 12 Clusters.

Rnd 3: Slip st in first ch-2 sp, ch 1, 3 sc in same sp, sc in next Cluster, (3 sc in next ch-2 sp, sc in next Cluster) around; join with slip st to first sc: 48 sc.

Rnd 4: Slip st in next sc, ch 5, dc in same st, ch 1, (skip next sc, dc in next sc, ch 1) 3 times, skip next sc, ★ (dc, ch 2, dc) in next sc, ch 1, (skip next sc, dc in next sc, ch 1) 3 times, skip next sc; repeat from ★ around; join with slip st to first dc: 30 dc.

Rnds 5-7: Work same as Motif A, Rnds 7-9.

ASSEMBLY

Following Placement Diagram and placing each Motif A with Pansies facing the same direction, join Motifs together forming strips as follows:

With **right** sides together, matching sts and working through outside loops of **both** thicknesses, join Color A with slip st in any corner sc; ch 1, sc in same st and in each st across to next corner sc; finish off.

Join strips in same manner.

EDGING

Rnd 1: With **right** side facing and working in Back Loops Only, join Color A with slip st in any corner sc; ch 1, 3 sc in same st, sc in each sc around working 3 sc in each corner sc; join with slip st to first sc, finish off.

Rnd 2: With **right** side facing, join MC with slip st in any corner sc; ch 7, sc in fourth ch from hook, (dc, work Picot, dc) in same st, skip next 2 sc, [(dc, work Picot, dc) in next sc, skip next 2 sc] across to next corner sc, ★ dc in corner sc, (work Picot, dc) twice in same st, skip next 2 sc, [(dc, work Picot, dc) in next sc, skip next 2 sc] across to next corner sc; repeat from ★ around; join with slip st to third ch of beginning ch-7, finish off.

PLACEMENT DIAGRAM

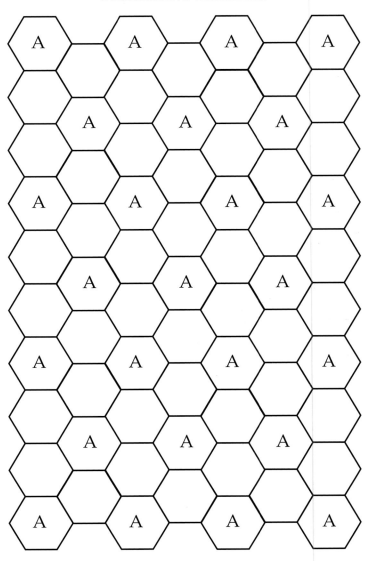

PANSY BASKET TISSUE COVER

MATERIALS

Worsted Weight Yarn, approximately:
MC (Brown) - 1½ ounces, (40 grams, 85 yards)
CC (Green) - 1 ounce, (30 grams, 55 yards)
Sport Weight Yarn, approximately:
Color A (Lilac) - ¾ ounce, (20 grams, 75 yards)
Color B (Green) - 16 yards
Color C (Black) - 7 yards
Color D (Yellow) - 2 yards
Crochet hooks, size C (2.75 mm) **and** size G (4.00 mm)
or sizes needed for gauge
Ribbon bow
Yarn needle
2 - 16" lengths of 22 gauge wire

GAUGE: With larger size hook, 8 sc and 8 rows = 2"
Pansy = 2½"

COVER

Using larger size hook and CC, ch 20 **loosely**; being careful not to twist ch, join with slip st to form a ring.
Rnd 1 (Right side): Ch 1, sc in first 4 chs, 3 sc in next ch, (sc in next 4 chs, 3 sc in next ch) around; do **not** join, place marker (**see Markers, page 138**): 28 sc.
Note: Loop a short piece of yarn around any stitch to mark last round as **right** side.
Rnd 2: Sc in next 5 sc, 3 sc in next sc, (sc in next 6 sc, 3 sc in next sc) 3 times, sc in next sc: 36 sc.
Rnd 3: Sc in next 7 sc, 3 sc in next sc, (sc in next 8 sc, 3 sc in next sc) 3 times, sc in next sc: 44 sc.
Rnd 4: Sc in next 9 sc, 3 sc in next sc, (sc in next 10 sc, 3 sc in next sc) 3 times, sc in next sc: 52 sc.
Rnd 5: Sc in next 11 sc, 3 sc in next sc, (sc in next 12 sc, 3 sc in next sc) 3 times, sc in next sc: 60 sc.
Rnd 6: Sc in next 13 sc, 3 sc in next sc, (sc in next 14 sc, 3 sc in next sc) 3 times, sc in next sc: 68 sc.
Rnd 7: Sc in next 15 sc, 2 sc in next sc, (sc in next 16 sc, 2 sc in next sc) 3 times, sc in next sc: 72 sc.
Rnds 8-15: Sc in each sc around; at end of Rnd 15, change to MC in last sc (**Fig. 24a, page 138**).
Rnd 16: Sc in each sc around; remove marker, slip st in next sc.
Rnd 17 (Edging): Ch 2 (**counts as first hdc, now and throughout**), turn; working in Back Loops Only (**Fig. 22, page 138**), hdc in next sc and in each sc around; join with slip st to first hdc.
Rnd 18: Ch 1, working from **left** to **right**, work reverse sc in each st around (**Figs. 19a-d, page 136**); join with slip st to first st, finish off.

Rnd 19: Fold Edging toward work. With **right** side facing and working in free loops on Rnd 16 (**Fig. 23a, page 138**), join MC with slip st in any sc; ch 2, hdc in next sc and in each sc around; join with slip st to first hdc.
Rnds 20 and 21: Ch 1, work FPhdc around first 4 sts (**Fig. 14, page 135**), work BPhdc around next 4 sts (**Fig. 15, page 135**), ★ work FPhdc around next 4 sts, work BPhdc around next 4 sts; repeat from ★ around; join with slip st to first FPhdc.
Rnds 22 and 23: Ch 1, work BPhdc around first 4 sts, work FPhdc around next 4 sts, ★ work BPhdc around next 4 sts, work FPhdc around next 4 sts; repeat from ★ around; join with slip st to first BPhdc.
Repeat Rnds 20-23 once or until sides measure approximately 5¼" from Rnd 7.
Last Rnd: Slip st in each st around; join with slip st to first st, finish off.

HANDLE

Using larger size hook and MC, ch 58 **loosely**.
Row 1 (Right side): Hdc in third ch from hook and in each ch across: 57 sts.
Note: Mark last row as **right** side.
Row 2: Ch 1, do **not** turn; working from **left** to **right** and working over wire (**Fig. 25, page 138**), work reverse sc in each hdc across; finish off leaving a long end for sewing.
Row 3: With **right** side facing, working in free loops of beginning ch (**Fig. 23b, page 138**) and working over second wire, join MC with slip st in first ch on left; ch 1, work reverse sc in same st and in each st across; finish off leaving a long end for sewing.
Bend wires on each end to wrong side.

PANSY (Make 5)

With Color C and using smaller size hook, ch 4; join with slip st to form a ring.
Rnd 1 (Right side): Ch 2, 2 hdc in ring, (ch 3, 3 hdc in ring) 3 times changing to Color D in last hdc worked, ch 5, sc **around** ring in sp **between** second and third hdc groups (**Fig. 1, page 16**), ch 5; join with slip st to first hdc, finish off.
Note: Mark last round as **right** side.
Rnd 2: With **right** side facing, join Color A with slip st in first ch-5 loop; ch 1, [sc, ch 3, hdc, ch 1, (dc, ch 1) 6 times, hdc, ch 3, sc] in same loop and in next loop, skip next hdc, sc in next hdc, ★ (4 hdc, ch 1, 4 hdc) in next ch-3 sp, skip next hdc, sc in next hdc, skip next hdc; repeat from ★ around; join with slip st to first sc.
Edging: Ch 3, (sc in next sp, ch 3) 9 times, skip next sc, sc in next sc, (ch 3, sc in next sp) 9 times, slip st in next sc; finish off.

LEAF (Make 15)

With Color B and using smaller size hook, ch 8 **loosely**; sc in third ch from hook, hdc in next ch, dc in last 4 chs; finish off leaving a long end for sewing.

FINISHING

Using photo as a guide for placement, sew Handle to sides of Cover sliding ends of wire through sides of Cover. Sew Pansies and Leaves to Cover as desired. Add bow to Handle.

Quick PANSY SACHET

Finished Size: Approximately 5" in diameter

MATERIALS

Bedspread Weight Cotton Thread (size 10), approximately:
- MC (White) - 45 yards
- Color A (Lilac) - 22 yards
- Color B (Green) - 2 yards
- Color C (Black) - 1 yard
- Color D (Yellow) - ½ yard

Steel crochet hook, size 6 (1.80 mm) **or** size needed for gauge
¾ yard of ⅛" ribbon
Cotton balls or polyester fiberfill
Tapestry needle
Scented oil

GAUGE: Front or Back, Rnds 1-3 = 1½"

PATTERN STITCHES

BEGINNING CLUSTER

Ch 2, ★ YO, insert hook in st or sp indicated, YO and pull up a loop, YO and draw through 2 loops on hook; repeat from ★ once **more**, YO and draw through all 3 loops on hook *(Figs. 10a & b, page 134)*.

CLUSTER

★ YO, insert hook in st or sp indicated, YO and pull up a loop, YO and draw through 2 loops on hook; repeat from ★ 2 times **more**, YO and draw through all 4 loops on hook.

FRONT

Work same as Pansy Afghan Motif A, page 36, through Rnd 9; at end of Rnd 9, do **not** finish off.

Rnd 10 (Eyelet rnd): Slip st in next sc, ch 5, dc in same st, ch 1, skip next sc, (dc in next sc, ch 1, skip next sc) 7 times, ★ (dc, ch 2, dc) in next sc, ch 1, skip next sc, (dc in next sc, ch 1, skip next sc) 7 times; repeat from ★ around; join with slip st to first dc: 54 sps.

Rnd 11: Slip st in next ch-2 sp, ch 1, 3 sc in same sp, sc in next dc, (sc in next ch-1 sp and in next dc) across to next ch-2 sp, ★ 3 sc in next ch-2 sp, sc in next dc, (sc in next ch-1 sp and in next dc) across to next ch-2 sp; repeat from ★ around; join with slip st to first sc, finish off: 120 sc.

Rnd 12: With **right** side facing, join MC with slip st in any corner sc; ch 1, (sc, ch 3) twice in same st, (skip next sc, sc in next sc, ch 3) 9 times, skip next sc, ★ (sc, ch 3) twice in next sc, (skip next sc, sc in next sc, ch 3) 9 times, skip next sc; repeat from ★ around; join with slip st to first sc: 66 ch-3 sps.

Rnd 13: Slip st in next ch-3 sp, ch 1, sc in same sp, ch 2, work (Cluster, ch 4, sc in fourth ch from hook, Cluster) in next ch-3 sp, ch 2, ★ sc in next ch-3 sp, ch 2, work (Cluster, ch 4, sc in fourth ch from hook, Cluster) in next ch-3 sp, ch 2; repeat from ★ around; join with slip st to first sc, finish off.

BACK

Work same as Pansy Afghan Motif B, through Rnd 7; at end of Rnd 7, do **not** finish off.

Rnd 8 (Eyelet rnd): Work same as Front, Rnd 10; finish off.

FINISHING

See Washing and Blocking, page 140.
Sprinkle scented oil on the fiberfill.

JOINING

With **wrong** sides together and matching spaces, weave ribbon through Eyelet rnd, stuffing before closing. Tie ribbon in a bow to secure.

THE DINING ROOM

Set the scene for intimate dining with these handcrafted table dressings. (Below and opposite top)
*Perfect for those special dinners, our handy casserole cozy holds a standard-size baking dish,
and the matching cutlery caddy keeps utensils neatly separated and close at hand. These fast-to-
stitch projects are crafted using fabric strips and a large hook.* (Opposite bottom) *It's fun — and
easy — to fashion our lovely table setting by adding a lacy edging to a purchased place mat.
The same frilly edging is worked around a plastic ring to gather a coordinating napkin.*

FRILLY NAPKIN RING AND PLACE MAT EDGING

Finished Size: Napkin Ring - 4" in diameter
Place Mat Edging - 1¼" wide

MATERIALS

Bedspread Weight Cotton Thread (size 10), approximately:
Napkin Ring - 30 yards **each**
Place Mat Edging - 135 yards **each** (for an Edging 50" long)
Steel crochet hooks, sizes 7 (1.65 mm) **and** 10 (1.30 mm)
or sizes needed for gauge
2" Plastic ring
Purchased place mat (ours measures 12½" x 17")
Straight pins
Sewing needle and thread

GAUGE: With smaller size hook, 15 sc = 1"
With larger size hook, 9 dc = 1"

NAPKIN RING

Rnd 1 (Right side)**:** With smaller size hook, join thread with slip st around ring; ch 1, 95 sc in ring; join with slip st to first sc.

Note: Loop a short piece of thread around any stitch to mark last round as **right** side.

Rnd 2: With larger size hook, ch 3, skip next sc, dc in next sc, ch 4, skip next 2 sc, ★ dc in next sc, skip next sc, dc in next sc, ch 4, skip next 2 sc; repeat from ★ around; join with slip st to top of beginning ch-3: 19 ch-4 sps.

Rnd 3: Slip st in next dc and in next ch-4 sp, ch 1, [sc, ch 2, dc, ch 2, (tr, ch 2) twice, dc, ch 2, sc] in same sp and in each ch-4 sp around; join with slip st to first sc: 38 tr.

Rnd 4: ★ Ch 3, skip next ch-2 sp, sc in next ch-2 sp, ch 5, in next ch-2 sp work (sc, ch 3, slip st in last sc worked, sc, ch 5, slip st in last sc worked, sc, ch 3, slip st in last sc worked, sc), ch 5, sc in next ch-2 sp, ch 3, sc in sp **between** next 2 sc; repeat from ★ around; join with slip st to base of beginning ch-3, finish off.

PLACE MAT EDGING
BEGINNING CHAIN

With larger size hook, make a chain to fit around the place mat. The number of chains must be divisible by 5. For example, as in ours, 450 (5 goes into 450, 90 times evenly). Count the chains and adjust as needed. Being careful not to twist ch, join with slip st to form a ring.

Rnd 1 (Right side)**:** Ch 1, sc in each ch around; join with slip st to first sc.

Note: Loop a short piece of thread around any stitch to mark last round as **right** side.

Rnds 2-4: With smaller size hook, work same as Napkin Ring.

FINISHING

See Washing and Blocking, page 140.

Using photo as a guide, pin Edging along hem line on right side of place mat and sew in place.

Quick CASSEROLE COZY

Finished Size: To fit a 9" x 13" casserole dish

MATERIALS

100% Cotton Fabric, 44/45" wide, approximately:
4½ yards
Crochet hook, size P (10.00 mm) **or** size needed for gauge
2 yards of 1½" grosgrain ribbon

Prepare fabric and tear into 2" strips *(see Preparing Fabric Strips and Joining Fabric Strips, page 139)*.

GAUGE: 6 sc and 6 rows = 4"

Ch 7 **loosely**.

Rnd 1 (Right side)**:** Sc in second ch from hook, (ch 2, sc) twice in same st, sc in last 5 chs, (ch 2, sc) twice in same st; working in free loops of beginning ch *(Fig. 23b, page 138)*, sc in next 4 chs; do **not** join, place fabric marker *(see Markers, page 138)*: 14 sc.

Note #1: Loop a short piece of fabric around any stitch to mark last round as **right** side.

Note #2: Work in Back Loops Only throughout *(Fig. 22, page 138)*.

Rnds 2-5: Sc in each sc around working (sc, ch 2, sc) in each corner ch-2 sp: 46 sc.

Rnd 6: Sc in each sc around working 2 sc in each corner ch-2 sp; remove marker, slip st in next sc: 54 sc.

Rnds 7-9: Ch 1, sc in each sc around; join with slip st to first sc.

Rnd 10: Ch 3, skip next sc, (slip st in next sc, ch 3, skip next sc) around; join with slip st to base of beginning ch-3, finish off.

Beginning in center of one long side, weave ribbon between sc on Rnd 9. Pull ends of ribbon tight around casserole dish and tie in a bow to secure. Trim ends.

Quick CUTLERY CADDY

Finished Size: Approximately 5" high x 3¹/₂" in diameter **each**

MATERIALS
100% Cotton Fabric, 44/45" wide, approximately: 3¹/₂ yards
Crochet hook, size P (10.00 mm) **or** size needed for gauge
1¹/₂ yards of 1¹/₂" grosgrain ribbon

Prepare fabric and tear into 2" strips *(see Preparing Fabric Strips and Joining Fabric Strips, page 139)*.

GAUGE: Rnds 1 and 2 = 3¹/₂"

HOLDER (Make 3)

Rnd 1 (Right side): Ch 2, 7 sc in second ch from hook; do **not** join, place fabric marker *(see Markers, page 138)*. *Note:* Loop a short piece of fabric around any stitch to mark last round as **right** side.

Rnd 2: 2 Sc in each sc around: 14 sc.

Rnd 3: Sc in Back Loop Only of each sc around *(Fig. 22, page 138)*.

Rnds 4-7: Sc in both loops of each sc around; at end of Rnd 7, remove marker, slip st in next sc.

Rnd 8: Ch 3, skip next sc, (slip st in next sc, ch 3, skip next sc) around; join with slip st to base of beginning ch-3, finish off.

Beginning with any Holder and working between sc on Rnd 6, weave ribbon between 7 sc, continue to weave through 7 sc on Rnd 6 on each Holder in same manner to form a group; tie ribbon in a bow to secure. Trim ends.

SHELL RUG

Continued from page 33.

Row 2 AND ALL WRONG SIDE ROWS THROUGH ROW 28: Ch 1, turn; sc in each st across.

Row 3: Ch 3 **(counts as first dc, now and throughout)**, turn; (work FPtr around dc in row **below** next sc, 2 dc in next sc) 4 times, dc in next 2 sc, work FPtr around dc in row **below** next sc, (2 dc in next sc, work FPtr around dc in row **below** next sc) 3 times, dc in last sc: 26 sts.

Row 5: Ch 3, turn; work FPtr around next FPtr, (dc in next sc, 2 dc in next sc, work FPtr around next FPtr) 3 times, 2 dc in next sc, dc in next 2 sc, 2 dc in next sc, work FPtr around next FPtr, (dc in next sc, 2 dc in next sc, work FPtr around next FPtr) 3 times, dc in last sc: 34 sts.

Row 7: Ch 3, turn; work FPtr around next FPtr, ★ dc in each sc across to next FPtr, work FPtr around next FPtr; repeat from ★ across to last sc, dc in last sc.

Row 9: Ch 3, turn; work FPtr around next FPtr, (dc in next 2 sc, 2 dc in next sc, work FPtr around next FPtr) 3 times, 2 dc in next sc, dc in next 4 sc, 2 dc in next sc, work FPtr around next FPtr, (dc in next 2 sc, 2 dc in next sc, work FPtr around next FPtr) 3 times, dc in last sc: 42 sts.

Rows 11 and 13: Repeat Row 7.

Row 15: Ch 3, turn; work FPtr around next FPtr, (dc in next 3 sc, 2 dc in next sc, work FPtr around next FPtr) 3 times, 2 dc in next sc, dc in next 6 sc, 2 dc in next sc, work FPtr around next FPtr, (dc in next 3 sc, 2 dc in next sc, work FPtr around next FPtr) 3 times, dc in last sc: 50 sts.

Rows 17, 19, and 21: Repeat Row 7.

Row 23: Ch 3, turn; work FPtr around next FPtr, (dc in next 5 sc, work FPtr around next FPtr) 3 times, 2 dc in next sc, dc in next 8 sc, 2 dc in next sc, work FPtr around next FPtr, (dc in next 5 sc, work FPtr around next FPtr) 3 times, dc in last sc: 52 sts.

Rows 25 and 27: Repeat Row 7.

Row 29: Ch 1, turn; sc in first sc, work FPsc around next FPtr, (sc in next sc, 2 dc in each of next 3 sc, sc in next sc, work FPsc around next FPtr) twice, sc in next sc, dc in next 4 sc, work FPtr around next FPtr, dc in next 12 sc, work FPtr around next FPtr, dc in next 4 sc, sc in next sc, work FPsc around next FPtr, leave remaining 13 sts unworked.

Row 30: Turn; slip st in first st, sc in next 24 sts, slip st in next st, leave remaining sts unworked.

Row 31: Ch 1, turn; work FPsc around first FPsc, sc in next sc, 2 dc in each of next 3 sc, sc in next sc, work FPsc around next FPtr, sc in next 12 sc, work FPsc around next FPtr, leave remaining sts unworked.

Row 32: Turn; slip st in first st, sc in next 12 sc, slip st in next st, leave remaining sts unworked.

Row 33: Ch 1, turn; work FPsc around first FPsc, sc in next sc, 2 hdc in each of next 2 sc, 2 dc in each of next 2 sc, dc in next 2 sc, 2 dc in each of next 2 sc, 2 hdc in each of next 2 sc, sc in next sc, work FPsc around next FPsc, sc in next sc, 2 dc in each of next 3 sc, sc in next sc, work FPsc around next FPsc, sc in next sc, (2 dc in each of next 3 sc, sc in next sc, work FPsc around next FPtr, sc in next sc) twice; finish off.

Lower Edge: With **right** side facing, having beginning ch toward the left, and working in end of rows, join yarn with slip st in end of Row 6; sc in same row, 2 hdc in next row, dc in next row, 2 dc in next row, tr in next row, 5 tr in last row; working in free loops of beginning ch *(Fig. 23b, page 138)*, tr in next 10 chs; working in end of rows, 5 tr in first row, tr in next row, 2 dc in next row, dc in next row, 2 hdc in next row, (sc, slip st) in next row; finish off.

PINEAPPLE TABLE TOPPER

Continued from page 29.

Rnd 38: Ch 3, dc in next 5 dc, ★ † ch 3, skip next ch-3 sp, (sc in next ch-3 sp, ch 3) 6 times, dc in next 6 dc, ch 3, skip next ch-3 sp, (sc in next ch-3 sp, ch 3) 4 times †, dc in next 6 dc; repeat from ★ 18 times **more**, then repeat from † to † once; join with slip st to first dc.

Rnd 39: Ch 3, dc in next 5 dc, ★ † ch 3, skip next ch-3 sp, (sc in next ch-3 sp, ch 3) 5 times, dc in next 6 dc, ch 5, skip next ch-3 sp, (sc in next ch-3 sp, ch 5) 3 times †, dc in next 6 dc; repeat from ★ 18 times **more**, then repeat from † to † once; join with slip st to first dc.

Rnd 40: Ch 3, ★ † decrease twice, dc in next dc, ch 3, skip next ch-3 sp, (sc in next ch-3 sp, ch 3) 4 times, dc in next dc, decrease twice, dc in next dc, ch 7, skip next loop, (sc in next loop, ch 7) twice †, dc in next dc; repeat from ★ 18 times **more**, then repeat from † to † once; join with slip st to first dc.

Rnd 41: Ch 3, dc in next 3 dc, ★ † ch 3, skip next ch-3 sp, (sc in next ch-3 sp, ch 3) 3 times, dc in next 4 dc, ch 10, skip next loop, sc in next loop, ch 10 †, dc in next 4 dc; repeat from ★ 18 times **more**, then repeat from † to † once; join with slip st to first dc.

Rnd 42: Ch 3, dc in next 3 dc, ★ † ch 3, skip next ch-3 sp, (sc in next ch-3 sp, ch 3) twice, dc in next 4 dc, ch 10, (sc in next loop, ch 10) twice †, dc in next 4 dc; repeat from ★ 18 times **more**, then repeat from † to † once; join with slip st to first dc.

Rnd 43: Ch 2, dc in next dc, decrease, ★ † ch 3, skip next ch-3 sp, sc in next ch-3 sp, ch 3, decrease twice, ch 10, (sc in next loop, ch 10) 3 times †, decrease twice; repeat from ★ 18 times **more**, then repeat from † to † once; skip beginning ch-2 and join with slip st to first dc.

Rnd 44: Work beginning tr Cluster, (ch 10, sc in next loop) 4 times, ★ ch 10, work tr Cluster, (ch 10, sc in next loop) 4 times; repeat from ★ around, ch 5, dtr in top of beginning tr Cluster to form last loop: 100 loops.

Rnd 45: Ch 1, sc in same loop, ch 10, (sc in next loop, ch 10) around; join with slip st to first sc.

Rnd 46: Slip st in first 3 chs, ch 3, (dc, ch 4, slip st in third ch from hook, ch 1, 2 dc) in same loop, ch 5, ★ (2 dc, ch 4, slip st in third ch from hook, ch 1, 2 dc) in next loop, ch 5; repeat from ★ around; join with slip st to first dc, finish off.

See Washing and Blocking, page 140.

PRETTY PILLOWS

Finished Size: Pillow #1 - approximately 14" in diameter
Pillow #2 - approximately 15" in diameter

MATERIALS
Bedspread Weight Cotton Thread (size 10), approximately:
Pillow #1 - 430 yards
Pillow #2 - 650 yards
Crochet hook, size E (3.50 mm) **or** size needed for gauge
Pillow #1 - 14" round pillow or ½ yard 44/45" wide fabric and polyester fiberfill
Pillow #2 - ⅝ yard 44/45" wide fabric and polyester fiberfill

---

PATTERN STITCHES
DECREASE
★ YO, insert hook in **next** dc, YO and pull up a loop, YO and draw through 2 loops on hook; repeat from ★ once **more**, YO and draw through all 3 loops on hook **(counts as one dc)**.

BEGINNING CLUSTER (uses first 4 dc)
Ch 3, ★ YO twice, insert hook in **next** dc, YO and pull up a loop, (YO and draw through 2 loops on hook) twice; repeat from ★ 2 times **more**, YO and draw through all 4 loops on hook *(Figs. 11a & b, page 134)*.

CLUSTER (uses next 4 dc)
★ YO twice, insert hook in **next** dc, YO and pull up a loop, (YO and draw through 2 loops on hook) twice; repeat from ★ 3 times **more**, YO and draw through all 5 loops on hook.

2-DC CLUSTER
★ YO, insert hook in sp indicated, YO and pull up a loop, YO and draw through 2 loops on hook; repeat from ★ once **more**, YO and draw through all 3 loops on hook *(Figs. 10a & b, page 134)*.

PILLOW #1
GAUGE: Rnds 1-4 = 3½"

Note: Pillow is worked holding 2 strands of thread together.

BACK
Ch 5; join with slip st to form a ring.

Rnd 1 (Right side)**:** Ch 1, 10 sc in ring; join with slip st to first sc.

Note: Loop a short piece of thread around any stitch to mark last round as **right** side.

Rnd 2: Ch 1, sc in same st, (ch 5, sc in next sc) around, ch 2, dc in first sc to form last loop: 10 loops.

Rnd 3: Ch 1, sc in same loop, (ch 5, sc in next loop) around, ch 2, dc in first sc to form last loop.

Rnd 4: Ch 3 **(counts as first dc, now and throughout)**, (dc, ch 2, 2 dc) in same loop, ch 5, sc in next loop, ★ ch 5, (2 dc, ch 2, 2 dc) in next loop, ch 5, sc in next loop; repeat from ★ around, ch 2, dc in first dc to form last loop: 10 loops.

Rnd 5: Ch 1, sc in same loop, ch 5, (2 dc, ch 2, 2 dc) in next ch-2 sp, ch 5, ★ (sc in next loop, ch 5) twice, (2 dc, ch 2, 2 dc) in next ch-2 sp, ch 5; repeat from ★ around to last loop, sc in last loop, ch 2, dc in first sc to form last loop: 15 loops.

Rnd 6: Ch 1, sc in same loop, ch 5, sc in next loop, ch 3, (dc in next 2 dc, ch 3) twice, sc in next loop, ★ (ch 5, sc in next loop) twice, ch 3, (dc in next 2 dc, ch 3) twice, sc in next loop; repeat from ★ around, ch 2, dc in first sc to form last loop.

Rnd 7: Ch 1, sc in same loop, ch 5, sc in next loop, ch 3, skip next ch-3 sp, 2 dc in each of next 2 dc, ch 3, (tr, ch 3) twice in next ch-3 sp, 2 dc in each of next 2 dc, ch 3, skip next ch-3 sp, ★ sc in next loop, ch 5, sc in next loop, ch 3, skip next ch-3 sp, 2 dc in each of next 2 dc, ch 3, (tr, ch 3) twice in next ch-3 sp, 2 dc in each of next 2 dc, ch 3, skip next ch-3 sp; repeat from ★ around; join with slip st to first sc.

Rnd 8: Slip st in first loop, ch 1, sc in same loop, ch 3, skip next ch-3 sp, 2 dc in next dc, dc in next 3 dc, ch 3, skip next ch-3 sp, dc in next ch-3 sp, (ch 1, dc) 7 times in same sp, ch 3, skip next ch-3 sp, dc in next 3 dc, 2 dc in next dc, ch 3, skip next ch-3 sp, ★ sc in next loop, ch 3, skip next ch-3 sp, 2 dc in next dc, dc in next 3 dc, ch 3, skip next ch-3 sp, dc in next ch-3 sp, (ch 1, dc) 7 times in same sp, ch 3, skip next ch-3 sp, dc in next 3 dc, 2 dc in next dc, ch 3, skip next ch-3 sp; repeat from ★ around; join with slip st to first sc.

Rnd 9: Slip st in next 3 chs and in next dc, ch 3, dc in same st and in next 4 dc, ch 3, (sc in next ch-1 sp, ch 3) 7 times, skip next ch-3 sp, dc in next 4 dc, 2 dc in next dc, ch 1, ★ 2 dc in next dc, dc in next 4 dc, ch 3, (sc in next ch-1 sp, ch 3) 7 times, skip next ch-3 sp, dc in next 4 dc, 2 dc in next dc, ch 1; repeat from ★ around; join with slip st to first dc.

Rnd 10: Ch 3, dc in next 5 dc, ch 3, skip next ch-3 sp, (sc in next ch-3 sp, ch 3) 6 times, ★ (dc in next 6 dc, ch 3) twice, skip next ch-3 sp, (sc in next ch-3 sp, ch 3) 6 times; repeat from ★ around to last 6 dc, dc in last 6 dc, ch 3; join with slip st to first dc.

Rnd 11: Ch 3, dc in next 5 dc, ch 3, skip next ch-3 sp, (sc in next ch-3 sp, ch 3) 5 times, dc in next 6 dc, ch 3, sc in next ch-3 sp, ch 3, ★ dc in next 6 dc, ch 3, skip next ch-3 sp, (sc in next ch-3 sp, ch 3) 5 times, dc in next 6 dc, ch 3, sc in next ch-3 sp, ch 3; repeat from ★ around; join with slip st to first dc.

Rnd 12: Ch 3, dc in next 5 dc, ch 3, skip next ch-3 sp, (sc in next ch-3 sp, ch 3) 4 times, dc in next 6 dc, ch 3, (sc in next ch-3 sp, ch 3) twice, ★ dc in next 6 dc, ch 3, skip next ch-3 sp, (sc in next ch-3 sp, ch 3) 4 times, dc in next 6 dc, ch 3, (sc in next ch-3 sp, ch 3) twice; repeat from ★ around; join with slip st to first dc.

Rnd 13: Ch 2, dc in next 5 dc, ch 3, skip next ch-3 sp, (sc in next ch-3 sp, ch 3) 3 times, dc in next 4 dc, decrease, ch 3, (sc in next ch-3 sp, ch 3) 3 times, ★ decrease, dc in next 4 dc, ch 3, skip next ch-3 sp, (sc in next ch-3 sp, ch 3) 3 times, dc in next 4 dc, decrease, ch 3, (sc in next ch-3 sp, ch 3) 3 times; repeat from ★ around; skip beginning ch-2 and join with slip st to first dc.

Rnd 14: Ch 2, dc in next 4 dc, ch 3, skip next ch-3 sp, (sc in next ch-3 sp, ch 3) twice, dc in next 3 dc, decrease, ch 3, (sc in next ch-3 sp, ch 3) 4 times, ★ decrease, dc in next 3 dc, ch 3, skip next ch-3 sp, (sc in next ch-3 sp, ch 3) twice, dc in next 3 dc, decrease, ch 3, (sc in next ch-3 sp, ch 3) 4 times; repeat from ★ around; skip beginning ch-2 and join with slip st to first dc.

Rnd 15: Ch 3, dc in next 3 dc, ch 5, skip next ch-3 sp, sc in next ch-3 sp, ch 5, dc in next 4 dc, ch 3, (sc in next ch-3 sp, ch 3) 5 times, ★ dc in next 4 dc, ch 5, skip next ch-3 sp, sc in next ch-3 sp, ch 5, dc in next 4 dc, ch 3, (sc in next ch-3 sp, ch 3) 5 times; repeat from ★ around; join with slip st to first dc.

Rnd 16: Ch 3, dc in next 3 dc, ch 3, sc in next sc, ch 3, dc in next 4 dc, ch 3, (sc in next ch-3 sp, ch 3) 6 times, ★ dc in next 4 dc, ch 3, sc in next sc, ch 3, dc in next 4 dc, ch 3, (sc in next ch-3 sp, ch 3) 6 times; repeat from ★ around; join with slip st to first dc.

Rnd 17: Work beginning Cluster, ch 1, work Cluster, ch 7, sc in next ch-3 sp, (ch 4, sc in next ch-3 sp) 6 times, ch 7, ★ work Cluster, ch 1, work Cluster, ch 7, sc in next ch-3 sp, (ch 4, sc in next ch-3 sp) 6 times, ch 7; repeat from ★ around; join with slip st to top of beginning Cluster.

Rnd 18: Slip st in first ch-1 sp, ch 1, sc in same sp, (ch 5, sc in next ch-sp) around, ch 2, dc in first sc to form last loop.

Rnd 19: Ch 1, sc in same loop, ch 5, (sc in next loop, ch 5) around; join with slip st to first sc, finish off.

FRONT

Work same as Back; at end of Rnd 19, do **not** finish off.

FINISHING

Make pillow form if desired, page 140.

JOINING

Ch 1, hold Front and Back with **wrong** sides together and Front facing; matching pattern and working through **both** pieces, (3 sc, ch 3, slip st in sc just made, 2 sc) in first loop and in each loop around inserting pillow form before closing; join with slip st to first sc, finish off.

PILLOW #2

GAUGE: Rnds 1-3 = 4"

Note: Pillow is worked holding 2 strands of thread together.

BACK

Ch 8; join with slip st to form a ring.

Rnd 1 (Right side): Ch 3 (**counts as first dc, now and throughout**), 15 dc in ring; join with slip st to first dc: 16 dc.
Note: Loop a short piece of thread around any stitch to mark last round as **right** side.

Rnd 2: Ch 12, (dc in next 2 dc, ch 9) around to last dc, dc in last dc; join with slip st to third ch of beginning ch-12: 8 loops.

Rnd 3: Slip st in first 2 chs, ch 3, dc in next 2 chs, ch 3, skip next ch, dc in next 3 chs, skip next 2 dc and next ch, ★ dc in next 3 chs, ch 3, skip next ch, dc in next 3 chs, skip next 2 dc and next ch; repeat from ★ around; join with slip st to first dc: 48 dc.

Rnd 4: Slip st in next dc, ch 3, dc in next dc, (2 dc, ch 3, 2 dc) in next ch-3 sp, dc in next 2 dc, skip next 2 dc, ★ dc in next 2 dc, (2 dc, ch 3, 2 dc) in next ch-3 sp, dc in next 2 dc, skip next 2 dc; repeat from ★ around; join with slip st to first dc: 64 dc.

Rnd 5: Slip st in next dc, ch 3, dc in next 2 dc, (2 dc, ch 3, 2 dc) in next ch-3 sp, dc in next 3 dc, skip next 2 dc, ★ dc in next 3 dc, (2 dc, ch 3, 2 dc) in next ch-3 sp, dc in next 3 dc, skip next 2 dc; repeat from ★ around; join with slip st to first dc: 80 dc.

Rnd 6: Slip st in next dc, ch 3, dc in next 3 dc, (2 dc, ch 3, 2 dc) in next ch-3 sp, dc in next 4 dc, skip next 2 dc, ★ dc in next 4 dc, (2 dc, ch 3, 2 dc) in next ch-3 sp, dc in next 4 dc, skip next 2 dc; repeat from ★ around; join with slip st to first dc: 96 dc.

Rnd 7: Slip st in next dc, ch 3, dc in next 4 dc, (2 dc, ch 3, 2 dc) in next ch-3 sp, dc in next 5 dc, skip next 2 dc, ★ dc in next 5 dc, (2 dc, ch 3, 2 dc) in next ch-3 sp, dc in next 5 dc, skip next 2 dc; repeat from ★ around; join with slip st to first dc: 112 dc.

Rnd 8: Slip st in next dc, ch 3, dc in next 5 dc, (2 dc, ch 3, 2 dc) in next ch-3 sp, dc in next 6 dc, skip next 2 dc, ★ dc in next 6 dc, (2 dc, ch 3, 2 dc) in next ch-3 sp, dc in next 6 dc, skip next 2 dc; repeat from ★ around; join with slip st to first dc: 128 dc.

Rnd 9: Slip st in next 2 dc, ch 3, dc in next 5 dc, (2 dc, ch 3, 2 dc) in next ch-3 sp, dc in next 6 dc, ch 3, skip next 4 dc, ★ dc in next 6 dc, (2 dc, ch 3, 2 dc) in next ch-3 sp, dc in next 6 dc, ch 3, skip next 4 dc; repeat from ★ around; join with slip st to first dc: 128 dc.

Rnd 10: Slip st in next 3 dc, ch 3, dc in next 4 dc, (2 dc, ch 3, 2 dc) in next ch-3 sp, dc in next 5 dc, ch 3, (dc, ch 5, dc) in next ch-3 sp, ch 3, skip next 3 dc, ★ dc in next 5 dc, (2 dc, ch 3, 2 dc) in next ch-3 sp, dc in next 5 dc, ch 3, (dc, ch 5, dc) in next ch-3 sp, ch 3, skip next 3 dc; repeat from ★ around; join with slip st to first dc.

Rnd 11: Slip st in next 3 dc, ch 3, dc in next 3 dc, (2 dc, ch 3, 2 dc) in next ch-3 sp, dc in next 4 dc, ch 3, skip next ch-3 sp, 7 dc in next loop, ch 3, skip next ch-3 sp and next 3 dc, ★ dc in next 4 dc, (2 dc, ch 3, 2 dc) in next ch-3 sp, dc in next 4 dc, ch 3, skip next ch-3 sp, 7 dc in next loop, ch 3, skip next ch-3 sp and next 3 dc; repeat from ★ around; join with slip st to first dc: 152 dc.

Rnd 12: Slip st in next 3 dc, ch 3, dc in next 2 dc, (2 dc, ch 3, 2 dc) in next ch-3 sp, dc in next 3 dc, ch 3, skip next 3 dc, dc in next dc, (ch 1, dc in next dc) 6 times, ch 3, skip next 3 dc, ★ dc in next 3 dc, (2 dc, ch 3, 2 dc) in next ch-3 sp, dc in next 3 dc, ch 3, skip next 3 dc, dc in next dc, (ch 1, dc in next dc) 6 times, ch 3, skip next 3 dc; repeat from ★ around; join with slip st to first dc: 136 dc.

Rnd 13: Slip st in next 3 dc, ch 3, dc in next dc, (2 dc, ch 3, 2 dc) in next ch-3 sp, dc in next 2 dc, ch 5, work 2-dc Cluster in next ch-1 sp, (ch 2, work 2-dc Cluster in next ch-1 sp) 5 times, ch 5, skip next ch-3 sp and next 3 dc, ★ dc in next 2 dc, (2 dc, ch 3, 2 dc) in next ch-3 sp, dc in next 2 dc, ch 5, work 2-dc Cluster in next ch-1 sp, (ch 2, work 2-dc Cluster in next ch-1 sp) 5 times, ch 5, skip next ch-3 sp and next 3 dc; repeat from ★ around; join with slip st to first dc: 48 2-dc Clusters.

Rnd 14: Slip st in next 3 dc, ch 3, (2 dc, ch 3, 2 dc) in next ch-3 sp, dc in next dc, ch 5, work 2-dc Cluster in next ch-2 sp, (ch 2, work 2-dc Cluster in next ch-2 sp) 4 times, ch 5, skip next 3 dc, ★ dc in next dc, (2 dc, ch 3, 2 dc) in next ch-3 sp, dc in next dc, ch 5, work 2-dc Cluster in next ch-2 sp, (ch 2, work 2-dc Cluster in next ch-2 sp) 4 times, ch 5, skip next 3 dc; repeat from ★ around; join with slip st to first dc, finish off.

FRONT

Work same as Back; at end of Rnd 14, do **not** finish off.

FINISHING

Make pillow form if desired, page 140.

JOINING

Rnd 1: Slip st in next 2 dc and in next ch-3 sp, ch 1, hold Front and Back with **wrong** sides together and Front facing; matching pattern and working through **both** pieces, sc in same sp, ch 5, sc in next loop, ch 5, sc in next ch-2 sp, (ch 3, sc in next ch-2 sp) 3 times, ★ (ch 5, sc in next ch-sp) 4 times, (ch 3, sc in next ch-2 sp) 3 times; repeat from ★ around to last loop inserting pillow form before closing, ch 5, sc in last loop, ch 5; join with slip st to first sc: 56 ch-sps.

Rnd 2: Slip st in first loop, ch 1, 5 sc in same loop and in next loop, (2 sc, ch 3, slip st in sc just made, sc) in each of next 3 ch-3 sps, ★ 5 sc in each of next 4 loops, (2 sc, ch 3, slip st in sc just made, sc) in each of next 3 ch-3 sps; repeat from ★ around to last 2 loops, 5 sc in each of last 2 loops; join with slip st to first sc, finish off.

LACY COASTER

Finished Size: Approximately 5¼" in diameter

MATERIALS
Bedspread Weight Cotton Thread (size 10), approximately 45 yards **each**
Steel crochet hook, size 6 (1.80 mm) **or** size needed for gauge

GAUGE: Rnds 1-5 = 2"

PATTERN STITCHES
DECREASE
★ YO, insert hook in **next** dc, YO and pull up a loop, YO and draw through 2 loops on hook; repeat from ★ once **more**, YO and draw through all 3 loops on hook (**counts as one dc**).
BEGINNING CLUSTER (uses first 4 dc)
Ch 3, ★ YO twice, insert hook in **next** dc, YO and pull up a loop, (YO and draw through 2 loops on hook) twice; repeat from ★ 2 times **more**, YO and draw through all 4 loops on hook (*Figs. 11a & b, page 134*).
CLUSTER (uses next 4 dc)
★ YO twice, insert hook in **next** dc, YO and pull up a loop, (YO and draw through 2 loops on hook) twice; repeat from ★ 3 times **more**, YO and draw through all 5 loops on hook.

Ch 5; join with slip st to form a ring.

Rnd 1 (Right side)**:** Ch 1, 10 sc in ring; join with slip st to first sc.

Note: Loop a short piece of thread around any stitch to mark last round as **right** side.

Rnd 2: Ch 1, sc in same st, (ch 5, sc in next sc) around, ch 2, dc in first sc to form last loop: 10 loops.

Rnd 3: Ch 1, sc in same loop, (ch 5, sc in next loop) around, ch 2, dc in first sc to form last loop.

Rnd 4: Ch 3 (**counts as first dc, now and throughout**), (dc, ch 2, 2 dc) in same loop, ch 5, sc in next loop, ★ ch 5, (2 dc, ch 2, 2 dc) in next loop, ch 5, sc in next loop; repeat from ★ around, ch 2, dc in first dc to form last loop: 10 loops.

Rnd 5: Ch 1, sc in same loop, ch 5, (2 dc, ch 2, 2 dc) in next ch-2 sp, ch 5, ★ (sc in next loop, ch 5) twice, (2 dc, ch 2, 2 dc) in next ch-2 sp, ch 5; repeat from ★ around to last loop, sc in last loop, ch 2, dc in first sc to form last loop: 15 loops.

Rnd 6: Ch 1, sc in same loop, ch 5, sc in next loop, ch 3, (dc in next 2 dc, ch 3) twice, sc in next loop, ★ (ch 5, sc in next loop) twice, ch 3, (dc in next 2 dc, ch 3) twice, sc in next loop; repeat from ★ around, ch 2, dc in first sc to form last loop.

Rnd 7: Ch 1, sc in same loop, ch 5, sc in next loop, ch 3, skip next ch-3 sp, 2 dc in each of next 2 dc, ch 3, (tr, ch 3) twice in next ch-3 sp, 2 dc in each of next 2 dc, ch 3, skip next ch-3 sp, ★ sc in next loop, ch 5, sc in next loop, ch 3, skip next ch-3 sp, 2 dc in each of next 2 dc, ch 3, (tr, ch 3) twice in next ch-3 sp, 2 dc in each of next 2 dc, ch 3, skip next ch-3 sp; repeat from ★ around; join with slip st to first sc.

Rnd 8: Slip st in first loop, ch 1, sc in same loop, ch 3, skip next ch-3 sp, 2 dc in next dc, dc in next 3 dc, ch 3, skip next ch-3 sp, dc in next ch-3 sp, (ch 1, dc) 4 times in same sp, ch 3, dc in next 3 dc, 2 dc in next dc, ch 3, skip next ch-3 sp, ★ sc in next loop, ch 3, skip next ch-3 sp, 2 dc in next dc, dc in next 3 dc, ch 3, skip next ch-3 sp, dc in next ch-3 sp, (ch 1, dc) 4 times in same sp, ch 3, dc in next 3 dc, 2 dc in next dc, ch 3, skip next ch-3 sp; repeat from ★ around; join with slip st to first sc.

Rnd 9: Slip st in first 3 chs and in next dc, ch 3, dc in next 4 dc, ch 3, (sc in next ch-1 sp, ch 3) 4 times, skip next ch-3 sp, dc in next 5 dc, ch 1, ★ dc in next 5 dc, ch 3, (sc in next ch-1 sp, ch 3) 4 times, skip next ch-3 sp, dc in next 5 dc, ch 1; repeat from ★ around; join with slip st to first dc.

Rnd 10: Ch 2, dc in next 4 dc, ch 4, skip next ch-3 sp, sc in next ch-3 sp, (ch 3, sc in next ch-3 sp) twice, ch 4, dc in next 3 dc, decrease, ch 3, sc in next ch-1 sp, ch 3, ★ decrease, dc in next 3 dc, ch 4, skip next ch-3 sp, sc in next ch-3 sp, (ch 3, sc in next ch-3 sp) twice, ch 4, dc in next 3 dc, decrease, ch 3, sc in next ch-1 sp, ch 3; repeat from ★ around; skip beginning ch-2 and join with slip st to first dc.

Rnd 11: Ch 3, dc in next 3 dc, ch 4, skip next ch-4 sp, sc in next ch-3 sp, ch 3, sc in next ch-3 sp, ch 4, dc in next 4 dc, ch 3, (sc in next ch-3 sp, ch 3) twice, ★ dc in next 4 dc, ch 4, skip next ch-4 sp, sc in next ch-3 sp, ch 3, sc in next ch-3 sp, ch 4, dc in next 4 dc, ch 3, (sc in next ch-3 sp, ch 3) twice; repeat from ★ around; join with slip st to first dc.

Rnd 12: Ch 3, dc in next 3 dc, ch 5, skip next ch-4 sp, sc in next ch-3 sp, ch 5, dc in next 4 dc, ch 3, sc in next ch-3 sp, (ch 5, sc in next ch-3 sp) twice, ch 3, ★ dc in next 4 dc, ch 5, skip next ch-4 sp, sc in next ch-3 sp, ch 5, dc in next 4 dc, ch 3, sc in next ch-3 sp, (ch 5, sc in next ch-3 sp) twice, ch 3; repeat from ★ around; join with slip st to first dc.

Rnd 13: Ch 3, dc in next 3 dc, ch 3, sc in next sc, ch 3, dc in next 4 dc, ch 5, (sc in next ch-sp, ch 5) 4 times, ★ dc in next 4 dc, ch 3, sc in next sc, ch 3, dc in next 4 dc, ch 5, (sc in next ch-sp, ch 5) 4 times; repeat from ★ around; join with slip st to first dc.

Rnd 14: Work beginning Cluster, ch 1, work Cluster, ch 7, sc in next loop, (ch 5, slip st in third ch from hook, ch 3, sc in next loop) 4 times, ch 7, ★ work Cluster, ch 1, work Cluster, ch 7, sc in next loop, (ch 5, slip st in third ch from hook, ch 3, sc in next loop) 4 times, ch 7; repeat from ★ around; join with slip st to top of beginning Cluster, finish off.

See Washing and Blocking, page 140.

47

gifts for all

A handmade gift says "you're special" to a friend or family member. We've assembled lots of thoughtful ideas for everyone in this collection, including a handsome jar topper for Dad, a lacy doily and tissue cover for Mom, and a handy kitchen set for a new neighbor. For whatever reason you need a present, you'll find the perfect token among these gifts for all.

FLOWERPOT LACE

Shell and cluster stitches form a flower-like motif on this sunny flowerpot cover. Fashioned in bedspread weight cotton thread, the pretty cover is finished with ribbons laced through the eyelet rounds. Presented with a blooming plant, it's a lovely gift for a secret pal.

Finished Size: Approximately 3¹/₂" high (Body)

MATERIALS
Bedspread Weight Cotton Thread (size 10),
   approximately 180 yards
Steel crochet hook, size 5 (1.90 mm) **or** size needed
   for gauge
1¹/₂ yards of ¹/₈" ribbon
Flower pot - 4" top diameter x 3" to 3¹/₂" high

GAUGE: 14 dc and 7 rows = 2"

PATTERN STITCHES
CLUSTER
★ YO, insert hook in st indicated, YO and pull up a loop, YO and draw through 2 loops on hook; repeat from ★ 5 times **more**, YO and draw through all 7 loops on hook *(Figs. 10a & b, page 134)*.
SHELL
(2 Dc, ch 2, 2 dc) in st or sp indicated.
DOUBLE SHELL
2 Dc in sp indicated, (ch 2, 2 dc) twice in **same** sp.
V-ST
(Dc, ch 2, dc) in sp indicated.
DECREASE (uses next 3 sps)
★ YO twice, insert hook in **next** ch-3 sp, YO and pull up a loop, (YO and draw through 2 loops on hook) twice; repeat from ★ 2 times **more**, YO and draw through all 4 loops on hook.

BODY

Ch 84 **loosely**; being careful not to twist ch, join with slip st to form a ring.

Rnd 1 (Right side)**:** Ch 3 **(counts as first dc, now and throughout)**, dc in next ch and in each ch around; join with slip st to first dc: 84 dc.

Note: Loop a short piece of thread around any stitch to mark last round as **right** side.

Rnd 2 (Eyelet rnd)**:** Ch 4 **(counts as first dc plus ch 1, now and throughout)**, skip next dc, (dc in next dc, ch 1, skip next dc) around; join with slip st to first dc: 42 ch-1 sps.

Rnd 3: Ch 3, dc in next ch and in each st around; join with slip st to first dc: 84 dc.

Rnd 4: Ch 3, dc in next dc, work Cluster in next dc, ★ dc in next 11 dc, work Cluster in next dc; repeat from ★ 5 times **more**, dc in last 9 dc; join with slip st to first dc: 7 Clusters.

Rnd 5: Ch 3, work Cluster in next dc, dc in next Cluster, work Cluster in next dc, ★ dc in next 9 dc, work Cluster in next dc, dc in next Cluster, work Cluster in next dc; repeat from ★ 5 times **more**, dc in last 8 dc; join with slip st to first dc: 14 Clusters.

Rnd 6: Ch 3, dc in next Cluster, work Cluster in next dc, ★ dc in next 11 sts, work Cluster in next dc; repeat from ★ 5 times **more**, dc in last 9 sts; join with slip st to first dc: 7 Clusters.

Rnd 7: Ch 3, dc in next dc and in each st around; join with slip st to first dc: 84 dc.

Rnds 8 and 9: Repeat Rnds 2 and 3.

Rnd 10: Slip st in next 2 dc, ch 3, (dc, ch 2, 2 dc) in same st, skip next 2 dc, (work Shell in next dc, skip next 2 dc) around; join with slip st to first dc: 28 Shells.

Rnd 11: Slip st in next dc and in next ch-2 sp, ch 4, dc in same sp, (ch 1, dc in same sp) 6 times, sc in next Shell (ch-2 sp), ★ dc in next Shell, (ch 1, dc in same sp) 7 times, sc in next Shell; repeat from ★ around; join with slip st to first dc: 14 sc.

Rnd 12: Ch 1, sc in same st, (sc in next ch-1 sp, sc in next dc) 7 times, skip next sc, ★ sc in next dc, (sc in next ch-1 sp, sc in next dc) 7 times, skip next sc; repeat from ★ around; join with slip st to first sc, finish off.

RUFFLE

Rnd 1: With **right** side facing and working in free loops of beginning ch *(Fig. 23b, page 138)*, join thread with slip st in second ch; ch 3, (dc, ch 2, 2 dc) in same st, skip next 2 chs, (work Shell in next ch, skip next 2 chs) around; join with slip st to first dc: 28 Shells.

Rnd 2: Slip st in next dc and in next ch-2 sp, ch 5 **(counts as first dc plus ch 2, now and throughout)**, dc in same sp, work Shell in next Shell, ★ work V-St in next 3 Shells, work Shell in next Shell; repeat from ★ 5 times **more**, work V-St in last 2 Shells; join with slip st to first dc: 7 Shells and 21 V-Sts.

Rnd 3: Slip st in first ch-2 sp, ch 5, dc in same sp, ★ † work Shell in next Shell, work V-St in next V-St (ch-2 sp), 7 dc in next V-St †, work V-St in next V-St; repeat from ★ 5 times **more**, then repeat from † to † once; join with slip st to first dc: 7 7-dc groups.

Rnd 4: Slip st in first ch-2 sp, ch 5, dc in same sp, ★ † ch 1, work Double Shell in next Shell, ch 1, work V-St in next V-St, ch 1, (dc in next dc, ch 1) 7 times †, work V-St in next V-St; repeat from ★ 5 times **more**, then repeat from † to † once; join with slip st to first dc.

Rnd 5: Slip st in first ch-2 sp, ch 5, dc in same sp, ★ † ch 1, work Shell in next 2 ch-2 sps, ch 1, work V-St in next V-St, ch 1, skip next ch-1 sp, sc in next ch-1 sp, (ch 3, sc in next ch-1 sp) 5 times, ch 1 †, work V-St in next V-St; repeat from ★ 5 times **more**, then repeat from † to † once; join with slip st to first dc.

Rnd 6: Slip st in first ch-2 sp, ch 5, dc in same sp, ★ † ch 3, work Shell in next 2 Shells, ch 3, work V-St in next V-St, ch 3, skip next ch-1 sp, (sc in next ch-3 sp, ch 3) 5 times †, work V-St in next V-St; repeat from ★ 5 times **more**, then repeat from † to † once; join with slip st to first dc.

Rnd 7: Slip st in first ch-2 sp, ch 5, dc in same sp, ★ † ch 3, work Double Shell in next 2 Shells, ch 3, work V-St in next V-St, ch 3, skip next ch-3 sp, (sc in next ch-3 sp, ch 3) 4 times †, work V-St in next V-St; repeat from ★ 5 times **more**, then repeat from † to † once; join with slip st to first dc.

Rnd 8: Slip st in first ch-2 sp, ch 5, dc in same sp, ★ † ch 3, work Shell in next 4 ch-2 sps, ch 3, work V-St in next V-St, skip next ch-3 sp, decrease †, work V-St in next V-St; repeat from ★ 5 times **more**, then repeat from † to † once; join with slip st to first dc, finish off.

FINISHING

See Washing and Blocking, page 140.
Weave ribbon through both Eyelet rnds on Body.
Insert pot in Cover and pull ribbons to gather Cover around pot.
Tie each ribbon in a bow to secure Cover to pot.

Quick HAPPY HOUSEWARMING!

Crocheted in worsted weight yarn, this handy set makes a thoughtful housewarming gift. The round hot pad is crocheted using front post double crochet stitches. A coordinating pot holder has the same pretty pattern and is finished with a loop for hanging.

Finished Size: Hot Pad - 9" in diameter
Pot Holder - 8" in diameter

MATERIALS
Worsted Weight Yarn, approximately:
MC (White) - 3½ ounces, (100 grams, 230 yards)
CC (Blue) - 1 ounce, (30 grams, 65 yards)
Crochet hook, size G (4.00 mm) **or** size needed for gauge

GAUGE: Rnds 1 and 2 of Front = 2¼"

PATTERN STITCH
FRONT POST DOUBLE CROCHET *(abbreviated FPdc)*
YO, insert hook from **front** to **back** around post of st indicated *(Fig. 13, page 135)*, YO and pull up a loop **even** with loop on hook, (YO and draw through 2 loops on hook) twice.

HOT PAD
FRONT
Rnd 1 (Right side): With CC, ch 4, 11 dc in fourth ch from hook; join with slip st to top of beginning ch: 12 sts.
Note: Loop a short piece of yarn around any stitch to mark last round as **right** side.
Rnd 2: Ch 3 **(counts as first dc, now and throughout)**, dc in same st, 2 dc in next dc and in each dc around; join with slip st to first dc, finish off: 24 dc.
Rnd 3: With **right** side facing, join MC with slip st in any dc; ch 3, work FPdc around same st, (dc in next dc, work FPdc around same st) around; join with slip st to first dc: 48 sts.
Rnd 4: Ch 3, dc in same st, work FPdc around next FPdc, (2 dc in next dc, work FPdc around next FPdc) around; join with slip st to first dc, finish off: 72 sts.

Rnd 5: With **right** side facing and working in Back Loops Only **(Fig. 22, page 138)**, join CC with slip st in first dc; ch 3, dc in next 10 sts, 2 dc in next st, (dc in next 11 sts, 2 dc in next st) around; join with slip st to first dc, finish off: 78 dc.

Rnd 6: With **right** side facing, join MC with slip st in first dc; ch 3, dc in next dc, work FPdc around next dc, (dc in next 2 dc, work FPdc around next dc) around; join with slip st to first dc: 26 FPdc.

Rnd 7: Ch 3, 2 dc in next dc, work FPdc around next FPdc, (dc in next dc, 2 dc in next dc, work FPdc around next FPdc) around; join with slip st to first dc: 104 sts.

Rnd 8: Ch 3, dc in next 2 dc, work FPdc around next FPdc, (dc in next 3 dc, work FPdc around next FPdc) around; join with slip st to first dc, finish off.

BACK

Rnd 1 (Right side)**:** With MC, ch 4, 11 dc in fourth ch from hook; join with slip st to top of beginning ch: 12 sts.

Note: Mark last round as **right** side.

Rnds 2 and 3: Ch 3, dc in same st, 2 dc in next dc and in each dc around; join with slip st to first dc: 48 dc.

Rnd 4: Ch 1, sc in first 7 dc, 2 sc in next dc, (sc in next 7 dc, 2 sc in next dc) around; do **not** join, place marker **(see Markers, page 138)**: 54 sc.

Rnd 5: (Sc in next 8 sc, 2 sc in next sc) around: 60 sc.

Rnd 6: (Sc in next 9 sc, 2 sc in next sc) around: 66 sc.

Rnd 7: (Sc in next 10 sc, 2 sc in next sc) around: 72 sc.

Rnd 8: (Sc in next 11 sc, 2 sc in next sc) around: 78 sc.

Rnd 9: (Sc in next 12 sc, 2 sc in next sc) around: 84 sc.

Rnd 10: (Sc in next 13 sc, 2 sc in next sc) around: 90 sc.

Rnd 11: (Sc in next 14 sc, 2 sc in next sc) around: 96 sc.

Rnd 12: (Sc in next 15 sc, 2 sc in next sc) around: 102 sc.

Rnd 13: (Sc in next 50 sc, 2 sc in next sc) twice: 104 sc.

Rnd 14: Sc in each sc around; slip st in next sc, finish off.

JOINING

Rnd 1: With **wrong** sides together, Front facing and working through inside loops only of **both** pieces, join CC with slip st in any st; ch 1, sc in each st around; join with slip st to Back Loop Only of first sc.

Rnd 2: Ch 1, sc in Back Loop Only of each sc around; join with slip st to both loops of first sc, finish off.

POT HOLDER

FRONT

Rnds 1-7: Work same as Hot Pad: 104 sts.
Finish off.

BACK

Rnds 1-5: Work same as Hot Pad: 60 sc.

Rnd 6: (Sc in next 4 sc, 2 sc in next sc) around: 72 sc.

Rnd 7: (Sc in next 5 sc, 2 sc in next sc) around: 84 sc.

Rnd 8: (Sc in next 6 sc, 2 sc in next sc) around: 96 sc.

Rnd 9: (Sc in next 11 sc, 2 sc in next sc) around: 104 sc.

Rnd 10: Sc in each sc around; slip st in next sc, finish off.

JOINING

Rnd 1: Work same as Hot Pad.

Rnd 2: Ch 1, sc in Back Loop Only of each sc around; join with slip st to both loops of first sc, ch 9, skip next 2 sc, slip st in both loops of next sc; finish off.

Quick PETITE TISSUE COVER

A lovely accessory for a lady's dressing table, this lacy tissue cover is created using bedspread weight cotton thread. Purse-size tissues fit nicely inside the petite holder, which is worked in shell stitches and accented with satin bows.

Finished Size: Approximately 2¹⁄₂" x 5¹⁄₄"

MATERIALS

Bedspread Weight Cotton Thread (size 10), approximately 50 yards
Crochet hook, size 5 (1.90 mm) **or** size needed for gauge
1 yard of ¹⁄₈" ribbon
Purse-size tissues

GAUGE: In pattern, (V-St, Shell) twice and 7 rows = 2"

PATTERN STITCHES

V-ST
(Dc, ch 2, dc) in st or sp indicated.

SHELL
5 Dc in sp indicated.

BODY

Ch 46 **loosely**.

Row 1 (Right side): Dc in sixth ch from hook, (ch 1, skip next ch, dc in next ch) across: 21 sps.

Note: Loop a short piece of thread around any stitch to mark last row as **right** side.

Row 2: Ch 4 **(counts as first dc plus ch 1, now and throughout)**, dc in next dc, skip next ch-1 sp, work V-St in next ch-1 sp, ★ skip next ch-1 sp, work Shell in next ch-1 sp, skip next ch-1 sp, work V-St in next ch-1 sp; repeat from ★ 3 times **more**, skip next ch-1 sp, dc in next dc, ch 1, skip next ch, dc in next ch: 4 Shells.

Row 3: Ch 4, turn; dc in next dc, work Shell in next V-St (ch-2 sp), ★ work V-St in center dc of next Shell, work Shell in next V-St; repeat from ★ across, dc in next dc, ch 1, dc in last dc.

Row 4: Ch 4, turn; dc in next dc, work V-St in center dc of next Shell, ★ work Shell in next V-St, work V-St in center dc of next Shell; repeat from ★ across, dc in next dc, ch 1, dc in last dc.

Rows 5-20: Repeat Rows 3 and 4, 8 times.

Row 21: Ch 4, turn; dc in next dc, ch 1, (dc, ch 1) twice in next V-St, ★ working across next Shell, (skip next dc, dc in next dc, ch 1) twice, (dc, ch 1) twice in next V-St; repeat from ★ across, dc in next dc, ch 1, dc in last dc; finish off: 21 ch-1 sps.

EDGING

With **wrong** side facing, fold ends of Body up, placing beginning ch and Row 21 on each side of center row. Working through **both** thicknesses and matching sps on end of rows carefully (5 sps **each** side of center), join thread with slip st in first sp; ch 2, 2 dc in same sp, (slip st, ch 2, 2 dc) in next sp and in each sp across to last sp, slip st in last sp; finish off. Repeat for other end.

FINISHING

Insert tissues (without packaging) into Cover.

Cut ribbon in half.

Begin with center of each ribbon in sps at opposite ends. Lace ribbon through every other sp on Rows 1 and 21, criss-crossing as if lacing a shoe, and leaving 7 center sps on each row free; tie each ribbon in a bow.

BABY BROTHER

With his rosy cheeks and big smile, this soft crocheted doll makes a great buddy for a child who's adjusting to the arrival of a new sibling. Dressed in a newborn-size sleeper, he'll help teach big brother or sister how to handle the new baby safely.

Finished Size: Approximately 23" tall

MATERIALS
Worsted Weight Yarn, approximately:
   MC (Peach) - 5 ounces, (140 grams, 330 yards)
   CC (Brown) - 12 yards
Crochet hook, size I (5.50 mm) **or** size needed for gauge
Embroidery floss - blue and pink
Pink felt
Yarn and tapestry needles
Brown sewing thread
Polyester fiberfill
Cardboard - 1¾" x 5"
Sleeper (size 0-3 months)

GAUGE: 14 sc and 13 rows = 4"

PATTERN STITCHES
CLUSTER
★ YO, insert hook in st indicated, YO and pull up a loop, YO and draw through 2 loops on hook; repeat from ★ 2 times **more**, YO and draw through all 4 loops on hook *(Figs. 10a & b, page 134)*.
Note: Always push Cluster to **right** side unless otherwise specified.

SC DECREASE
Pull up a loop in next 2 sts, YO and draw through all 3 loops on hook **(counts as one sc)**.

DC DECREASE (uses next 2 sts)
★ YO, insert hook in **next** st, YO and pull up a loop, YO and draw through 2 loops on hook; repeat from ★ once **more**, YO and draw through all 3 loops on hook **(counts as one dc)**.

LEFT LEG
With MC, ch 6 **loosely**.
Rnd 1 (Right side): Sc in second ch from hook and in next 2 chs, 2 sc in next ch, 5 sc in next ch; working in free loops of beginning ch *(Fig. 23b, page 138)*, 2 sc in next ch, sc in next 2 chs, 2 sc in next ch; do **not** join, place marker *(see Markers, page 138)*: 16 sc.
Rnd 2: 2 Sc in next sc, sc in next 4 sc, 2 sc in next sc, (sc in next sc, 2 sc in next sc) twice, sc in next 5 sc, 2 sc in next sc: 21 sc.

Rnd 3: 2 Sc in next sc, sc in next 6 sc, (hdc, dc) in next sc, hdc in next sc, 2 sc in each of next 3 sc, hdc in next sc, (dc, hdc) in next sc, sc in next 6 sc, 2 sc in next sc: 28 sts.
Rnd 4: 2 Sc in next sc, sc in next 8 sts, (sc, tr, sc) in next dc, (work Cluster in next st, sc in next st) twice, 3 dc in next sc, drop loop from hook, insert hook in first dc of 3-dc group, hook dropped loop and draw through, sc in next sc, 5 dc in next sc, drop loop from hook, insert hook in first dc of 5-dc group, hook dropped loop and draw through, sc in next 11 sts: 31 sts.
Rnd 5: Sc in next 9 sc, sc decrease, skip next tr, YO, insert hook in next sc, YO and pull up a loop, YO and draw through 2 loops on hook, skip next st, YO, insert hook in next sc, YO and pull up a loop, YO and draw through 2 loops on hook, YO and draw through all 3 loops on hook, dc decrease twice, sc decrease twice, sc in next 8 sc: 23 sts.
Rnd 6: Sc decrease, sc in next 7 sc, sc decrease, (sc in next st, sc decrease) twice, sc in next 6 sc: 19 sts.
Rnd 7: Sc decrease, (sc in next 6 sc, sc decrease) twice, sc in next sc: 16 sc.
Rnds 8 and 9: Sc in each sc around.
Rnd 10: (Sc in next 3 sc, 2 sc in next sc) around: 20 sc.
Rnds 11-16: Sc in each sc around.
Rnd 17: (Sc in next 3 sc, sc decrease) around: 16 sc.
Rnd 18: Sc in next 15 sc, slip st in next sc, remove marker.
Note: Begin working in rows for knee.
Row 1: Turn; skip first slip st, sc in next 8 sc, slip st in next sc, leave remaining 6 sc unworked.
Rows 2 and 3: Turn; skip first slip st, sc in next 8 sc, slip st in same sc as previous slip st.
Note: Begin working in rounds.
Rnd 1: Turn; skip first slip st, sc in next 8 sc, sc in same sc as previous slip st, sc in next 6 sc on Rnd 18, sc in same sc as slip st on Row 1; do **not** join, place marker: 16 sc.
Rnd 2: (Sc in next 3 sc, 2 sc in next sc) around: 20 sc.
Rnd 3: (Sc in next 4 sc, 2 sc in next sc) around: 24 sc.
Rnds 4-10: Sc in each sc around.
Rnd 11: Sc in next 14 sc, slip st in next sc, leave remaining 9 sts unworked; finish off.

RIGHT LEG
Work same as Left Leg through Rnd 3: 28 sts.

Rnd 4: Sc in next 11 sts, 5 dc in next sc, drop loop from hook, insert hook in first dc of 5-dc group, hook dropped loop and draw through, sc in next sc, 3 dc in next sc, drop loop from hook, insert hook in first dc of 3-dc group, hook dropped loop and draw through, (sc in next st, work Cluster in next st) twice, (sc, tr, sc) in next dc, sc in next 8 sts, 2 sc in next st: 31 sts.

Rnd 5: Sc in next 8 sc, sc decrease twice, dc decrease twice, YO, insert hook in next sc, YO and pull up a loop, YO and draw through 2 loops on hook, skip next st, YO, insert hook in next sc, YO and pull up a loop, YO and draw through 2 loops on hook, YO and draw through all 3 loops on hook, skip next tr, sc decrease, sc in next 9 sc: 23 sts.

Rnd 6: Sc in next 6 sc, sc decrease, (sc in next st, sc decrease) twice, sc in next 7 sc, sc decrease: 19 sts.
Complete same as Left Leg; do **not** finish off.
Stuff Legs.

BODY

Joining Row: Ch 1, fold Rnd 11 of Leg in half with ch 1 at fold; matching sts and working through **both** thicknesses, sc in each sc across Right Leg; fold Rnd 11 of Left Leg in half with toes pointing away from you; matching sts and working through **both** thicknesses, sc in each sc across Left Leg: 24 sc.

Rnd 1 (Right side)**:** Ch 1, turn; sc in Front Loop Only of each sc across *(Fig. 22, page 138)*, turn; working in free loops *(Fig. 23a, page 138)*, 2 sc in each sc across; do **not** join, place marker: 72 sc.

Rnds 2-12: Sc in each sc around.

Rnd 13: Sc in next 14 sc, work Cluster in next sc, push Cluster to **wrong** side (belly button), sc in each sc around.

Rnds 14-16: Sc in each st around.

Rnd 17: (Sc in next 10 sc, sc decrease) around: 66 sc.

Rnd 18: Sc in each sc around.

Rnd 19: (Sc in next 9 sc, sc decrease) around: 60 sc.

Rnd 20: Sc in each st around.

Rnd 21: (Sc in next 8 sc, sc decrease) around: 54 sc.

Rnd 22: Sc in each sc around.

Rnd 23: (Sc in next 7 sc, sc decrease) around: 48 sc.

Rnd 24: Sc in each sc around.

Rnd 25: (Sc in next 6 sc, sc decrease) around: 42 sc.

Rnd 26: Sc in each sc around.

Rnd 27: (Sc in next 5 sc, sc decrease) around: 36 sc.

Rnd 28: Sc in each sc around.

Rnd 29: (Sc in next 4 sc, sc decrease) around: 30 sc.

Rnds 30-32: Sc in each sc around; do **not** finish off.
Stuff Body.

HEAD

Rnd 1: 2 Sc in each sc around: 60 sc.

Rnds 2-7: Sc in each sc around.

Rnd 8: Sc in first 23 sc, work Cluster in next sc (nose), sc in each sc around.

Rnds 9-19: Repeat Rnds 20-30 of Body: 30 sc.

Rnd 20: (Sc in next sc, sc decrease) around: 20 sc.
Stuff Head.

Rnd 21: Sc decrease around; slip st in next sc, finish off leaving a long end for sewing: 10 sc.

Thread yarn needle with end and weave through remaining sts; gather tightly and secure.

RIGHT ARM

With MC, ch 18 **loosely**; being careful not to twist ch, join with slip st to form a ring.

Rnd 1 (Right side)**:** Sc in each ch around; do **not** join, place marker: 18 sc.

Rnds 2-7: Sc in each sc around.

Rnd 8: (Sc in next 7 sc, sc decrease) twice: 16 sc.

Rnd 9: Sc in each sc around.

Note: Begin working in rows for elbow.

Row 1: Sc in next 12 sc, slip st in next sc, leave remaining 3 sc unworked, remove marker.

Row 2: Turn; skip first slip st, sc in next 8 sc, slip st in next sc, leave remaining sc unworked.

Rows 3 and 4: Turn; skip first slip st, sc in next 8 sc, slip st in same sc as previous slip st.

Note: Begin working in rounds.

Rnd 1: Turn; skip first slip st, sc in next 8 sc, sc in same sc as previous slip st, sc in next 6 sc on Rnd 9, sc in same sc as slip st on Row 2; do **not** join, place marker.

Rnds 2-8: Sc in each sc around: 16 sc.

Rnds 9 and 10: (Sc in next 2 sc, sc decrease) around: 9 sc.

Rnd 11: (Sc in next 2 sc, 2 sc in next sc) around: 12 sc.

Rnds 12 and 13: Sc in each sc around.

Rnd 14: Ch 2, skip next 2 sc (for Thumb), sc in each sc around: 12 sts.
Stuff Arm.

Rnd 15: Sc in next 2 chs, (sc in next 3 sc, sc decrease) twice; do **not** finish off: 10 sts.

FINGERS

Sc in next sc, slip st in next sc, ch 5 **loosely**, sc in second ch from hook and in each ch across (finger), fold Rnd 15 in half with ch-5 at fold; ★ matching sts and working through **both** thicknesses, slip st in next sc, ch 6 **loosely**, sc in second ch from hook and in each ch across (finger); repeat from ★ once **more**, slip st in next sc, ch 4 **loosely**, sc in second ch from hook and in each ch across (finger), slip st in last sc; finish off.

Continued on page 58.

ELEGANT HANDKERCHIEF

*O*ur elegant handkerchief is fashioned by adding a dainty edging to a square of linen.
Triple picot stitches, worked in fine cotton thread, create the feminine trim.

Finished Size: Approximately ⁵/₈" wide

MATERIALS
Cotton Crochet Thread (size 30), approximately 55 yards
Steel crochet hook, size 13 (0.85 mm)
Handkerchief linen - 11" square

Note: Gauge is not important. Edging can be smaller or larger
without changing the overall effect.

PREPARING HANDKERCHIEF
Press edges of linen ⅛" to wrong side; press ⅛" to wrong side
again.
Note: When working sc on first round of Edging, insert hook
through linen, ⅛" from pressed edge.

PATTERN STITCHES
BEGINNING TRIPLE PICOT
Ch 15, slip st in tenth ch from hook, (ch 10, slip st in same
ch) twice.
TRIPLE PICOT
Ch 10, slip st in adjacent loop of **previous** Triple Picot, ch 5,
slip st in tenth ch from hook, (ch 10, slip st in same ch)
twice.

EDGING
Rnd 1 (Right side): With **right** side of linen facing, join thread
with slip st in any corner; ch 1, 2 sc in same corner, work
114 sc evenly spaced across to next corner, ★ 3 sc in next
corner, work 114 sc evenly spaced across to next corner; repeat
from ★ 2 times **more**, sc in same corner as first sc; join with
slip st to first sc: 468 sc.
Rnd 2: Ch 1, sc in same st, (ch 5, skip next 2 sc, sc in next sc)
around to last 2 sc, ch 2, skip last 2 sc, dc in first sc to form
last loop: 156 loops.
Rnd 3: Ch 1, sc in same loop, work beginning Triple Picot,
ch 5, sc in next loop, ★ (work Triple Picot, ch 5, skip next
loop, sc in next loop) across to next corner sc, work
Triple Picot, ch 5, sc in next loop; repeat from ★ 2 times
more, (work Triple Picot, ch 5, skip next loop, sc in next loop)
across to last loop, ch 10, slip st in adjacent loop of **previous**
Triple Picot, ch 5, slip st in tenth ch from hook, ch 10, slip st in
same ch, ch 5, slip st in adjacent loop of **beginning**
Triple Picot, ch 5, slip st in same ch, ch 5; join with slip st to
first sc, finish off.

See Washing and Blocking, page 140.

BABY BROTHER

Continued from page 56.

THUMB

Rnd 1: Join MC with sc in first skipped sc on Rnd 13 of Arm *(see Joining With Sc, page 137)*, sc in next sc, sc in free loop of next 2 chs; do **not** join: 4 sc.

Rnd 2: Sc in next 2 sc, sc decrease; slip st in next sc, finish off.

LEFT ARM

Work same as Right Arm.

FINGERS

Sc in next 7 sc, slip st in next sc, ch 4 **loosely**, sc in second ch from hook and in each ch across (finger), fold Rnd 15 in half with ch-4 at fold; ★ matching sts and working through **both** thicknesses, slip st in next sc, ch 6 **loosely**, sc in second ch from hook and in each ch across (finger); repeat from ★ once **more**, slip st in next sc, ch 5 **loosely**, sc in second ch from hook and in each ch across (finger), slip st in last sc; finish off.

THUMB

Work same as Right Hand.

EAR (Make 2)

Rnd 1 (Right side)**:** With MC, ch 2, 6 sc in second ch from hook; do **not** join, place marker.

Rnd 2: 2 Sc in each sc around: 12 sc.

Joining Rnd: Ch 1, fold Ear in half with ch-1 at fold; matching sts and working through **both** thicknesses, sc in each sc across; finish off leaving a long end for sewing: 6 sc.

FINISHING

Using photo as a guide for placement, sew Ears to Head. Fold beginning ch of Arm in half; sew each Arm to Body. Cut cheeks from pink felt using pattern. Sew to face using pink embroidery floss and Blanket St *(Figs. 35a & b, page 141)*. Add facial features using blue embroidery floss and Satin St for eyes *(Fig. 34, page 141)* and pink embroidery floss and Outline St for mouth *(Figs. 32a & b, page 141)*.

HAIR

Wind CC **loosely** and **evenly** around the cardboard until the card is filled, then cut across one end; repeat as needed. Thread tapestry needle with sewing thread.
Holding several 3¹/₂" strands of CC at a time, stitch across center of strands working from side to side on top of Head.

Quick MALLARD JAR TOPPER

Remind Dad that he's special by giving him a jar of his favorite goodies topped with this handsome mallard. The miniature duck is lightly stuffed for extra appeal.

MATERIALS

Bedspread Weight Cotton Thread (size 10), approximately:
  MC (Ecru) - 15 yards
  Color A (Green) - 5 yards
  Color B (Brown) - 9 yards
  Color C (Gold) - 1 yard
Crochet hook, size 6 (1.80 mm) **or** size needed for gauge
Glue
2⁵/₈" Circle self-sticking mounting board
Ribbons - 14" each color
Polyester fiberfill
Sewing needle and thread
Black embroidery floss

GAUGE: Rnds 1 and 2 of Cover = 1"

PATTERN STITCH
DECREASE
Pull up a loop in next 2 sts, YO and draw through all 3 loops on hook **(counts as one sc)**.

COVER

Rnd 1 (Right side)**:** With MC, ch 4, 17 dc in fourth ch from hook; join with slip st to top of beginning ch: 18 sts.

Note: Loop a short piece of thread around any stitch to mark last round as **right** side.

Rnd 2: Ch 3 **(counts as first dc, now and throughout)**, dc in same st, 2 dc in next dc and in each dc around; join with slip st to first dc: 36 dc.

Rnd 3: Ch 3, dc in next 2 dc, 2 dc in next dc, (dc in next 3 dc, 2 dc in next dc) around; join with slip st to first dc: 45 dc.

Rnd 4: Ch 3, dc in next 3 dc, 2 dc in next dc, (dc in next 4 dc, 2 dc in next dc) around; join with slip st to first dc: 54 dc.

Rnd 5: Ch 3, dc in next 4 dc, 2 dc in next dc, (dc in next 5 dc, 2 dc in next dc) around; join with slip st to first dc: 63 dc.

Rnd 6: Ch 3, dc in next 5 dc, 2 dc in next dc, (dc in next 6 dc, 2 dc in next dc) around; join with slip st to first dc, finish off: 72 dc.

Cheek

MALLARD

HEAD

Rnd 1 (Right side): With Color A, ch 2, 6 sc in second ch from hook; do **not** join, place marker *(see Markers, page 138)*.

Rnd 2: 2 Sc in each sc around: 12 sc.

Rnd 3: (Sc in next sc, 2 sc in next sc) around: 18 sc.

Rnds 4-7: Sc in each sc around.

Rnd 8: (Decrease, sc in next sc) around: 12 sc.

Rnd 9: Sc in each sc around; drop Color A, slip st in next sc changing to MC *(Fig. 24b, page 138)*.

Rnd 10: Ch 1, sc in each sc around; cut MC, join with slip st to first sc changing to Color A.

Rnd 11: Ch 1, sc in each sc around; join with slip st to first sc, finish off.

BODY

Row 1: With **right** side facing, join Color B with slip st in same st as joining, ch 17 **loosely**; sc in second ch from hook and in each ch across; sc in next 12 sc of Head; working in free loops of beginning ch *(Fig. 23b, page 138)*, sc in next 16 chs; do **not** join: 44 sc.

Row 2: Turn; slip st in first 3 sc, ch 1, working in Front Loops Only *(Fig. 22, page 138)*, sc in same st and in next 18 sc, 2 sc in each of next 2 sc, sc in next 19 sc, leave last 2 sc unworked: 42 sc.

Row 3: Ch 1, turn; sc in Back Loop Only of each sc across.

Row 4: Turn; slip st in first 3 sc, ch 1, sc in Front Loop Only of same st and in each sc across to last 2 sc, leave last 2 sc unworked: 38 sc.

Row 5: Ch 1, turn; sc in Back Loop Only of each sc across.

Rows 6 and 7: Repeat Rows 4 and 5: 34 sc.

Finish off.

BEAK

With Color C, ch 4, slip st in second ch from hook, sc in last 2 chs; finish off.

FINISHING

Sew Beak to Head.

With embroidery floss, add French Knot eyes *(Fig. 37, page 142)*.

Stuff Mallard lightly and sew to right side of Cover.

Attach Cover to mounting board.

Tie ribbons around jar lid.

TULIP DOILY

Featuring a charming tulip design, this hexagon-shaped doily brings Victorian elegance to any room. The old-fashioned piece is worked using bedspread weight cotton thread and finished with an edging of dainty picots.

Finished Size: Approximately 13" in diameter

MATERIALS

Bedspread Weight Cotton Thread (size 10),
    approximately 135 yards
Steel crochet hook, size 3 (2.10 mm) **or** size needed
    for gauge

GAUGE: Rnds 1-3 = 1¹/₂"

PATTERN STITCHES

DECREASE (uses next 2 dc)
★ YO, insert hook in **next** dc, YO and pull up a loop, YO and draw through 2 loops on hook; repeat from ★ once **more**, YO and draw through all 3 loops on hook **(counts as one dc)**.

DOUBLE DECREASE (uses next 3 dc)
★ YO, insert hook in **next** dc, YO and pull up a loop, YO and draw through 2 loops on hook; repeat from ★ 2 times **more**, YO and draw through all 4 loops on hook **(counts as one dc)**.

CLUSTER (uses next 6 dc)
★ YO, insert hook in **next** dc, YO and pull up a loop, YO and draw through 2 loops on hook; repeat from ★ 5 times **more**; YO and draw through all 7 loops on hook **(Figs. 11a & b, page 134)**.

Ch 6; join with slip st to form a ring.

Rnd 1 (Right side)**:** Ch 1, (sc in ring, ch 3) 6 times; join with slip st to first sc.

Rnd 2: Slip st in first ch-3 sp, ch 1, (sc, ch 3) twice in same sp and in each ch-3 sp around; join with slip st to first sc: 12 ch-3 sps.

Rnds 3 and 4: Slip st in first ch-3 sp, ch 1, sc in same sp, ch 3, (sc in next ch-3 sp, ch 3) around; join with slip st to first sc.

Rnd 5: Slip st in first ch-3 sp, ch 1, sc in same sp, (ch 6, sc in next ch-3 sp) around, ch 3, dc in first sc to form last loop.

Rnd 6: Ch 1, sc in same loop, (ch 6, sc in next loop) around, ch 3, dc in first sc to form last loop.

Rnd 7: Ch 1, sc in same loop, (ch 7, sc in next loop) around, ch 3, tr in first sc to form last loop.

Rnd 8: Ch 3 **(counts as first dc, now and throughout)**, (2 dc, ch 3, 3 dc) in same sp, ch 6, sc in next loop, ch 6,

★ (3 dc, ch 3, 3 dc) in next loop, ch 6, sc in next loop, ch 6; repeat from ★ around; join with slip st to first dc: 6 sc.

Rnd 9: Ch 3, dc in same st, 2 dc in each of next 2 dc, ch 3, sc in next ch-3 sp, ch 3, 2 dc in each of next 3 dc, ch 3, (sc in next loop, ch 3) twice, ★ 2 dc in each of next 3 dc, ch 3, sc in next ch-3 sp, ch 3, 2 dc in each of next 3 dc, ch 3, (sc in next loop, ch 3) twice; repeat from ★ around; join with slip st to first dc.

Rnd 10: Ch 3, dc in next 5 dc, ch 3, (sc in next ch-3 sp, ch 3) twice, dc in next 6 dc, ch 3, skip next ch-3 sp, sc in next ch-3 sp, ch 3, ★ dc in next 6 dc, ch 3, (sc in next ch-3 sp, ch 3) twice, dc in next 6 dc, ch 3, skip next ch-3 sp, sc in next ch-3 sp, ch 3; repeat from ★ around; join with slip st to first dc.

Rnd 11: Ch 3, dc in next 5 dc, ch 3, skip next ch-3 sp, 2 dc in next ch-3 sp, ch 3, dc in next 6 dc, ch 3, (sc in next ch-3 sp, ch 3) twice, ★ dc in next 6 dc, ch 3, skip next ch-3 sp, 2 dc in next ch-3 sp, ch 3, dc in next 6 dc, ch 3, (sc in next ch-3 sp, ch 3) twice; repeat from ★ around; join with slip st to first dc.

Rnd 12: Ch 3, dc in next 5 dc, ch 3, dc in next 2 dc, ch 3, dc in next 6 dc, ch 3, (sc in next ch-3 sp, ch 3) 3 times, ★ dc in next 6 dc, ch 3, dc in next 2 dc, ch 3, dc in next 6 dc, ch 3, (sc in next ch-3 sp, ch 3) 3 times; repeat from ★ around; join with slip st to first dc.

Rnd 13: Ch 2, dc in next dc, decrease twice, ch 4, 3 dc in next dc, ch 3, 3 dc in next dc, ch 4, decrease 3 times, ch 3, (sc in next ch-3 sp, ch 3) 4 times, ★ decrease 3 times, ch 4, 3 dc in next dc, ch 3, 3 dc in next dc, ch 4, decrease 3 times, ch 3, (sc in next ch-3 sp, ch 3) 4 times; repeat from ★ around; skip beginning ch-2 and join with slip st to first dc.

Rnd 14: Ch 2, decrease, ch 3, 2 dc in each of next 3 dc, ch 1, 3 dc in next ch-3 sp, ch 1, 2 dc in each of next 3 dc, ch 3, work double decrease, ch 3, (sc in next ch-3 sp, ch 3) 5 times, ★ work double decrease, ch 3, 2 dc in each of next 3 dc, ch 1, 3 dc in next ch-3 sp, ch 1, 2 dc in each of next 3 dc, ch 3, work double decrease, ch 3, (sc in next ch-3 sp, ch 3) 5 times; repeat from ★ around; skip beginning ch-2 and join with slip st to top of first decrease.

Rnd 15: Slip st in first ch-3 sp, ch 1, sc in same sp, ch 3, decrease 3 times, ch 3, 2 dc in each of next 3 dc, ch 3, decrease 3 times, ch 3, ★ (sc in next ch-3 sp, ch 3) 8 times, decrease 3 times, ch 3, 2 dc in each of next 3 dc, ch 3, decrease 3 times, ch 3; repeat from ★ around to last 7 ch-3 sps, (sc in next ch-3 sp, ch 3) 7 times; join with slip st to first sc.

Rnd 16: Slip st in first ch-3 sp, ch 1, sc in same sp, ch 3, work double decrease, ch 3, sc in next ch-3 sp, ch 4, work Cluster, ch 4, sc in next ch-3 sp, ch 3, work double decrease, ch 3, ★ (sc in next ch-3 sp, ch 3) 9 times, work double decrease, ch 3, sc in next ch-3 sp, ch 4, work Cluster, ch 4, sc in next ch-3 sp, ch 3, work double decrease, ch 3; repeat from ★ around to last 8 ch-3 sps, (sc in next ch-3 sp, ch 3) 8 times; join with slip st to first sc.

Rnd 17: Slip st in first ch-3 sp, ch 1, sc in same sp, ch 3, sc in next ch-3 sp, (ch 5, slip st in third ch from hook, ch 2, sc in next ch-3 sp) 3 times, ★ (ch 3, sc in next ch-3 sp) 11 times, (ch 5, slip st in third ch from hook, ch 2, sc in next ch-3 sp) 3 times; repeat from ★ around to last 9 ch-3 sps, ch 3, (sc in next ch-3 sp, ch 3) 9 times; join with slip st to first sc.

Rnd 18: Ch 9, (tr in next sc, ch 5) around; join with slip st to fourth ch of beginning ch-9: 84 loops.

Rnd 19: Ch 9, (tr in next tr, ch 5) around; join with slip st to fourth ch of beginning ch-9.

Rnd 20: Slip st in first loop, ch 1, (3 sc, ch 3, slip st in third ch from hook, 3 sc) in same loop and in each loop around; join with slip st to first sc, finish off.

See Washing and Blocking, page 140.

61

COUNTRY BREAD CLOTH

Cheer up a special friend with a batch of homemade muffins delivered in a basket lined with this country bread cloth. The cozy warmer is crafted by adding a colorful edging, crocheted with bedspread weight cotton thread, to a coordinating plaid fabric square.

Finished Size: Approximately 21" square

MATERIALS
Bedspread Weight Cotton Thread (size 10),
   approximately 265 yards
Steel crochet hook, size 6 (1.80 mm) **or** size needed
   for gauge
Fabric - 17" square
Washable fabric marker
Sewing needle and thread

GAUGE: 16 dc and 8 rows = 2"

PREPARING BREAD CLOTH

Press edges of fabric ¼" to wrong side; press ¼" to wrong side again. Hem with matching sewing thread.
Along **each** side of square, make a mark at every inch.
With a single strand of bedspread weight cotton thread, make 4 backstitches between each inch mark on fabric **(Figs. 36a & b, page 141)**: 64 sts **each** side.

PATTERN STITCH
CLUSTER
★ YO twice, insert hook in loop indicated, YO and pull up a loop, (YO and draw through 2 loops on hook) twice; repeat from ★ 2 times **more**, YO and draw through all 4 loops on hook **(Figs. 10a & b, page 134)**.

EDGING

Rnd 1 (Right side): With **right** side of fabric facing, join thread with slip st in first backstitch **before** any corner; ch 8 **(counts as first dc plus ch 5, now and throughout)**, ★ 2 dc in each backstitch across to within one backstitch of next corner, 3 dc in last backstitch, ch 5; repeat from ★ 2 times **more**, 2 dc in each backstitch across, 2 dc in same backstitch as beginning ch-8; join with slip st to first dc: 129 dc **each** side.

Rnd 2: Slip st in first corner ch-5 sp, ch 8, dc in same sp, ch 1, dc in next dc, ch 1, ★ (skip next dc, dc in next dc, ch 1) across to next corner ch-5 sp, (dc, ch 5, dc) in corner ch-5 sp, ch 1, dc in next dc, ch 1; repeat from ★ 2 times **more**, (skip next dc, dc in next dc, ch 1) across; join with slip st to first dc: 66 ch-1 sps **each** side.

Rnd 3: Slip st in first corner ch-5 sp, ch 8, 2 dc in same sp, dc in each dc and in each ch-1 sp across to next corner ch-5 sp, ★ (2 dc, ch 5, 2 dc) in corner ch-5 sp, dc in each dc and in each ch-1 sp across to next corner ch-5 sp; repeat from ★ around, dc in same corner as beginning ch-8; join with slip st to first dc: 137 dc **each** side.

Rnd 4: Repeat Rnd 2: 70 ch-1 sps **each** side.

Rnd 5: Ch 3 **(counts as first dc, now and throughout)**, (2 dc, ch 5, 2 dc) in first corner ch-5 sp, ★ † dc in next dc, dc in next ch-1 sp, dc in next dc, ch 5, skip next 2 ch-1 sps, sc in next ch-1 sp, (sc in next dc, sc in next ch-1 sp) 3 times, ch 5, skip next 2 dc, dc in next dc, dc in next ch-1 sp †, repeat from † to † across to within one dc of next corner ch-5 sp, dc in next dc, (2 dc, ch 5, 2 dc) in next corner ch-5 sp; repeat from ★ 2 times **more**, then repeat from † to † across; join with slip st to first dc.

Rnd 6: Slip st in next 2 dc, ch 3, (2 dc, ch 5, 2 dc) in first corner ch-5 sp, dc in next dc, ch 3, ★ † skip next 3 dc, dc in next dc, 2 dc in next ch-5 sp, ch 5, skip next sc, sc in next 5 sc, ch 5, 2 dc in next ch-5 sp, dc in next dc, ch 3 †, repeat from † to † across to within 4 dc of next corner ch-5 sp, skip next 3 dc, dc in next dc, (2 dc, ch 5, 2 dc) in next corner ch-5 sp, dc in next dc, ch 3; repeat from ★ 2 times **more**, then repeat from † to † across to last 3 dc, skip last 3 dc; join with slip st to first dc.

Rnd 7: Slip st in next 2 dc, ch 3, (2 dc, ch 5, 2 dc) in first corner ch-5 sp, dc in next dc, ch 5, sc in next ch-3 sp, ch 5, ★ † skip next 2 dc, dc in next dc, 2 dc in next ch-5 sp, ch 5, skip next sc, sc in next 3 sc, ch 5, 2 dc in next ch-5 sp, dc in next dc, ch 5, sc in next ch-3 sp, ch 5 †, repeat from † to † across to within 3 dc of next corner ch-5 sp, skip next 2 dc, dc in next dc, (2 dc, ch 5, 2 dc) in next corner ch-5 sp, dc in next dc, ch 5, sc in next ch-3 sp, ch 5; repeat from ★ 2 times **more**, then repeat from † to † across to last 2 dc, skip last 2 dc; join with slip st to first dc.

Rnd 8: Slip st in next 2 dc, ch 3, (2 dc, ch 5, 2 dc) in first corner ch-5 sp, dc in next dc, ch 5, sc in next ch-5 sp, ch 7, sc in next ch-5 sp, ch 5, ★ † skip next 2 dc, dc in next dc, 2 dc in next ch-5 sp, ch 5, skip next sc, sc in next sc, ch 5, 2 dc in next ch-5 sp, dc in next dc, ch 5, sc in next ch-5 sp, ch 7, sc in next ch-5 sp, ch 5 †, repeat from † to † across to within 3 dc of

next corner ch-5 sp, skip next 2 dc, dc in next dc, (2 dc, ch 5, 2 dc) in next corner ch-5 sp, dc in next dc, ch 5, sc in next ch-5 sp, ch 7, sc in next ch-5 sp, ch 5; repeat from ★ 2 times **more**, then repeat from † to † across to last 2 dc, skip last 2 dc; join with slip st to first dc.

Rnd 9: Slip st in next 2 dc, ch 3, (2 dc, ch 5, 2 dc) in first corner ch-5 sp, dc in next dc, ch 3, skip next ch-5 sp, (work Cluster, ch 3) 5 times in next loop, ★ † skip next 2 dc, dc in next dc, 2 dc in each of next 2 ch-5 sps, dc in next dc, ch 3,

skip next ch-5 sp, (work Cluster, ch 3) 5 times in next loop †, repeat from † to † across to within 3 dc of next corner ch-5 sp, skip next 2 dc, dc in next dc, (2 dc, ch 5, 2 dc) in next corner ch-5 sp, dc in next dc, ch 3, skip next ch-5 sp, (work Cluster, ch 3) 5 times in next loop; repeat from ★ 2 times **more**, then repeat from † to † across to last 2 dc, skip last 2 dc; join with slip st to first dc, finish off.

See Washing and Blocking, page 140.

just for fun

These innovative designs give you lots of fun ideas for accenting your life with crochet. You'll find several projects, like our seasonal magnets, that are not only quick to stitch, but they also help you use up scrap yarn. There's even a clever rug that you can craft from recycled plastic bags! This whimsical collection provides a variety of ways to enjoy your stitching time.

KID-PLEASING PLAID AFGHAN

Fashioned with fun in mind, this reversible plaid afghan is worked in kid-pleasing colors. Stripes of yellow, green, white, and blue crisscross the bright red throw, creating the look of tartan plaid. A playful accent for a child's room, the heavy, durable cover-up will be enjoyed for years.

Finished Size: Approximately 48" x 67"

MATERIALS

Worsted Weight Yarn, approximately:
MC (Red) - 29 ounces, (820 grams, 1,905 yards)
Color A (White) - 4¹/₂ ounces, (130 grams, 295 yards)
Color B (Blue) - 6 ounces, (170 grams, 395 yards)
Color C (Yellow) - 3 ounces, (90 grams, 200 yards)
Color D (Green) - 2¹/₂ ounces, (70 grams, 165 yards)
Crochet hook, size H (5.00 mm) **or** size needed for gauge

GAUGE: 15 tr and 5 rows = 4"

BODY

With MC, ch 184 **loosely**.

Row 1 (Right side): Tr in fifth ch from hook **(4 skipped chs count as first tr)**, tr in next 8 chs, ★ † ch 2, skip next 2 chs, tr in next 7 chs, (ch 2, skip next 2 chs, tr in next ch, ch 2) twice, skip next 2 chs †, tr in next 31 chs, ch 2, skip next 2 chs, tr in next ch, ch 2, skip next 2 chs, tr in next 19 chs; repeat from ★ once **more**, then repeat from † to † once, tr in each ch across: 149 tr.

Note: Loop a short piece of yarn around any stitch to mark last row as **right** side and bottom edge.

Row 2: Ch 4 **(counts as first tr, now and throughout)**, turn; tr in next 9 tr, ★ † ch 2, (skip next ch-2 sp, tr in next tr, ch 2) twice, skip next ch-2 sp, tr in next 7 tr, ch 2, skip next ch-2 sp †, tr in next 19 tr, ch 2, skip next ch-2 sp, tr in next tr, ch 2, skip next ch-2 sp, tr in next 31 tr; repeat from ★ once **more**, then repeat from † to † once, tr in each st across.

Row 3: Ch 4, turn; tr in next 9 tr, ★ † ch 2, skip next ch-2 sp, tr in next 7 tr, ch 2, (skip next ch-2 sp, tr in next tr, ch 2) twice, skip next ch-2 sp †, tr in next 31 tr, ch 2, skip next ch-2 sp, tr in next tr, ch 2, skip next ch-2 sp, tr in next 19 tr; repeat from ★ once **more**, then repeat from † to † once, tr in each tr across.

Row 4: Repeat Row 2.

Row 5 (Eyelet row): Ch 6 **(counts as first tr plus ch 2, now and throughout)**, turn; skip next 2 tr, tr in next tr, (ch 2, skip next 2 tr, tr in next tr) twice, ★ † ch 2, skip next ch-2 sp, tr in next tr, (ch 2, skip next 2 tr, tr in next tr) twice, (ch 2, skip next ch-2 sp, tr in next tr) 3 times †, (ch 2, skip next 2 tr, tr in next tr) 10 times, (ch 2, skip next ch-2 sp, tr in next tr) twice, (ch 2, skip next 2 tr, tr in next tr) 6 times; repeat from ★ once **more**, then repeat from † to † once, (ch 2, skip next 2 tr, tr in next tr) across: 60 ch-2 sps.

Rows 6 and 7 (Eyelet rows): Ch 6, turn; skip next ch-2 sp, tr in next tr, (ch 2, skip next ch-2 sp, tr in next tr) across.

Row 8: Ch 4, turn; (tr in next 2 chs, tr in next tr) 3 times, ★ † (ch 2, skip next ch-2 sp, tr in next tr) 3 times, (tr in next 2 chs, tr in next tr) twice, ch 2, skip next ch-2 sp, tr in next tr †, (tr in next 2 chs, tr in next tr) 6 times, (ch 2, skip next ch-2 sp, tr in next tr) twice, (tr in next 2 chs, tr in next tr) 10 times; repeat from ★ once **more**, then repeat from † to † once, (tr in next 2 chs, tr in next tr) across: 149 tr.

Rows 9-17: Repeat Row 3 once, then repeat Rows 2 and 3, 4 times **more**.

Row 18 (Eyelet row): Ch 6, turn; skip next 2 tr, tr in next tr, (ch 2, skip next 2 tr, tr in next tr) twice, ★ † (ch 2, skip next ch-2 sp, tr in next tr) 3 times, (ch 2, skip next 2 tr, tr in next tr) twice, ch 2, skip next ch-2 sp, tr in next tr †, (ch 2, skip next 2 tr, tr in next tr) 6 times, (ch 2, skip next ch-2 sp, tr in next tr) twice, (ch 2, skip next 2 tr, tr in next tr) 10 times; repeat from ★ once **more**, then repeat from † to † once, (ch 2, skip next 2 tr, tr in next tr) across: 60 ch-2 sps.

Rows 19 and 20: Repeat Rows 7 and 8.

Rows 21-25: Repeat Row 3 once, then repeat Rows 2 and 3 twice.

Row 26: Repeat Row 18.

Row 27: Ch 4, turn; (tr in next 2 chs, tr in next tr) 3 times, ★ † ch 2, skip next ch-2 sp, tr in next tr, (tr in next 2 chs, tr in next tr) twice, (ch 2, skip next ch-2 sp, tr in next tr) 3 times †, (tr in next 2 chs, tr in next tr) 10 times, (ch 2, skip next ch-2 sp, tr in next tr) twice, (tr in next 2 chs, tr in next tr) 6 times; repeat from ★ once **more**, then repeat from † to † once, (tr in next 2 chs, tr in next tr) across.

Row 28: Repeat Row 2.

Rows 29-83: Repeat Rows 5-28 twice, then repeat Rows 5-11 once **more**.
Finish off.

STRIPES

Note: Always join yarn and finish off leaving a 4" end for fringe.

Referring to Placement Diagram for color placement, work all Vertical Lines of one color and then all Horizontal Lines of the same color. Work colors in the following sequence: White, Blue, Yellow, Green.

PLACEMENT DIAGRAM

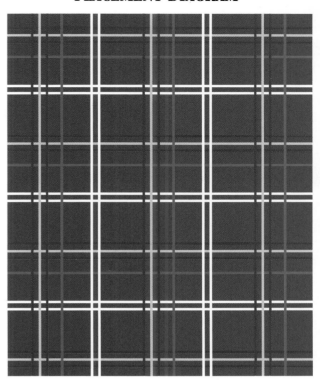

VERTICAL LINE
Front Stripe: Hold afghan with **right** side facing and top edge toward you; working upward, join yarn with slip st around first ch-2; (ch 3 **loosely**, sc around next skipped ch-2) across; finish off.

Back Stripe: Hold afghan with **wrong** side facing and bottom edge toward you; working to **left** of Front Stripe and around same skipped ch-2, join yarn with slip st around skipped ch-2 of beginning ch; working upward, (ch 3 **loosely**, sc around next skipped ch-2) across; finish off.

HORIZONTAL LINE
Front Stripe: Hold afghan with **right** side facing and bottom edge toward the left; join yarn with slip st around post of first tr of Eyelet row; working upward, (ch 3 **loosely**, sc around post of next tr) across; finish off.

Back Stripe: Hold afghan with **wrong** side facing and bottom edge toward the left; working to **right** of Front Stripe and around same tr, join yarn with slip st around post of first tr; working upward, (ch 3 **loosely**, sc around post of next tr) across; finish off.

Add additional fringe to each end of every Stripe Line around afghan using 3 strands of matching color, each 9" long *(Figs. 30a & b, page 140)*, and add fringe to both ends of afghan, evenly spacing fringe between Stripes and using 4 strands of MC, each 9" long.

SUNFLOWER BASKET

Pick our pretty sunflower basket to bring nature's delights indoors! The petals of the cheery carrier are stiffened and slightly curved to form a shallow basket. It's perfect for displaying on your table.

Finished Size: Approximately 9" in diameter after shaping and 6" tall

MATERIALS
Cotton Crochet Thread (size 3), approximately:
   MC (Gold) - 110 yards
   Color A (Brown) - 10 yards
   Color B (Green) - 22 yards
Steel crochet hook, size 0 (3.25 mm) **or** size needed for gauge
3 - 18" lengths of 22 gauge wire
Tapestry needle
Starching materials: Commercial fabric stiffener, blocking board, plastic wrap, resealable plastic bag, 9" plastic foam ring, terry towel, paper towels, and stainless steel pins

GAUGE: Rnds 1-5 = 3"

PATTERN STITCHES
CROSS ST
Skip next dc, dc in next dc, working **around** last dc, dc in skipped dc *(Fig. 1)*.

Fig. 1

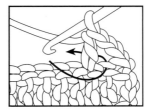

DECREASE (uses next 2 dc)
★ YO, insert hook in **next** st, YO and pull up a loop, YO and draw through 2 loops on hook; repeat from ★ once **more**, YO and draw through all 3 loops on hook.

BOTTOM

With Color A, ch 6; join with slip st to form a ring.

Rnd 1 (Right side): Ch 3, (hdc, ch 1) 7 times in ring; join with slip st to second ch of beginning ch-3: 8 ch-1 sps.

Note: Loop a short piece of thread around any stitch to mark last round as **right** side.

Rnd 2: Slip st in first ch-1 sp, ch 3, hdc in same sp, (hdc, ch 1, hdc) in next ch-1 sp and in each ch-1 sp around; join with slip st to second ch of beginning ch-3: 8 ch-1 sps.

Rnd 3: Slip st in first ch-1 sp, ch 3, hdc in same sp, ch 2, ★ (hdc, ch 1, hdc) in next ch-1 sp, ch 2; repeat from ★ around; join with slip st to second ch of beginning ch-3: 16 sps.

Rnd 4: Slip st in first ch-1 sp, ch 3, hdc in same sp, ch 1, (hdc, ch 1) twice in next sp and in each sp around; join with slip st to second ch of beginning ch-3, finish off: 32 ch-1 sps.

Rnd 5: With **right** side facing and working in Back Loops Only *(Fig. 22, page 138)*, join MC with slip st in same st as joining; ch 1, sc in same st and in each ch and in each hdc around; join with slip st to first sc: 64 sc.

Rnd 6: Ch 3 **(counts as first dc, now and throughout)**, working in both loops, dc in same st and in next 6 sc, ★ 2 dc in each of next 2 sc, dc in next 6 sc; repeat from ★ around to last sc, 2 dc in last sc; join with slip st to first dc: 80 dc.

Rnd 7: Ch 3, dc in next dc, work 3 Cross Sts, dc in next 2 dc, ch 2, ★ dc in next 2 dc, work 3 Cross Sts, dc in next 2 dc, ch 2; repeat from ★ around; join with slip st to first dc: 8 ch-2 sps.

Rnd 8: Ch 5, **turn**; 2 dc in next dc, dc in next dc, work 3 Cross Sts, dc in next dc, ★ 2 dc in next dc, ch 2, 2 dc in next dc, dc in next dc, work 3 Cross Sts, dc in next dc; repeat from ★ around, dc in same st as beginning ch-5; join with slip st to third ch of beginning ch-5.

Rnd 9: Ch 3, turn; dc in same st, work 5 Cross Sts, 2 dc in next dc, ch 3, ★ 2 dc in next dc, work 5 Cross Sts, 2 dc in next dc, ch 3; repeat from ★ around; join with slip st to first dc.

Rnd 10: Ch 3, turn; working around beginning ch-3, dc in st to the **right**, ch 3, (work 7 Cross Sts, ch 3) 7 times, work 6 Cross Sts; join with slip st to first dc.

Rnd 11: Ch 3, turn; working around beginning ch-3, dc in st to the **right**, work 6 Cross Sts, ch 3, (work 7 Cross Sts, ch 3) around; join with slip st to first dc.

Rnd 12: Ch 3, turn; working around beginning ch-3, dc in st to the **right**, ch 4, (work 7 Cross Sts, ch 4) 7 times, work 6 Cross Sts; join with slip st to first dc, do **not** finish off.

FIRST PETAL

Row 1: Slip st in next dc, ch 2, turn; dc in next dc, work 5 Cross Sts, decrease, leave remaining sts unworked.

Row 2: Ch 2, turn; decrease, work 3 Cross Sts, decrease, hdc in next dc, leave turning ch unworked.

Row 3: Ch 2, turn; dc in next st, work 3 Cross Sts, decrease; finish off.

REMAINING 7 PETALS

Row 1: With **right** side facing, join MC with slip st in first unworked dc on Rnd 12; ch 2, dc in next dc, work 5 Cross Sts, decrease, leave remaining sts unworked.

Rows 2 and 3: Work same as First Petal; on last Petal, do **not** finish off.

EDGING

Ch 1, do **not** turn; working in end of rows, ★ 2 sc in each of first 3 rows, 4 sc in next ch-4 sp, 2 sc in each of next 3 rows, sc in next 8 sts; repeat from ★ around; join with slip st to first sc, finish off.

HANDLE

CENTER SECTION

Fold up 1" on each end of wire and twist to secure.

With Color B, ch 91 **loosely**.

Row 1 (Right side): Working over first wire *(Fig. 25, page 138)*, sc in back ridge of second ch from hook and in each ch across *(Fig. 2a, page 133)*; finish off leaving a long end for sewing: 90 sc.

Note: Mark last row as **right** side.

FIRST SIDE

Foundation Chain: With **right** side facing, join Color B with slip st in tenth sc from **left** edge, ch 9 **loosely**; finish off.

With **right** side facing, join Color B with slip st in tenth sc from **right** edge, ch 10 **loosely**.

Row 1: Working over second wire, sc in back ridge of second ch from hook and in next 8 chs, sc in same sc as joining and in each sc across to Foundation Chain, sc in same sc as joining, sc in back ridge of last 9 chs; finish off leaving a long end for sewing: 90 sc.

SECOND SIDE

Working in both loops of beginning ch *(Fig. 23b, page 138)*, work same as First Side.

FINISHING

Using photo as a guide for placement, sew Handle to Bottom, joining Center Section to center 2 sc between Petals and joining First and Second Sides to side of Petals leaving 5 sc from Center Section free.

See Starching and Blocking, page 143.

Quick PINCUSHION BONNET

Pretty as a spring bonnet, this dainty pincushion keeps pins and needles safely in one spot. Sewing enthusiasts will love the notion, which is worked in bedspread weight cotton thread and lightly stuffed before finishing. A delicate floral spray lends a charming touch.

Finished Size: Approximately 6" in diameter

MATERIALS
Bedspread Weight Cotton Thread (size 10),
   approximately 120 yards
Steel crochet hook, size 6 (1.80 mm) **or** size needed
   for gauge
Polyester fiberfill
Tapestry needle
Finishing materials: Ribbon, flowers

GAUGE: Rnds 1 and 2 of Cushion = 1"

PATTERN STITCH
DECREASE (uses next 2 sts)
★ YO, insert hook in **next** st, YO and pull up a loop, YO and draw through 2 loops on hook; repeat from ★ once **more**, YO and draw through all 3 loops on hook **(counts as one dc)**.

CUSHION

Rnd 1 (Right side)**:** Ch 4, 15 dc in fourth ch from hook; join with slip st to top of beginning ch: 16 sts.

Rnd 2: Ch 3 **(counts as first dc, now and throughout)**, dc in same st, 2 dc in each dc around; join with slip st to first dc: 32 dc.

Rnd 3: Ch 3, dc in same st and in next dc, (2 dc in next dc, dc in next dc) around; join with slip st to first dc: 48 dc.

Rnd 4: Ch 3, dc in same st and in next 2 dc, (2 dc in next dc, dc in next 2 dc) around; join with slip st to first dc: 64 dc.

Rnd 5: Ch 3, dc in same st and in next 3 dc, (2 dc in next dc, dc in next 3 dc) around; join with slip st to Back Loop Only of first dc *(Fig. 22, page 138)*: 80 dc.

Rnd 6: Ch 3, dc in Back Loop Only of next dc and in each dc around; join with slip st to both loops of first dc.

Rnds 7-9: Ch 3, dc in both loops of next dc and in each dc around; join with slip st to first dc.

Rnd 10: Ch 3, dc in next dc and in each dc around; join with slip st to Back Loop Only of first dc.

Rnd 11: Ch 2, working in Back Loops Only, dc in next 4 dc, (decrease, dc in next 3 dc) around; skip beginning ch-2 and join with slip st to both loops of first dc: 64 dc.

Rnd 12: Ch 2, working in both loops, dc in next 3 dc, (decrease, dc in next 2 dc) around; skip beginning ch-2 and join with slip st to first dc: 48 dc.

Stuff Cushion **lightly** and shape.

Rnd 13: Ch 2, dc in next 2 dc, (decrease, dc in next dc) around; skip beginning ch-2 and join with slip st to first dc: 32 dc.

Rnd 14: Ch 2, dc in next dc, decrease around; skip beginning ch-2 and join with slip st to first dc: 16 dc.

Rnd 15: Ch 2, dc in next st, decrease around; skip beginning ch-2 and join with slip st to first dc, finish off leaving a long end for sewing: 8 dc.

Add additional stuffing, if necessary.

Thread needle with end and weave through remaining sts; gather tightly and secure.

TRIM

With top toward you and working in free loops on Rnd 5 **(Fig. 23a, page 138)**, join thread with slip st in any dc; ch 1, working from **left** to **right**, work reverse sc in each st around **(Figs. 19a-d, page 136)**; join with slip st to first st, finish off.

BRIM

Rnd 1: With top toward you and working in free loops on Rnd 10, join thread with slip st in any dc; ch 3, dc in next dc, ch 3, skip next 2 dc, (dc in next 2 dc, ch 3, skip next 2 dc) around; join with slip st to first dc: 20 ch-3 sps.

Rnd 2: Ch 3, dc in next dc and in next ch, ch 3, skip next ch, dc in next ch, ★ dc in next 2 dc and in next ch, ch 3, skip next ch, dc in next ch; repeat from ★ around; join with slip st to first dc: 80 dc.

Rnd 3: Ch 3, dc in next 2 dc and in next ch, ch 3, skip next ch, dc in next ch, ★ dc in next 4 dc and in next ch, ch 3, skip next ch, dc in next ch; repeat from ★ around to last dc, dc in last dc; join with slip st to first dc: 120 dc.

Rnd 4: Ch 3, dc in next 3 dc and in next ch, ch 3, skip next ch, dc in next ch, ★ dc in next 6 dc and in next ch, ch 3, skip next ch, dc in next ch; repeat from ★ around to last 2 dc, dc in last 2 dc; join with slip st to first dc: 160 dc.

Rnd 5: Ch 3, dc in next 4 dc, ch 3, skip next 2 chs, dc in next ch, ch 3, ★ skip next 2 dc, dc in next 6 dc, ch 3, skip next 2 chs, dc in next ch, ch 3; repeat from ★ around to last 3 dc, skip next 2 dc, dc in last dc; join with slip st to first dc: 140 dc.

Rnd 6: Slip st in next dc, ch 3, dc in next 3 dc, ch 3, (skip next 2 chs, dc in next ch, ch 3) twice, skip next 2 dc, ★ dc in next 4 dc, ch 3, (skip next 2 chs, dc in next ch, ch 3) twice, skip next 2 dc; repeat from ★ around; join with slip st to first dc: 120 dc.

Rnd 7: Slip st in next 2 dc, ch 3, dc in next dc, ch 3, (skip next 2 chs, dc in next ch, ch 3) 3 times, skip next 2 dc, ★ dc in next 2 dc, ch 3, (skip next 2 chs, dc in next ch, ch 3) 3 times, skip next 2 dc; repeat from ★ around; join with slip st to first dc: 80 ch-3 sps.

Rnd 8: Ch 1, sc in same st and in next dc, 3 sc in each of next 4 ch-3 sps, ★ sc in next 2 dc, 3 sc in each of next 4 ch-3 sps; repeat from ★ around; join with slip st to first sc, finish off.

FINISHING

Using photo as a guide for placement, place ribbon around Cushion and glue in place. Add flowers and bows as desired.

Quick COLORFUL BAG RUG

Unique home fashions are in the bag — or rather, made out of them — when you craft this colorful bath mat using plastic bags and a jumbo hook! Worked in rounds of double crochets, the eye-catching rug can be created from new garbage bags or recycled shopping bags.

Finished Size: 24" in diameter

MATERIALS
Plastic Garbage or Shopping Bag Strips, approximately:
 MC (Red) - 100 yards
 CC (White) - 70 yards
Crochet hook, size S
Optional: Rotary cutter and mat

PREPARING PLASTIC STRIPS
Lay each bag flat on a hard surface and cut bottom and handles (if any) off. Do **not** cut sides.

Cut across each bag forming 6" wide strips **(Fig. 1a, page 71)**, ending with a circle of plastic **(Fig. 1b, page 71)**.

Note: A rotary cutter and mat can be used to cut approximately 10 bags at the same time.

Link the strips together by pulling one strip through the loop of another strip and then back through itself *(Fig. 1c)*; pull tightly to form knot.

Fig. 1a

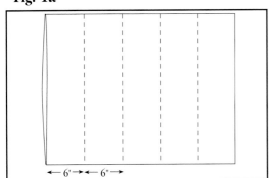

Fig. 1b

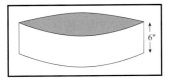

Fig. 1c

GAUGE: Rnds 1 and 2 = 7½"

Rnd 1 (Right side)**:** With CC, ch 4, 9 dc in fourth ch from hook; join with slip st to top of beginning ch: 10 sts.

Rnd 2: Ch 3 **(counts as first dc, now and throughout)**, dc in same st, 2 dc in next dc and in each dc around; join with slip st to first dc changing to MC *(Fig. 24b, page 138)*: 20 dc.

Rnd 3: Ch 3, dc in same st and in next dc, (2 dc in next dc, dc in next dc) around; join with slip st to first dc: 30 dc.

Rnd 4: Ch 3, dc in same st and in next 2 dc, (2 dc in next dc, dc in next 2 dc) around; join with slip st to first dc changing to CC: 40 dc.

Rnd 5: Ch 3, dc in same st and in next 4 dc, (2 dc in next dc, dc in next 4 dc) around; join with slip st to first dc: 48 dc.

Rnd 6: Ch 3, dc in same st and in next 3 dc, (2 dc in next dc, dc in next 3 dc) around; join with slip st to first dc changing to MC: 60 dc.

Rnd 7: Ch 3, dc in next dc, 2 dc in next dc, (dc in next 2 dc, 2 dc in next dc) around; join with slip st to first dc: 80 dc.

Rnd 8: Ch 1, sc in same st and in next dc, hdc in next dc, dc in next dc, hdc in next dc, ★ sc in next 2 dc, hdc in next dc, dc in next dc, hdc in next dc; repeat from ★ around; join with slip st to first sc, finish off.

PLAYTIME DINOSAUR

Add adventure to a child's day with this "dino-riffic" dinosaur! Sure to stimulate young imaginations, the prehistoric playmate is crocheted with fabric strips and stuffed.

Finished Size: Approximately 28" long x 10" high

MATERIALS

100% Cotton Fabric, 44/45" wide, approximately:
   MC (Brown) - 7½ yards
   Color A (Tan) - 4 yards
   Color B (Black) - ¹⁄₁₆ yard
Crochet hook, size K (6.50 mm) **or** size needed for gauge
2 - 18 mm eyes
Polyester fiberfill
Yarn needle
Sewing needle and thread

Prepare fabric and cut into 1" strips *(see Preparing Fabric Strips and Joining Fabric Strips, page 139)*.

GAUGE: 8 sc and 8 rows = 4"

PATTERN STITCH

DECREASE
Pull up a loop in next 2 sts, YO and draw through all 3 loops on hook **(counts as one sc)**.

HEAD AND BODY

Rnd 1 (Right side): With MC, ch 2, 6 sc in second ch from hook; do **not** join, place fabric marker *(see Markers, page 138)*.

Rnd 2: (Sc in next sc, 2 sc in next sc) around: 9 sc.

Rnd 3: Sc in next 2 sc, 2 sc in next sc, ★ sc in next sc changing to Color B *(Fig. 24a, page 138)*, sc in next sc changing to MC, 2 sc in next sc; repeat from ★ once **more**: 12 sc.

Rnd 4: Sc in next 6 sc, 3 sc in next sc, sc in next sc, 3 sc in next sc, sc in next 3 sc: 16 sc.

Rnd 5: (Sc in next 5 sc, decrease) twice, sc in next 2 sc: 14 sc.

Rnd 6: Sc in each sc around.

Rnd 7: (Sc in next sc, 2 sc in next sc) around: 21 sc.

Rnd 8: Sc in each sc around.

Rnd 9: Sc in next 14 sc, 4 sc in next sc, sc in next 6 sc: 24 sc.

Rnds 10-13: Sc in each sc around.

Rnd 14: (Sc in next 4 sc, decrease) around: 20 sc.

Rnd 15: Sc in each sc around.

Rnd 16: (Sc in next 3 sc, decrease) around: 16 sc.

Rnds 17 and 18: Sc in each sc around.

Rnd 19: (Sc in next 3 sc, 2 sc in next sc) around: 20 sc.

Rnd 20: Sc in next sc, 2 sc in next sc, sc in next 11 sc, 2 sc in next sc, (sc in next sc, 2 sc in next sc) 3 times: 25 sc.

Rnd 21: Sc in each sc around.

Rnd 22: 2 Sc in next sc, sc in next 16 sc, (2 sc in next sc, sc in next sc) 4 times: 30 sc.

Rnds 23 and 24: Sc in each sc around.

Rnd 25: (Sc in next sc, 2 sc in next sc) twice, sc in next 13 sc, 2 sc in next sc, (sc in next sc, 2 sc in next sc) 6 times: 39 sc.

Rnds 26-30: Sc in each sc around.

Rnd 31: Sc in next 2 sc, 2 sc in next sc, sc in next 16 sc, (2 sc in next sc, sc in next 3 sc) 5 times: 45 sc.

Rnds 32-35: Sc in each sc around; at end of Rnd 35, slip st in next sc, finish off leaving a long end for sewing.

TAIL

Rnd 1: With MC, ch 2, 6 sc in second ch from hook; do **not** join, place marker.

Rnd 2: (2 Sc in next sc, sc in next sc) around: 9 sc.

Rnds 3 and 4: Sc in each sc around.

Rnd 5: (2 Sc in next sc, sc in next 2 sc) around: 12 sc.

Rnds 6 and 7: Sc in each sc around.

Rnd 8: (2 Sc in next sc, sc in next 3 sc) around: 15 sc.

Rnds 9 and 10: Sc in each sc around.

Rnd 11: (2 Sc in next sc, sc in next 4 sc) around: 18 sc.

Rnds 12-15: Sc in each sc around.

Rnd 16: Sc in next 16 sc, leave remaining 2 sc unworked.

Note: Begin working in rows.

Row 1: Ch 1, turn; decrease, sc in next 12 sc, decrease: 14 sc.

Rows 2-5: Ch 1, turn; decrease, sc in each sc across to last 2 sc, decrease: 6 sc.

Note: Begin working in rounds.

Rnd 1: Ch 1, turn; sc in each sc across; work 6 sc evenly spaced across end of rows; sc in next 2 sc on Rnd 15; work 6 sc evenly spaced across end of rows; do **not** join, place marker: 20 sc.

Rnd 2: (Sc in next 4 sc, 2 sc in next sc) around: 24 sc.

Rnds 3 and 4: Sc in each sc around.

Note: Begin working in rows.

Row 1: Sc in next 2 sc, leave remaining 22 sc unworked.

Row 2: Ch 1, turn; decrease, sc in next 18 sc, decrease, leave remaining 2 sc unworked: 20 sc.

Rows 3-8: Ch 1, turn; decrease, sc in each sc across to last 2 sc, decrease; place marker around last st worked on Row 8: 8 sc.
Note: Begin working in rounds.

Rnd 1: Ch 1, turn; sc in each sc across; work 8 sc evenly spaced across end of rows; sc in next 2 sc on Row 1; work 7 sc evenly spaced across end of rows; do **not** join, place marker: 25 sc.

Rnd 2: (Sc in next 4 sc, 2 sc in next sc) around: 30 sc.

Rnd 3: Sc in next 3 sc, 2 sc in next sc, sc in next 13 sc, 2 sc in next sc, (sc in next 3 sc, 2 sc in next sc) 3 times: 35 sc.

Rnd 4: Sc in next 4 sc, 2 sc in next sc, sc in next 14 sc, 2 sc in next sc, (sc in next 4 sc, 2 sc in next sc) 3 times: 40 sc.

Rnd 5: Sc in next 4 sc, 2 sc in next sc, sc in next 19 sc, 2 sc in next sc, (sc in next 4 sc, 2 sc in next sc) 3 times; slip st in next sc, finish off leaving a long end for sewing: 45 sc.

RIGHT BACK LEG

Rnd 1: With Color A, ch 2, 6 sc in second ch from hook; do **not** join, place marker.

Rnd 2: 2 Sc in each sc around: 12 sc.

Rnd 3: (Sc in next 2 sc, 2 sc in next sc) around: 16 sc.

Rnd 4: (Sc in next 3 sc, 2 sc in next sc) around; slip st in next sc: 20 sc.

Rnd 5: Ch 1, **turn**; sc in FLO of first 3 sc *(Fig. 22, page 138)*, (slip st, ch 2, dc, ch 2, slip st) in BLO of next sc (toe), ★ sc in FLO of next sc, (slip st, ch 2, dc, ch 2, slip st) in BLO of next sc (toe); repeat from ★ 2 times **more**, sc in FLO of last 10 sc; join with slip st to first sc: 4 toes.

Rnd 6: Ch 1, **turn**; sc in both loops of first 10 sc, hdc in free loop of next sc on Rnd 4 (behind toe) *(Fig. 23a, page 138)*, (sc in next sc, hdc in free loop of next sc on Rnd 4) 3 times, sc in last 3 sc; join with slip st to first sc changing to MC *(Fig. 24b, page 138)*, place marker: 20 sts.

Rnds 7-10: Sc in each sc around.
Note: Begin working in rows.

Row 1: Sc in next 6 sc, remove marker, ch 1, turn; decrease, sc in next 13 sc, decrease, leave remaining 3 sc unworked: 15 sc.

Row 2: Ch 1, turn; sc in each sc across.

Row 3: Ch 1, turn; decrease, sc in each sc across to last 2 sc, decrease: 13 sc.

Rows 4-11: Repeat Rows 2 and 3, 4 times; at end of Row 11, finish off leaving a long end for sewing: 5 sc.

LEFT BACK LEG

Rnds 1-10: Work same as Right Back Leg.

Note: Begin working in rows.

Row 1: Sc in next sc, ch 1, turn; decrease, sc in next 13 sc, decrease, leave remaining 3 sc unworked: 15 sc.

Rows 2-11: Work same as Right Back Leg.

LEFT FRONT LEG

Rnd 1: With Color A, ch 2, 6 sc in second ch from hook; do **not** join, place marker.

Rnd 2: 2 Sc in each sc around: 12 sc.

Rnd 3: (Sc in next sc, 2 sc in next sc) around; slip st in next sc: 18 sc.

Rnd 4: Ch 1, turn; sc in FLO of first 2 sc, (slip st, ch 2, dc, ch 2, slip st) in BLO of next sc (toe), ★ sc in FLO of next sc, (slip st, ch 2, dc, ch 2, slip st) in BLO of next sc (toe); repeat from ★ 2 times **more**, sc in FLO of last 9 sc; join with slip st to first sc: 4 toes.

Rnd 5: Ch 1, turn; sc in both loops of first 9 sc, hdc in free loop of next sc on Rnd 3, (sc in next sc, hdc in free loop of next sc on Rnd 3) 3 times, sc in last 2 sc; join with slip st to first sc changing to MC, place marker: 18 sts.

Rnds 6-8: Sc in each sc around.

Note: Begin working in rows.

Row 1: Slip st in next sc, ch 1, turn; decrease, sc in next 10 sc, decrease, leave remaining 4 sts unworked: 12 sc.

Row 2: Ch 1, turn; sc in each sc across.

Row 3: Ch 1, turn; decrease, sc in each sc across to last 2 sc, decrease: 10 sc.

Rows 4-8: Repeat Rows 2 and 3 twice, then repeat Row 2 once **more**: 6 sc.

Row 9: Ch 1, turn; decrease across: 3 sc.

Row 10: Ch 1, turn; sc in each sc across; finish off leaving a long end for sewing.

RIGHT FRONT LEG

Rnds 1-8: Work same as Left Front Leg.

Note: Begin working in rows.

Row 1: Sc in next 5 sc, slip st in next sc, ch 1, turn; decrease, sc in next 10 sc, decrease, leave remaining 4 sc unworked: 12 sc.

Rows 2-10: Work same as Left Front Leg.

PLATES

LARGE (Make 10)

With Color A, ch 6 **loosely**.

Row 1 (Right side): Sc in second ch from hook and in each ch across: 5 sc.

Note: Loop a short piece of fabric around any stitch to mark last row as **right** side.

Row 2: Ch 1, turn; sc in each sc across.

Row 3: Ch 1, turn; decrease, sc in next sc, decrease: 3 sc.

Row 4: Ch 1, turn; sc in each sc across.

Row 5: Ch 1, turn; pull up a loop in each sc across, YO and draw through all 4 loops on hook; finish off.

Edging: With **right** side facing and working in end of rows, join Color A with slip st in first row; ch 1, 2 sc in same row, sc in next 3 rows, 3 sc in next row, sc in next 3 rows, 2 sc in last row; finish off leaving a long end for sewing.

SMALL (Make 8)

With Color A, ch 4 **loosely**.

Row 1 (Right side): Sc in second ch from hook and in each ch across: 3 sc.

Note: Mark last row as **right** side.

Row 2: Ch 1, turn; sc in each sc across.

Row 3: Ch 1, turn; pull up a loop in each sc across, YO and draw through all 4 loops on hook; finish off.

Edging: With **right** side facing and working in end of rows, join Color A with slip st in first row; ch 1, 2 sc in same row, sc in next row, 3 sc in next row, sc in next row, 2 sc in last row; finish off leaving a long end for sewing.

SPIKES

LARGE (Make 3)

Rnd 1: With Color A, ch 2, 6 sc in second ch from hook; do **not** join, place marker.

Rnds 2-5: Sc in each sc around.

Rnd 6: (Sc in next 2 sc, 2 sc in next sc) twice; slip st in next sc, finish off leaving a long end for sewing: 8 sc.

Stuff **lightly**.

SMALL (Make 2)

Work same as Large Spike through Rnd 4; at end of Rnd 4, slip st in next sc, finish off leaving a long end for sewing.

Stuff **lightly**.

FINISHING

Add eyes.

Stuff Head, Body, Tail, and Legs.

Using photo as a guide for placement, sew Tail to Body.

Sew Legs in place with toes facing forward.

Sew a Large Spike to tip of Tail.

Sew 2 Small Spikes on each side of Large Spike near Tail.

Sew remaining 2 Large Spikes on each side of Tail.

Starting at Tail and working toward Neck, with wrong side facing inward, sew a double row of Plates in the following sequence: 1 Small, 5 Large, 3 Small.

Quick POPPY POT HOLDER

With its familiar red and black colors, this vibrant poppy pot holder will brighten your kitchen. The easy-to-make pad is crocheted with rug yarn for extra durability.

Finished Size: Approximately 7¹/₂" in diameter

MATERIALS
Rug Yarn, approximately:
  MC (Red) - 40 yards
  CC (Black) - 5 yards
Crochet hook, size H (5.00 mm) **or** size needed for gauge

GAUGE: Rnds 1 and 2 (Center) = 2¹/₂"

CENTER

Rnd 1 (Right side): With CC, ch 2, 6 sc in second ch from hook; join with slip st to first sc.

Note: Loop a short piece of yarn around any stitch to mark last round as **right** side.

Rnd 2: Ch 3 **(counts as first dc, now and throughout)**, 2 dc in same st, 3 dc in next sc and in each sc around; join with slip st to first dc, finish off: 18 dc.

PETALS

Rnd 1: With **right** side facing and working in Back Loops Only **(Fig. 22, page 138)**, join MC with slip st in any dc; ch 3, dc in same st, 2 dc in each of next 2 dc, ch 1, (2 dc in each of next 3 dc, ch 1) around; join with slip st to both loops of first dc: 36 dc.

Rnd 2: Working in both loops, ch 3, dc in same st, 2 dc in each of next 5 dc, ch 1, (2 dc in each of next 6 dc, ch 1) around; join with slip st to first dc: 72 dc.

Rnd 3: Ch 3, dc in same st and in next 10 dc, 2 dc in next dc, ch 1, ★ 2 dc in next dc, dc in next 10 dc, 2 dc in next dc, ch 1; repeat from ★ around; join with slip st to first dc: 84 dc.

Rnd 4: Slip st in next 3 dc, ch 1, sc in same st, (ch 2, sc in next dc) 3 times, ch 8 (hanger), sc in next dc, (ch 2, sc in next dc) 3 times, skip next 6 dc, ★ sc in next dc, (ch 2, sc in next dc) 7 times, skip next 6 dc; repeat from ★ around; join with slip st to first sc, finish off.

Quick FOUR-SEASON FRIDGIES

Celebrate the joys of the seasons with this cute collection of magnets. Worked with worsted weight yarn, these attention-getters are ideal for posting notes and reminders or simply perking up the refrigerator door.

MATERIALS
Worsted Weight Yarn, approximately:
  15 to 30 yards **total** assorted colors for **each** Fridgie
Crochet hook, size F (3.75 mm)
Yarn needle
Finishing materials: Adhesive magnetic strips, glue, 6 mm and 3 mm black beads, paper clip or wire, 3" chenille stem, black and white embroidery floss, black buttons, and black felt

Note: Gauge is not important. Fridgies can be smaller or larger without changing the overall effect.

PATTERN STITCH
DECREASE
Pull up a loop in next 2 sts, YO and draw through all 3 loops on hook **(counts as one sc)**.

STRAWBERRY
BERRY (Make 2)
With Red, ch 4 **loosely**.
Row 1 (Right side)**:** Sc in second ch from hook and in each ch across: 3 sc.
*Note: Loop a short piece of yarn around any stitch to mark last row as **right** side.*
Row 2: Ch 1, turn; sc in each sc across.
Row 3: Ch 1, turn; 2 sc in first sc, sc in next sc, 2 sc in last sc: 5 sc.
Row 4: Ch 1, turn; 2 sc in first sc, sc in next 3 sc, 2 sc in last sc: 7 sc.
Rows 5-7: Ch 1, turn; sc in each sc across.
Row 8: Ch 1, turn; decrease, sc in next 3 sc, decrease: 5 sc.
Edging: Ch 1, turn; sc evenly around entire piece; join with slip st to first sc, finish off leaving a long end for sewing.

STEM AND LEAVES
With Green, ch 3 **loosely**, sc in second ch from hook and in next ch (Stem), ★ ch 4 **loosely**, slip st in second ch from hook, sc in next 2 chs; repeat from ★ 4 times **more**; finish off leaving a long end for sewing: 5 Leaves.

Whipstitch Berries together **(Fig. 28b, page 140)**.
Sew Stem and Leaves to top of Berry.

With Yellow, add straight stitches to front of Berry for seeds **(Fig. 33, page 141)**.
Attach a long magnetic strip to back.

BUTTERFLY
BODY
With Black, ch 3 **loosely**; being careful not to twist ch, join with slip st to form a ring.
Rnd 1 (Right side)**:** Ch 1, 2 sc in each ch around; do **not** join, place marker **(see Markers, page 138)**: 6 sc.
Rnds 2-9: Sc in each sc around.
Rnd 10: (Slip st in next sc, skip next sc) 3 times; join with slip st to first slip st, finish off.

WING (Make 8)
With Yellow, ch 3 **loosely**.
Row 1 (Right side)**:** Sc in second ch from hook and in next ch: 2 sc.
*Note: Loop a short piece of yarn around any stitch to mark last row as **right** side.*
Row 2: Ch 1, turn; 2 sc in each sc across: 4 sc.
Row 3: Ch 1, turn; sc in each sc across.
Row 4: Ch 1, turn; 2 sc in first sc, sc in next 2 sc, 2 sc in last sc: 6 sc.
Row 5: Ch 1, turn; sc in each sc across.
Row 6: Ch 1, turn; decrease, sc in next 2 sc, decrease: 4 sc.
Row 7: Ch 1, turn; sc in each sc across.
Row 8: Ch 1, turn; decrease twice; finish off: 2 sc.
Edging: With **right** side facing, join Black with slip st in any st; ch 1, sc evenly around entire piece; join with slip st to first sc, finish off leaving a long end for sewing.

Whipstitch 2 Wing pieces together **(Fig. 28b, page 140)**. Repeat for remaining Wings.
Using photo as a guide for placement, flatten Body and sew Wings to side of Body; tack 1" of top and bottom Wings together beginning at Body.
With black embroidery floss, embroider veins on Wings using Outline Stitch **(Figs. 32a & b, page 141)**.
With white embroidery floss, add French knots around outer edges of Wings **(Fig. 37, page 142)**.
Fold chenille stem in half and insert it into top of Body; tack in place and bend top of stem to form curves.
Attach a long magnetic strip to back.

Shovel driveway!

rake leaves!

BROWN-EYED SUSAN

FLOWER (Make 2)

With Brown, ch 3 **loosely**; being careful not to twist ch, join with slip st to form a ring.

Rnd 1 (Right side): Ch 1, 2 sc in each ch around; do **not** join, place marker *(see Markers, page 138)*: 6 sc.

Note: Loop a short piece of yarn around any stitch to mark last round as **right** side.

Rnd 2: 2 Sc in each sc around; slip st in next sc, finish off: 12 sc.

Rnd 3: With **right** side facing, join Yellow with slip st in same st as slip st, ★ ch 8 **loosely**, slip st in second ch from hook, sc in next ch, hdc in last 5 chs, slip st in next sc on Rnd 2; repeat from ★ around working last slip st in first sc; finish off leaving a long end for sewing: 12 petals.

LEAF (Make 2)

With Green, ch 9 **loosely**; 2 dc in third ch from hook and in each of next 2 chs, hdc in next 2 chs, sc in next ch, (sc, ch 2, sc) in last ch; working in free loops of beginning ch *(Fig. 23b, page 138)*, sc in next ch, hdc in next 2 chs, 2 dc in each of next 2 chs, 3 dc in next ch; join with slip st to top of beginning ch, finish off leaving a long end for sewing.

Whipstitch Brown-eyed Susan together *(Fig. 28b, page 140)*. Using photo as a guide for placement, sew Leaves to back of Flower.
Attach a long magnetic strip to back.

WATERMELON

With Pink, ch 3 **loosely**; being careful not to twist ch, join with slip st to form a ring.

Rnd 1 (Right side): Ch 1, 2 sc in each ch around; join with slip st to first sc: 6 sc.

Note: Loop a short piece of yarn around any stitch to mark last round as **right** side.

Rnds 2 and 3: Ch 1, turn; 2 sc in each sc around; join with slip st to first sc: 24 sc.

Rnd 4: Ch 1, turn; sc in first sc, 2 sc in next sc, (sc in next sc, 2 sc in next sc) around; join with slip st to first sc: 36 sc.

Rnds 5 and 6: Ch 1, turn; sc in each sc around; join with slip st to first sc.

Rnd 7: Ch 1, turn; sc in first 2 sc, 2 sc in next sc, (sc in next 2 sc, 2 sc in next sc) around; join with slip st to first sc: 48 sc.

Rnd 8: Ch 1, turn; sc in each sc around; join with slip st to first sc, finish off.

Rnd 9: With **wrong** side facing, join Light Green with slip st in first sc; ch 1, 2 sc in same st, sc in next 11 sc, (2 sc in next sc, sc in next 11 sc) around; join with slip st to first sc, finish off: 52 sc.

Rnd 10: With **right** side facing, join Dark Green with slip st in first sc; ch 1, 2 sc in same st, sc in next 3 sc, (2 sc in next sc, sc in next 3 sc) around; join with slip st to first sc, finish off leaving a long end for sewing: 65 sc.

Fold piece in half with **wrong** side to the inside and whipstitch edge together *(Fig. 28b, page 140)*.
Glue 3 mm beads to front.
Attach a long magnetic strip to back.

APPLE

BODY (Make 2)

With Red, ch 3 **loosely**; being careful not to twist ch, join with slip st to form a ring.

Rnd 1 (Right side): Ch 1, 2 sc in each ch around; do **not** join, place marker *(see Markers, page 138)*: 6 sc.

Note: Loop a short piece of yarn around any stitch to mark last round as **right** side.

Rnd 2: 2 Sc in each sc around: 12 sc.

Rnd 3: Sc in next 2 sc, (2 hdc in each of next 3 sc, sc in next 2 sc) twice: 18 sts.

Rnd 4: Sc in next 2 sc, 2 hdc in each of next 3 hdc, (sc in next 2 sts, 2 sc in next hdc) twice, sc in next 2 hdc, 2 hdc in each of next 3 hdc, sc in next 2 sc: 26 sts.

Rnd 5: Sc in next 2 sc, 2 hdc in each of next 3 hdc, sc in next 4 sts, (2 sc in each of next 2 sc, sc in next 4 sts) twice, 2 hdc in each of next 3 hdc, sc in next 2 sc; slip st in next sc, finish off leaving a long end for sewing: 36 sts.

STEM

With Brown, ch 4 **loosely**; 2 sc in second ch from hook, slip st in last 2 chs; finish off leaving a long end for sewing.

LEAF

With Green, ch 6 **loosely**; 2 hdc in third ch from hook, hdc in next ch, sc in next ch, (sc, ch 2, sc) in last ch; working in free loops of beginning ch *(Fig. 23b, page 138)*, sc in next ch, hdc in next ch, 2 hdc in next ch, slip st in next ch, ch 2 (stem); finish off leaving a long end for sewing.

Whipstitch Apple together *(Fig. 28b, page 140)*.
Sew Stem and Leaf to top of Apple.
Attach a long magnetic strip to back.

JACK-O'-LANTERN

PUMPKIN (Make 2)

With Orange, ch 3 **loosely**; being careful not to twist ch, join with slip st to form a ring.

Rnd 1 (Right side): Ch 1, 2 sc in each ch around; do **not** join, place marker *(see Markers, page 138)*: 6 sc.

Note: Loop a short piece of yarn around any stitch to mark last round as **right** side.

Rnd 2: 2 Sc in each sc around: 12 sc.
Rnd 3: (Sc in next 3 sc, 2 hdc in each of next 3 sc) twice: 18 sts.
Rnd 4: (Sc in next 3 sc, 2 sc in each of next 6 hdc) twice: 30 sc.
Rnd 5: ★ Sc in next 3 sc, (hdc in next sc, 2 hdc in next sc) 6 times; repeat from ★ once **more**; slip st in next sc, finish off leaving a long end for sewing: 42 sts.

STEM

With **right** side of one Pumpkin facing (front), join Green with slip st in same st as last slip st; ch 3, (2 dc, ch 3, slip st) in same st; finish off.

LEAF (Make 1 **each**: Yellow, Green, Red, and Brown)
Ch 7 **loosely**; slip st in second ch from hook and in next ch, (ch 2, slip st in second ch from hook and in next ch of beginning ch) 4 times; working in free loops of beginning ch *(Fig. 23b, page 138)*, slip st in next ch, (ch 2, slip st in second ch from hook and in next ch of beginning ch) 3 times; finish off leaving a long end for sewing.

Whipstitch Pumpkin together *(Fig. 28b, page 140)*.
Cut facial features from black felt using patterns and glue to front.
Using photo as a guide for placement, sew Leaves to Jack-O'-Lantern. Attach a long magnetic strip to back.

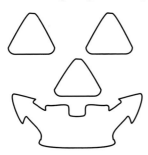

SKI HAT

Rnd 1 (Right side)**:** With Green, ch 4, 9 dc in fourth ch from hook; join with slip st in top of beginning ch changing to White, do **not** cut Green *(Fig. 24b, page 138)*: 10 sts.
Rnd 2: Ch 3 **(counts as first dc, now and throughout)**, dc in same st, 2 dc in next dc and in each dc around; join with slip st to first dc changing to Green: 20 dc.
Rnd 3: Ch 3, dc in next dc and in each dc around; join with slip st to first dc changing to White.
Rnd 4: Ch 3, dc in next 2 dc, 2 dc in next dc, (dc in next 3 dc, 2 dc in next dc) around; join with slip st to first dc changing to Green: 25 dc.
Rnd 5: Ch 3, dc in next dc and in each dc around; join with slip st to first dc.
Rnd 6: Ch 1, turn; sc in Back Loop Only of each dc around *(Fig. 22, page 138)*; join with slip st to first sc, finish off.

Using Green and White, make a 1¹/₂" pom-pom *(Figs. 29a & b, page 140)*. Sew pom-pom to top of Hat.

Flatten Hat and stitch opening closed.
Attach a long magnetic strip to back.

SNOWMAN

BODY (Make 2)
With White, ch 3 **loosely**; being careful to not twist ch, join with slip st to form a ring.
Rnd 1 (Right side)**:** Ch 1, 2 sc in each ch around; do **not** join, place marker *(see Markers, page 138)*: 6 sc.
Rnds 2 and 3: 2 Sc in each sc around: 24 sc.
Rnd 4: (Sc in next sc, 2 sc in next sc) around; slip st in next sc, finish off leaving a long end for sewing: 36 sc.

HEAD (Make 2)
Work same as Body through Rnd 3; at end of Rnd 3, slip st in next sc, finish off: 24 sc.

ARM (Make 2)
With Brown, ch 5 **loosely**, slip st in second ch from hook and in next ch, (ch 3, slip st in second ch from hook and in next ch) twice, slip st in last 2 chs of beginning ch-5; finish off leaving a long end for sewing.

NOSE
With Orange, ch 2, slip st in second ch from hook; finish off leaving a long end for sewing.

SCARF
With Red, ch 32 leaving 1¹/₂" of yarn at each end; finish off. Fray ends of yarn and trim.

EARMUFF (Make 2)
With Green, ch 3 **loosely**; being careful not to twist ch, join with slip st to form a ring.
Rnd 1 (Right side)**:** Ch 1, 2 sc in each ch around; do **not** join, place marker: 6 sc.
Rnd 2: 2 Sc in each sc around: 12 sc.
Rnd 3: Decrease 6 times; slip st in next sc, finish off leaving a long end for sewing: 6 sc.

Whipstitch Head together *(Fig. 28b, page 140)*.
Whipstitch Body together.
Using photo as a guide for placement, sew Head and Arms to Body. Sew Nose and Earmuffs to Head.
Glue 6 mm beads to Head and buttons to Body.
Cut paper clip or wire to measure approximately 3". Insert ends of wire into top of each Earmuff and glue in place curving wire approximately ¹/₄" above Head.
Tie Scarf around neck.
Attach a long magnetic strip to back.

rock-a-bye collection

Celebrate a little one's arrival with precious crocheted gifts and accessories. Our sweet collection includes booties to keep tiny toes toasty warm, snuggly afghans to wrap an infant in love, and a precious little lamb to guide baby to dreamland. Whether stitched for a boy or a girl, these creations are sure to become keepsakes of this wonderful occasion.

CUDDLY SET

*S*nuggly soft, this precious set will surround a little one with love. The gently textured afghan, worked in worsted weight brushed acrylic yarn, features cluster stitch variations and a delicate picot finish. The sweet lamb makes a cuddly bedtime buddy for baby.*

Finished Size: Afghan - approximately 35" x 35"
Lamb - approximately 7" tall

MATERIALS
Worsted Weight Brushed Acrylic Yarn, approximately:
  Afghan
    19 ounces, (540 grams, 855 yards)
  Lamb
    MC (White) - 2 ounces, (60 grams, 90 yards)
    Color A (Black) - ¹/₂ ounce, (15 grams, 25 yards)
    Color B (Lilac) - 7 yards
Crochet hooks, sizes E (3.50 mm) **and** H (5.00 mm) **or**
  sizes needed for gauge
¹/₂ yard of ³/₈" ribbon
Polyester fiberfill
Yarn needle

AFGHAN

PATTERN STITCHES
5-DC CLUSTER
★ YO, insert hook in dc indicated, YO and pull up a loop, YO and draw through 2 loops on hook; repeat from ★ 4 times **more**, YO and draw through all 6 loops on hook **(Figs. 10a & b, page 134)**.
PICOT
Ch 3, slip st in last sc worked.

GAUGE: With larger size hook, 12 dc = 4" and 5 rows = 3"

With larger size hook, ch 10; being careful not to twist ch, join with slip st to form a ring.
Rnd 1 (Right side)**:** Ch 6 **(counts as first dc plus ch 3, now and throughout)**, (5 dc in ring, ch 3) 3 times, 4 dc in ring; join with slip st to first dc: 20 dc.

Rnd 2: Slip st in first ch-3 sp, ch 6, 2 dc in same sp, dc in next 2 dc, work 5-dc Cluster in next dc, dc in next 2 dc, ★ (2 dc, ch 3, 2 dc) in next ch-3 sp, dc in next 2 dc, work 5-dc Cluster in next dc, dc in next 2 dc; repeat from ★ 2 times **more**, dc in same sp as first dc; join with slip st to first dc: 4 5-dc Clusters.

Rnd 3 AND ALL ODD NUMBERED RNDS THROUGH RND 25: Slip st in first ch-3 sp, ch 6, 2 dc in same sp, dc in each st across to next corner ch-3 sp, ★ (2 dc, ch 3, 2 dc) in corner ch-3 sp, dc in each st across to next corner ch-3 sp; repeat from ★ 2 times **more**, dc in same sp as first dc; join with slip st to first dc.

Rnd 4: Slip st in first ch-3 sp, ch 6, 2 dc in same sp, dc in next 3 dc, work 5-dc Cluster in next dc, dc in next 5 dc, work 5-dc Cluster in next dc, dc in next 3 dc, ★ (2 dc, ch 3, 2 dc) in next corner ch-3 sp, dc in next 3 dc, work 5-dc Cluster in next dc, dc in next 5 dc, work 5-dc Cluster in next dc, dc in next 3 dc; repeat from ★ 2 times **more**, dc in same sp as first dc; join with slip st to first dc: 8 5-dc Clusters.

Rnd 6: Slip st in first ch-3 sp, ch 6, 2 dc in same sp, dc in next 3 dc, work 5-dc Cluster in next dc, dc in next 13 dc, work 5-dc Cluster in next dc, dc in next 3 dc, ★ (2 dc, ch 3, 2 dc) in next corner ch-3 sp, dc in next 3 dc, work 5-dc Cluster in next dc, dc in next 13 dc, work 5-dc Cluster in next dc, dc in next 3 dc; repeat from ★ 2 times **more**, dc in same sp as first dc; join with slip st to first dc.

Rnd 8: Slip st in first ch-3 sp, ch 6, 2 dc in same sp, dc in next 3 dc, work 5-dc Cluster in next dc, (dc in next 10 dc, work 5-dc Cluster in next dc) twice, dc in next 3 dc, ★ (2 dc, ch 3, 2 dc) in next corner ch-3 sp, dc in next 3 dc, work 5-dc Cluster in next dc, (dc in next 10 dc, work 5-dc Cluster in next dc) twice, dc in next 3 dc; repeat from ★ 2 times **more**, dc in same sp as first dc; join with slip st to first dc: 12 5-dc Clusters.

Rnd 10: Slip st in first ch-3 sp, ch 6, 2 dc in same sp, ★ † dc in next 3 dc, work 5-dc Cluster in next dc, dc in next 11 dc, work 5-dc Cluster in next dc, dc in next 5 dc, work 5-dc Cluster in next dc, dc in next 11 dc, work 5-dc Cluster in next dc, dc in next 3 dc †, (2 dc, ch 3, 2 dc) in next corner ch-3 sp; repeat from ★ 2 times **more**, then repeat from † to † once, dc in same sp as first dc; join with slip st to first dc: 16 5-dc Clusters.

Rnd 12: Slip st in first ch-3 sp, ch 6, 2 dc in same sp, ★ † dc in next 3 dc, work 5-dc Cluster in next dc, dc in next 11 dc, work 5-dc Cluster in next dc, dc in next 13 dc, work 5-dc Cluster in next dc, dc in next 11 dc, work 5-dc Cluster in next dc, dc in next 3 dc †, (2 dc, ch 3, 2 dc) in next corner ch-3 sp; repeat from ★ 2 times **more**, then repeat from † to † once, dc in same sp as first dc; join with slip st to first dc.

Rnd 14: Slip st in first ch-3 sp, ch 6, 2 dc in same sp, ★ † dc in next 3 dc, work 5-dc Cluster in next dc, dc in next 11 dc, work 5-dc Cluster in next dc, (dc in next 10 dc, work

5-dc Cluster in next dc) twice, dc in next 11 dc, work 5-dc Cluster in next dc, dc in next 3 dc †, (2 dc, ch 3, 2 dc) in next corner ch-3 sp; repeat from ★ 2 times **more** then repeat from † to † once, dc in same sp as first dc; join with slip st to first dc: 20 5-dc Clusters.

Rnd 16: Slip st in first ch-3 sp, ch 6, 2 dc in same sp, ★ † dc in next 3 dc, work 5-dc Cluster in next dc, (dc in next 11 dc, work 5-dc Cluster in next dc) twice, dc in next 5 dc, work 5-dc Cluster in next dc, (dc in next 11 dc, work 5-dc Cluster in next dc) twice, dc in next 3 dc †, (2 dc, ch 3, 2 dc) in next corner ch-3 sp; repeat from ★ 2 times **more**, then repeat from † to † once, dc in same sp as first dc; join with slip st to first dc: 24 5-dc Clusters.

Rnd 18: Slip st in first ch-3 sp, ch 6, 2 dc in same sp, ★ † dc in next 3 dc, work 5-dc Cluster in next dc, dc in next 18 dc, work 5-dc Cluster in next dc, (dc in next 11 dc, work 5-dc Cluster in next dc) twice, dc in next 18 dc, work 5-dc Cluster in next dc, dc in next 3 dc †, (2 dc, ch 3, 2 dc) in next corner ch-3 sp; repeat from ★ 2 times **more**, then repeat from † to † once, dc in same sp as first dc; join with slip st to first dc: 20 5-dc Clusters.

Rnd 20: Slip st in first ch-3 sp, ch 6, 2 dc in same sp, ★ † dc in next 3 dc, work 5-dc Cluster in next dc, dc in next 27 dc, work 5-dc Cluster in next dc, dc in next 13 dc, work 5-dc Cluster in next dc, dc in next 27 dc, work 5-dc Cluster in next dc, dc in next 3 dc †, (2 dc, ch 3, 2 dc) in next corner ch-3 sp; repeat from ★ 2 times **more**, then repeat from † to † once, dc in same sp as first dc; join with slip st to first dc: 16 5-dc Clusters.

Rnd 22: Slip st in first ch-3 sp, ch 6, 2 dc in same sp, ★ † dc in next 3 dc, work 5-dc Cluster in next dc, dc in next 35 dc, work 5-dc Cluster in next dc, dc in next 5 dc, work 5-dc Cluster in next dc, dc in next 35 dc, work 5-dc Cluster in next dc, dc in next 3 dc †, (2 dc, ch 3, 2 dc) in next corner ch-3 sp; repeat from ★ 2 times **more**, then repeat from † to † once, dc in same sp as first dc; join with slip st to first dc.

Rnd 24: Slip st in first ch-3 sp, ch 6, 2 dc in same sp, dc in next 3 dc, work 5-dc Cluster in next dc, (dc in next 42 dc, work 5-dc Cluster in next dc) twice, dc in next 3 dc, ★ (2 dc, ch 3, 2 dc) in next corner ch-3 sp, dc in next 3 dc, work 5-dc Cluster in next dc, (dc in next 42 dc, work 5-dc Cluster in next dc) twice, dc in next 3 dc; repeat from ★ 2 times **more**, dc in same sp as first dc; join with slip st to first dc: 12 5-dc Clusters.

Rnd 26: Slip st in first ch-3 sp, ch 1, ★ (2 sc, work Picot, 2 sc) in corner ch-3 sp, sc in next dc, work Picot, (sc in next 3 dc, work Picot) across to within one dc of next corner ch-3 sp, sc in next dc; repeat from ★ around; join with slip st to first sc, finish off.

Continued on page 84.

Quick BABY'S BIBLE COVER

Enhanced with tiny pearls, this dainty cover is designed for holding baby's first Bible. The lacy jacket features a pretty shell pattern stitched in bedspread weight cotton thread.

Finished Size: Approximately 4³/4" x 7"

MATERIALS
    Bedspread Weight Cotton Thread (size 10), approximately 85 yards
    Steel crochet hook, size 7(1.65 mm) **or** size needed for gauge
    2 - 5" lengths of 1¹/2" satin ribbon
    Straight pins
    Sewing needle and thread
    35 - 3 mm pearls
    Bible: 3" wide x 4¹/2" long x ⁵/8" deep

GAUGE: 6 Shells and 10 rows = 2"

PATTERN STITCH
SHELL
(2 Dc, ch 2, sc) in st or sp indicated.

Ch 58 **loosely**.
Row 1 (Right side): (Dc, ch 2, sc) in fourth ch from hook, (skip next 2 chs, work Shell in next ch) across: 19 ch-2 sps.

Note: Loop a short piece of thread around any stitch to mark last row as **right** side.
Row 2: Turn; slip st in first ch-2 sp, ch 3 **(counts as first dc, now and throughout)**, (dc, ch 2, sc) in same sp, work Shell in each Shell (ch-2 sp) across: 19 Shells.
Rows 3-22: Repeat Row 2, 20 times.
Edging: Turn; slip st in first ch-2 sp, ch 3, (dc, ch 2, sc) in same sp, work Shell in each Shell across; working in end of rows, work Shell in first row, (skip next row, work Shell in next row) across to last row, work Shell in last row; working over beginning ch, work Shell in each ch-2 sp across; working in end of rows, work Shell in first row, (skip next row, work Shell in next row) across to last row, work Shell in last row; join with slip st to first dc, finish off: 62 Shells.

Fold cut ends of ribbons under ¹/4" and pin ribbons to wrong side of Cover with folded edges on Rows 1 and 22 and long edge along outer edge of Cover. Sew ribbons in place, stitching along folded edges and outer edges, leaving inside edge of each ribbon free.
Using photo as a guide for placement, sew pearls randomly to Cover.
Insert Bible.

CUDDLY SET

Continued from page 82.

LAMB

PATTERN STITCHES

DECREASE

Pull up a loop in next 2 sts, YO and draw through all 3 loops on hook **(counts as one sc)**.

3-DC CLUSTER

★ YO, insert hook in st indicated, YO and pull up a loop, YO and draw through 2 loops on hook; repeat from ★ 2 times **more**, YO and draw through all 4 loops on hook.

GAUGE: With smaller size hook, 10 sc and 10 rows = 2"

HEAD

Rnd 1 (Right side)**:** With smaller size hook and MC, ch 2, 8 sc in second ch from hook; do **not** join, place marker **(see Markers, page 138)**.

Rnd 2: 2 Sc in each sc around: 16 sc.

Rnd 3: (Sc in next sc, 2 sc in next sc) around: 24 sc.

Rnd 4: (Sc in next 2 sc, 2 sc in next sc) around: 32 sc.

Rnds 5-11: Sc in each sc around.

Rnd 12: Decrease around: 16 sc.

Rnd 13: Sc in each sc around; slip st in next sc, finish off leaving a long end for sewing.

Stuff **firmly**.

BODY

Rnds 1-4: Work same as Head: 32 sc.

Rnd 5: (Sc in next sc, work 3-dc Cluster in next sc) around to last 2 sc, decrease: 15 3-dc Clusters.

Rnd 6: Work 3-dc Cluster in next sc, (sc in next st, work 3-dc Cluster in next sc) around: 16 3-dc Clusters.

Rnd 7: Sc in next 3-dc Cluster, (work 3-dc Cluster in next sc, sc in next 3-dc Cluster) around: 15 3-dc Clusters.

Rnds 8-13: Repeat Rnds 6 and 7, 3 times.

Rnd 14: Sc in next 3 sts, (decrease, sc in next 2 sts) around: 24 sc.

Rnd 15: (Decrease, sc in next sc) around: 16 sc.

Stuff **firmly**.

Rnd 16: Decrease around: 8 sc.

Rnd 17: Decrease around; slip st in next sc, finish off leaving a long end for sewing: 4 sc.

Thread needle with end and weave through remaining sts; gather tightly and secure.

LEG (Make 4)

Rnd 1 (Right side)**:** With smaller size hook and Color A, ch 2, 6 sc in second ch from hook; do **not** join, place marker.

Rnd 2: 2 Sc in each sc around: 12 sc.

Rnd 3: Sc in next 2 sc, work 3-dc Cluster in each of next 2 sc (hoof), sc in each sc around: 12 sts.

Rnds 4 and 5: Sc in each st around.

Rnd 6: Sc in next 10 sc, decrease changing to MC **(Fig. 24a, page 138)**: 11 sc.

Rnds 7 and 8: Repeat Rnds 6 and 7 of Body: 5 3-dc Clusters.

Rnd 9: Sc in each st around.

Stuff **firmly**.

Rnd 10: Decrease, (sc in next sc, decrease) around; slip st in next sc, finish off leaving a long end for sewing: 7 sc.

MUZZLE

Rnd 1 (Right side)**:** With smaller size hook and Color A, ch 2, 6 sc in second ch from hook; do **not** join, place marker.

Rnd 2: 2 Sc in each sc around: 12 sc.

Rnd 3: Sc in each sc around.

Rnd 4: (Sc in next sc, 2 sc in next sc) around: 18 sc.

Rnd 5: Sc in each sc around; slip st in next sc, finish off leaving a long end for sewing.

EAR (Make 2)

With smaller size hook and Color A, ch 7 **loosely**.

Rnd 1 (Right side)**:** Sc in second ch from hook and in next ch, hdc in next 3 chs, 8 dc in last ch; working in free loops of beginning ch **(Fig. 23b, page 138)**, hdc in next 3 chs, sc in next 2 chs, ch 1; join with slip st to first sc, finish off leaving a long end for sewing.

TAIL

With smaller size hook and MC, ch 7 **loosely**.

Rnd 1 (Right side)**:** Sc in second ch from hook and in next ch, work 3-dc Cluster in next 3 chs, work 3-dc Cluster 3 times in last ch; working in free loops of beginning ch, work 3-dc Cluster in next 3 chs, sc in next 2 chs, ch 1; join with slip st to first sc, finish off leaving a long end for sewing.

FLOWER (Make 2)

Rnd 1: With smaller size hook and Color B, ch 4, 5 dc in fourth ch from hook; join with slip st to top of beginning ch: 6 sts.

Rnd 2 (Wrong side)**:** Ch 1, (2 dc, ch 1, slip st) in same st as joining, (slip st, ch 1, 2 dc, ch 1, slip st) in next dc and in each dc around pushing center to front; finish off leaving a long end for sewing.

FINISHING

Using photo as a guide for placement, sew Head to Body. Sew Muzzle to Head stuffing lightly before closing. Sew Ears to Head. Sew Tail and Flowers to Body. With MC, add Turkey Loop Stitch to top of Head between Ears **(Fig. 31, page 141)**. With Color A, add French Knot eyes **(Fig. 37, page 142)**. Sew Legs to Body with hooves facing forward. Tie ribbon in a bow around neck.

Quick FOR TINY TOES

Tiny toes will appreciate the warmth of these cozy booties. Ideal for shower gifts, both styles are made using baby fingering weight yarn for softness. The booties are trimmed with satin ribbons woven through eyelet rounds on the cuffs.

Finished Size: 3 to 6 months

MATERIALS
Baby Fingering Weight Yarn, approximately:
  Solid
    1½ ounces, (40 grams, 262 yards)
  Striped
    MC (White) - 1½ ounces, (40 grams, 262 yards)
    CC (Blue) - 11 yards
  Crochet hook, size D (3.25 mm) **or** size needed for gauge
  1 yard of ¼" ribbon for **each** pair

GAUGE: 12 dc and 6 rows = 2"

PATTERN STITCH
CLUSTER
★ YO, insert hook in sp indicated, YO and pull up a loop, YO and draw through 2 loops on hook; repeat from ★ once **more**, YO and draw through all 3 loops on hook *(Figs. 10a & b, page 134)*.

SOLID BOOTIE
SOLE
With MC, ch 14 **loosely**.

Rnd 1 (Right side): 3 Sc in second ch from hook, sc in next 3 chs, hdc in next 3 chs, dc in next 5 chs, 7 dc in last ch; working in free loops of beginning ch *(Fig. 23b, page 138)*, dc in next 5 chs, hdc in next 3 chs, sc in next 3 chs; join with slip st to first sc: 32 sts.

Note: Loop a short piece of yarn around any stitch to mark last round as **right** side.

Rnd 2: Ch 3 **(counts as first dc, now and throughout)**, turn; dc in same st and in next 11 sts, 2 dc in each of next 7 dc, dc in next 11 sts, 2 dc in each of last 2 sc; join with slip st to first dc: 42 dc.

Rnd 3: Ch 3, turn; 2 dc in next dc, dc in next dc, 2 dc in next dc, dc in next 12 dc, 2 dc in next dc, (dc in next dc, 2 dc in next dc) 6 times, dc in next 12 dc, 2 dc in last dc; join with slip st to Back Loop Only of first dc *(Fig. 22, page 138)*: 52 dc.

SIDES

Rnd 1: Ch 3, do **not** turn; dc in Back Loop Only of next dc and in each dc around; join with slip st to both loops of first dc.

Rnd 2: Ch 3, turn; dc in both loops of next dc and in each dc around; join with slip st to first dc.

Rnd 3: Ch 3, turn; dc in next 33 dc, place marker around last dc worked for Instep placement, dc in last 18 dc; join with slip st to first dc, finish off.

INSTEP

Row 1: With **wrong** side facing, join MC with slip st in marked dc; ch 3, dc in next 9 dc, leave remaining dc unworked: 10 dc.

Rows 2-4: Ch 3, turn; dc in next dc and in each dc across. Finish off leaving a long end for sewing.

With **right** side of Instep and Side together and beginning in seventh dc from Instep, sew Instep to Sides.

CUFF

Fold Bootie in half to find center back stitch.

Rnd 1: With **right** side facing, join MC with slip st in dc at center back; ch 1, sc in same st and in each dc across to Instep seam, sc in seam and in next 10 dc of Instep, sc in seam and in each dc around; join with slip st to first sc: 40 sc.

Rnd 2 (Eyelet rnd)**:** Ch 4, skip next sc, (dc in next sc, ch 1, skip next sc) around; join with slip st to third ch of beginning ch-4: 20 ch-1 sps.

Rnd 3: Ch 6, dc in same st, ch 2, skip next dc, ★ (dc, ch 3, dc) in next dc, ch 2, skip next dc; repeat from ★ around; join with slip st to third ch of beginning ch-6: 10 ch-3 sps.

Rnd 4: (Slip st, ch 2, dc, ch 3, work Cluster) in first ch-3 sp, ch 1, dc in next ch-2 sp, ch 1, ★ work (Cluster, ch 3, Cluster) in next ch-3 sp, ch 1, dc in next ch-2 sp, ch 1; repeat from ★ around; skip beginning ch-2 and join with slip st to first dc.

Rnd 5: Ch 1, ★ (hdc, 3 dc, hdc) in next ch-3 sp, ch 1, sc in next dc, ch 1; repeat from ★ around; join with slip st to first hdc, finish off.

Weave ribbon tie through Eyelet rnd.

STRIPED BOOTIE

Work same as Solid Bootie through Rnd 2 of Cuff.

Rnd 3: Ch 1, sc in same st, (ch 5, skip next dc, sc in next dc) around to last dc, ch 2, skip last dc, dc in first sc to form last loop: 10 loops.

Rnd 4: Ch 1, (sc, ch 2, 3 dc) in same loop, (sc in center ch of next loop, ch 2, 3 dc in same loop) around; join with slip st to first sc, finish off.

Rnd 5: With **wrong** side facing, join CC with slip st in first ch-2 sp; ch 2, 4 dc in same sp, (slip st, ch 2, 4 dc) in next ch-2 sp and in each ch-2 sp around; join with slip st to first slip st, finish off.

Rnd 6: With **right** side facing, join MC with slip st in first ch-2 sp; ch 4, slip st in third ch from hook, 4 dc in same ch-2 sp, ★ slip st in next ch-2 sp, ch 4, slip st in third ch from hook, 4 dc in same ch-2 sp; repeat from ★ around; join with slip st to first slip st, finish off.

Weave ribbon tie through Eyelet rnd.

Quick DOWNY-SOFT AFGHANS

*B*aby *is sure to have sweet dreams when covered with one of these downy-soft afghans. Worked holding two strands of baby fingering weight yarn, both feature a pretty "V" design that's created with front post treble crochets.*

Finished Size: Approximately 30" x 40"

MATERIALS

Baby Fingering Weight Yarn, approximately:
   Solid
      15 ounces, (430 grams, 2,140 yards)
   Striped
      MC (White) - 11 ounces, (310 grams, 1,570 yards)
      Color A (Blue) - 2 ounces, (60 grams, 285 yards)
      Color B (Pink) - 2 ounces, (60 grams, 285 yards)
Crochet hook, size K (6.50 mm) **or** size needed for gauge

Note: Entire Afghan is worked holding 2 strands of yarn together.

GAUGE: In pattern, 13 dc = 4" and 12 rows (1 repeat) = 4½"

BODY

*Note: For Striped Afghan, work in the following Color Sequence: 2 Rows using two strands MC (**Fig. 24a, page 138**), ★ 2 rows using one strand MC **and** one strand Color A, 2 rows using one strand MC **and** one strand Color B, 2 rows using two strands MC; repeat from ★ throughout.*

Ch 96 **loosely**.

Row 1 (Right side)**:** Dc in fourth ch from hook and in each ch across: 94 sts.

Row 2: Ch 1, turn; sc in each st across.

Row 3: Ch 3 **(counts as first dc, now and throughout)**, turn; dc in next sc, (ch 2, skip next 2 sc, dc in next 2 sc) across: 23 ch-2 sps.

Row 4: Ch 1, turn; sc in first 2 dc, (ch 2, sc in next 2 dc) across.

Row 5: Ch 1, turn; sc in first 2 sc, ★ working in **front** of ch-2 sps of previous 2 rows, work 2 FPtr around center sc in row **below** *(Fig. 18, page 136)*, sc in next 2 sc; repeat from ★ across: 46 FPtr.

Row 6: Ch 1, turn; sc in each sc and in each FPtr across.

Row 7: Ch 3, turn; dc in next sc and in each sc across.

Row 8: Ch 1, turn; sc in each dc across.

Row 9: Ch 3, turn; dc in next 3 sc, ch 2, (skip next 2 sc, dc in next 2 sc, ch 2) across to last 6 sc, skip next 2 sc, dc in last 4 sc: 22 ch-2 sps.

Row 10: Ch 1, turn; sc in first 4 dc, ch 2, (sc in next 2 dc, ch 2) across to last 4 dc, sc in last 4 dc.

Row 11: Ch 1, turn; sc in first 4 sc, working in **front** of ch-2 sps of previous 2 rows, work 2 FPtr around center sc in row **below**,

★ sc in next 2 sc, working in **front** of ch-2 sps of previous 2 rows, work 2 FPtr around center sc in row **below**; repeat from ★ across to last 4 sc, sc in last 4 sc: 44 FPtr.

Row 12: Ch 1, turn; sc in each sc and in each FPtr across.

Row 13: Ch 3, turn; dc in next sc and in each sc across.

Rows 14-104: Repeat Rows 2-13, 7 times, then repeat Rows 2-8 once **more**; do **not** finish off.

EDGING

Rnd 1: Ch 1, turn; (sc, ch 2, sc) in first sc, sc in each sc across to last sc, (sc, ch 2, sc) in last sc; work 122 sc evenly spaced across end of rows; working in free loops of beginning ch *(Fig. 23b, page 138)*, (sc, ch 2, sc) in first ch, sc in each ch across to last ch, (sc, ch 2, sc) in last ch; work 122 sc evenly spaced across end of rows; join with slip st to first sc: 436 sc.

Rnd 2: Slip st in first corner ch-2 sp, ch 1, ★ (sc, hdc, dc, hdc, sc) in corner sp, ch 1, [skip next 2 sc, (sc, dc, sc) in next sc, ch 1] across to within 1 sc of next corner ch-2 sp, skip next sc; repeat from ★ around; join with slip st to first sc, finish off.

*E*mbroidered bluebirds and daisies dress up these darling bubble suits for sizes 3, 6, and 12 months. Fashioned with sport weight yarn using simple crochet stitches, the wee wearables are ideal for playtime or outings to Grandma's house.

Finished Size: 3 months 6 months 12 months
Finished Length: 16" 18½" 21"

Size Note: Instructions are written for size 3 months with sizes 6 and 12 months in braces. Instructions will be easier to read if you circle all the numbers pertaining to your size.

MATERIALS
Sport Weight Yarn, approximately:
    MC (Blue or Pink) - 3{4½-5} ounces,
        [100{130-140} grams, 330{425-470} yards]
    CC (White) - 1¼{1½-1¾} ounces
        [35{40-50} grams, 120{140-165} yards]
    For embroidery:
        Pink Suit - small amount **each** Yellow and Green
        Blue Suit - small amount **each** Pink, Green, Gold,
            and Dark Blue
Crochet hook, size F (3.75 mm) **or** size needed for gauge
Yarn needle
6" length of snap tape for **each**
3 - ½" buttons **each**
Sulky® Solvy stabilizer
Sewing needle and thread

GAUGE: 20 dc and 10 rows = 4"
        sc, (ch 1, sc) 10 times and 19 rows = 4"

PATTERN STITCH
DECREASE
Working in sc and ch-1 sps, pull up a loop in next 2 sts, YO and draw through all 3 loops on hook (**counts as one sc**).

YOKE

With CC, ch 53{58-60} **loosely**.

Row 1 (Right side): Sc in second ch from hook and in each ch across: 52{57-59} sc.

Note: Loop a short piece of yarn around any stitch to mark last row as **right** side.

Row 2: Ch 3 (**counts as first dc, now and throughout**), turn; dc in next 2{2-3} sc, 2 dc in next sc, (dc in next 4 sc, 2 dc in next sc) across to last 3{3-4} sc, dc in last 3{3-4} sc: 62{68-70} dc.

Row 3: Ch 3, turn; dc in next 2{0-1} dc, 2 dc in next dc, (dc in next 4 dc, 2 dc in next dc) across to last 3{1-2} dc, dc in last 3{1-2} dc: 74{82-84} dc.

Row 4: Ch 3, turn; dc in next 3{1-2} dc, 2 dc in next dc, (dc in next 5 dc, 2 dc in next dc) across to last 3{1-2} dc, dc in last 3{1-2} dc: 86{96-98} dc.

Row 5: Ch 3, turn; dc in next 3{1-2} dc, 2 dc in next dc, (dc in next 6 dc, 2 dc in next dc) across to last 4{2-3} dc, dc in last 4{2-3} dc: 98{110-112} dc.

Row 6: Ch 3, turn; dc in next 4{2-3} dc, 2 dc in next dc, (dc in next 7 dc, 2 dc in next dc) across to last 4{2-3} dc, dc in last 4{2-3} dc: 110{124-126} dc.

Row 7: Ch 3, turn; dc in next 4{2-3} dc, 2 dc in next dc, (dc in next 8 dc, 2 dc in next dc) across to last 5{3-4} dc, dc in last 5{3-4} dc: 122{138-140} dc.

Row 8: Ch 3, turn; dc in next 5{3-4} dc, 2 dc in next dc, (dc in next 9 dc, 2 dc in next dc) across to last 5{3-4} dc, dc in last 5{3-4} dc: 134{152-154} dc.

Row 9: Ch 3, turn; dc in next 5{3-4} dc, 2 dc in next dc, (dc in next 10 dc, 2 dc in next dc) across to last 6{4-5} dc, dc in last 6{4-5} dc: 146{166-168} dc.

Row 10: Ch 3, turn; dc in next 6{4-5} dc, 2 dc in next dc, (dc in next 11 dc, 2 dc in next dc) across to last 6{4-5} dc, dc in last 6{4-5} dc: 158{180-182} dc.

Row 11: Ch 3, turn; dc in next 6{4-5} dc, 2 dc in next dc, (dc in next 12 dc, 2 dc in next dc) across to last 7{5-6} dc, dc in last 7{5-6} dc: 170{194-196} dc.

Size 12 Months Only - Row 12: Ch 3, turn; dc in next 6 dc, 2 dc in next dc, (dc in next 13 dc, 2 dc in next dc) across to last 6 dc, dc in last 6 dc: 210 dc.

All Sizes: Finish off.

BODY

Rnd 1: With **wrong** side facing, skip first 59{67-73} dc and join MC with slip st in next dc; ch 1, sc in same st, ch 1, (skip next dc, sc in next dc, ch 1) 26{29-31} times, skip next 32{38-42} dc (armhole), (sc in next dc, ch 1, skip next dc) 13{15-16} times; working across sts on left Back, sc in first dc, ch 1, (skip next dc, sc in next dc, ch 1) 13{14-15} times, skip last 32{38-42} dc (armhole); join with slip st to first sc: 54{60-64} sc.

Rnd 2: Ch 1, turn; sc in first ch-1 sp, ch 1, (skip next sc, sc in next ch-1 sp, ch 1) around; join with slip st to first sc.
Repeat Rnd 2 until piece measures approximately 11{13-15}" from beginning ch, ending by working a **wrong** side round.

BACK LEG SHAPING

Note: Begin working in rows.
Row 1: Ch 1, turn; slip st in first ch-1 sp, decrease beginning in next sc, ch 1, (skip next sc, sc in next ch-1 sp, ch 1) 24{27-29} times, skip next sc, decrease, leave remaining sts unworked: 26{29-31} sc.
Row 2 (Decrease row): Ch 1, turn; decrease, ch 1, (skip next sc, sc in next ch-1 sp, ch 1) across to last 2 sc, skip next sc, decrease: 25{28-30} sc.
Repeat Row 2, 6{7-8} times: 19{21-22} sc.
Next 3 Rows: Turn; slip st in first 4 sts, ch 1, sc in same ch-1 sp, (ch 1, skip next sc, sc in next ch-1 sp) across to last 2 sc, leave remaining sts unworked: 10{12-13} sc.
Next Row: Ch 1, turn; sc in first sc, (ch 1, skip next sc, sc in next ch-1 sp) across to last sc, sc in last sc.
Repeat last row until piece measures approximately 15{17½-20}" from beginning ch, ending by working a **wrong** side row, do **not** finish off.

LOWER BAND

Row 1: Ch 1, turn; sc in each sc and in each ch-1 sp across: 18{22-24} sc.
Rows 2-5: Ch 1, turn; sc in each sc across.
Finish off.

FRONT LEG SHAPING

Row 1: With **right** side facing, skip 3{5-7} sc from Back and join MC with slip st in next ch-1 sp; ch 1, sc in same sp, (ch 1, skip next sc, sc in next ch-1 sp) across to last 3{5-7} sc, leave remaining sts unworked: 21{20-18} sc.
Row 2 (Decrease row): Ch 1, turn; decrease, ch 1, (skip next sc, sc in next ch-1 sp, ch 1) across to last 2 sc, skip next sc, decrease: 20{19-17} sc.
Repeat Row 2, 10{7-4} times: 10{12-13} sc.

UPPER BAND

Row 1: Ch 1, turn; sc in first sc, (ch 1, skip next sc, sc in next ch-1 sp) across to last sc, sc in last sc.
Repeat Row 1 until piece measures approximately 15{17½-20}" from beginning ch, ending by working a **wrong** side row; do **not** finish off.

LOWER BAND

Work same as Back.

SLEEVE

Rnd 1: With **wrong** side facing, join MC with slip st in first dc on armhole; ch 1, sc in same st, ch 1, skip next dc, (sc in next dc, ch 1, skip next dc) around; join with slip st to first sc: 16{19-21} sc.
Rnd 2: Ch 1, turn; sc in first ch-1 sp, ch 1, (skip next sc, sc in next ch-1 sp, ch 1) around; join with slip st to first sc.
Repeat Rnd 2 until Sleeve measures approximately 1½{1¾-2}" from Yoke, ending by working a **wrong** side round.
Last Rnd: Ch 1, turn; sc in each sc and in each ch-1 sp around; join with slip st to first sc, finish off.
Repeat for second Sleeve.

FINISHING

LEG BAND

Row 1: With **right** side facing, join MC with slip st in end of last row on either Lower Band; ch 1, work 60{70-75} sc evenly spaced across Leg opening.
Row 2: Ch 1, turn; sc in first 2 sc, decrease, (sc in next 3 sc, decrease) across to last sc, sc in last sc: 48{56-60} sc.
Row 3: Ch 1, turn; sc in each sc across; finish off.
Repeat for second Leg opening.

BACK EDGING

Row 1: With **wrong** side facing; join CC with slip st in corner at left Back neck edge; ch 1, work 21{21-23} sc evenly spaced across end of rows, work 21{21-23} sc evenly spaced across end of rows of right Back: 42{42-46} sc.
For Girl's Only - Row 2: Ch 1, turn; sc in first sc, ch 3, skip next 2 sc (buttonhole), ★ sc in next 6{6-7} sc, ch 3, skip next 2 sc; repeat from ★ once **more**, sc in next sc, decrease, sc in each sc across; finish off.
For Boy's Only - Row 2: Ch 1, turn; sc in first 20{20-22} sc, decrease, sc in next sc, ch 3, skip next 2 sc (buttonhole), ★ sc in next 6{6-7} sc, ch 3, skip next 2 sc; repeat from ★ once **more**, sc in last sc; finish off.

Sew buttons to side opposite buttonholes.
Sew snap tape to each Lower Band, lapping Front over Back.
With MC, sew opening closed between Body and Sleeve.
Trace embroidery diagram of your choice from page 142 onto Sulky® Solvy stabilizer, using manufacturers instructions.
Centering design, baste stabilizer to front of Yoke. Embroider design on stabilizer. Remove stabilizer by tearing or cutting away large areas. Remaining stabilizer may be removed by submerging Bubble Suit in water for 30 seconds to 2 minutes, then shape and air dry.

FLORAL ENSEMBLE

*As pretty as a spring garden, this floral set will make mother and baby feel extra special.
The delightful throw is created holding two strands of yarn and enhanced with rows of dainty
flowers that are worked in as you stitch. A matching bottle cover completes the ensemble.*

Finished Size: Afghan - approximately 35" x 47"
Bottle Cover - approximately 6¹/₂" tall

MATERIALS
Baby Fingering Weight Yarn, approximately:
  Afghan
    MC (White) - 17 ounces, (480 grams, 2,430 yards)
    Color A (Yellow) - 8 ounces,
      (230 grams, 1,145 yards)
    Color B (Green) - ³/₄ ounce, (20 grams, 110 yards)

Bottle Cover
  MC (White) - ¹/₂ ounce, (15 grams, 70 yards)
  Color A (Yellow) - 30 yards
  Color B (Green) - 3 yards
Crochet hooks, sizes C (2.75 mm) **and** size H (5.00 mm)
  or sizes needed for gauge
¹/₂ yard of ¹/₈" ribbon
Yarn needle

PATTERN STITCH

DECREASE

YO, insert hook in **same** sc, YO and pull up a loop, YO and draw through 2 loops on hook, YO, skip next sc, insert hook in next sc, YO and pull up a loop, YO and draw through 2 loops on hook, YO and draw through all 3 loops on hook.

AFGHAN

GAUGE: With larger size hook, 8 sc = 2"

Note: Entire Afghan is worked holding 2 strands of yarn together.

BODY

With MC and larger size hook, ch 133 **loosely**.

Row 1 (Right side)**:** Dc in fourth ch from hook **(3 skipped chs count as first dc)** and in each ch across: 131 dc.

Note: Loop a short piece of yarn around any stitch to mark last row as **right** side.

Row 2: Ch 1, turn; sc in first dc, (dc in next dc, sc in next dc) across.

Row 3: Ch 3 **(counts as first dc, now and throughout)**, turn; dc in next st and in each st across.

Rows 4 and 5: Repeat Rows 2 and 3 changing to Color A at end of Row 5 *(Fig. 24a, page 138)*.

Row 6: Ch 1, turn; sc in each st across.

Row 7: Ch 1, turn; sc in first sc, (tr in next sc, sc in next sc pushing tr to right side) across.

Row 8: Ch 1, turn; sc in each st across changing to MC in last sc.

Rows 9 and 10: Ch 1, turn; sc in each sc across.

Row 11: Ch 1, turn; sc in first 8 sc changing to Color B in last sc worked, do **not** cut MC, ★ † sc in next sc, ch 10, slip st in tenth ch from hook, (ch 9, slip st in same ch) twice changing to MC in last st worked †, sc in next 18 sc changing to Color B in last sc worked, do **not** cut MC; repeat from ★ 5 times **more**, then repeat from † to † once, sc in last 8 sc: 21 loops.

Rows 12-14: Ch 1, turn; holding loops to **right** side, sc in each sc across: 131 sc.

Row 15: Ch 1, turn; sc in first 5 sc, ★ † holding next loop in front of next sc, sc in both loop **and** in sc, sc in next 5 sc, skip next loop, holding next loop in front of next sc, sc in both loop **and** in sc †, sc in next 12 sc; repeat from ★ 5 times **more**, then repeat from † to † once, sc in last 5 sc.

Rows 16-18: Ch 1, turn; sc in each sc across.

Row 19: Ch 1, turn; sc in first 8 sc changing to Color A in last sc worked, do **not** cut MC, ★ † dc in center loop, (ch 3, slip st in last dc worked, dc in same loop) 4 times changing to MC in last dc worked, skip next sc †, sc in next 18 sc changing to Color A in last sc worked, do **not** cut MC; repeat from ★ 5 times **more**, then repeat from † to † once, sc in last 8 sc: 7 flowers.

Row 20: Ch 1, turn; sc in first 8 sc, ch 1, skip next flower, (sc in next 18 sc, ch 1, skip next flower) across to last 8 sc, sc in last 8 sc: 124 sc.

Row 21: Ch 1, turn; sc in first 8 sc, holding flower in front of next ch-1 sp, sc in both Back Loop Only of center dc **and** in ch-1 sp *(Fig. 22, page 138)*, ★ sc in next 18 sc, holding flower in front of next ch-1 sp, sc in both Back Loop Only of center dc **and** in ch-1 sp; repeat from ★ across to last 8 sc, sc in last 8 sc: 131 sc.

Rows 22 and 23: Ch 1, turn; sc in each sc across changing to Color A at end of Row 23.

Rows 24-26: Repeat Rows 6-8.

Row 27: Ch 3, turn; dc in next sc and in each sc across.

Rows 28-47: Repeat Rows 2 and 3, 10 times.

Rows 48-157: Repeat Rows 6-47 twice, then repeat Rows 6-31 once **more**.

Finish off.

EDGING

Rnd 1: With **wrong** side facing, join Color A with slip st in any corner st; ch 1, sc evenly around working 3 sc in each corner (total sc must be a multiple of 2); join with slip st to Front Loop Only of first sc.

Rnd 2: Ch 6, turn; dc in fourth ch from hook, working in Back Loops Only, (decrease, ch 4, dc in top of decrease) around to last sc, dc in same st as last decrease, skip last sc; join with slip st to second ch of beginning ch-6, finish off.

Rnd 3: With **right** side facing, holding Rnd 2 forward, and working in free loops of Rnd 1 *(Fig. 23a, page 138)*, join Color A with slip st in first sc; ch 6, dc in fourth ch from hook, (decrease, ch 4, dc in top of decease) around to last sc, dc in same st as last decrease, skip last sc; join with slip st to second ch of beginning ch-6, finish off.

BOTTLE COVER

GAUGE: With smaller size hook, Rnds 1-3 of Bottom = 2"
 11 sc = 2"

BOTTOM

With smaller size hook and MC, ch 2; join with slip st to form a ring.

Rnd 1 (Right side)**:** Ch 3 **(counts as first dc, now and throughout)**, 11 dc in ring; join with slip st to first dc: 12 dc.

Note: Loop a short piece of yarn around any stitch to mark last round as **right** side.

Rnd 2: Ch 3, dc in same st, 2 dc in each dc around; join with slip st to first dc: 24 dc.

Rnd 3: Ch 3, 2 dc in next dc, (dc in next dc, 2 dc in next dc) around; join with slip st to first dc: 36 dc.

SIDES

Rnd 1: Slip st from **back** to **front** around post of first dc, ch 3, work BPdc around next dc and around each dc around *(Fig. 17, page 136)*; join with slip st to first dc.

Rnd 2: Ch 1, turn; sc in first st, dc in next st, (sc in next st, dc in next st) around; join with slip st to first sc.

Rnd 3: Ch 3, turn; dc in next st and in each st around; join with slip st to first dc.

Rnds 4 and 5: Repeat Rnds 2 and 3 changing to Color A at end of Rnd 5 *(Fig. 24b, page 138)*.

Rnd 6: Ch 1, turn; sc in each st around; join with slip st to first sc.

Rnd 7: Ch 1, turn; sc in first sc, tr in next sc, (sc in next sc pushing tr to right side, tr in next sc) around; join with slip st to first sc.

Rnd 8: Ch 1, turn; sc in each st around; join with slip st to first sc changing to MC.

Rnds 9 and 10: Ch 1, turn; sc in each sc around; join with slip st to first sc.

Rnd 11: Ch 1, turn; sc in first 6 sc changing to Color B in last sc worked, do **not** cut MC, ★ † sc in next sc, ch 10, slip st in tenth ch from hook, (ch 9, slip st in same ch) twice changing to MC in last st worked †, sc in next 11 sc changing to Color B in last sc worked, do **not** cut MC; repeat from ★ once **more**, then repeat from † to † once, sc in last 5 sc; join with slip st to first sc: 9 loops.

Rnds 12-14: Ch 1, turn; holding loops to **right** side, sc in each sc around; join with slip st to first sc: 36 sc.

Rnd 15: Ch 1, turn; sc in first 3 sc, ★ † holding next loop in front of next sc, sc in both loop **and** in sc, sc in next 5 sc, skip next loop, holding next loop in front of next sc, sc in both loop **and** in sc †, sc in next 5 sc; repeat from ★ once **more**, then repeat from † to † once, sc in last 2 sc; join with slip st to first sc.

Rnds 16-18: Ch 1, turn; sc in each sc around; join with slip st to first sc.

Rnd 19: Ch 1, turn; sc in first 6 sc changing to Color A in last sc worked, do **not** cut MC, ★ † dc in center loop, (ch 3, slip st in last dc worked, dc in same loop) 4 times changing to MC in last dc worked, skip next sc †, sc in next 11 sc changing to Color A in last sc worked, do **not** cut MC; repeat from ★ once **more**, then repeat from † to † once, sc in last 5 sc; join with slip st to first sc: 3 flowers.

Rnd 20: Ch 1, turn; sc in first 6 sc, ch 1, skip next flower, (sc in next 11 sc, ch 1, skip next flower) twice, sc in last 5 sc; join with slip st to first sc: 33 sc.

Rnd 21: Ch 1, turn; sc in first 6 sc, holding flower in front of next ch-1 sp, sc in both Back Loop Only of center dc **and** in ch-1 sp *(Fig. 22, page 138)*, ★ sc in next 11 sc, holding flower in front of next ch-1 sp, sc in both Back Loop Only of center dc **and** in ch-1 sp; repeat from ★ once **more**, sc in last 5 sc; join with slip st to first sc: 36 sc.

Rnds 22 and 23: Ch 1, turn; sc in each sc around; join with slip st to first sc changing to Color A at end of Rnd 23.

Rnds 24-26: Repeat Rnds 6-8.

Rnd 27: Ch 3, turn; dc in next sc and in each sc around; join with slip st to first dc.

Rnds 28-31: Repeat Rnds 2-5.

Rnd 32: Ch 1, do **not** turn; sc in each dc around; join with slip st to Front Loop Only of first sc.

Rnd 33: Ch 6, turn; dc in fourth ch from hook, working in Back Loops Only, (decrease, ch 4, dc in top of decrease) around to last sc, dc in same st as last decrease, skip last sc; join with slip st to second ch of beginning ch-6, finish off.

Rnd 34: With **right** side facing, holding Rnd 33 forward, and working in free loops of Rnd 32 *(Fig. 23a, page 138)*, join Color A with slip st in first sc; ch 6, dc in fourth ch from hook, (decrease, ch 4, dc in top of decease) around to last sc, dc in same st as last decrease; join with slip st to second ch of beginning ch-6, finish off.

Weave ribbon through dc on Rnd 31 and tie in a bow.

fashion corner

Wake up your wardrobe with these stylish crocheted wearables. From a light spring cardigan for her or a cozy winter sweater for him to fanciful footwear for children, there's something to brighten everyone's day. This crocheted collection makes a fashion forecast for fun!

DELICATE CARDIGAN

*M*ake a statement for style when you wear this feminine cardigan! The airy cover-up — designed for small, medium, and large sizes — uses clusters to create its delicate motifs. Stitched in neutral with cotton thread, it can be worn during any season.

Size:	Small	Medium	Large
Finished Chest			
Measurement:	36"	42"	48"

Size Note: Instructions are written for size Small with sizes Medium and Large in braces. Instructions will be easier to read if you circle all the numbers pertaining to your size.

MATERIALS
Cotton Crochet Thread (size 5), approximately:
   24{27-29} ounces, [680{770-820} grams,
      2,060{2,315-2,485} yards]
Crochet hook, size E (3.50 mm) **or** size needed for gauge
5 - ³/₈" buttons
Sewing needle and thread

GAUGE: Rnds 1 and 2 of Motif (Flower) = 1³/₄"
   One Motif slightly stretched = 3"

PATTERN STITCHES
BEGINNING CLUSTER
Ch 2, ★ YO, insert hook in same sp, YO and pull up a loop, YO and draw through 2 loops on hook; repeat from ★ once **more**, YO and draw through all 3 loops on hook **(Figs. 10a & b, page 134)**.

CLUSTER
★ YO, insert hook in sp indicated, YO and pull up a loop, YO and draw through 2 loops on hook; repeat from ★ 2 times **more**, YO and draw through all 4 loops on hook.
SCALLOP
Slip st in st indicated, ch 3, 2 dc in same st.

MOTIF [Make 134{154-164}]
Ch 6; join with slip st to form a ring.
Rnd 1 (Right side)**:** Ch 6, (dc in ring, ch 3) 7 times; join with slip st to third ch of beginning ch-6: 8 ch-3 sps.
Note: Loop a short piece of thread around any stitch to mark last round as **right** side.
Rnd 2: Slip st in first ch-3 sp, (ch 1, sc, ch 2, 3 dc, ch 2, sc) in same sp and in each ch-3 sp around, sc in first sc to form last sp: 8 Petals.
Rnd 3: Ch 1, sc in same sp, ch 5, (sc in next ch-1 sp between Petals, ch 5) around; join with slip st to first sc: 8 loops.
Rnd 4: Slip st in first loop, work (beginning Cluster, ch 3, Cluster) in same sp, ch 5, sc in next loop, ch 5, ★ work (Cluster, ch 3, Cluster) in next loop, ch 5, sc in next loop, ch 5; repeat from ★ around; join with slip st to top of beginning Cluster.

Rnds 5 and 6: Slip st in first ch-3 sp, work (beginning Cluster, ch 3, Cluster) in same sp, ch 5, ★ (sc in next loop, ch 5) across to next ch-3 sp, work (Cluster, ch 3, Cluster) in ch-3 sp, ch 5; repeat from ★ 2 times **more**, (sc in next loop, ch 5) across; join with slip st to top of beginning Cluster. Finish off.

HALF MOTIF [Make 6{2-6}]

Ch 4; join with slip st to form a ring.
Row 1: Ch 6, dc in ring, (ch 3, dc in ring) 4 times: 5 sps.
Row 2 (Right side)**:** Turn; slip st in first ch-3 sp, (ch 1, sc, ch 2, 3 dc, ch 2, sc) in same sp and in each sp across: 5 Petals.
Note: Mark last row as **right** side.
Row 3: Ch 1, turn; sc in first sc, ch 5, (sc in next ch-1 sp between Petals, ch 5) across, sc in last sc: 5 loops.
Row 4: Turn; slip st in first loop, work (beginning Cluster, ch 3, Cluster) in same loop, ★ ch 5, sc in next loop, ch 5, work (Cluster, ch 3, Cluster) in next loop; repeat from ★ once **more**.
Rows 5 and 6: Turn; slip st in first ch-3 sp, work (beginning Cluster, ch 3, Cluster) in same sp, ★ ch 5, (sc in next loop, ch 5) across to next ch-3 sp, work (Cluster, ch 3, Cluster) in ch-3 sp; repeat from ★ once **more**.
Finish off.

ASSEMBLY

Using Placement Diagram as a guide, join Motifs and Half Motifs together forming strips, then join strips, leaving edges of Motifs along dotted lines unjoined.

Join Motifs as follows:
With **right** sides together and working through **both** pieces, join thread with slip st in corner ch-3 sp; ch 1, sc in same sp, ch 4, (sc in next loop, ch 4) across to next corner ch-3 sp, sc in corner ch-3 sp; finish off.

Join strips as follows:
With **right** sides together and working through **both** pieces, join thread with slip st in corner ch-3 sp; ch 1, sc in same sp, ch 4, (sc in next loop, ch 4) across to next corner ch-3 sp, sc in corner ch-3 sp, ★ ch 1, sc in corner ch-3 sp of next Motif, ch 4, (sc in next loop, ch 4) across to next corner ch-3 sp, sc in corner ch-3 sp; repeat from ★ across; finish off.

Small and Large Sizes Only
Join underarm and side seams in same manner as joining strips.

Medium Size Only
Beginning at bottom edge, join Front to Back at side, in the same manner as joining strips. Join underarm from wrist to center of sixth Motif, then join top of last Motif to Sleeve.

Repeat for second side.

PLACEMENT DIAGRAMS

Small

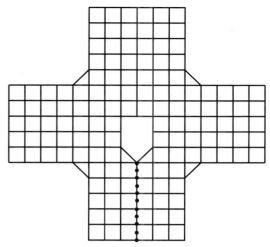

Medium

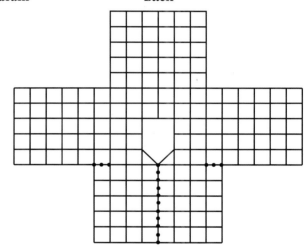

Large

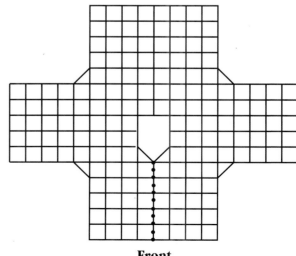

Continued on page 98.

Quick FEMININE SCARF

Welcome chilly weather with this classy mini muffler! Worked in shell stitches to create its familiar pineapple pattern, the toasty neck-warmer makes a chic accent. It's fast to finish, so you can make several to coordinate with all of your outerwear.

Finished Size: Approximately 5" x 32"

MATERIALS
Sport Weight Yarn, approximately:
  1¼ ounces, (35 grams, 120 yards)
  Crochet hook, size H (5.00 mm) **or** size needed for gauge

GAUGE: Rows 1-9 = 5"

PATTERN STITCHES
BEGINNING SHELL
Ch 3 **(counts as first dc, now and throughout)**,
(dc, ch 1, 2 dc) in same sp.
SHELL
(2 Dc, ch 1, 2 dc) in sp indicated.
PICOT
Ch 3, slip st in third ch from hook.

FIRST HALF
Ch 17 **loosely**.
Row 1: Sc in second ch from hook, (ch 3, skip next 2 chs, sc in next ch) across: 5 ch-3 sps.
Row 2 (Right side): Turn; slip st in first ch-3 sp, work beginning Shell, ch 1, skip next ch-3 sp, 6 tr in next ch-3 sp, ch 1, skip next ch-3 sp, work Shell in last ch-3 sp.
Note: Loop a short piece of yarn around any stitch to mark last row as **right** side.
Row 3: Turn; slip st in first 2 dc and in next ch-1 sp, work beginning Shell, ch 1, sc in next tr, (ch 3, sc in next tr) 5 times, ch 1, work Shell in next Shell (ch-1 sp).
Row 4: Turn; slip st in first 2 dc and in next ch-1 sp, work beginning Shell, ch 1, sc in next ch-3 sp, (ch 3, sc in next ch-3 sp) 4 times, ch 1, work Shell in next Shell.

Row 5: Turn; slip st in first 2 dc and in next ch-1 sp, work beginning Shell, ch 2, sc in next ch-3 sp, (ch 3, sc in next ch-3 sp) 3 times, ch 2, work Shell in next Shell.

Row 6: Turn; slip st in first 2 dc and in next ch-1 sp, work beginning Shell, ch 2, sc in next ch-3 sp, (ch 3, sc in next ch-3 sp) twice, ch 2, work Shell in next Shell.

Row 7: Turn; slip st in first 2 dc and in next ch-1 sp, work beginning Shell, ch 3, (sc in next ch-3 sp, ch 3) twice, work Shell in next Shell.

Row 8: Turn; slip st in first 2 dc and in next ch-1 sp, work beginning Shell, ch 4, skip next ch-3 sp, sc in next ch-3 sp, ch 4, work Shell in next Shell.

Row 9: Turn; slip st in first 2 dc and in next ch-1 sp, work beginning Shell, ch 3, skip next 2 ch-4 sps, work Shell in next Shell.

Row 10: Turn; slip st in first 2 dc and in next ch-1 sp, work beginning Shell, ch 1, 6 tr in next ch-3 sp, ch 1, work Shell in next Shell.

Rows 11-25: Repeat Rows 3-10 once, then repeat Rows 3-9 once **more**.

Row 26: Turn; slip st in first 2 dc and in next ch-1 sp, work beginning Shell, skip next ch-3 sp, work Shell in next Shell.

Row 27: Turn; slip st in first 2 dc and in next ch-1 sp, ch 3, slip st in next Shell.

Row 28: Turn; slip st in ch-3 sp, work beginning Shell, finish off.

SECOND HALF

Row 1: With **right** side facing and working over beginning ch, join yarn with slip st in first ch-3 sp; work beginning Shell in same sp, ch 1, skip next ch-3 sp, 6 tr in next ch-3 sp, ch 1, skip next ch-3 sp, work Shell in last ch-3 sp.

Rows 2-24: Work same as First Half, Rows 3-10 twice, then repeat Rows 3-9 once **more**.

Rows 25-27: Work same as First Half, Rows 26-28.

EDGING

With **right** side facing, join yarn with slip st in first dc on either point; ch 1, sc in same st, work Picot, ★ skip next dc, sc in next ch-1 sp, work Picot 3 times, sc in same sp, work Picot, skip next dc, sc in next dc, work Picot; working in end of rows, (sc in top of next dc, work Picot) across to beginning ch-3 sp, (sc, work Picot) twice in ch-3 sp, (sc in top of next dc, work Picot) across; repeat from ★ once **more**; join with slip st to first sc, finish off.

DELICATE CARDIGAN

Continued from page 96.

EDGING

Rnd 1: With **right** side facing, join thread with slip st in corner ch-3 sp of bottom left front; ch 1, 3 sc in same sp, sc in next Cluster, 3 sc in next loop, (sc in next sc, 3 sc in next loop) 3 times, sc in next Cluster, ★ sc in next 2 ch-3 sps, sc in next Cluster, 3 sc in next loop, (sc in next sc, 3 sc in next loop) 3 times, sc in next Cluster; repeat from ★ across to next corner ch-3 sp, 3 sc in corner ch-3 sp, † sc in next Cluster, 3 sc in next loop, (sc in next sc, 3 sc in next loop) 3 times, sc in next Cluster, sc in next 2 ch-3 sps †, repeat from † to † across to next Half Motif, sc in next Cluster, work 25 sc evenly spaced across end of rows, sc in next Cluster, sc in next 3 ch-3 sps, (repeat from † to † twice, sc in next ch-3 sp) 3 times, sc in next Cluster, work 25 sc evenly spaced across end of rows, sc in next Cluster, sc in next 2 ch-3 sps, repeat from † to † 4 times, sc in next Cluster, 3 sc in next loop, (sc in next sc, 3 sc in next loop) 3 times, sc in next Cluster; join with slip st to first sc: 596{634-672} sc.

Rnd 2: Ch 1, sc in first sc, 2 sc in next sc, sc in each sc across bottom edge to next corner sc, 2{3-2} sc in corner sc, sc in next 17 sc, ch 3 (buttonhole), skip next 3 sc, (sc in next 16 sc, ch 3, skip next 3 sc) 4 times, sc in next sc, 3 sc in next sc, sc in next 174 sc, 3 sc in next sc, sc in each sc across; join with slip st to first sc: 587{626-663} sc.

Rnd 3: Ch 3, 2 dc in same st, (skip next 2 sc, work Scallop in next sc) across to first buttonhole, skip next ch-3 sp, ★ work Scallop in next sc, (skip next 2 sc, work Scallop in next sc) 5 times, skip next ch-3 sp; repeat from ★ 3 times **more**, (work Scallop in next sc, skip next 2 sc) across; join with slip st to base of beginning ch-3, finish off: 199{212-225} Scallops.

CUFF

Rnd 1: With **right** side facing, join thread with slip st in ch-3 sp to **right** of any joining on Sleeve; ch 1, sc in same sp and in next ch-3 sp, 3 sc in each of next 4 loops, (sc in next 2 ch-3 sps, 3 sc in each of next 4 loops) around; join with slip st to first sc: 70 sc.

Rnds 2 and 3: Ch 1, 2 sc in first sc, sc next sc and in each sc around; join with slip st to first sc: 72 sc.

Rnd 4: Ch 3, 2 dc in same st, skip next 2 sc, (work Scallop in next sc, skip next 2 sc) around; join with slip st to base of beginning ch-3, finish off: 24 Scallops.

Repeat for second Cuff.

Sew buttons opposite buttonholes.

HIS·AND·HERS PULLOVERS

Make one to share and one to wear when you stitch these pullovers for him or her. Cozy additions to a cool-weather wardrobe, they're fashioned with worsted weight yarn and finished with classic ribbing. Instructions are given for sizes 32 to 46.

Size: 32 34 36 38 40 42 44 46
Finished Chest
   Measurement: 36" 38" 40" 42" 44" 46" 48" 50"

Size Note: Instructions are written for sizes 32, 34, 36, and 38 in first braces with sizes 40, 42, 44 and 46 in second braces. Instructions will be easier to read if you circle all the numbers pertaining to your size.

MATERIALS
Worsted Weight Yarn, approximately:
   {21-22-23-24}{25-26-28-29} ounces,
     [{600-620-650-680}{710-740-800-820} grams,
   {1,380-1,445-1,510-1,575}
   {1,640-1,705-1,840-1,905} yards]
Crochet hook, size I (5.50 mm) **or** size needed for gauge
Yarn needle

GAUGE: In pattern, 14 sts and 10 rows = 4"

PATTERN STITCH
DECREASE
★ YO, insert hook in **next** sc, YO and pull up a loop, YO and draw through 2 loops on hook; repeat from ★ once **more**, YO and draw through all 3 loops on hook **(counts as one dc)**.

BACK

Ch {65-69-73-75}{79-83-87-89} sts **loosely**.
Row 1 (Right side): Dc in fourth ch from hook and in each ch across: {63-67-71-73}{77-81-85-87} sts.
Note: Loop a short piece of yarn around any stitch to mark last row as **right** side.
Row 2: Ch 1, turn; sc in first dc, dc in next dc, (slip st in next dc, dc in next dc) across to last st, sc in last st.
Row 3: Ch 3 **(counts as first dc, now and throughout)**, turn; [YO, insert hook in same st, YO and pull up a loop, YO and draw through 2 loops on hook, YO, insert hook in next dc, YO and pull up a loop, YO and draw through 2 loops on hook, YO and draw through all 3 loops on hook **(counts as one dc)**], dc in next st and in each st across.
Repeat Rows 2 and 3 for pattern until Back measures approximately {21-21½-22-22½}{23-23½-24-24½}", ending by working a **wrong** side row.

RIGHT NECK SHAPING

Row 1: Work in pattern across {19-21-23-23}{25-27-29-29} sts, leave remaining sts unworked.
Rows 2-4: Work across in pattern.
Finish off.

LEFT NECK SHAPING

Row 1: With **right** side facing, skip {25-25-25-27}{27-27-27-29} sts from Right Neck Shaping and join yarn with slip st in next st; work across in pattern: {19-21-23-23}{25-27-29-29} sts.
Rows 2-4: Work across in pattern.
Finish off.

FRONT

Work same as Back until Front measures approximately {19½-20-20½-21}{21½-22-22½-23}", ending by working a **wrong** side row.

LEFT NECK SHAPING

Row 1: Work in pattern across {19-21-23-23}{25-27-29-29} sts, leave remaining sts unworked.
Rows 2-8: Work across in pattern.
Finish off.

RIGHT NECK SHAPING

Row 1: With **right** side facing, skip {25-25-25-27}{27-27-27-29} sts from Left Neck Shaping and join yarn with slip st in next st; work across in pattern: {19-21-23-23}{25-27-29-29} sts.
Rows 2-8: Work across in pattern.
Finish off.

SLEEVE (Make 2)

Ch {39-39-41-41}{43-43-45-45} sts **loosely**.
Row 1 (Right side): Dc in fourth ch from hook and in each ch across: {37-37-39-39}{41-41-43-43} sts.
Note: Mark last row as **right** side.
Row 2: Ch 1, turn; sc in first dc, dc in next dc, (slip st in next dc, dc in next dc) across to last st, sc in last st.
Row 3 (Increase row): Ch 3, dc in same st and in each st across to last sc, 2 dc in last sc: {39-39-41-41}{43-43-45-45} sts.
Repeat Rows 2 and 3, {15-15-16-16}{16-16-17-17} times: {69-69-73-73}{75-75-79-79} sts.
Work even until Sleeve measures approximately {15¼-15¼-16¼-16¼}{16¼-16¼-16¾-16¾}", ending by working a **wrong** side row; finish off.

FINISHING

Whipstitch shoulder seams *(Fig. 28a, page 140)*.
Whipstitch Sleeves to Pullover, matching center of Sleeve to shoulder seam and beginning {10-10-10½-10½}{10¾-10¾-11¼-11¼}" down from shoulder seam.
Whipstitch underarm and side in one continuous seam.

BOTTOM RIBBING

Rnd 1: With **right** side facing and working in free loops of beginning ch *(Fig. 23b, page 138)*, join yarn with slip st in first ch on Back; ch 1, sc in same st and in each ch around; join with slip st to first sc: {126-134-142-146}{154-162-170-174} sc.
Rnd 2: Ch 3, dc in next sc and in each sc around; join with slip st to first dc.
Rnds 3-5: Ch 3, work FPdc around next st *(Fig. 16, page 136)*, ★ work BPdc around next st *(Fig. 17, page 136)*, work FPdc around next st; repeat from ★ around; join with slip st to first dc. Finish off.

SLEEVE RIBBING

Rnd 1: With **right** side facing and working in free loops of beginning ch, join yarn with slip st in first ch; ch 1, work {36-36-39-39}{39-39-42-42} sc evenly spaced around; join with slip st to first sc.
Rnd 2: Ch 2, dc in next 2 sc, (decrease, dc in next sc) around; skip beginning ch-2 and join with slip st to first dc: {24-24-26-26}{26-26-28-28} dc.
Rnds 3-5: Work same as Bottom Ribbing.
Finish off.

NECK RIBBING

Rnd 1: With **right** side facing, join yarn with slip st at right shoulder seam; ch 1, work 3 sc evenly spaced across end of rows, place marker, work {23-23-23-25}{25-25-25-27} sc evenly spaced across Back, place marker, work 11 sc evenly spaced across end of rows, place marker, work {23-23-23-25}{25-25-25-27} sc evenly spaced across Front, place marker, work 8 sc evenly spaced across end with slip st to first sc: {68-68-68-72}{72-72-72-76}

Rnd 2: Ch 3, (dc in each sc across to within one s decrease) 4 times, dc in each sc across; join with dc: {64-64-64-68}{68-68-68-72} dc.

Rnds 3-5: Work same as Bottom Ribbing.

Finish off.

Quick SLIPPERS FOR KIDS

Easy to stitch, these sassy slippers for kids are as much fun to wear as they are to make! Pom-poms and long single and double crochets worked in black create a bold accent on the booties. Soft and comfortable, they're made of long-wearing worsted weight yarn.

Size:	Small	Medium	Large
Sole length:	6½"	7"	7½"

Size Note: Instructions are written for size Small with sizes Medium and Large in braces. Instructions will be easier to read if you circle all the numbers pertaining to your size. If only one number is given, it applies to all sizes.

MATERIALS

Worsted Weight Yarn, approximately:
   MC (Red) - 3{3½-4} ounces,
     [90{100-110} grams, 170{200-225} yards]
   CC (Black) - 40 yards
Crochet hook, size G (4.00 mm) **or** size needed for gauge
Yarn needle

PATTERN STITCHES

DECREASE
Pull up a loop in next 2 sts, YO and draw through all 3 loops on hook (counts as one sc).

LONG DOUBLE CROCHET (abbreviated Long dc)
YO, insert hook in st on row below next st, YO and pull up a loop even with loop on hook (Fig. 5, page 133), (YO and draw through 2 loops on hook) twice.

LONG SINGLE CROCHET (abbreviated Long sc)
Insert hook in st on row below next st, YO and pull up a loop even with loop on hook, YO and draw through both loops on hook.

SOLE

Holding 2 strands of MC together, ch 16{18-21} loosely.

Rnd 1 (Right side): 3 Sc in second ch from hook, sc in each ch across to last ch, 3 sc in last ch; working in free loops of beginning ch (Fig. 23b, page 138), sc in each ch across; join with slip st to first sc: 32{36-42} sc.

Note: Loop a short piece of yarn around any stitch to mark last round as right side.

Rnd 2: Ch 1, turn; sc in next 7{7-8} sc, hdc in next 5{7-9} sc, 2 hdc in each of next 5 sc, hdc in next 5{7-9} sc, sc in next 7{7-8} sc, 2 sc in each of last 3 sc; join with slip st to first sc: 40{44-50} sts.

Rnd 3: Ch 1, turn; 2 sc in each of next 5 sc, sc in next 8{8-9} sc, hdc in next 7{9-11} hdc, 2 hdc in each of next 5 hdc, hdc in next 7{9-11} hdc, sc in last 8{8-9} sts; join with slip st to first sc: 50{54-60} sts.

Rnd 4: Ch 1, turn; sc in next 8 sc, hdc in next 10{11-14} hdc, 2 hdc in each of next 3{5-5} hdc, hdc in next 10{11-14} hdc, sc in next 12{12-11} sts, 2 sc in each of next 3{4-5} sc, sc in last 4{3-3} sc; finish off: 56{63-70} sts.

TOP

Rnd 1: With right side facing and working in Back Loops Only (Fig. 22, page 138), join 1 strand of MC with slip st in center back sc; ch 2 (counts as first hdc, now and throughout), hdc in next sc and in each st around; join with slip st to first hdc.

Rnd 2: Ch 2, do not turn; working in both loops, hdc in next hdc and in each hdc around; join with slip st to first hdc, finish off.

Rnd 3: With right side facing, join 1 strand of CC with slip st in same st as joining; ch 1, sc in same st and in next 2 hdc, work Long dc, sc in next 2 hdc, work Long sc, ★ sc in next 3 hdc, work Long dc, sc in next 2 hdc, work Long sc; repeat from ★ around; join with slip st to first sc, finish off.

Rnd 4: With right side facing, join 1 strand of MC with slip st in Back Loop Only of first sc; ch 2, hdc in Back Loop Only of next 2 sc, hdc in both loops of next st, hdc in Back Loop Only of next 2 sc, hdc in both loops of next st, ★ hdc in Back Loop Only of next 3 sc, hdc in both loops of next st, hdc in Back Loop Only of next 2 sc, hdc in both loops of next st; repeat from ★ around; join with slip st to first hdc.

Rnd 5: Ch 2, working in both loops, hdc in next hdc and in each hdc around; join with slip st to first hdc.

Rnd 6: Ch 2, hdc in next 25{28-33} hdc, decrease 5 times, hdc in each hdc around; join with slip st to first hdc: 51{58-65} sts.

Rnd 7: Ch 2, hdc in next 23{26-31} hdc, decrease 5 times, hdc in each hdc around; join with slip st to first hdc: 46{53-60} sts.

Rnd 8: Ch 2, hdc in next 11{13-13} hdc, dc in next 5{6-7} hdc, hdc in next 7{7-11} hdc, decrease 3 times, hdc in next 7{7-10} hdc, dc in next 5{6-7} hdc, hdc in each hdc around; join with slip st to first hdc: 43{50-57} sts.

Rnd 9: Ch 2, hdc in next 15{18-20} sts, 2 dc in next dc, skip next 17{17-24} sts, 2 dc in next dc, hdc in each st around; join with slip st to first hdc, finish off: 28{35-35} sts.

TRIM

Rnd 1: With right side facing, join 1 strand of CC with slip st in center back hdc; ch 1, sc in same st and in next 2 hdc, work Long dc, sc in next 2 sts, work Long sc, ★ sc in next 3 sts, work Long dc, sc in next 2 sts, work Long sc; repeat from ★ around; join with slip st to first sc.

Rnd 2: Ch 1, sc in each st around; join with slip st to Front Loop Only of first sc.

Rnd 3: Ch 3, turn; (slip st in Back Loop Only of next sc, ch 3) around; join with slip st to base of first slip st.

Rnd 4: Turn; working in free loops on Rnd 2 (Fig. 23a, page 138), slip st in each st around; join with slip st to first slip st, finish off.

Sew seam.

With CC, make two 1 1/2" pom-poms (Figs. 29a & b, page 140) and attach to Slippers.

$\mathcal{Q}$uick TULIP GARDEN SWEATSHIRT

A garden of pretty tulips blooms on this cozy crewneck that's just right for early spring weather. It's created by inserting a panel of crocheted flowers in the front of a sweatshirt and adding single crochet ribbing along the neck, sleeves, and bottom.

MATERIALS

Worsted Weight Yarn, approximately:
  6 ounces, (170 grams, 405 yards) (for size Medium)
Crochet hooks, sizes E (3.50 mm) **and** G (4.00 mm) **or** sizes needed for gauge
Adult sweatshirt
Seam ripper
Tape measure
Yarn needle
Erasable marking pen
Straight pins
Sewing needle and thread
Sewing machine

GAUGE: With larger size hook, 8 sts = 2"
  Panel = 5$^{1}/_{4}$" wide

SWEATSHIRT PREPARATION

Use seam ripper to remove ribbing from bottom, neck, and sleeves of sweatshirt. Try on sweatshirt. Crocheted Sleeve Ribbing will extend approximately 2$^{3}/_{4}$" below edge of sleeve and Bottom Ribbing will extend approximately 3$^{1}/_{4}$" below edge of body. If sleeves and body will be too long, determine desired length of body and sleeves, and place a pin to mark each length.

PATTERN STITCHES

FRONT POST DOUBLE CROCHET (abbreviated **FPdc**)
YO, insert hook from **front** to **back** around post of st indicated **(Fig. 13, page 135)**, YO and pull up a loop **even** with loop on hook, (YO and draw through 2 loops on hook) twice. Skip st behind FPdc.

DECREASE
Pull up a loop in each of next 2 dc, YO and draw through all 3 loops on hook **(counts as one sc)**.

PANEL

With larger size hook, ch 22 **loosely**.

Row 1 (Right side)**:** Sc in second ch from hook and in each ch across: 21 sc.

Note: Loop a short piece of yarn around any stitch to mark last row as **right** side.

Row 2: Ch 2, turn; dc in first 11 sts, (ch 10, dc) 3 times in same st as last dc, dc in last 10 sts: 24 dc.

Row 3: Ch 1, turn; sc in first 2 dc, work FPdc around st in row **below** next dc, sc in next dc, work FPdc around st in row **below** next dc, sc in next 4 dc, decrease 3 times working **behind** ch-10 loops, sc in next 4 dc, work FPdc around st in row **below** next dc, sc in next dc, work FPdc around st in row **below** next dc, sc in last 2 dc, leave turning ch unworked **(now and throughout)**: 21 sts.

Row 4: Ch 2, turn; dc in each st across.

Row 5: Ch 1, turn; sc in first 2 dc, work FPdc around FPdc below next dc, sc in next dc, work FPdc around FPdc below next dc, sc in next 2 dc, holding next loop in front of next dc, sc in both loop **and** in next dc, sc in next 5 dc, skip next loop, holding next loop in front of next dc, sc in both loop **and** in next dc, sc in next 2 dc, work FPdc around FPdc below next dc, sc in next dc, work FPdc around FPdc below next dc, sc in last 2 dc.

Row 6: Ch 2, turn; dc in each st across.

Row 7: Ch 1, turn; sc in first 2 dc, work FPdc around FPdc below next dc, sc in next dc, work FPdc around FPdc below next dc, sc in next 5 dc, holding center loop in front of next dc, 6 dc in both loop **and** in next dc, drop loop from hook, insert hook in first dc of 6-dc group, hook dropped loop and draw through, ch 1 to close, sc in next 5 dc, work FPdc around FPdc below next dc, sc in next dc, work FPdc around FPdc below next dc, sc in last 2 dc.

Row 8: Ch 2, turn; dc in first 10 sts, dc in next ch, dc in last 10 sts.

Row 9: Ch 1, turn; sc in first 2 dc, work FPdc around FPdc below next dc, sc in next dc, work FPdc around FPdc below next dc, sc in next 11 dc, work FPdc around FPdc below next dc, sc in next dc, work FPdc around FPdc below next dc, sc in last 2 dc.

Repeat Rows 2-9 until Panel measures approximately same as determined length of sweatshirt front, ending by working Row 9; finish off. Adjust length of sweatshirt if needed.

ASSEMBLY

1. Lay sweatshirt flat; draw lines across sweatshirt bottom and sleeves at determined lengths, adding 1/4" for seam allowances.
2. Cut sweatshirt bottom and sleeves off at drawn lines.
3. Cut strip from center front of sweatshirt, 1/2" less than width of Panel.
4. Zigzag stitch **all** raw edges.
5. With right sides together, sew Panel to sweatshirt using a 1/4" seam.

SLEEVE RIBBING (Make 2)

With smaller size hook, ch 14 **loosely**.

Row 1 (Right side)**:** Sc in second ch from hook and in each ch across: 13 sc.

Note: Mark last row as **right** side.

Row 2: Ch 1, turn; sc in Back Loop Only of each sc across **(Fig. 22, page 138)**; do **not** finish off.

On **right** side of sweatshirt, measure around sleeve opening. Multiply this measurement by .667. Repeat Row 2 until Ribbing is approximately the same length as determined measurement, ending by working a **wrong** side row.

Joining Row: With **right** sides together and working in Back Loops Only of last row **and** in free loops of beginning ch **(Fig. 23b, page 138)**, slip st in each st across; finish off.

BOTTOM RIBBING

With smaller size hook, ch 16 **loosely**.

Row 1 (Right side)**:** Sc in second ch from hook and in each ch across: 15 sc.

Note: Mark last row as **right** side.

Row 2: Ch 1, turn; sc in Back Loop Only of each sc across; do **not** finish off.

On **right** side of sweatshirt, measure around bottom opening. Multiply this measurement by .667. Repeat Row 2 until Ribbing is approximately the same length as determined measurement, ending by working a **wrong** side row.

Joining Row: With **right** sides together and working in Back Loops Only of sc on last row **and** in free loops of beginning ch, slip st in each st across; finish off.

Continued on page 107.

TOPS FOR TODDLERS

Toddlers will look precious in these pullovers for girls or boys. Splashed with color, the sweaters have rich texture that's created using treble crochet clusters. They're stitched in baby fingering weight yarn for softness next to a little one's sensitive skin.

Size:	2	4	6
Finished Chest			
Measurement:	25"	27"	29"

Size Note: Instructions are written for size 2 with sizes 4 and 6 in braces. Instructions will be easier to read if you circle all the numbers pertaining to your size.

MATERIALS

Baby Fingering Weight Yarn, approximately:

2-Color

MC (Navy) - 6{7-8} ounces,
  [170{200-230} grams, 860{1,000-1,145} yards]

CC (Red) - 1¼{1½-1¾} ounces,
  [35{40-50} grams, 180{215-250} yards]

4-Color

MC (Light Blue) - 4{5-5½} ounces,
  [110{140-160} grams, 570{715-785} yards]

Color A (White) - ¾{1-1} ounce,
  [20{30-30} grams, 110{145-145} yards]

Color B (Red) - 1½{1¾-2} ounces,
  [40{50-60} grams, 215{250-285} yards]

Color C (Navy) - 1{1¼-1½} ounces,
  [30{35-40} grams, 145{180-215} yards]

Crochet hooks, sizes C (2.75 mm) **and** D (3.25 mm) **or** sizes needed for gauge

Yarn needle

GAUGE: With larger size hook, in pattern,
  (ch 2, tr) 4 times = 2" and 8 rows = 1¾"

PATTERN STITCHES

TR CLUSTER

★ YO twice, insert hook in st or sp indicated, YO and pull up a loop, (YO and draw through 2 loops on hook) twice; repeat from ★ once **more**, YO and draw through all 3 loops on hook *(Figs. 10a & b, page 134)*.

DC CLUSTER

★ YO, insert hook in sp indicated, YO and pull up a loop, YO and draw through 2 loops on hook; repeat from ★ once **more**, YO and draw through all 3 loops on hook.

BACK

RIBBING

With smaller size hook and MC, ch 15 **loosely**.

Row 1: Sc in second ch from hook and in each ch across: 14 sc.

Row 2: Ch 1, turn; sc in Back Loop Only of each sc across *(Fig. 22, page 138)*.

Repeat Row 2 until 38{41-44} ribs [76{82-88} rows] are complete; do **not** finish off.

BODY

Change to larger size hook.

Row 1 (Right side): Ch 1, work 76{82-88} sc evenly spaced across end of rows.

Note: Loop a short piece of yarn around any stitch to mark last row as **right** side.

Row 2: Ch 6 **(counts as first tr plus ch 2, now and throughout)**, turn; skip next 2 sc, tr in next sc, (ch 2, skip next 2 sc, tr in next sc) across: 25{27-29} ch-2 sps.

Row 3: Ch 1, turn; sc in first tr, ★ working **behind** next ch-2 sp, work tr Cluster in each of next 2 skipped sc on row **below**, sc in next tr; repeat from ★ across: 50{54-58} tr Clusters.

Row 4: Ch 6, turn; skip next 2 sts, tr in next sc, (ch 2, skip next 2 sts, tr in next sc) across: 25{27-29} ch-2 sps.

Row 5: Ch 1, turn; sc in first tr, ★ working **behind** next ch-2 sp, work 2 tr Clusters in ch-2 sp **below**, sc in next tr; repeat from ★ across: 50{54-58} tr Clusters.

Repeat Rows 4 and 5 for pattern, 21{23-25} times; do **not** finish off.

LEFT NECK SHAPING

Row 1: Ch 6, turn; skip next 2 sts, tr in next sc, (ch 2, skip next 2 sts, tr in next sc) 7{8-9} times, ch 3, skip next 2 sts, slip st in next sc, leave remaining sts unworked: 9{10-11} sps.

Row 2: Ch 1, turn; working **behind** first ch-3 sp, work (dc Cluster, tr Cluster) in ch-2 sp **below**, sc in next tr, ★ working **behind** next ch-2 sp, work 2 tr Clusters in ch-2 sp **below**, sc in next tr; repeat from ★ across: 18{20-22} Clusters.

Row 3: Ch 6, turn; skip next 2 sts, tr in next sc, ★ ch 2, skip next 2 sts, tr in next sc; repeat from ★ across to last sc, ch 3, slip st in last sc: 8{9-10} sps.

Row 4: Repeat Row 2; finish off: 16{18-20} Clusters.

RIGHT NECK SHAPING

Row 1: With **wrong** side facing, skip 6 sc from Left Neck Shaping and join MC with slip st in next sc; ch 3, skip next 2 sts, tr in next sc, (ch 2, skip next 2 sts, tr in next sc) across: 9{10-11} sps.

Row 2: Ch 1, turn; sc in first tr, ★ working **behind** next ch-2 sp, work 2 tr Clusters in ch-2 sp **below**, sc in next tr; repeat from ★ across to last ch-3 sp, working **behind** last ch-3 sp, work (tr Cluster, dc Cluster) in ch-2 sp **below**, slip st in last st: 18{20-22} Clusters.

Row 3: Ch 1, turn; slip st in first 2 Clusters and in next sc, ch 3, skip next 2 sts, tr in next sc, (ch 2, skip next 2 sts, tr in next sc) across: 8{9-10} sps.

Row 4: Repeat Row 2; finish off: 16{18-20} Clusters.

FRONT

Work same as Back through Row 3 of Body.

Row 4: Ch 6, turn; skip next 2 sts, tr in next sc, ★ ch 2, skip next 2 sts, tr in next sc; repeat from ★ across to last 3 sts changing to CC in last tr worked *(Fig. 24a, page 138)*, drop MC, do **not** cut yarn unless otherwise instructed, ch 2, skip next 2 sts, tr in last sc: 25{27-29} ch-2 sps.

Row 5: Ch 1, turn; sc in first tr, working **behind** next ch-2 sp, work 2 tr Clusters in ch-2 sp **below**, sc in next tr changing to MC, drop CC, ★ working **behind** next ch-2 sp, work 2 tr Clusters in ch-2 sp **below**, sc in next tr; repeat from ★ across.

Row 6: Ch 6, turn; skip next 2 sts, tr in next sc, ★ ch 2, skip next 2 sts, tr in next sc; repeat from ★ across to last 2 MC Clusters changing to CC in last tr worked, drop MC, (ch 2, skip next 2 sts, tr in next sc) across.

Row 7: Ch 1, turn; sc in first tr, (working **behind** next ch-2 sp, work 2 tr Clusters in ch-2 sp **below**, sc in next tr) across to first MC ch-2 sp changing to MC in last sc worked, drop CC, ★ working **behind** next ch-2 sps, work 2 tr Clusters in ch-2 sp **below**, sc in next tr; repeat from ★ across.

Repeat Rows 6 and 7, 18{20-22} times; do **not** finish off.

RIGHT NECK SHAPING

Note: Continue to work in established diagonal pattern.

Row 1: Ch 6, turn; skip next 2 sts, tr in next sc, (ch 2, skip next 2 sts, tr in next sc) 8{9-10} times, ch 3, skip next 2 sts, slip st in next sc, leave remaining sts unworked: 10{11-12} sps.

Rows 2-6: Repeat Rows 2 and 3 of Back Left Neck Shaping twice, then repeat Row 2 once **more**: 16{18-20} Clusters.

Rows 7 and 8: Repeat Rows 4 and 5 of Back Body: 14{16-18} Clusters.

Finish off.

LEFT NECK SHAPING

Row 1: With **wrong** side facing, skip 4 sc from Right Neck Shaping and join CC with slip st in next sc; ch 3, skip next 2 sts, tr in next sc, (ch 2, skip next 2 sts, tr in next sc) across: 10{11-12} sps.

Rows 2-6: Repeat Rows 2 and 3 of Back Right Neck Shaping twice, then repeat Row 2 once **more**: 16{18-20} Clusters.

Row 7: Ch 1, turn; slip st in first 2 Clusters and in next sc, ch 6, skip next 2 sts, tr in next sc, (ch 2, skip next 2 sts, tr in next sc) across: 7{8-9} sps.

Row 8: Repeat Row 5 of Back Body: 14{16-18} Clusters. Finish off.

SLEEVE (Make 2)

RIBBING

With smaller size hook and MC, ch 11 **loosely**.

Row 1: Sc in second ch from hook and in each ch across: 10 sc.

Row 2: Ch 1, turn; sc in Back Loop Only of each sc across.

Repeat Row 2 until Ribbing measures approximately 5¼{5½ -5½}".

BODY

Change to larger size hook.

Row 1 (Right side): Ch 1, work 37{37-43} sc evenly spaced across end of rows.

Note: Mark last row as **right** side.

Row 2: Ch 6, turn; skip next 2 sc, tr in next sc, (ch 2, skip next 2 sc, tr in next sc) across: 12{12-14} ch-2 sps.

Row 3: Ch 1, turn; sc in first tr, ★ working **behind** next ch-2 sp, work tr Cluster in each of next 2 skipped sc on row **below**, sc in next tr; repeat from ★ across: 24{24-28} tr Clusters.

Row 4: Ch 6, turn; skip next 2 sts, tr in next sc, (ch 2, skip next 2 sts, tr in next sc) across: 12{12-14} ch-2 sps.

Row 5: Ch 1, turn; sc in first tr, ★ working **behind** next ch-2 sp, work 2 tr Clusters in ch-2 sp **below**, sc in next tr; repeat from ★ across: 24{24-28} tr Clusters.

Rows 6-9: Repeat Rows 4 and 5, twice.

Row 10 (Increase row): Ch 6, turn; tr in first sc, ch 2, skip next 2 sts, (tr in next sc, ch 2, skip next 2 sts) across to last sc, (tr, ch 2, tr) in last sc: 14{14-16} ch-2 sps.

Row 11: Ch 1, turn; sc in first tr, working **behind** first ch-2 sp, work 2 tr Clusters in first sc on row **below**, sc in next tr, ★ working **behind** next ch-2 sp, work 2 tr Clusters in ch-2 sp **below**, sc in next tr; repeat from ★ across to last ch-2 sp, working **behind** last ch-2 sp, work 2 tr Clusters in last sc on row **below**, sc in last tr: 28{28-32} tr Clusters.

Repeat Rows 6-11, 4{5-5} times: 44{48-52} tr Clusters.

Repeat Rows 4 and 5 for pattern until Sleeve measures approximately 9½{10½-11½}" from bottom edge, ending by working Row 5; finish off.

FINISHING

Sew shoulder seams.

NECK RIBBING

Foundation Rnd: With **right** side facing and using smaller size hook, join MC with slip st at right shoulder seam; ch 1, work 8 sc evenly spaced along Right Back Neck edge, work 22 sc evenly spaced across Back, work 8 sc evenly spaced along Left Back Neck edge, work 16 sc evenly spaced along Left Front Neck edge, work 16 sc evenly spaced across Front, work 16 sc evenly spaced along Right Front Neck edge; join with slip st to first sc: 86 sc.

Ch 6{6-8} **loosely**.

Row 1: Sc in second ch from hook and in each ch across, slip st in first 2 sc on Foundation Rnd: 7{7-9} sts.

Row 2: Turn; skip first 2 slip sts, sc in Back Loop Only of each sc across: 5{5-7} sc.

Row 3: Ch 1, turn; sc in Back Loop Only of each sc across, slip st in next 2 sc on Foundation Rnd: 7{7-9} sts.

Repeat Rows 2 and 3 around, ending by working Row 2.

Last Row: Ch 1, turn; sc in Back Loop Only of each sc across, slip st in last sc on Foundation Rnd; finish off leaving a long end for sewing.

Whipstitch seam on Neck Ribbing *(Fig. 28a, page 140)*. Whipstitch Sleeves to Top, matching center of Sleeve to shoulder seam and beginning 5½{6-6½}" down from shoulder seam. Whipstitch underarm and side in one continuous seam.

TULIP GARDEN SWEATSHIRT

Continued from page 104.

NECK RIBBING

With smaller size hook, ch 8 **loosely**.

Row 1 (Right side): Sc in second ch from hook and in each ch across: 7 sc.

Note: Mark last row as **right** side.

Row 2: Ch 1, turn; sc in Back Loop Only of each sc across; do **not** finish off.

On **right** side of sweatshirt, measure around neck opening. Multiply this measurement by .667. Repeat Row 2 until Ribbing is approximately the same length as determined measurement, ending by working a **wrong** side row.

Joining Row: With **right** sides together and working in Back Loops Only of sc on last row **and** in free loops of beginning ch, slip st in each st across; finish off.

With **right** sides together and stretching each Ribbing to fit opening, sew Ribbings to sweatshirt using a ¼" seam.

hooked on holidays

*Celebrate a year of holidays with these festive projects!
Our fun-filled assortment includes delightful decorations and
great gift ideas, too. For Valentine's Day, cute frames surround
special photos with love, and a pair of patriotic mascots brings
spirit to the Fourth of July. Wheat-sheaf patterns enrich
a Thanksgiving doily, and a three-dimensional Christmas tree
makes a charming centerpiece. With these unique projects — and
so many more — it's easy to become hooked on holidays!*

VALENTINE'S DAY

*You'll love displaying your sweetheart's photo in one of these frilly magnetic frames. Stitched in
bedspread weight cotton thread, they're just the right size to take to the office or place on the refrigerator
door. With three styles from which to choose, you can always keep your loved one close to your heart!*

Quick SWEETHEART FRAMES

Finished Size: Heart - approximately 4³/4" wide x 4¹/2" high
Oval - approximately 4¹/2" wide x 5" high
Round - approximately 4¹/2" in diameter

MATERIALS
Bedspread Weight Cotton Thread (size 10), approximately:
Heart or Round - 35 yards **each**
Oval - 45 yards
Steel crochet hook, size 7 (1.65 mm) **or** size needed
for gauge
Magnetic strips
Cardboard
Heart: ¹/2 yard of ¹/8" ribbon

GAUGE: 9 sc = 1"

PATTERN STITCHES
DC DECREASE (uses next 2 sts)
★ YO, insert hook in **next** st, YO and pull up a loop, YO and
draw through 2 loops on hook; repeat from ★ once **more**,
YO and draw through all 3 loops on hook (**counts as
one dc**).
DOUBLE DECREASE (uses next 3 sts)
★ YO, insert hook in **next** st, YO and pull up a loop, YO and
draw through 2 loops on hook; repeat from ★ 2 times
more, YO and draw through all 4 loops on hook.
SC DECREASE
Pull up a loop in next 2 sts, YO and draw through all 3 loops
on hook (**counts as one sc**).
SHELL
(2 Dc, ch 4, 2 dc) in st indicated.
V-ST
(Dc, ch 1, dc) in st indicated.

HEART FRAME

Ch 9 **loosely**.

Rnd 1: 2 Hdc in third ch from hook, sc in next ch, slip st in next ch, skip next ch, slip st in next ch, sc in next ch, 5 hdc in last ch; working in free loops of beginning ch *(Fig. 23b, page 138)*, sc in next 2 chs, 3 sc in next ch, sc in next 2 chs, 2 hdc in next ch; join with slip st to top of beginning ch: 21 sts.

Note: Loop a short piece of thread around any stitch to mark last round as back.

Rnd 2: Ch 2, hdc in same st, hdc in next hdc, sc in next 2 sts, slip st in next 2 slip sts, sc in next 2 sts, hdc in next hdc, 2 hdc in next hdc, 3 dc in next hdc, 2 hdc in next hdc, sc in next 3 sc, 3 hdc in next sc, sc in next 3 sc, 2 hdc in next hdc, 3 dc in last hdc; join with slip st top of beginning ch-2: 31 sts.

Rnd 3: Ch 3 **(counts as first dc, now and throughout)**, dc in same st, 3 dc in next hdc, hdc in next hdc, sc in next sc, slip st in next sc, skip next 2 slip sts, slip st in next sc, sc in next sc, hdc in next hdc, 3 dc in next hdc, 2 dc in each of next 5 sts, dc in next 5 sts, (dc, tr, dc) in next hdc, dc in next 5 sts, 2 dc in each of last 4 sts; join with slip st to first dc: 45 sts.

Rnd 4: Ch 3, dc in same st and in next dc, 2 dc in each of next 2 dc, hdc in next 2 sts, sc in next sc, skip next 2 slip sts, sc in next sc, hdc in next 2 sts, 2 dc in each of next 2 dc, dc in next dc, 2 dc in next dc, 3 dc in next dc, (dc in next dc, 2 dc in next dc) 3 times, dc in next 7 dc, (dc, tr, dc) in next tr, dc in next 7 dc, (2 dc in next dc, dc in next dc) 3 times, 3 dc in last dc; join with slip st to first dc: 61 sts.

Rnd 5: Ch 3, dc in same st, (dc in next dc, 2 dc in next dc) twice, hdc in next 2 dc, sc in next 2 sts, skip next 2 sc, sc in next 2 hdc, hdc in next 2 dc, 2 dc in next dc, (dc in next dc, 2 dc in next dc) 5 times, dc in next 2 dc, 2 dc in next dc, dc in next 11 dc, (dc, tr, dc) in next tr, dc in next 11 dc, 2 dc in next dc, dc in next 2 dc, (2 dc in next dc, dc in next dc) 3 times; join with slip st to first dc: 75 sts.

Rnd 6: Ch 1, **turn**; working in Back Loops Only *(Fig. 22, page 138)*, sc in first 63 sts, skip next 2 sc, sc in last 10 sts; join with slip st to first sc: 73 sc.

Rnd 7 (Eyelet rnd): Ch 5, skip next sc, working in both loops, dc in next sc, (ch 2, skip next sc, dc in next sc) 11 times, ch 1, skip next sc, (dc, ch 1, tr, ch 1, dc) in next sc, ch 1, (skip next sc, dc in next sc, ch 2) 16 times, skip next sc, dc in next sc, ch 1, skip next sc, dc decrease, ch 1, skip next sc, (dc in next sc, ch 2, skip next sc) 4 times; join with slip st to third ch of beginning ch-5: 38 sps.

Rnd 8: Ch 1, sc in same st, ch 3, (sc in next dc, ch 3) 13 times, (sc, ch 3, sc) in next tr, (ch 3, sc in next dc) around, ch 1, hdc in first sc to form last sp: 39 sps.

Rnd 9: Ch 1, sc in same sp, ch 4, (sc in next ch-3 sp, ch 4) 14 times, (sc, ch 4, sc) in next ch-3 sp, (ch 4, sc in next ch-3 sp) around, ch 1, dc in first sc to form last sp: 40 sps.

Rnd 10: Ch 1, sc in same sp, ch 5, slip st in third ch from hook, ch 2, (sc in next ch-4 sp, ch 5, slip st in third ch from hook, ch 2) around; join with slip st to first sc, finish off.

FRONT EDGING

With back facing, Rnds 6-10 forward, and working in free loops on Rnd 5 *(Fig. 23a, page 138)*, join thread with slip st in same st as joining; ch 2, dc in next st, dc decrease 5 times, (dc, tr, dc) in same st as last decrease worked, dc decrease 7 times, dc in next dc, (dc decrease, dc in next dc) 7 times, work double decrease, (dc in next dc, dc decrease) 8 times; skip beginning ch-2 and join with slip st to first dc, finish off.

OVAL FRAME

Ch 5 **loosely**.

Rnd 1: Sc in third ch from hook and in next ch, (hdc, dc, hdc) in last ch; working in free loops of beginning ch *(Fig. 23b, page 138)*, sc in next ch, (sc, hdc, dc) in next ch; join with slip st to top of beginning ch: 10 sts.

Note: Loop a short piece of thread around any stitch to mark last round as back.

Rnd 2: Ch 2 **(counts as first hdc, now and throughout)**, hdc in same st and in next 2 sc, 2 hdc in next hdc, 3 dc in next dc, 2 hdc in next hdc, hdc in next 2 sc, 2 hdc in next hdc, 3 dc in last dc; join with slip st to first hdc: 18 sts.

Rnd 3: Ch 2, hdc in same st and in next 4 hdc, 2 hdc in next hdc, dc in next dc, 3 dc in next dc, dc in next dc, 2 hdc in next hdc, hdc in next 4 hdc, 2 hdc in next hdc, dc in next dc, 3 dc in next dc, dc in last dc; join with slip st to first hdc: 26 sts.

Rnd 4: Ch 2, hdc in same st and in next 6 hdc, 2 hdc in next hdc, dc in next dc, (2 dc in next dc, dc in next dc) twice, 2 hdc in next hdc, hdc in next 6 hdc, 2 hdc in next hdc, dc in next dc, (2 dc in next dc, dc in next dc) twice; join with slip st to first hdc: 34 sts.

Rnd 5: Ch 3 **(counts as first dc, now and throughout)**, hdc in same st and in next hdc, † 2 hdc in next hdc, hdc in next 4 hdc, 2 hdc in next hdc, hdc in next hdc, (hdc, dc) in next hdc, dc in next dc, (2 dc in next dc, dc in next dc) 3 times †, (dc, hdc) in next hdc, hdc in next hdc, repeat from † to † once; join with slip st to first dc: 48 sts.

Rnd 6: Ch 3, dc in same st and in next hdc, † 2 hdc in next hdc, hdc in next 8 hdc, 2 hdc in next hdc, dc in next hdc, (2 dc in next dc, dc in next dc) twice, 2 dc in each of next 4 dc, dc in next dc †, (2 dc in next dc, dc in next st) twice, repeat from † to † once, 2 dc in next dc, dc in last dc; join with slip st to first dc: 68 sts.

Rnd 7: Ch 2, hdc in next st and in each st around; join with slip st to first hdc.

Rnd 8: Ch 2, hdc in next 19 hdc, dc in next hdc, (2 dc in next hdc, dc in next hdc) 6 times, hdc in next 21 hdc, dc in next hdc, (2 dc in next hdc, dc in next hdc) 6 times, hdc in last hdc; join with slip st to first hdc: 80 sts.

Rnd 9: Ch 1, **turn**; working in Back Loops Only *(Fig. 22, page 138)*, sc in each st around; join with slip st to first sc.

Rnd 10: Ch 4, working in both loops, dc in same st, ch 3, skip next 3 sc, work Shell in next sc, ch 3, skip next 3 sc, (work V-St in next sc, ch 3, skip next 3 sc, work Shell in next sc, ch 3, skip next 3 sc) around; join with slip st to third ch of beginning ch-4: 10 Shells.

Rnd 11: Ch 1, sc in same st, sc in next ch-1 sp and in next dc, skip next ch-3 sp, dc in next Shell (ch-4 sp), (ch 1, dc) 7 times in same sp, skip next ch-3 sp, ★ sc in next dc, sc in next ch-1 sp and in next dc, skip next ch-3 sp, dc in next Shell, (ch 1, dc) 7 times in same sp, skip next ch-3 sp; repeat from ★ around; join with slip st to first sc.

Rnd 12: Slip st in next sc, ch 1, sc in same st and in next sc, (sc in next ch-1 sp, ch 3, slip st in sc just worked, sc in next dc) 7 times, skip next sc, ★ sc in next 2 sc, (sc in next ch-1 sp, ch 3, slip st in sc just worked, sc in next dc) 7 times, skip next sc; repeat from ★ around; join with slip st to first sc, finish off.

FRONT EDGING

Rnd 1: With back facing, Rnds 9-12 forward, and working in free loops on Rnd 8 *(Fig. 23a, page 138)*, join thread with slip st in same st as joining; ch 2, dc in next 15 hdc, dc decrease, (dc in next st, dc decrease) 8 times, dc in next 14 hdc, (dc decrease, dc in next st) 8 times; skip beginning ch-2 and join with slip st to first dc: 62 dc.

Rnd 2: Ch 1, sc in first 18 dc, sc decrease, (sc in next dc, sc decrease) 3 times, sc in next 20 dc, sc decrease, (sc in next dc, sc decrease) 3 times, sc in last 2 dc; join with slip st to first sc, finish off: 54 sc.

ROUND FRAME

Rnd 1: Ch 2, 6 sc in second ch from hook; do **not** join, place marker *(see Markers, page 138)*.

Note: Loop a short piece of thread around any stitch to mark last round as back.

Rnd 2: 2 Sc in each sc around: 12 sc.

Rnd 3: (Sc in next sc, 2 sc in next sc) around: 18 sc.

Rnd 4: (Sc in next 2 sc, 2 sc in next sc) around: 24 sc.

Rnd 5: (Sc in next 3 sc, 2 sc in next sc) around: 30 sc.

Rnd 6: (Sc in next 4 sc, 2 sc in next sc) around: 36 sc.

Rnd 7: (Sc in next 5 sc, 2 sc in next sc) around: 42 sc.

Rnd 8: (Sc in next 6 sc, 2 sc in next sc) around: 48 sc.

Rnd 9: (Sc in next 5 sc, 2 sc in next sc) around: 56 sc.

Rnd 10: (Sc in next 3 sc, 2 sc in next sc) around; slip st in next sc: 70 sc.

Rnd 11: Ch 1, **turn**; working in Back Loops Only *(Fig. 22, page 138)*, sc in each sc around; join with slip st to first sc.

Rnd 12: Ch 1, working in both loops, 2 sc in same st, sc in next 6 sc, (2 sc in next sc, sc in next 6 sc) around; join with slip st to first sc: 80 sc.

Rnd 13: Ch 1, sc in same st, ch 4, skip next 4 sc, 4 dc in next sc, ch 4, skip next 4 sc, ★ sc in next sc, ch 4, skip next 4 sc, 4 dc in next sc, ch 4, skip next 4 sc; repeat from ★ around; join with slip st to first sc: 8 sc.

Rnd 14: Ch 4, dc in same st, ch 1, 3 dc in each of next 4 dc, ch 1, ★ work V-St in next sc, ch 1, 3 dc in each of next 4 dc, ch 1; repeat from ★ around; join with slip st to third ch of beginning ch-4.

Rnd 15: Ch 1, ★ sc in next ch-1 sp, ch 4, slip st in sc just worked, skip next dc, sc in next 5 dc, hdc in next dc, ch 3, slip st in hdc just worked, dc in next dc, ch 4, slip st in dc just worked, hdc in next dc, ch 3, slip st in hdc just worked, sc in next 4 dc, skip next dc; repeat from ★ around; join with slip st to first sc, finish off.

FRONT EDGING

With back facing, Rnds 11-15 forward, and working in free loops on Rnd 10 *(Fig. 23a, page 138)*, join thread with slip st in same st as joining; ch 2, dc in next st, dc decrease around; skip beginning ch-2 and join with slip st to first dc, finish off: 35 sts.

FINISHING

See Washing and Blocking, page 140.

Cut cardboard to fit inside of Front Edging of each Frame.

Cut photo to fit and insert into frame.

Attach a long magnetic strip to back of each Frame.

Heart: Weave ribbon through Eyelet round and tie in a bow.

EASTER

These inspirational bookmarks are thoughtful reminders of the Easter story. Perfect for marking a special scripture, they're fashioned with white cotton thread and gold metallic braid.

Quick CROSS BOOKMARKS

Finished Size: Cross #1 - approximately 5" long
Cross #2 - approximately 5¹/₂" long
Cross #3 - approximately 5³/₄" long

MATERIALS
Cotton Crochet Thread (size 20), approximately:
Cross #1 (White) - 13 yards
Cross #2 (White) - 21 yards
Cross #3 (White) - 37 yards
Metallic Braid (size 8), approximately:
Cross #1 (Gold) - 28 yards
Cross #2 (Gold) - 12 yards
Cross #3 (Gold) - 3 yards
Steel crochet hook, size 8 (1.50 mm)

GAUGE: Gauge is not important. Crosses can be smaller or larger without changing the overall effect.

PATTERN STITCHES
CLUSTER
★ YO, insert hook in dc indicated, YO and pull up a loop, YO and draw through 2 loops on hook; repeat from ★ once **more**, YO and draw through all 3 loops on hook **(Figs. 10a & b, page 134)**.
PICOT
Ch 3, slip st in sc just worked.

CROSS #1
FIRST MOTIF
With Gold, ch 5; join with slip st to form a ring.
Rnd 1 (Right side)**:** Ch 3 **(counts as first dc, now and throughout)**, 2 dc in ring, ch 3, (3 dc in ring, ch 3) 3 times; join with slip st to first dc: 12 dc.
Note: Loop a short piece of thread around any stitch to mark last round as **right** side.
Rnd 2: Ch 3, dc in same st and in next dc, 2 dc in next dc, ch 2, dc in next ch-3 sp, ch 2, ★ 2 dc in next dc, dc in next dc, 2 dc in next dc, ch 2, dc in next ch-3 sp, ch 2; repeat from ★ around; join with slip st to first dc: 24 dc.
Rnd 3: Ch 3, working in Back Loops Only **(Fig. 22, page 138)**, dc in same st and in next 3 dc, 2 dc in next dc, ch 2, work (Cluster, ch 3, Cluster) in next dc, ch 2, ★ 2 dc in next dc,

dc in next 3 dc, 2 dc in next dc, ch 2, work (Cluster, ch 3, Cluster) in next dc, ch 2; repeat from ★ around; join with slip st to first dc, finish off.

REMAINING 5 MOTIFS
Work same as First Motif through Rnd 2.
Refer to Assembly Diagram for joining sequence.
Rnd 3 (Joining rnd)**:** Ch 3, working in Back Loops Only, dc in same st and in next 3 dc, 2 dc in next dc, ch 2, ★ work (Cluster, ch 3, Cluster) in next dc, ch 2, 2 dc in next dc, dc in next 3 dc, 2 dc in next dc, ch 2; repeat from ★ once **more**, work Cluster in next dc, ch 1, slip st in center ch of corner ch-3 on **previous Motif**, ch 1, work Cluster in same dc on **new Motif**, ch 2, dc in next dc, slip st in adjacent dc on **previous Motif**, dc in same dc on **new Motif**, dc in next 3 dc, 2 dc in next dc, slip st in adjacent dc on **previous Motif**, ch 2, work Cluster in next dc on **new Motif**, ch 1, slip st in center ch of corner ch-3 on **previous Motif**, ch 1, work Cluster in same dc on **new Motif**, ch 2; join with slip st to first dc, finish off.

ASSEMBLY DIAGRAM

```
      +---+
      | 4 |
  +---+---+---+
  | 6 | 3 | 5 |
  +---+---+---+
      | 2 |
      +---+
      | 1 |
      +---+
```

EDGING
Rnd 1: With **right** side facing, join White with slip st in any st, ch 1, sc evenly around working 3 sc in corners (total sc must be a multiple of 2); join with slip st to first sc.
Rnd 2: Ch 1, sc in same st, work Picot, skip next sc, ★ sc in next sc, work Picot, skip next sc; repeat from ★ around; join with slip st to first sc, finish off.

CROSS #2
CENTER
With White, ch 8; join with slip st to form a ring.
Rnd 1: Ch 3 **(counts as first dc, now and throughout)**, 4 dc in ring, ch 3, (5 dc in ring, ch 3) 3 times; join with slip st to first dc: 20 dc.

112

TOP

Row 1: Ch 3, dc in same st and in next 3 dc, 2 dc in next dc, leave remaining sts unworked: 7 dc.

Rows 2-5: Ch 3, turn; dc in same st and in each dc across to last dc, 2 dc in last dc: 15 dc.

Row 6 (Right side): Ch 3, turn; dc in same st, 2 dc in next dc, 2 tr in each of next 2 dc, tr in next 7 dc, 2 tr in each of next 2 dc, 2 dc in each of last 2 dc: 23 sts.

Note: Loop a short piece of thread around any stitch to mark last row as **right** side.

Row 7: Ch 1, turn; slip st in first 8 sts, ch 4 **(counts as first tr, now and throughout)**, tr in next 8 tr, leave remaining 7 sts unworked: 9 tr.

Row 8: Ch 3, turn; ★ YO twice, insert hook in **next** tr, YO and pull up a loop, (YO and draw through 2 loops on hook) twice; repeat from ★ 7 times **more**, YO and draw through all 9 loops on hook, ch 1 to close, finish off.

LEFT SIDE

Row 1: With **right** side facing, join White with slip st in first dc of next 5-dc group on Center; ch 3, dc in same st, 2 dc in next dc, dc in next dc, 2 dc in each of next 2 dc, leave remaining sts unworked: 9 dc.

Row 2: Ch 3, turn; dc in same st and in next dc, 2 dc in next dc, dc in next 3 dc, 2 dc in next dc, dc in next dc, 2 dc in last dc: 13 dc.

Row 3: Ch 3, turn; dc in same st and in next 11 dc, 2 dc in last dc: 15 dc.

Row 4: Ch 1, turn; slip st in first 5 dc, ch 4, tr in next 6 dc, leave remaining 4 sts unworked: 7 tr.

Row 5: Ch 3, turn; ★ YO twice, insert hook in **next** tr, YO and pull up a loop, (YO and draw through 2 loops on hook) twice; repeat from ★ 5 times **more**, YO and draw through all 7 loops on hook, ch 1 to close, finish off.

BOTTOM

Row 1: With **wrong** side facing, skip next 5-dc group and join White with slip st in next dc on Center (opposite Top); ch 3, dc in same st and in next 3 dc, 2 dc in last dc: 7 dc.

Row 2: Ch 3, turn; dc in next dc and in each dc across.

Row 3: Ch 3, turn; dc in same st and in each dc across to last dc, 2 dc in last dc: 9 dc.

Rows 4-9: Repeat Rows 2 and 3, 3 times: 15 dc.

Rows 10-13: Ch 3, turn; dc in next dc and in each dc across.

Rows 14-16: Work same as Rows 6-8 of Top.

RIGHT SIDE

Row 1: With **right** side facing, join White with slip st in first dc of remaining 5-dc group on Center; ch 3, dc in same st, 2 dc in next dc, dc in next dc, 2 dc in each of last 2 dc: 9 dc.

Rows 2-5: Work same as Left Side.

EDGING

Rnd 1: With **right** side facing, join Gold with slip st in any st; ch 1, sc evenly around (total sc must be a multiple of 2); join with slip st to first sc.

Rnd 2: Ch 2, sc in second ch from hook, skip next sc, ★ slip st in next sc, ch 2, sc in second ch from hook, skip next sc; repeat from ★ around; join with slip st to first slip st, finish off.

CROSS #3

CENTER

Rnd 1 (Right side)**:** With Gold, ch 5; (2 dc, ch 1) 3 times in fifth ch from hook, dc in same ch; join with slip st to top of beginning ch: 4 ch-1 sps.

Note: Loop a short piece of thread around any stitch to mark last round as **right** side.

Rnd 2: Slip st in first ch-1 sp, ch 10 **loosely**, dc in fourth ch from hook and in next 6 chs (bottom of Cross), skip next 2 dc, ★ slip st in next ch-1 sp, ch 6 **loosely**, dc in fourth ch from hook and in next 2 chs, skip next 2 dc; repeat from ★ 2 times **more**; join with slip st to first st.

Rnd 3: Ch 16, slip st around skipped chs on end of bottom ch-10, ch 12, ★ tr in next ch-1 sp on Rnd 1, ch 5, slip st around skipped chs on end of next ch-6, ch 5; repeat from ★ around; join with slip st to fourth ch of beginning ch-16, finish off: 8 sps.

BOTTOM

Row 1: With **right** side facing, skip next 5 chs and join White with slip st in next ch, ch 1, 6 sc in same loop, sc in next slip st, 6 sc in next loop: 13 sc.

Row 2: Ch 3 (**counts as first dc, now and throughout**), turn; skip next sc, (2 dc, ch 1, 2 dc) in next sc, skip next 3 sc, (dc, ch 2, dc) in next sc, skip next 3 sc, (2 dc, ch 1, 2 dc) in next sc, skip next sc, dc in last sc: 12 dc.

Row 3: Ch 3, turn; (dc, ch 2, dc) in next ch-1 sp, (2 dc, ch 1, 2 dc) in next ch-2 sp, (dc, ch 2, dc) in next ch-1 sp, skip next 2 dc, dc in last dc: 10 dc.

Row 4: Ch 3, turn; (2 dc, ch 1, 2 dc) in next ch-2 sp, (dc, ch 2, dc) in next ch-1 sp, (2 dc, ch 1, 2 dc) in next ch-2 sp, skip next dc, dc in last dc: 12 dc.

Rows 5-8: Repeat Rows 3 and 4, twice.

Row 9: Ch 3, turn; dc in same st, (dc, ch 2, dc) in next ch-1 sp, (2 dc, ch 1, 2 dc) in next ch-2 sp, (dc, ch 2, dc) in next ch-1 sp, skip next 2 dc, 2 dc in last dc: 12 dc.

Row 10: Ch 3, turn; dc in next dc, (2 dc, ch 1, 2 dc) in next ch-2 sp, (dc, ch 2, dc) in next ch-1 sp, (2 dc, ch 1, 2 dc) in next ch-2 sp, skip next dc, dc in last 2 dc: 14 dc.

Row 11: Ch 3, turn; dc in same st and in next dc, (dc, ch 2, dc) in next ch-1 sp, (2 dc, ch 1, 2 dc) in next ch-2 sp, (dc, ch 2, dc) in next ch-1 sp, skip next 2 dc, dc in next dc, 2 dc in last dc: 14 dc.

Row 12: Ch 3, turn; dc in next 2 dc, (2 dc, ch 1, 2 dc) in next ch-2 sp, (dc, ch 2, dc) in next ch-1 sp, (2 dc, ch 1, 2 dc) in next ch-2 sp, skip next dc, dc in last 3 dc: 16 dc.

Row 13: Ch 3, turn; dc in same st and in next 2 dc, (dc, ch 2, dc) in next ch-1 sp, (2 dc, ch 1, 2 dc) in next ch-2 sp, (dc, ch 2, dc) in next ch-1 sp, skip next 2 dc, dc in next 2 dc, 2 dc in last dc: 16 dc.

Rnd 14: Ch 3, turn; skip next dc, (dc, ch 2, dc) in next dc, (2 dc, ch 1, 2 dc) in next ch-2 sp, (dc, ch 2, dc) in next ch-1 sp, (2 dc, ch 1, 2 dc) in next ch-2 sp, skip next 2 dc, (dc, ch 2, dc) in next dc, skip next dc, dc in last dc: 16 dc.

Rnd 15: Ch 3, turn; (2 dc, ch 1, 2 dc) in next ch-2 sp, ★ (dc, ch 2, dc) in next ch-1 sp, (2 dc, ch 1, 2 dc) in next ch-2 sp; repeat from ★ once **more**, skip next dc, dc in last dc; finish off.

RIGHT SIDE

Row 1: With **right** side facing, join White with slip st in next ch-5 sp on Center; ch 1, 6 sc in same sp, sc in next slip st, 6 sc in next ch-5 sp: 13 sc.

Rows 2-4: Work same as Rows 2-4 of Bottom.

Rows 5-7: Work same as Rows 9-11 of Bottom.

Row 8: Ch 3, turn; dc in same st and in next 2 dc, (2 dc, ch 1, 2 dc) in next ch-2 sp, (dc, ch 2, dc) in next ch-1 sp, (2 dc, ch 1, 2 dc) in next ch-2 sp, skip next dc, dc in next 2 dc, 2 dc in last dc; finish off: 18 dc.

TOP AND LEFT SIDE

Work same as Right Side.

EDGING

Rnd 1: With **right** side facing, join White with slip st in any st; ch 1, sc evenly around working 3 sc in each corner (total sc must be a multiple of 3); join with slip st to first sc.

Rnd 2: Ch 1, sc in first 2 sc, ch 3, skip next sc, ★ sc in next 2 sc, ch 3, skip next sc; repeat from ★ around; join with slip st to first sc, finish off.

PATRIOTIC DAYS

*S*how your patriotic pride with these popular political mascots. Wearing spirited ribbons,
the Democratic donkey and the Republican elephant are Yankee-Doodle dandies!

POLITICAL MASCOTS

Finished Size: Approximately 7¹/₂" tall

MATERIALS
Worsted Weight Yarn, approximately:
  Donkey
    MC (Brown) - 1¹/₄ ounces, (35 grams, 70 yards)
    CC (Dark Brown) - 15 yards
  Elephant
    MC (Grey) - 3 ounces, (90 grams, 170 yards)
    CC (Light Grey) - 4 yards
Crochet hook, size I (5.50 mm) **or** size needed for gauge

Polyester fiberfill
Yarn needle
Donkey: 2 - 6 mm buttons for eyes
  Black embroidery floss
  Cardboard
  ¹/₂ yard of ³/₄" ribbon
Elephant: 2 - 8 mm eyes
  ³/₄ yard of 1" ribbon

GAUGE: 7 sc and 7 rows = 2"

DONKEY

BODY
Rnd 1 (Right side): With MC, ch 2, 6 sc in second ch from hook; do **not** join, place marker **(see Markers, page 138)**.
Rnd 2: 2 Sc in each sc around: 12 sc.
Rnd 3: (Sc in next sc, 2 sc in next sc) around: 18 sc.
Rnd 4: (Sc in next 5 sc, 2 sc in next sc) around: 21 sc.
Rnds 5-7: Sc in each sc around.
Rnd 8: (Sc in next 5 sc, decrease) around: 18 sc.
Rnds 9-13: Sc in each sc around.
Rnd 14: (Sc in next 5 sc, 2 sc in next sc) around: 21 sc.
Rnds 15-17: Sc in each sc around.
Rnd 18: (Sc in next 5 sc, decrease) around: 18 sc.
Stuff Body as needed.
Rnd 19: (Sc in next sc, decrease) around: 12 sc.
Rnd 20: Decrease around: 6 sc.
Add additional stuffing, if necessary.
Rnd 21: (Skip next sc, slip st in next sc) around; finish off.

HEAD
Rnd 1 (Right side): With MC, ch 2, 6 sc in second ch from hook; do **not** join, place marker.
Rnd 2: (Sc in next sc, 2 sc in next sc) around: 9 sc.
Rnds 3 and 4: Sc in each sc around.
Rnd 5: (Sc in next 2 sc, 2 sc in next sc) around: 12 sc.
Rnd 6: Sc in each sc around.
Rnd 7: (Sc in next 3 sc, 2 sc in next sc) around: 15 sc.
Rnd 8: Sc in each sc around.
Rnd 9: (Sc in next 4 sc, 2 sc in next sc) around: 18 sc.
Rnd 10: (Sc in next 5 sc, 2 sc in next sc) around: 21 sc.
Rnd 11: (Sc in next 6 sc, 2 sc in next sc) around: 24 sc.
Rnd 12: Sc in each sc around.
Stuff Head as needed.
Rnds 13 and 14: Decrease around: 6 sc.
Add additional stuffing, if necessary.
Rnd 15: (Skip next sc, slip st in next sc) around; finish off.

NECK
With MC and leaving a long end for sewing, ch 18 **loosely**; being careful not to twist ch, join with slip st to form a ring.
Rnd 1 (Right side): Ch 1, sc in each ch around; do **not** join, place marker: 18 sc.
Rnds 2 and 3: Sc in each sc around; at end of Rnd 3, slip st in next sc, finish off leaving a long end for sewing.

LEG (Make 4)
Rnd 1 (Right side): With CC, ch 2, 6 sc in second ch from hook; do **not** join, place marker.
Rnd 2: (Sc in next 2 sc, 2 sc in next sc) twice changing to MC in last sc **(Fig. 24a, page 138)**: 8 sc.
Rnds 3-8: Sc in each sc around.
Rnd 9: (Sc in next 3 sc, 2 sc in next sc) twice: 10 sc.
Rnds 10-12: Sc in each sc around.
Rnd 13: (Decrease, sc in next 3 sc) twice: 8 sc.
Rnds 14 and 15: Sc in each sc around.
Rnd 16: (Sc in next 3 sc, 2 sc in next sc) twice: 10 sc.
Rnd 17: (Sc in next 4 sc, 2 sc in next sc) twice; slip st in next sc, finish off leaving a long end for sewing: 12 sc.
Stuff **firmly**.

EAR (Make 2)
With MC, ch 8 **loosely**; sc in second ch from hook, hdc in each ch across; finish off leaving a long end for sewing.

TAIL
With MC, ch 11 **loosely**; slip st in back ridge of second ch from hook and in each ch across **(Fig. 2a, page 133)**; finish off leaving a long end for sewing.
Cut 3 strands of CC each 2" long. Hold strands together and fold in half. With crochet hook, draw the folded end up through end of Tail and pull the loose ends through the folded end; draw the knot up **tightly**. Trim to 1".

FINISHING
Sew Neck to Body and stuff lightly. Sew Head to Neck, with nose pointing down.
Sew Ears to Head.
With embroidery floss, add straight stitch nostrils **(Fig. 33, page 141)**.
Add eyes. Sew Legs and Tail to Body.

Mane
Cut a piece of cardboard 1¹/₂" x 4". Wind CC **loosely** and evenly around the cardboard until the card is filled, then cut across one end; repeat as needed.
Thread yarn needle with a long strand of CC. Holding 6 strands of CC together at a time, sew each group to Head and Neck, forming 2 rows. Trim to desired length.

Tie ribbon in a knot around neck and trim ends.

ELEPHANT

TRUNK AND HEAD

Rnd 1 (Right side): With MC, ch 2, 6 sc in second ch from hook; join with slip st to Back Loop Only of first sc *(Fig. 22, page 138)*.

Rnd 2: Ch 1, sc in Back Loop Only of each sc around; do not join, place marker *(see Markers, page 138)*.
Note: Stuff as needed while working entire piece.

Rnds 3-10: Sc in both loops of each sc around.

Rnd 11: (Sc in next 2 sc, 2 sc in next sc) twice: 8 sc.

Rnds 12-18: Sc in each sc around.

Rnd 19: (Sc in next 3 sc, 2 sc in next sc) twice: 10 sc.

Rnds 20-22: Sc in each sc around.

Rnd 23: (Sc in next 4 sc, 2 sc in next sc) twice: 12 sc.

Rnd 24: (Sc in next sc, 2 sc in next sc) around: 18 sc.

Rnds 25 and 26: Sc in each sc around.

Rnd 27: (Sc in next 2 sc, 2 sc in next sc) around: 24 sc.

Rnd 28: (Sc in next 3 sc, 2 sc in next sc) around: 30 sc.

Rnd 29: (Sc in next 4 sc, 2 sc in next sc) around: 36 sc.

Rnds 30-34: Sc in each sc around.

Rnd 35: (Sc in next 4 sc, decrease) around: 30 sc.

Rnd 36: (Sc in next 3 sc, decrease) around: 24 sc.

Rnd 37: (Sc in next 2 sc, decrease) around: 18 sc.

Rnd 38: (Sc in next sc, decrease) around: 12 sc.

Rnd 39: Decrease around: 6 sc.

Rnd 40: (Skip next sc, slip st in next sc) around; finish off.

BODY

Rnd 1 (Right side): With MC, ch 2, 6 sc in second ch from hook; do not join, place marker.

Rnd 2: 2 Sc in each sc around: 12 sc.

Rnd 3: (Sc in next sc, 2 sc in next sc) around: 18 sc.

Rnd 4: (Sc in next 2 sc, 2 sc in next sc) around: 24 sc.

Rnd 5: (Sc in next 3 sc, 2 sc in next sc) around: 30 sc.

Rnd 6: (Sc in next 4 sc, 2 sc in next sc) around: 36 sc.

Rnds 7-22: Sc in each sc around.

Rnd 23: (Sc in next 4 sc, decrease) around: 30 sc.

Rnd 24: (Sc in next 3 sc, decrease) around: 24 sc.

Rnd 25: (Sc in next 2 sc, decrease) around: 18 sc.
Stuff Body as needed.

Rnd 26: (Sc in next sc, decrease) around: 12 sc.

Rnd 27: Decrease around: 6 sc.
Add additional stuffing, if necessary.

Rnd 28: (Skip next sc, slip st in next sc) around; finish off.

LEG (Make 4)

Rnd 1 (Right side): With MC, ch 2, 6 sc in second ch from hook; do not join, place marker.

Rnd 2: 2 Sc in each sc around: 12 sc.

Rnd 3: (Sc in next sc, 2 sc in next sc) around; slip st in Back Loop Only of next sc: 18 sc.

Rnd 4: Ch 1, working in Back Loops Only, sc in first 5 sc changing to CC in last sc worked, drop MC *(Fig. 24a, page 138)*, work Popcorn (toe), ★ sc in next sc changing to CC, drop MC, work Popcorn; repeat from ★ 3 times **more**; cut CC, sc in last 4 sc; do not join, place marker.

Rnd 5: Sc in each sc and in each Popcorn around: 18 sc.

Rnd 6: Sc in next 6 sc, decrease 3 times, sc in next 6 sc: 15 sc.

Rnds 7-13: Sc in each sc around.

Rnd 14: (Sc in next 4 sc, 2 sc in next sc) around: 18 sc.

Rnd 15: (Sc in next 5 sc, 2 sc in next sc) around: 21 sc.

Rnd 16: (Sc in next 6 sc, 2 sc in next sc) around; slip st in next sc, finish off leaving a long end for sewing: 24 sc.
Stuff Leg **firmly**.

EAR (Make 4)

With MC, ch 4 **loosely**.

Row 1 (Right side): Sc in second ch from hook and in each ch across: 3 sc.
Note: Loop a short piece of yarn around any stitch to mark last row as **right** side.

Row 2: Ch 1, turn; 2 sc in first sc, sc in next sc, 2 sc in last sc: 5 sc.

Rows 3 and 4: Ch 1, turn; sc in each sc across.

Row 5: Ch 1, turn; 2 sc in first sc, sc in next 3 sc, 2 sc in last sc: 7 sc.

Rows 6-11: Ch 1, turn; sc in each sc across.

Rows 12 and 13: Ch 1, turn; decrease, sc in each sc across to last 2 sc, decrease: 3 sc.

Edging: Ch 1, do **not** turn; sc evenly around; join with slip st to first sc, finish off.

TAIL

With MC, ch 15 **loosely**; slip st in back ridge of second ch from hook and in each ch across *(Fig. 2a, page 133)*; finish off leaving a long end for sewing.
Cut 3 strands of MC each 2" long. Hold strands together and fold in half. With crochet hook, draw the folded end up through end of Tail and pull the loose ends through the folded end; draw the knot up **tightly**. Trim to 1".

FINISHING

Beginning at side, whipstitch 2 Ears together, matching shaping *(Fig. 28b, page 140)*; leave a long end for sewing.
Repeat for second Ear.

Sew Head to Body with Trunk pointing down. Sew Ears to Head. Add eyes.
Sew Legs to Body, with toes pointing forward.
Sew Tail to Body.
Tie ribbon in a bow around neck.

Brew up some Halloween fun with this "spook-tacular" black cat and the magnets shown on page 121! More delightful than frightful, our green-eyed kitty will add mischief to your celebration. The cat is crocheted in worsted weight yarn and then stuffed to be extra cuddly.

BOO KITTY

Finished Size: Approximately 6½" tall x 8" long

MATERIALS

Worsted Weight Yarn, approximately:
MC (Black) - 3 ounces, (90 grams, 170 yards)
Color A (Pink) - 3 yards
Color B (Green) - 1 yard
Crochet hook, size H (5.00 mm) **or** size needed for gauge
Yarn needle
Polyester fiberfill
Purchased whiskers
¾ yard of 1½" ribbon

GAUGE: Rnds 1-4 of Body = 2"

PATTERN STITCH
DECREASE
Pull up a loop in next 2 sc, YO and draw through all 3 loops on hook **(counts as one sc)**.

BODY

With MC, ch 3 **loosely**; being careful not to twist ch, join with slip st to form a ring.
Rnd 1 (Right side): Ch 1, 2 sc in each ch around; do **not** join, place marker **(see Markers, page 138)**: 6 sc.
Rnd 2: 2 Sc in each sc around: 12 sc.
Rnd 3: (Sc in next sc, 2 sc in next sc) around: 18 sc.
Rnd 4: (Sc in next 2 sc, 2 sc in next sc) around: 24 sc.
Rnd 5: (Sc in next 3 sc, 2 sc in next sc) around: 30 sc.
Rnd 6: (Sc in next 4 sc, 2 sc in next sc) around: 36 sc.
Rnd 7: (Sc in next 5 sc, 2 sc in next sc) around: 42 sc.
Rnds 8-21: Sc in each sc around.
Stuff Body as needed.
Rnd 22: (Sc in next 5 sc, decrease) around: 36 sc.
Rnd 23: (Sc in next 4 sc, decrease) around: 30 sc.
Rnd 24: (Sc in next 3 sc, decrease) around: 24 sc.
Rnd 25: (Sc in next 2 sc, decrease) around: 18 sc.
Add additional stuffing, if necessary.
Rnd 26: (Sc in next sc, decrease) around: 12 sc.
Rnd 27: Decrease around: 6 sc.
Rnd 28: (Slip st in next sc, skip next sc) 3 times; slip st in next sc, finish off.

HEAD

Work same as Body through Rnd 7: 42 sc.
Rnds 8-12: Sc in each sc around.
Rnd 13: (Sc in next 5 sc, decrease) around: 36 sc.
Rnd 14: Decrease around; slip st in next sc, finish off leaving a long end for sewing: 18 sc.
Stuff Head as needed.

LEG (Make 4)

With MC, ch 3 **loosely**; being careful not to twist ch, join with slip st to form a ring.
Rnd 1 (Right side): Ch 1, 2 sc in each ch around; do **not** join, place marker: 6 sc.
Rnd 2: 2 Sc in each sc around: 12 sc.
Rnd 3: (Sc in next sc, 2 sc in next sc) around: 18 sc.
Rnd 4: (Sc in next 2 sc, 2 sc in next sc) around: 24 sc.
Rnds 5-7: Sc in each sc around.
Rnd 8: Sc in next 6 sc, decrease 6 times, sc in next 6 sc: 18 sc.
Rnds 9-14: Sc in each sc around; at end of Rnd 14, slip st in next sc, finish off leaving a long end for sewing.
Stuff Leg **firmly**.

EAR (Make 2)
INNER
Row 1 (Right side): With Color A, ch 2, 2 sc in second ch from hook.
Note: Loop a short piece of yarn around any stitch to mark last row as **right** side.
Row 2: Ch 1, turn; 2 sc in each sc across: 4 sc.
Rows 3 and 4: Ch 1, turn; sc in each sc across.
Row 5: Ch 1, turn; 2 sc in first sc, sc in next 2 sc, 2 sc in last sc; finish off.

OUTER
With MC, work same as Inner Ear; at end of Row 5, do **not** finish off.

EDGING
With **wrong** side of Inner and Outer Ears together, with Inner Ear facing, and working through both pieces, ch 1, sc evenly around entire Ear working 2 sc in each corner; join with slip st to first sc, finish off leaving a long end for sewing.

CHEEK (Make 2)

With MC, ch 3 **loosely**; being careful not to twist ch, join with slip st to form a ring.

Rnd 1 (Right side): Ch 1, 2 sc in each ch around; do **not** join, place marker: 6 sc.

Rnd 2: 2 Sc in each sc around: 12 sc.

Rnd 3: (Sc in next 2 sc, 2 sc in next sc) around: 16 sc.

Rnd 4: Sc in each sc around; slip st in next sc, finish off leaving a long end for sewing.

TAIL

With MC, ch 3 **loosely**; being careful not to twist ch, join with slip st to form a ring.

Rnd 1 (Right side): Ch 1, 2 sc in each ch around; do **not** join, place marker: 6 sc.

Rnd 2: 2 Sc in each sc around: 12 sc.

Note: Stuff as needed while working entire Tail.

Rnds 3-22: Sc in each sc around; at end of Rnd 22, slip st in next sc, finish off leaving a long end for sewing.

FINISHING

Using photo as a guide for placement, sew Head, Legs, and Tail to Body.

Sew Cheeks to Head, stuffing lightly before closing.

Sew Ears to top of Head, placing 2 sts apart.

With Color A, add Satin Stitch nose *(Fig. 34, page 141)*.

With Color B and MC, add Satin Stitch eyes.

Add 2 whiskers to each side of Head at Cheek, attaching in same manner as fringe *(Figs. 30a & b, page 140)*.

Tie ribbon in a bow around neck.

HAUNTING MAGNETS

Finished Size: Ghost - approximately 4"
Jack-O'-Lantern - approximately 3"
Witch - approximately 4¹/₄"

MATERIALS

Worsted Weight Yarn, approximately:
Ghost
White - 7 yards
Jack-O'-Lantern
Orange - 7 yards
Green - 1 yard
Witch
Green - 6 yards
Black - 4 yards
Orange - 2 yards
Crochet hook, size G (4.00 mm) **or** size needed for gauge
Yarn needle
Black felt - small amount
Magnetic strip - 1" **each**
Glue gun
Ghost: 2 - 10 mm oval wiggle eyes
Witch: 1 - 15 mm oval wiggle eye

GAUGE: 8 sc and 8 rows = 2"

GHOST
HEAD

With White, ch 5; join with slip st to form a ring.
Rnd 1 (Right side): Ch 1, (sc, hdc, dc, 3 tr, dc, hdc, sc) in ring; do **not** join or finish off.

BODY

Row 1: Ch 7 **loosely**, slip st in second ch from hook, sc in each ch across, slip st in ring: 5 sc.
Row 2: Ch 1, turn; skip first slip st, sc in each sc across, leave last slip st unworked.
Row 3: Ch 2, turn; slip st in second ch from hook, sc in each sc across, slip st in ring.
Row 4: Ch 1, turn; skip first slip st, sc in each sc across, leave last slip st unworked.
Row 5: Ch 7 **loosely**, turn; slip st in second ch from hook, sc in each ch and in each sc across, slip st in ring: 10 sc.
Row 6: Ch 1, turn; skip first slip st, sc in each sc across, leave last slip st unworked.
Rows 7-9: Repeat Rows 3 and 4 once, then repeat Row 3 once **more**.
Row 10: Ch 1, turn; skip first slip st, sc in next 5 sc, leave remaining 5 sc unworked: 5 sc.

Rows 11-13: Repeat Rows 3 and 4 once, then repeat Row 3 once **more**.
Finish off.

JACK-O'-LANTERN
PUMPKIN

With Orange, ch 4 **loosely**; being careful not to twist ch, join with slip st to form a ring.
Rnd 1 (Right side): Ch 1, 2 sc in each ch around; do **not** join, place marker *(see Markers, page 138)*: 8 sc.
Rnd 2: 2 Sc in each sc around: 16 sc.
Rnd 3: (Sc in next sc, 2 sc in next sc) around: 24 sc.
Rnd 4: (Sc in next 2 sc, 2 sc in next sc) around: 32 sc.
Rnd 5: Hdc in each sc around; slip st in next hdc, finish off.

STEM AND LEAVES

With Green, ch 6 **loosely**; slip st in second ch from hook and in next 3 chs (Stem), leave last ch unworked, ★ ch 3, slip st in second ch from hook, skip last ch, slip st in last ch of Stem (Leaf); repeat from ★ 2 times **more**; finish off leaving a long end for sewing.

WITCH
HEAD

With Green, ch 4 **loosely**; being careful not to twist ch, join with slip st to form a ring.
Rnd 1 (Right side): Ch 1, 2 sc in same ch, 4 sc in next ch, 2 sc in next ch, 4 sc in last ch; do **not** join, place marker *(see Markers, page 138)*: 12 sc.
Note: Loop a short piece of yarn around any stitch to mark last round as **right** side.
Rnd 2: 2 Sc in each sc around: 24 sc.
Rnd 3: Sc in each sc around.
Rnd 4: Sc in next 5 sc, ch 4 **loosely**, slip st in second ch from hook, hdc in next 2 chs, sc in same st as last sc made (nose), sc in next 3 sc, ch 2, hdc in second ch from hook, sc in same st as last sc made (chin), sc in each sc around; slip st in next sc, finish off.

HAIR

With **wrong** side facing, join Orange with slip st in same st as last slip st; work Loop St in first 6 sc pulling loop to measure approximately 1" *(Figs. 12a-c, page 135)*, work Loop St in next 7 sc pulling loop to measure approximately 1³/₄", slip st in next sc; finish off.

HAT

Row 1: With Black, ch 3, 3 hdc in third ch from hook.
Row 2 (Right side): Ch 2 **(counts as first hdc, now and throughout)**, turn; hdc in next 2 hdc, leave turning ch unworked.
Note: Mark last row as **right** side.

Embellished with wiggle eyes and felt facial features, these magnets are sure to scare up lots of smiles!

Row 3: Ch 2, turn; hdc in same st and in next hdc, 2 hdc in last hdc: 5 hdc.

Row 4: Ch 2, turn; hdc in next hdc and in each hdc across.

Row 5: Ch 2, turn; hdc in same st and in next 3 hdc, 2 hdc in last hdc: 7 hdc.

Row 6: Ch 2, turn; hdc in next hdc and in each hdc across.

Row 7: Ch 3, turn; working in Back Loops Only *(Fig. 22, page 138)*, dc in same st, 2 dc in next hdc and in each hdc across; finish off leaving a long end for sewing.

FINISHING

Using photo as guide for placement: Add black felt facial features.

Ghost: Attach eyes.

Jack-O'-Lantern: Sew on Stem and Leaves.

Witch: Sew Hat to Head and attach eye.

Attach magnetic strip to back.

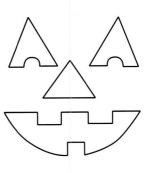

121

THANKSGIVING

Swaying fields of golden grain signal the beginning of the harvest season. During this time of thanksgiving, enrich your celebration with our beautiful doily. It's worked in bedspread weight cotton thread and features a pattern resembling sheaves of wheat.

WHEAT DOILY

Finished Size: Approximately 14" in diameter

MATERIALS

Bedspread Weight Cotton Thread (size 10), approximately 215 yards

Steel crochet hook, size 6 (1.80 mm) **or** size needed for gauge

GAUGE: Rnds 1-8 = 3¼"

PATTERN STITCHES

BEGINNING CLUSTER (uses first 3 dc)
Ch 2, ★ YO, insert hook in **next** dc, YO and pull up a loop, YO and draw through 2 loops on hook; repeat from ★ once **more**, YO and draw through all 3 loops on hook *(Figs. 11a &b, page 134)*.

CLUSTER (uses next 3 dc)
★ YO, insert hook in **next** dc, YO and pull up a loop, YO and draw through 2 loops on hook; repeat from ★ 2 times **more**, YO and draw through all 4 loops on hook.

BODY

Rnd 1 (Right side)**:** Ch 2, 6 sc in second ch from hook; join with slip st to first sc.

Rnds 2 and 3: Ch 1, 2 sc in each sc around; join with slip st to first sc: 24 sc.

Rnd 4: Ch 1, sc in same st, ch 3, skip next sc, (sc in next sc, ch 3, skip next sc) around; join with slip st to first sc: 12 ch-3 sps.

Rnd 5: Slip st in first ch-3 sp, ch 1, sc in same sp, ch 3, (sc in next ch-3 sp, ch 3) around; join with slip st to first sc.

Rnd 6: Slip st in first ch-3 sp, ch 1, (sc, ch 3) twice in same sp and in each ch-3 sp around; join with slip st to first sc: 24 ch-3 sps.

Rnd 7: Repeat Rnd 5.

Rnd 8: Slip st in first ch-3 sp, ch 1, (2 sc, ch 2, 2 sc) in same sp and in each ch-3 sp around; join with slip st to first sc: 24 ch-2 sps.

Rnd 9: Slip st in next sc and in next ch-2 sp, ch 8, (dc in next ch-2 sp, ch 5) around; join with slip st to third ch of beginning ch-8: 24 loops.

Rnd 10: Ch 3 (**counts as first dc, now and throughout**), (2 dc, ch 3, tr, ch 3, 3 dc) in same st, ch 3, sc in next dc, ch 3, ★ (3 dc, ch 3, tr, ch 3, 3 dc) in next dc, ch 3, sc in next dc, ch 3; repeat from ★ around; join with slip st to first dc: 12 tr.

Rnd 11: Work beginning Cluster, ch 3, (3 dc, ch 3, tr, ch 3, 3 dc) in next tr, ch 3, ★ (work Cluster, ch 3) twice, (3 dc, ch 3, tr, ch 3, 3 dc) in next tr, ch 3; repeat from ★ around to last 3 dc, work Cluster, ch 1, hdc in top of beginning Cluster to form last sp: 24 Clusters.

Rnd 12: Ch 7, work Cluster, ch 3, (3 dc, ch 3, tr, ch 3, 3 dc) in next tr, ch 3, work Cluster, ch 3, skip next ch-3 sp, ★ tr in next ch-3 sp, ch 3, work Cluster, ch 3, (3 dc, ch 3, tr, ch 3, 3 dc) in next tr, ch 3, work Cluster, ch 3, skip next ch-3 sp; repeat from ★ around; join with slip st to fourth ch of beginning ch-7.

Rnd 13: Ch 7, work Cluster, ch 3, (3 dc, ch 3, tr, ch 3, 3 dc) in next tr, ch 3, work Cluster, ch 3, ★ tr in next tr, ch 3, work Cluster, ch 3, (3 dc, ch 3, tr, ch 3, 3 dc) in next tr, ch 3, work Cluster, ch 3; repeat from ★ around; join with slip st to fourth ch of beginning ch-7.

Rnd 14: Ch 3, (2 dc, ch 3, tr, ch 3, 3 dc) in same st, ch 3, work Cluster, ch 3, ★ (3 dc, ch 3, tr, ch 3, 3 dc) in next tr, ch 3, work Cluster, ch 3; repeat from ★ around; join with slip st to first dc.

Rnd 15: Work beginning Cluster, ch 5, 3 dc in next tr, ch 5, ★ (work Cluster, ch 5) twice, 3 dc in next tr, ch 5; repeat from ★ around to last 3 dc, work Cluster, ch 2, dc in top of beginning Cluster to form last loop.

Rnd 16: Ch 1, sc in same loop, ch 5, sc in next loop, ch 5, work Cluster, ch 5, ★ (sc in next loop, ch 5) 3 times, work Cluster, ch 5; repeat from ★ around to last loop, sc in last loop, ch 2, dc in first sc to form last loop.

Rnds 17-19: Ch 1, sc in same loop, (ch 5, sc in next loop) around, ch 2, dc in first sc to form last loop: 96 loops.

Rnd 20: Ch 3, 2 dc in same st, ch 3, sc in next loop, ch 3, ★ 3 dc in center ch of next loop, ch 3, sc in next loop, ch 3; repeat from ★ around; join with slip st to first dc.

Rnd 21: Work beginning Cluster, ch 3, sc in next ch-3 sp, ch 4, slip st in third ch from hook, ch 1, sc in next ch-3 sp, ch 3, ★ work Cluster, ch 3, sc in next ch-3 sp, ch 4, slip st in third ch from hook, ch 1, sc in next ch-3 sp, ch 3; repeat from ★ around; join with slip st to top of beginning Cluster, finish off.

See Washing and Blocking, page 140.

CHRISTMAS

*O*ne of the joys of the holiday season is decorating our homes with handmade pieces we've grown to cherish. Sure to be added to those treasured keepsakes are the colorful creations in this collection. Our ruffled miniature tree is stitched with cotton thread and then stiffened. Sprigs of holly and shimmering trims provide a festive finish.

RUFFLED MINI TREE

Finished Size: Approximately 16" tall x 10" in diameter at base

MATERIALS
Bedspread Weight Cotton Thread (size 10), approximately 635 yards
Steel crochet hook, size 7 (1.65 mm) **or** size needed for gauge
Starching materials: Commercial fabric stiffener, 17" x 27½" heavy cardboard, transparent tape, plastic wrap, resealable plastic bag, terry towel, paper towels, and stainless steel pins
Protective coating materials: Porcelain glaze gloss finish, disposable plastic or rubber gloves, stiff paint brush, and waxed paper
Finishing materials: Glue gun, glass ornaments, holly sprigs, ribbon, and braid

GAUGE: Rnds 1-3 = 1½"

INNER CONE
Rnd 1 (Right side)**:** Ch 4, 5 dc in fourth ch from hook; join with slip st to top of beginning ch: 6 sts.
Note: Loop a short piece of thread around any stitch to mark last round as **right** side.
Rnd 2: Ch 4, tr in next dc and in each dc around; join with slip st to top of beginning ch-4.
Rnd 3: Ch 6, (dtr in next tr, ch 1) around; join with slip st to fifth ch of beginning ch-6.
Rnd 4: Ch 5 **(counts as first dtr, now and throughout)**, dtr in same st, ch 1, (2 dtr in next dtr, ch 1) around; join with slip st to first dtr: 12 dtr.
Rnd 5: Ch 6, (dtr in next dtr, ch 1) around; join with slip st to fifth ch of beginning ch-6.
Rnds 6 and 7: Ch 7, (dtr in next dtr, ch 2) around; join with slip st to fifth ch of beginning ch-7.
Rnd 8: Ch 5, dtr in same st, ch 2, (2 dtr in next dtr, ch 2) around; join with slip st to first dtr: 24 dtr.
Rnds 9 and 10: Ch 6, (dtr in next dtr, ch 1) around; join with slip st to fifth ch of beginning ch-6.
Rnds 11-14: Ch 7, (dtr in next dtr, ch 2) around; join with slip st to fifth ch of beginning ch-7.

Rnd 15: Ch 5, dtr in same st, ch 2, (dtr in next dtr, ch 2) twice, ★ 2 dtr in next dtr, ch 2, (dtr in next dtr, ch 2) twice; repeat from ★ around; join with slip st to first dtr: 32 dtr.
Rnds 16 and 17: Ch 7, (dtr in next dtr, ch 2) around; join with slip st to fifth ch of beginning ch-7.
Rnds 18-20: Ch 8, (dtr in next dtr, ch 3) around; join with slip st to fifth ch of beginning ch-8.
Rnd 21: Ch 9, (dtr in next dtr, ch 4) around; join with slip st to fifth ch of beginning ch-9; do **not** finish off.

Note: Layers are worked from bottom of Inner Cone to top.

FIRST LAYER (Bottom)
Rnd 1: Slip st in first ch-4 sp, ch 3, 3 dc in same sp, 4 dc in next ch-4 sp and in each ch-4 sp around; join with slip st to top of beginning ch-3: 128 sts.
Rnd 2: Ch 6, (dtr in next dc, ch 1) around; join with slip st to fifth ch of beginning ch-6.
Rnd 3: Slip st in first ch-1 sp, ch 1, sc in same sp, (ch 4, sc in next ch-1 sp) around, ch 1, dc in first sc to form last sp.
Rnds 4-6: Ch 1, sc in same sp, (ch 4, sc in next ch-4 sp) around, ch 1, dc in first sc to form last sp.
Rnd 7: Ch 7, dc in fourth ch from hook, dc in same sp, ★ dc in next ch-4 sp, ch 4, dc in fourth ch from hook, dc in same sp; repeat from ★ around; join with slip st to third ch of beginning ch-7, finish off.

SECOND LAYER
Rnd 1: With **right** side facing, join thread with slip st in any ch-3 sp on Rnd 18; ch 3, 3 dc in same sp, 4 dc in next ch-3 sp and in each ch-3 sp around; join with slip st to top of beginning ch-3: 128 sts.
Rnds 2-7: Repeat Rnds 2-7 of First Layer.

THIRD LAYER
Rnd 1: With **right** side facing, join thread with slip st in any ch-2 sp on Rnd 15; ch 3, 3 dc in same sp, 4 dc in next ch-2 sp and in each ch-2 sp around; join with slip st to top of beginning ch-3: 96 sts.
Rnds 2-7: Repeat Rnds 2-7 of First Layer.

FOURTH LAYER

Rnd 1: With **right** side facing, join thread with slip st in any ch-2 sp on Rnd 12; ch 3, 3 dc in same sp, 4 dc in next ch-2 sp and in each ch-2 sp around; join with slip st to top of beginning ch-3: 96 sts.

Rnds 2-7: Repeat Rnds 2-7 of First Layer.

FIFTH LAYER

Rnd 1: With **right** side facing, join thread with slip st in any ch-1 sp on Rnd 10; ch 5, (tr, ch 1) twice in same sp, (tr, ch 1) 3 times in next ch-1 sp and in each ch-1 sp around; join with slip st to fourth ch of beginning ch-5: 72 ch-1 sps.

Rnd 2: Slip st in first ch-1 sp, ch 1, sc in same sp, (ch 4, sc in next ch-1 sp) around, ch 1, dc in first sc to form last sp.

Rnds 3 and 4: Ch 1, sc in same sp, (ch 4, sc in next ch-4 sp) around, ch 1, dc in first sc to form last sp.
Rnd 5: Repeat Rnd 7 of First Layer.

SIXTH LAYER

Rnd 1: With **right** side facing, join thread with slip st in any ch-2 sp on Rnd 8; ch 5, (tr, ch 1) 3 times in same sp, (tr, ch 1) 4 times in next ch-2 sp and in each ch-2 sp around; join with slip st to fourth ch of beginning ch-5: 48 ch-1 sps.
Rnds 2-5: Repeat Rnds 2-5 of Fifth Layer.

SEVENTH LAYER

Rnd 1: With **right** side facing, join thread with slip st in any ch-2 sp on Rnd 6; ch 5, (tr, ch 1) 3 times in same sp, (tr, ch 1) 4 times in next ch-2 sp and in each ch-2 sp around; join with slip st to fourth ch of beginning ch-5: 48 ch-1 sps.
Rnds 2-5: Repeat Rnds 2-5 of Fifth Layer.

EIGHTH LAYER

Rnd 1: With **right** side facing, join thread with slip st in any ch-1 sp on Rnd 4; ch 5, (tr, ch 1) 3 times in same sp, (tr, ch 1) 4 times in next ch-1 sp and in each ch-1 sp around; join with slip st to fourth ch of beginning ch-5: 24 ch-1 sps.
Rnds 2-5: Repeat Rnds 2-5 of Fifth Layer.

NINTH LAYER (Top)

Rnd 1: With **right** side facing, join thread with slip st in any ch-1 sp on Rnd 3; ch 4, (dc, ch 1) twice in same sp, (dc, ch 1) 3 times in next ch-1 sp and in each ch-1 sp around; join with slip st to third ch of beginning ch-4: 18 ch-1 sps.
Rnds 2-5: Repeat Rnds 2-5 of Fifth Layer.

FINISHING

See Starching and Blocking, page 143.
Decorate as desired.

Quick CHEERY TREE SKIRT

Finished Size: Approximately 18" from top edge to bottom edge.

MATERIALS

Worsted Weight Yarn, approximately:
  MC (Red) - 27 ounces, (770 grams, 1,775 yards)
  Color A (Green) - 3 ounces, (90 grams, 195 yards)
  Color B (White) - 2 ounces, (60 grams, 130 yards)
Crochet hook, size N (9.00 mm) **or** size needed for gauge

Note: Entire Skirt is worked holding 4 strands of yarn together.

GAUGE: 7 sc and 8 rows = 4"

With MC, ch 25 **loosely**.
Row 1 (Right side): Sc in second ch from hook and in each ch across: 24 sc.
Note: Loop a short piece of yarn around any stitch to mark last row as **right** side.
Row 2: Ch 1, turn; 2 sc in first sc, sc in next 3 sc, (2 sc in next sc, sc in next 3 sc) across: 30 sc.
Row 3: Ch 1, turn; 2 sc in first sc, sc in next 4 sc, (2 sc in next sc, sc in next 4 sc) across: 36 sc.
Row 4: Ch 1, turn; 2 sc in first sc, sc in next 5 sc, (2 sc in next sc, sc in next 5 sc) across: 42 sc.
Row 5: Ch 1, turn; 2 sc in first sc, sc in next 6 sc, (2 sc in next sc, sc in next 6 sc) across changing to Color A in last sc *(Fig. 24a, page 138)*: 48 sc.
Row 6: Ch 1, turn; (sc, ch 1, sc) in first sc, ★ (ch 1, skip next sc, sc in next sc) 3 times, ch 1, skip next sc, (sc, ch 1, sc) in next sc; repeat from ★ across to last 7 sc, ch 1, (skip next sc, sc in next sc, ch 1) twice, skip next sc, sc in last 2 sc changing to Color B in last sc: 31 sc and 29 ch-1 sps.
Row 7: Ch 1, turn; sc in first sc, (ch 1, skip next sc, sc in next ch-1 sp) across to last sc, sc in last sc changing to Color A.
Row 8: Ch 1, turn; (sc, ch 1, sc) in first sc, (ch 1, skip next sc, sc in next ch-1 sp) 4 times, ★ ch 1, skip next sc, (sc, ch 1, sc) in next ch-1 sp, (ch 1, skip next sc, sc in next ch-1 sp) 4 times; repeat from ★ across to last sc, sc in last sc changing to MC: 37 sc and 35 ch-1 sps.
Row 9: Ch 1, turn; sc in first sc, (ch 1, skip next sc, sc in next ch-1 sp) across to last sc, sc in last sc.
Row 10: Ch 1, turn; 2 sc in first sc, sc in next sc, (sc in next ch-1 sp, sc in next sc) 5 times, ★ 2 sc in next ch-1 sp, sc in next sc, (sc in next ch-1 sp, sc in next sc) 5 times; repeat from ★ across: 78 sc.
Row 11: Ch 1, turn; 2 sc in first sc, sc in next 12 sc, (2 sc in next sc, sc in next 12 sc) across: 84 sc.
Row 12: Ch 1, turn; 2 sc in first sc, sc in next 13 sc, (2 sc in next sc, sc in next 13 sc) across: 90 sc.
Row 13: Ch 1, turn; 2 sc in first sc, sc in next 14 sc, (2 sc in next sc, sc in next 14 sc) across: 96 sc.
Row 14: Ch 1, turn; 2 sc in first sc, sc in next 15 sc, (2 sc in next sc, sc in next 15 sc) across: 102 sc.
Row 15: Ch 1, turn; 2 sc in first sc, sc in next 16 sc, (2 sc in next sc, sc in next 16 sc) across: 108 sc.
Row 16: Ch 1, turn; 2 sc in first sc, sc in next 17 sc, (2 sc in next sc, sc in next 17 sc) across: 114 sc.
Row 17: Ch 1, turn; 2 sc in first sc, sc in next 18 sc, (2 sc in next sc, sc in next 18 sc) across: 120 sc.
Row 18: Ch 1, turn; 2 sc in first sc, sc in next 19 sc, (2 sc in next sc, sc in next 19 sc) across: 126 sc.
Row 19: Ch 1, turn; 2 sc in first sc, sc in next 20 sc, (2 sc in next sc, sc in next 20 sc) across: 132 sc.

Worked holding four strands of yarn, this colorful striped skirt makes a cheery accent for your Christmas tree.

Row 20: Ch 1, turn; 2 sc in first sc, sc in next 21 sc, (2 sc in next sc, sc in next 21 sc) across: 138 sc.

Row 21: Ch 1, turn; 2 sc in first sc, sc in next 22 sc, (2 sc in next sc, sc in next 22 sc) across: 144 sc.

Row 22: Ch 1, turn; 2 sc in first sc, sc in next 23 sc, (2 sc in next sc, sc in next 23 sc) across: 150 sc.

Row 23: Ch 1, turn; 2 sc in first sc, sc in next 24 sc, (2 sc in next sc, sc in next 24 sc) across: 156 sc.

Row 24: Ch 1, turn; 2 sc in first sc, sc in next 25 sc, (2 sc in next sc, sc in next 25 sc) across: 162 sc.

Row 25: Ch 1, turn; 2 sc in first sc, sc in next 26 sc, (2 sc in next sc, sc in next 26 sc) across: 168 sc.

Row 26: Ch 1, turn; 2 sc in first sc, sc in next 27 sc, (2 sc in next sc, sc in next 27 sc) across: 174 sc.

Row 27: Ch 1, turn; 2 sc in first sc, sc in next 28 sc, (2 sc in next sc, sc in next 28 sc) across: 180 sc.

Row 28: Ch 1, turn; (sc, ch 1, sc) in first sc, ★ (ch 1, skip next sc, sc in next sc) 14 times, ch 1, skip next sc, (sc, ch 1, sc) in next sc; repeat from ★ 4 times **more**, (ch 1, skip next sc, sc in next sc) across to last 3 sc, ch 1, skip next sc, sc in last 2 sc changing to Color A in last sc: 97 sc and 95 ch-1 sps.

Row 29: Ch 1, turn; sc in first sc, (ch 1, skip next sc, sc in next ch-1 sp) across to last sc, sc in last sc changing to Color B.

Row 30: Ch 1, turn; (sc, ch 1, sc) in first sc, (ch 1, skip next sc, sc in next ch-1 sp) 15 times, ★ ch 1, skip next sc, (sc, ch 1, sc) in next ch-1 sp, (ch 1, skip next sc, sc in next ch-1 sp) 15 times; repeat from ★ across to last sc, sc in last sc changing to Color A: 103 sc and 101 ch-1 sps.

Row 31: Ch 1, turn; sc in first sc, (ch 1, skip next sc, sc in next ch-1 sp) across to last sc, sc in last sc changing to MC.

Row 32: Ch 1, turn; sc in first sc, ch 2, skip next sc, sc in next ch-1 sp, ★ (ch 1, skip next sc, sc in next ch-1 sp) 16 times, ch 2, skip next sc, sc in next ch-1 sp; repeat from ★ 4 times **more**, (ch 1, skip next sc, sc in next ch-1 sp) across to last sc, sc in last sc; finish off.

Quick SNOWFLAKE SACHETS

Finished Size: Approximately 4" in diameter

MATERIALS

Bedspread Weight Cotton Thread (size 10), approximately:

Snowflake #1

MC (Red) - 35 yards

CC (Ecru) - 13 yards

Snowflake #2

MC (Red) - 35 yards

CC (Ecru) - 15 yards

Snowflake #3

MC (Red) - 35 yards

CC (Ecru) - 18 yards

Steel crochet hook, size 6 (1.80 mm) **or** size needed for gauge

1/2 yard of 1/8" ribbon for **each**

Tapestry needle

Sewing needle and thread

4 - 5" squares of bridal net for **each**

Potpourri

GAUGE: Rnds 1 and 2 of Back = 1 1/4"

PATTERN STITCHES

CLUSTER

Ch 3, ★ YO, insert hook in third ch from hook, YO and pull up a loop, YO and draw through 2 loops on hook; repeat from ★ once **more**, YO and draw through all 3 loops on hook *(Figs. 10a & b, page 134)*.

5-TR CLUSTER (uses next 5 tr)

★ YO twice, insert hook in **next** tr, YO and pull up a loop, (YO and draw through 2 loops on hook) twice; repeat from ★ 4 **more**, YO and draw through all 6 loops on hook *(Figs. 11a & b, page 134)*.

2-TR CLUSTER

Ch 4, ★ YO twice, insert hook in fourth ch from hook, YO and pull up a loop, (YO and draw through 2 loops on hook) twice; repeat from ★ once **more**, YO and draw through all 3 loops on hook.

BEGINNING 3-TR CLUSTER

Ch 3, ★ YO twice, insert hook st or sp indicated, YO and pull up a loop, (YO and draw through 2 loops on hook) twice; repeat from ★ once **more**, YO and draw through all 3 loops on hook.

3-TR CLUSTER

★ YO twice, insert hook st or sp indicated, YO and pull up a loop, (YO and draw through 2 loops on hook) twice; repeat from ★ 2 times **more**, YO and draw through all 4 loops on hook.

2-PICOT LOOP

Ch 6, slip st in fifth ch from hook, ch 8, slip st in fifth ch from hook, ch 2.

4-PICOT LOOP

(Ch 5, slip st in fifth ch from hook) 4 times, ch 1.

BACK

With MC, ch 4; join with slip st to form a ring.

Rnd 1 (Right side): Ch 3, 11 dc in ring; join with slip st to top of beginning ch-3: 12 sts.

Note: Loop a short piece of thread around any stitch to mark last round as **right** side.

Rnd 2: Ch 5 **(counts as first dc plus ch 2, now and throughout)**, dc in same st, ch 2, dc in next dc, ch 2, ★ (dc, ch 2) twice in next dc, dc in next dc, ch 2; repeat from ★ around; join with slip st to first dc: 18 dc.

Rnd 3: Ch 5, dc in next dc, ch 2, (dc, ch 2) twice in next dc, ★ (dc in next dc, ch 2) twice, (dc, ch 2) twice in next dc; repeat from ★ around; join with slip st to first dc: 24 dc.

Rnd 4: Ch 5, dc in same st, ch 2, (dc in next dc, ch 2) 3 times, ★ (dc, ch 2) twice in next dc, (dc in next dc, ch 2) 3 times; repeat from ★ around; join with slip st to first dc: 30 dc.

Rnd 5: Ch 5, dc in next dc, ch 2, (dc, ch 2) twice in next dc, ★ (dc in next dc, ch 2) 4 times, (dc, ch 2) twice in next dc; repeat from ★ around to last 2 dc, (dc in next dc, ch 2) twice; join with slip st to first dc: 36 dc.

Rnd 6: Ch 5, dc in same st, ch 2, (dc in next dc, ch 2) 5 times, ★ (dc, ch 2) twice in next dc, (dc in next dc, ch 2) 5 times; repeat from ★ around; join with slip st to first dc: 42 dc.

Rnd 7: Ch 5, (dc in next dc, ch 2) 3 times, (dc, ch 2) twice in next dc, ★ (dc in next dc, ch 2) 6 times, (dc, ch 2) twice in next dc; repeat from ★ around to last 2 dc, (dc in next dc, ch 2) twice; join with slip st to first dc: 48 dc.

Rnd 8 (Eyelet rnd): Ch 5, (dc in next dc, ch 2) around; join with slip st to first dc, finish off: 48 ch-2 sps.

SNOWFLAKE #1 - FRONT

Rnd 1 (Right side): With CC, ch 2, sc in second ch from hook, (ch 6, sc in same ch) 5 times, ch 2, tr in first sc to form last loop: 6 loops.

Note: Mark last round as **right** side.

Rnd 2: Ch 8, dc in same loop, ch 6, ★ (dc, ch 5, dc) in next loop, ch 6; repeat from ★ around; join with slip st to third ch of beginning ch-8: 12 loops.

Filled with potpourri, these lacy ornaments also make sweet-smelling gifts and package tie-ons.

Rnd 3: Slip st in first loop, ch 6, (tr, ch 5, tr, ch 2, tr) in same loop, ch 1, sc in next ch-6 loop, ch 1, ★ (tr, ch 2, tr, ch 5, tr, ch 2, tr) in next ch-5 loop, ch 1, sc in next ch-6 loop, ch 1; repeat from ★ around; join with slip st to fourth ch of beginning ch-6.

Rnd 4: Ch 1, sc in same st, work Cluster, dc in next tr, work Cluster, (tr, work Cluster) 3 times in next loop, dc in next tr, work Cluster, sc in next tr and in next ch-1 sp, sc in next sc and in next ch-1 sp, ★ sc in next tr, work Cluster, dc in next tr, work Cluster, (tr, work Cluster) 3 times in next loop, dc in next tr, work Cluster, sc in next tr and in next ch-1 sp, sc in next sc and in next ch-1 sp; repeat from ★ around; join with slip st to first sc, finish off: 36 Clusters.

Rnd 5: With **right** side facing, skip first Cluster and join MC with sc in next dc *(see Joining With Sc, page 137)*; ch 9, skip next 4 Clusters, keeping chs **behind** Clusters, sc in next dc, ch 5, ★ skip next 2 Clusters, sc in next dc, ch 9, skip next 4 Clusters, keeping chs **behind** Clusters, sc in next dc, ch 5; repeat from ★ around; join with slip st to first sc: 12 loops.

Rnd 6: Ch 5, (skip next ch, dc in next ch, ch 2) 4 times, dc in next sc, ch 2, (skip next ch, dc in next ch, ch 2) twice, ★ dc in next sc, ch 2, (skip next ch, dc in next ch, ch 2) 4 times, dc in next sc, ch 2, (skip next ch, dc in next ch, ch 2) twice; repeat from ★ around; join with slip st to first dc: 48 ch-2 sps.

Rnd 7 (Eyelet rnd): Ch 5, dc in next dc, ch 2, holding next tip of Snowflake in front of next dc, dc in both center tr on Rnd 4 **and** in dc to join Snowflake, ch 2, ★ (dc in next dc, ch 2) 7 times, holding next tip of Snowflake in front of next dc, dc in both center tr on Rnd 4 **and** in dc, ch 2; repeat from ★ 4 times **more**, (dc in next dc, ch 2) around; join with slip st to first dc: 48 ch-2 sps.

Rnd 8 (Edging): Ch 2, dc in same st, (slip st, ch 2, dc) in next dc and in each dc around; join with slip st to first st, finish off.

SNOWFLAKE #2 - FRONT

Rnd 1 (Right side): With CC, ch 9, dc in ninth ch from hook, (ch 5, dc in same ch) 4 times, ch 2, dc in fourth ch of beginning ch-9 to form last loop: 6 loops.

Note: Mark last round as **right** side.

Rnd 2: Ch 1, (sc, ch 5, sc) in same loop, (ch 5, sc) twice in next loop and in each loop around, ch 2, dc in first sc to form last loop: 12 loops.

Rnd 3: Ch 1, sc in same loop, ch 4, 5 tr in next loop, ★ ch 4, sc in next loop, ch 4, 5 tr in next loop; repeat from ★ around, tr in first sc to form last sp: 30 tr.

Rnd 4: Ch 1, sc in same sp, ch 5, sc in next ch-4 sp, ch 5, work 5-tr Cluster, ★ ch 6, (sc in next ch-4 sp, ch 5) twice, work 5-tr Cluster; repeat from ★ around, ch 2, tr in first sc to form last loop: 6 5-tr Clusters.

Rnd 5: Ch 1, sc in same loop, work 2-tr Cluster, (tr, work 2-tr Cluster twice, tr) in next loop, work 2-tr Cluster, sc in next loop, ch 5, ★ sc in next loop, work 2-tr Cluster, (tr, work 2-tr Cluster twice, tr) in next loop, work 2-tr Cluster, sc in next loop, ch 5; repeat from ★ around; join with slip st to first sc, finish off: 24 2-tr Clusters.

Rnd 6: With **right** side facing, skip next 2-tr Cluster and join MC with slip st in next tr, ch 8, skip next 2 2-tr Clusters, keeping chs **behind** 2-tr Clusters, dc in next tr, ch 2, [tr, ch 2, (dc, ch 2) twice, tr] in next loop, ch 2, ★ skip next 2-tr Cluster, dc in next tr, ch 5, skip next 2 2-tr Clusters, keeping chs **behind** 2-tr Clusters, dc in next tr, ch 2, [tr, ch 2, (dc, ch 2) twice, tr] in next loop, ch 2; repeat from ★ around; join with slip st to third ch of beginning ch-8: 36 sps.

Rnd 7 (Eyelet rnd): Ch 5, (dc, ch 2) twice in next loop, dc in next dc, ch 2, ★ (skip next ch-2 sp, dc in next st, ch 2) 5 times, (dc, ch 2) twice in next loop, dc in next dc, ch 2; repeat from ★ 4 times **more**, (skip next ch-2 sp, dc in next st, ch 2) 4 times; join with slip st to third ch of beginning ch-5: 48 ch-2 sps.

Rnd 8 (Edging): Ch 2, dc in same st, (slip st, ch 2, dc) in next dc and in each dc around; join with slip st to first st, finish off.

SNOWFLAKE #3 - FRONT

Rnd 1 (Right side): With CC, ch 2, 6 sc in second ch from hook; join with slip st to first sc.

Note: Mark last round as **right** side.

Rnd 2: Work beginning 3-tr Cluster in same st, work 2-tr Cluster, ch 1, ★ work 3-tr Cluster in next sc, work 2-tr Cluster, ch 1; repeat from ★ around; join with slip st to top of beginning 3-tr Cluster: 12 Clusters.

Rnd 3: Ch 1, sc in same st, work 2-Picot Loop, skip next 2-tr Cluster, ★ sc in next 3-tr Cluster, work 2-Picot Loop, skip next 2-tr Cluster; repeat from ★ around; join with slip st to first sc: 12 Picots.

Rnd 4: Slip st in first 2 chs, ch 1, working **behind** next Picot, slip st in next ch, ch 1, 3 sc in same sp, ch 10, skip next 2 Picots, ★ 3 sc in next sp, ch 10, skip next 2 Picots; repeat from ★ around; join with slip st to first sc: 6 loops.

Rnd 5: Slip st in next 2 sc and in next loop, in same loop work [beginning 3-tr Cluster, ch 3, 3-tr Cluster, (4-Picot Loop, 3-tr Cluster) twice, ch 3, 3-tr Cluster], in next loop and in each loop around work [3-tr Cluster, ch 3, 3-tr Cluster, (4-Picot Loop, 3-tr Cluster) twice, ch 3, 3-tr Cluster]; join with slip st to top of beginning 3-tr Cluster, finish off: 30 Clusters.

Rnd 6: With **right** side facing, join MC with slip st in first ch-3 sp, ch 10 **(counts as first tr plus ch 6)**, skip next 3-tr Cluster, tr in next 3-tr Cluster, ch 6, tr in next ch-3 sp, ch 4, ★ tr in next ch-3 sp, ch 6, skip next 3-tr Cluster, tr in next 3-tr Cluster, ch 6, tr in next ch-3 sp, ch 4; repeat from ★ around; join with slip st to first tr: 18 tr.

Rnd 7 (Eyelet rnd): Ch 5, [(dc, ch 2) twice in next ch-6 loop, dc in next tr, ch 2] 2 times, dc in next ch-4 sp, ch 2, ★ dc in next tr, ch 2, [(dc, ch 2) twice in next ch-6 loop, dc in next tr, ch 2] 2 times, dc in next ch-4 sp, ch 2; repeat from ★ around; join with slip st to first dc: 48 ch-2 sps.

Rnd 8 (Edging): Ch 2, dc in same st, (slip st, ch 2, dc) in next dc and in each dc around; join with slip st to first st, finish off.

FINISHING

See Washing and Blocking, page 140.

POTPOURRI POUCH

Using Back for pattern, cut four pieces of bridal net, allowing ¼" seam allowance. Sew seam leaving a 2" opening for turning. Turn right side out having 2 layers for each side. Fill with potpourri and sew opening closed.

JOINING

With **wrong** sides together and matching spaces, weave ribbon through Eyelet rnd, inserting pouch before closing. Tie ribbon in a bow to secure.

Symbolizing bead garlands, ribbons of Christmasy colors make this fringed afghan especially merry!

MERRY AFGHAN

Finished Size: Approximately 49" x 65"

MATERIALS

Worsted Weight Yarn, approximately:
MC (White) - 25 ounces, (710 grams, 1,645 yards)
Color A (Red) - 12 ounces, (340 grams, 790 yards)
Color B (Green) - 11 ounces, (310 grams, 725 yards)
Crochet hook, size I (5.50 mm) **or** size needed for gauge

Note #1: Each row is worked across length of afghan.
Note #2: When changing colors at end of rows, leave a 7" end
for fringe.

COLOR SEQUENCE

2 Rows each Color A *(Fig. 24a, page 138)*, ★ MC, Color B,
MC, Color A; repeat from ★ throughout.

GAUGE: In pattern, 14 sts = 4"

With Color A, ch 229 **loosely.**
Row 1 (Right side)**:** Sc in second ch from hook and in next
3 chs, (dc in next 4 chs, sc in next 4 chs) across: 228 sts.
Note: Loop a short piece of yarn around any stitch to mark last
row as **right** side.
Row 2: Ch 1, turn; sc in first 4 sc, (dc in next 4 dc, sc in next
4 sc) across.
Row 3: Ch 3 **(counts as first dc, now and throughout)**,
turn; dc in next 3 sc, (sc in next 4 dc, dc in next 4 sc) across.
Row 4: Ch 3, turn; dc in next 3 dc, (sc in next 4 sc, dc in next
4 dc) across.
Row 5: Ch 1, turn; sc in first 4 dc, (dc in next 4 sc, sc in next
4 dc) across.
Repeat Rows 2-5 until afghan measures approximately 49",
ending by working Row 2 with Color A.
Finish off.

Add fringe using 2 or 3 strands of matching color, each 15" long
(Figs. 30a & b, page 140); attach in end of each row across
both ends of afghan.

general instructions

ABBREVIATIONS

BLO	Back Loop(s) Only
BPdc	Back Post double crochet(s)
BPhdc	Back Post half double crochet(s)
CC	Contrasting Color
ch(s)	chain(s)
dc	double crochet(s)
dtr	double treble crochet(s)
FLO	Front Loop(s) Only
FPdc	Front Post double crochet(s)
FPhdc	Front Post half double crochet(s)
FPtr	Front Post treble crochet(s)
hdc	half double crochet(s)
MC	Main Color
mm	millimeters
Rnd(s)	Round(s)
sc	single crochet(s)
sp(s)	space(s)
st(s)	stitch(es)
tr	treble crochet(s)
YO	yarn over

★ — work instructions following ★ as many **more** times as indicated in addition to the first time.

† to † — work all instructions from first † to second † **as many** times as specified.

( ) or [ ] — work enclosed instructions **as many** times as specified by the number immediately following **or** work all enclosed instructions in the stitch or space indicated **or** contains explanatory remarks.

work even — work without increasing or decreasing in the established pattern.

GAUGE

Correct gauge is essential for proper size or fit. Hook sizes given in instructions are merely guides and should never be used without first making a sample swatch as indicated. Then measure it, counting your stitches and rows or rounds carefully. If your swatch is smaller than specified, try again with a larger size hook; if larger, try again with a smaller size. Keep trying until you find the size that will give you the specified gauge. DO NOT HESITATE TO CHANGE HOOK SIZE TO OBTAIN CORRECT GAUGE. On garments and afghans, once proper gauge is obtained, measure width of piece approximately every 3" to be sure gauge remains consistent.

basic stitch guide

CHAIN

When beginning a first row of crochet in a chain, always skip the first chain from the hook, and work into the second chain from hook (for single crochet), third chain from hook (for half double crochet), or fourth chain from hook (for double crochet), etc. *(Fig. 1)*.

Fig. 1

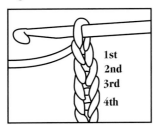

WORKING INTO THE CHAIN

Method 1: Insert hook into back ridge of each chain indicated *(Fig. 2a)*.
Method 2: Insert hook under top two strands of each chain *(Fig. 2b)*.

Fig. 2a   **Fig. 2b**

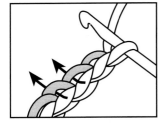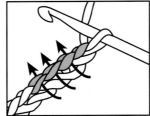

MAKING A BEGINNING RING

Chain amount indicated in instructions. Being careful not to twist chain, slip stitch in first chain to form a ring *(Fig. 3)*.

Fig. 3

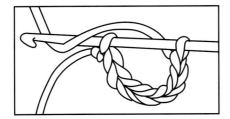

SINGLE CROCHET *(abbreviated sc)*

Insert hook in stitch or space indicated, YO and pull up a loop, YO and draw through both loops on hook *(Fig. 4)*.

Fig. 4

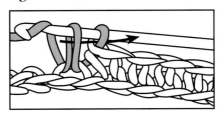

LONG STITCH

Work single crochet *(sc)* or double crochet *(dc)* inserting hook in stitch indicated in instructions *(Fig. 5)* and pulling up a loop even with loop on hook; complete as instructed.

Fig. 5

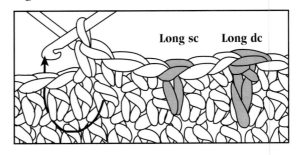

HALF DOUBLE CROCHET
(abbreviated hdc)

YO, insert hook in stitch or space indicated, YO and pull up a loop, YO and draw through all 3 loops on hook *(Fig. 6)*.

Fig. 6

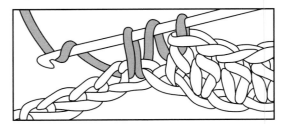

133

DOUBLE CROCHET *(abbreviated dc)*

YO, insert hook in stitch or space indicated, YO and pull up a loop, YO and draw through 2 loops on hook *(Fig. 7a)*, YO and draw through remaining 2 loops on hook *(Fig. 7b)*.

Fig. 7a

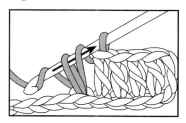

Fig. 7b

TREBLE CROCHET *(abbreviated tr)*

YO twice, insert hook in stitch or space indicated, YO and pull up a loop *(Fig. 8a)*, (YO and draw through 2 loops on hook) 3 times *(Fig. 8b)*.

Fig. 8a

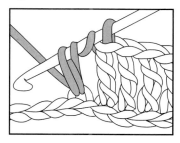

Fig. 8b

DOUBLE TREBLE CROCHET *(abbreviated dtr)*

YO three times, insert hook in stitch or space indicated, YO and pull up a loop *(Fig. 9a)*, (YO and draw through 2 loops on hook) 4 times *(Fig. 9b)*.

Fig. 9a

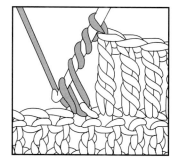

Fig. 9b

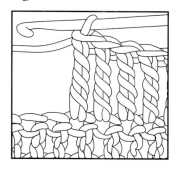

CLUSTER

A Cluster can be worked all in the same stitch or space *(Figs. 10a & b)*, **or** across several stitches *(Figs. 11a & b)*.

Fig. 10a

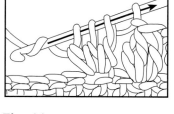

Fig. 10b

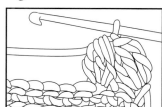

Fig. 11a

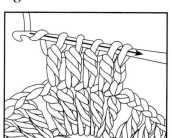

Fig. 11b

LOOP STITCH

Insert hook in next stitch, wrap yarn around index finger of left hand once **more**, insert hook through both loops on finger following direction indicated by arrow **(Fig. 12a)**, being careful to hook all loops **(Fig. 12b)**, draw through stitch pulling each loop as specified in instructions, remove finger from loop, YO and draw through all 3 loops on hook **(Loop St made, Fig. 12c)**.

Fig. 12a

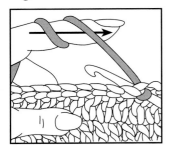

Fig. 12b

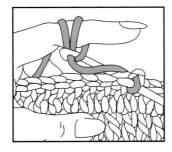

Fig. 12c

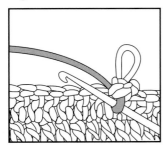

POST STITCH

Work around post of stitch indicated, inserting hook in direction of arrow **(Fig. 13)**.

Fig. 13

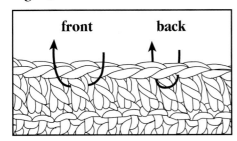

FRONT POST HALF DOUBLE CROCHET
(abbreviated FPhdc)

YO, insert hook from **front** to **back** around post of stitch indicated **(Fig. 13)**, YO and pull up a loop, YO and draw through all 3 loops on hook **(Fig. 14)**.

Fig. 14

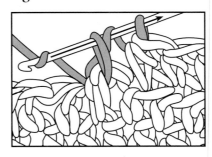

BACK POST HALF DOUBLE CROCHET
(abbreviated BPhdc)

YO, insert hook from **back** to **front** around post of stitch indicated **(Fig. 13)**, YO and pull up a loop, YO and draw through all 3 loops on hook **(Fig. 15)**.

Fig. 15

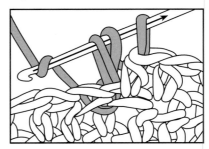

FRONT POST DOUBLE CROCHET
(abbreviated FPdc)

YO, insert hook from **front** to **back** around post of stitch indicated *(Fig. 13, page 135)*, YO and pull up a loop *(Fig. 16)*, (YO and draw through 2 loops on hook) twice.

Fig. 16

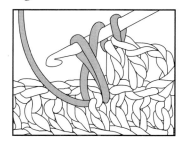

BACK POST DOUBLE CROCHET
(abbreviated BPdc)

YO, insert hook from **back** to **front** around post of stitch indicated *(Fig. 13, page 135)*, YO and pull up a loop *(Fig. 17)*, (YO and draw through 2 loops on hook) twice.

Fig. 17

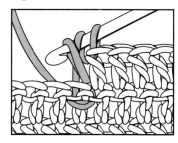

FRONT POST TREBLE CROCHET
(abbreviated FPtr)

YO twice, insert hook from **front** to **back** around post of stitch indicated *(Fig. 13, page 135)*, YO and pull up a loop *(Fig. 18)*, (YO and draw through 2 loops on hook) 3 times.

Fig. 18

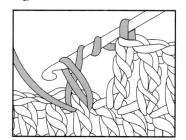

REVERSE SINGLE CROCHET
(abbreviated Reverse sc)

Working from **left** to **right**, insert hook in stitch to right of hook *(Fig. 19a)*, YO and draw through, under and to left of loop on hook (2 loops on hook) *(Fig. 19b)*, YO and draw through both loops on hook *(Fig. 19c)* (**Reverse sc made, Fig. 19d**).

Fig. 19a

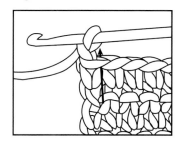

Fig. 19b

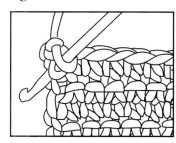

Fig. 19c

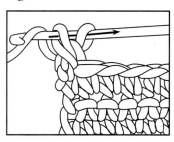

Fig. 19d

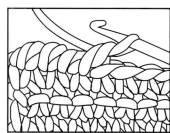

REVERSE HALF DOUBLE CROCHET
(abbreviated Reverse hdc)

Working from **left** to **right**, YO, insert hook in stitch indicated to right of hook *(Fig. 20a)*, YO and draw through, under and to left of loops on hook (3 loops on hook) *(Fig. 20b)*, YO and draw through all 3 loops on hook *(Fig. 20c)* (**Reverse hdc made, Fig. 20d**).

Fig. 20a

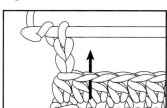

Fig. 20b

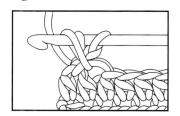

Fig. 20c

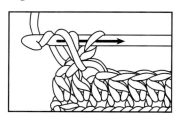

Fig. 20d

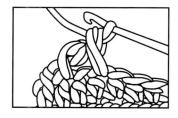

stitching tips

YARN

Yarn weight (type or size) is divided into four basic categories: **Fingering** (baby clothes), **Sport** (light-weight sweaters and afghans), **Worsted** (sweaters, afghans, toys), and **Bulky** (heavy sweaters, potholders, and afghans).

Baby yarn may either be classified as Fingering or Sport - check the label for the recommended gauge.

These weights have absolutely nothing to do with the number of plies. Ply refers to the number of strands that have been twisted together to make the yarn. There are fingering weight yarns consisting of four plies - and there are bulky weight yarns made of a single ply.

SUBSTITUTING YARN

Once you know the **weight** of the yarn specified for a particular pattern, **any** brand of the **same** weight may be used for that pattern.

You may wish to purchase a single skein first, and crochet a gauge swatch. Compare the gauge (remember, it **must** match the gauge in the pattern) and then compare the way the new yarn looks to the photographed item to be sure that you'll be satisfied with the finished results.

How many skeins to buy depends on the **yardage**. Compare the labels and don't hesitate to ask the shop owner for assistance. Ounces and grams can vary from one brand of the same weight yarn to another, but the yardage required to make a garment or item, in the size and pattern you've chosen, will always remain the same provided gauge is met and maintained.

DYE LOTS

Yarn is dyed in "lots" and then numbered. Different lots of the same color will vary slightly in shade and will be noticeable if crocheted in the same piece.

When buying yarn, it is important to check labels for the dye lot number. You should purchase enough of one color, from the same lot, to finish the entire project. It is a good practice to purchase an extra skein to be sure that you have enough to complete your project.

HOOKS

Crochet hooks used for working with **yarn** are made from aluminum, plastic, bone, or wood. They are lettered in sizes ranging from size B (2.25 mm) to the largest size Q (15.00 mm) - **the higher the letter, the larger the hook size**.

Crochet hooks used for **thread** work are most commonly made of steel. They are numbered in sizes ranging from size 00 (3.50 mm) to a very small size 14 (.75 mm) and, unlike aluminum hooks, **the higher the number, the smaller the hook size**.

HOW TO DETERMINE THE RIGHT SIDE

Many designs are made with the **front** of the stitch as the **right** side. Notice that the **front** of the stitches are smooth *(Fig. 21a)* and the **back** of the stitches are bumpy *(Fig. 21b)*. For easy identification, it may be helpful to loop a short piece of yarn, thread, or fabric around any stitch to mark **right** side.

Fig. 21a

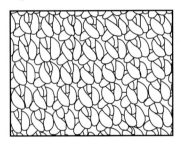

Fig. 21b

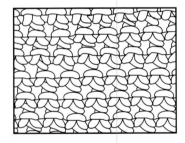

JOINING WITH SC

When instructed to join with sc, begin with a slip knot on hook. Insert hook in stitch or space indicated, YO and pull up a loop, yarn over and draw through both loops on hook.

MARKERS

Markers are used to help distinguish the beginning of each round being worked. Place a 2" scrap piece of yarn or fabric before the first stitch of each round, moving marker after each round is complete. Remove when no longer needed.

BACK OR FRONT LOOP ONLY

Work only in loop(s) indicated by arrow *(Fig. 22)*.

Fig. 22

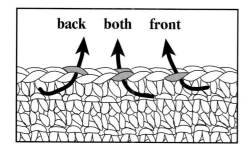

FREE LOOP

After working in Back or Front Loops Only on a row or round, there will be a ridge of unused loops. These are called the free loops. Later, when instructed to work in the free loops of the same row or round, work in these loops *(Fig. 23a)*. When instructed to work in a free loop of a beginning chain, work in loop indicated by arrow *(Fig. 23b)*.

Fig. 23a

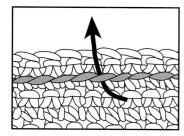

Fig. 23b

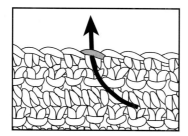

CHANGING COLORS

Work the last stitch to within one step of completion, hook new yarn *(Fig. 24a)* and draw through loops on hook. Cut old yarn and work over both ends unless otherwise specified. When working in rounds, drop old yarn and join with slip stitch to first stitch using new yarn *(Fig. 24b)*.

Fig. 24a

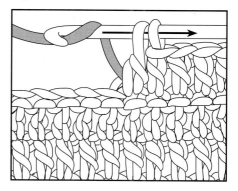

Fig. 24b

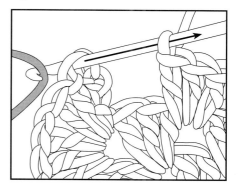

WORKING OVER WIRE

Place wire against chain or row indicated. Work stitches indicated over wire *(Fig. 25)*.

Fig. 25

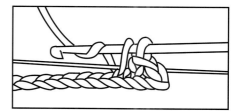

PREPARING FABRIC STRIPS

Fabric selected should be high quality, even weave 100% cotton, such as those sold for piecing quilts. Yardages given are based on fabrics 44/45" wide.

If the fabric is not pre-shrunk, it should be gently machine washed and dried. Straighten your fabric by pulling it across the bias. It may be necessary to lightly press the fabric.

To avoid joining strips often, we recommend that your strips be two yards or longer.

TEARING STRIPS

Tear off selvages, then tear into strips as instructed.

CUTTING STRIPS

1. Fold the fabric in half, short end to short end, as many times as possible, while still being able to cut through all thicknesses *(Fig. 26a)*.

Fig. 26a

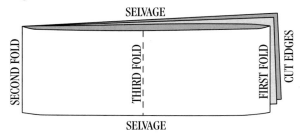

2. Cut off selvages, then cut fabric into 1" wide strips *(Fig. 26b)*. For quick results, a rotary cutter and mat may be used to cut several layers of fabric at one time.

Fig. 26b

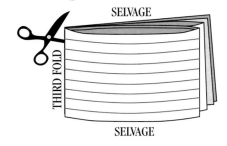

JOINING FABRIC STRIPS

The following is a technique for joining fabric strips without sewing strips together, and eliminates knots or ends to weave in later.

1. To join a new strip of fabric to working strip, cut a ½" slit, about ½" from ends of both fabric strips *(Fig. 27a)*.

Fig. 27a

2. With **right** sides up, place end of new strip over end of working strip and match slits *(Fig. 27b)*.

Fig. 27b

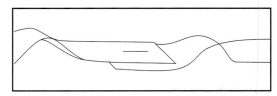

3. Pull free end of new strip through both slits from bottom to top *(Fig. 27c)*.

Fig. 27c

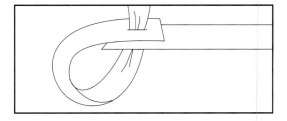

4. Pull new strip firmly to form a small knot *(Fig. 27d)*. Right sides of both strips should be facing up. Continue working with new strip.

Fig. 27d

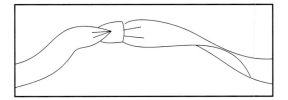

finishing

MAKING PILLOW FORM

Using crocheted piece for pattern, cut two pieces of fabric, allowing ¼" for seam allowance.

With **right** sides together, sew seam leaving a 2" opening for turning.

Turn form right side out; stuff firmly and sew opening closed.

WASHING AND BLOCKING

For a more professional look, thread projects should be washed and blocked. Using a mild detergent and warm water and being careful not to rub, twist, or wring, gently squeeze suds through the piece. Rinse several times in cool, clear water. Roll piece in a clean terry towel and gently press out the excess moisture. Lay piece on a flat surface and shape to proper size; where needed, pin in place using stainless steel pins. Allow to dry **completely**. Doilies can be spray starched for extra crispness.

WHIPSTITCH

With **wrong** sides together, and beginning in corner stitch, sew through both pieces once to secure the beginning of the seam, leaving an ample yarn end to weave in later. Insert needle from **front** to **back** through **both** loops of **each** piece *(Fig. 28a)* or through **inside** loops *(Fig. 28b)*. Bring needle around and insert it from **front** to **back** through the next loops of **both** pieces. Continue in this manner across to corner, keeping the sewing yarn fairly loose.

Fig. 28a

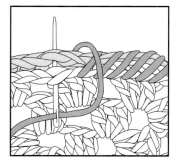

Fig. 28b

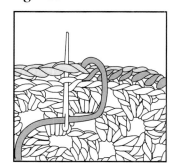

POM-POM

Cut a piece of cardboard 3" wide and as long as the diameter of your finished pom-pom is to be.

Wind the yarn around the cardboard until it is approximately ½" thick in the middle *(Fig. 29a)*.

Carefully slip the yarn off the cardboard and firmly tie an 18" length of yarn around the middle *(Fig. 29b)*. Leave yarn ends long enough to attach the pom-pom.

Cut the loops on both ends and trim the pom-pom into a smooth ball.

Fig. 29a

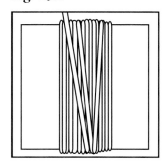

Fig. 29b

FRINGE

Cut a piece of cardboard 8" wide and half as long as specified in instructions for finished strands. Wind the yarn **loosely** and **evenly** around the cardboard until the card is filled, then cut across one end; repeat as needed. Hold the number of strands specified for one knot together and fold in half.

With **wrong** side facing and using a crochet hook, draw the folded end up through a row or stitch and pull the loose ends through the folded end *(Fig. 30a)*; draw the knot up **tightly** *(Fig. 30b)*. Repeat, spacing as specified. Lay flat on a hard surface and trim the ends.

Fig. 30a

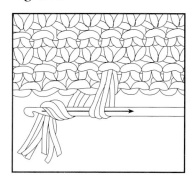

Fig. 30b

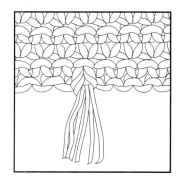

TURKEY LOOP STITCH

This stitch is composed of locked loops. Bring needle up through a stitch and back down through same stitch *(Point A)* forming a loop on **right** side of work. Bring needle up to either side of loop *(Point B)*, and back down through Point A locking stitch. Begin next stitch at Point B *(Fig. 31)*.

Fig. 31

OUTLINE STITCH

Bring needle up from wrong side at 1, leaving an end to be woven in later. Holding yarn or floss **above** the needle with thumb, insert needle down at 2 and up again at 3 (halfway between 1 and 2) *(Fig. 32a)*, pull through. Insert needle down at 4 and up again at 2, making sure the yarn or floss is **above** the needle *(Fig. 32b)*, pull through. Continue in same manner.

Fig. 32a   **Fig. 32b**

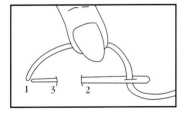 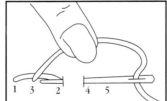

STRAIGHT STITCH

Straight Stitch is just what the name implies, a single, straight stitch. Bring needle up at 1 and go down at 2 *(Fig. 33)*. Continue in same manner.

Fig. 33

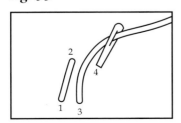

SATIN STITCH

Satin Stitch is a series of straight stitches worked side by side so they touch but do not overlap. Bring needle up at odd numbers and go down at even numbers *(Fig. 34)*.

Fig. 34

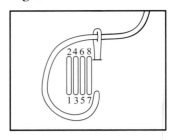

BLANKET STITCH

Bring needle up from wrong side at 1, even with edge of felt and leaving an end to be woven in later. Insert needle down at 2 and up again at 3, keeping floss below point of needle *(Fig. 35a)*. Continue in same manner, keeping stitches even *(Fig. 35b)*.

Fig. 35a   **Fig. 35b**

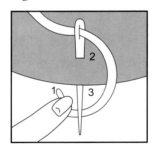 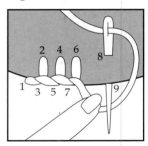

BACKSTITCH

Working from right to left, bring needle up at 1 leaving an end to be woven in later, go down at 2 and come up at 3 *(Fig. 36a)*. The second stitch is made by going down at 1 and coming up at 4 *(Fig. 36b)*. Continue in same manner.

Fig. 36a   **Fig. 36b**

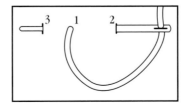 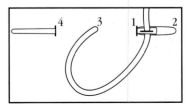

FRENCH KNOT

Bring needle up at 1. Wrap yarn desired number of times around needle and go down at 2, holding end of yarn with non-stitching fingers *(Fig. 37)*. Tighten knot; then pull needle through, holding yarn until it must be released.

Fig. 37

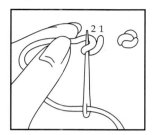

LAZY DAISY STITCH

Make all loops equal in length. Bring needle up at 1 and make a counterclockwise loop with the yarn. Go down at 1 and come up at 2, keeping the yarn below the point of the needle *(Fig. 38)*. Secure loop by bringing thread over loop and down at 3. Repeat for the desired number of petals or leaves.

Fig. 38

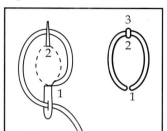

KEY

■	Satin Stitch
⟋	Lazy Daisy stitch
⁄	Outline stitch
╱	Straight stitch
●	French Knots
	Blue
	Dark Blue
	Green
	Pink
	Yellow

Fold

STARCHING & BLOCKING

TIPS

1. If using the same fabric stiffener for both white and colored items, starch the white items first, in case thread dye should bleed into the solution.
2. A good blocking board can make pinning easier. You can use heavy cardboard, an ironing board, ceiling board, etc.
3. Stainless steel pins with balls on the end will be easier to use and will help keep fingers from hurting. Fabric stiffener will permanently damage pins used for sewing. These can be set aside for all starching projects.
4. Fabric stiffener can be returned to the bottle after starching if it has not been contaminated with particles and dye. Clip one corner of the bag, then squeeze the bag, forcing the solution to flow into the bottle.
5. An acrylic spray can be used after starching to protect the piece from heat and humidity.

STARCHING

Read the following instructions before beginning.

1. Wash item using a mild detergent and warm water. Rinse thoroughly. Roll each piece in a clean terry towel and gently press out the excess moisture. Lay piece flat and allow to dry **completely**.
2. Pour fabric stiffener in a resealable plastic bag. Do not dilute stiffener. *Note:* This method is permanent and will not wash out.
3. Immerse dry piece in fabric stiffener, remove air, and seal the bag. Work solution thoroughly into each piece. Let soak for several hours or overnight.

BLOCKING

Good blocking techniques make a big difference in the quality of the finished piece. When pinning piece be careful not to split the threads when inserting pins between the stitches. Make sure curved parts are smooth, straight parts are straight and symmetrical components are equal. Use photo as a guide and use a generous quantity of pins to hold all of the components in place until dry.

Refer to further instructions on this page for specific projects.

SUNFLOWER BASKET

1. Remove Basket from solution and squeeze gently to remove as much excess stiffener as possible. Blot with a paper towel several times to remove excess from holes.
2. With **right** side facing, pin bottom of Basket through Rnd 11 to plastic covered blocking board, forming a 9" circle.
3. Place a 9" plastic foam ring covered with plastic wrap into Basket, or use plastic wrap to create a ring. Curve Petals upward and pin in place.
4. Allow to dry **completely**.

RUFFLED MINI TREE

1. Using heavy cardboard, form a cone that is pointed at top, 17" in height and 8 1/2" in diameter at base. Tape along edge to secure and cover with plastic wrap.
2. Remove Tree from solution and squeeze gently to remove as much excess stiffener as possible. Blot with a paper towel several times to remove excess from holes.
3. Place Tree over cone and pin at regular intervals. Working with one Layer at a time, shape each into evenly spaced ruffles, stuffing each ruffle with plastic wrap to hold its shape; pin in place.
4. Allow to dry **completely**.
5. Apply protective coating to protect and preserve Tree after starching.

PROTECTIVE COATING

1. Remove Tree from cardboard cone. Cover cone with waxed paper.
2. Wearing gloves and using a paintbrush, apply a light coat of porcelain glaze to entire surface. Remember to check and remove drips periodically.
3. Allow to dry **completely**.

A second coat may be applied only after first coat is **completely** dry.

Note: To **wash** Tree, rinse in cool or lukewarm water, then pat dry. Tree can be reshaped if necessary by using a hair dryer and shaping after area is warm. Allow to cool before using.

credits

We extend a warm *thank you* to the generous people who allowed us to photograph some of our projects at their homes: *Wrapped Up in Afghans* — Susan Wildung, Joan Gould, Nancy Gunn Porter, and Gail Wilcox. *All Through the House* — Shirley Held. *Gifts for All* — Nancy Gunn Porter. *Hooked on Holidays* — LaJauna Hernin.

To Magna IV Color Imaging of Little Rock, Arkansas, we say thank you for the superb color reproduction and excellent pre-press preparation. We want to especially thank photographers Larry Pennington, Ken West, Karen Shirey, and Mark Mathews of Peerless Photography, Little Rock, Arkansas, and Jerry R. Davis of Jerry Davis Photography, Little Rock, Arkansas, for their time, patience, and excellent work.

A special word of thanks goes to the talented designers who created the lovely projects in this book:

Linda Bailey: *Ruffled Mini Tree*, page 124
Mary Lamb Becker: *Pretty in Peach*, page 24, and
    Cheery Tree Skirt, page 126
Dianne Bee: *Sunflower Basket*, page 67
Joan Beebe: *Darling Bubble Suits*, page 88
Rose Marie Brooks: *Downy-Soft Afghans*, page 86
Christina Romo Carlisle: *Tops for Toddlers*, page 105
Maureen Egan Emlet: *Patchwork Sampler*, page 6
Nancy Fuller: *Kid-Pleasing Plaid Afghan*, page 64
Shobha Govindan: *Pretty Pillows*, page 44;
    Lacy Coaster, page 47; *Pincushion Bonnet,* page 69;
    and *Cross Bookmarks*, page 112
Anne Halliday: *Snowflake Sachets*, page 128
Cindy Harris: *Four-Season Fridgies*, page 76;
    Political Mascots, page 115; and *Boo Kitty*, page 118
Jan Hatfield: *Happy Housewarming!*, page 51
Alice Heim: *Elegant Handkerchief*, page 57
Carol L. Jensen: *Feminine Scarf*, page 97
Terry Kimbrough: *Shell Jar Topper*, page 32; *Shell Basket*,
    page 32; *Shell Towel Edging*, page 33; *Shell Rug*, page 33;
    Pansy Garden Afghan, page 36; *Pansy Sachet*, page 39;
    Petite Tissue Cover, page 52; *Mallard Jar Topper*, page 58;
    and *Poppy Pot Holder*, page 75
Jennine Korejko: *Snuggly Wraps*, page 12, and
    Slippers for Kids, page 101
Tammy Kreimeyer: *Playtime Dinosaur*, page 72, and
    Sweetheart Frames, page 108

Melissa Leapman: *Building Blocks Quilt*, page 10
Jean Leffler: *Baby Brother*, page 54
Linda Luder: *For Tiny Toes*, page 85
Kay Meadors: *Delicate Cardigan*, page 94, and
    Tulip Garden Sweatshirt, page 103
Sue Penrod: *Pansy Basket Tissue Cover*, page 38,
    and *Haunting Magnets*, page 120
Carole Prior: *Filet Ripples*, page 18, and *Merry Afghan*,
    page 131
Mary Jane Protus: *Brown-Eyed Susans*, page 20, and
    Handsome Stripes, page 22
Delsie Rhoades: *Pineapple Table Topper*, page 28;
    Flowerpot Lace, page 48; *Tulip Doily*, page 60;
    and *Wheat Doily*, page 122
Katherine Satterfield Robert: *Frilly Napkin Ring
    and Place Mat Edging*, page 42
Donna Scully: *His-and-Hers Pullovers*, page 99
Rena Stevens: *Bold Appeal*, page 16
C. Strohmeyer: *Floral Ensemble Bottle Cover*, page 93
Gail Tanquary: *Country Bread Cloth*, page 62
Carole Rutter Tippett: *Lacy Hexagons*, page 14
Beth Ann Webber: *Cuddly Set*, page 80
Maggie Weldon: *Casserole Cozy*, page 42, and
    Cutlery Caddy, page 43
Margie Wicker: *Baby's Bible Cover*, page 83
Mary Workman: *Colorful Bag Rug*, page 70

We extend a sincere *thank you* to the people who assisted in making and testing the projects for this book: Janet Akins, Anitta Armstrong, Jennie Black, June Clevenger, Helga Christensen, Liz Edmondson, Lee Ellis, Patricia Funk, Linda Graves, Naomi Greening, Raymelle Greening, Jean Hall, Kathleen Hardy, Lisa Hightower, Maedean Johnson, Frances Moore-Kyle, Ruth Landon, Ruby Lee, Pat Little, Faye Morgan, Carol McElroy, Sandy Pique, Dale Potter, Hilda Rivero, Rondi Rowell, Linda Shock, Donna Soellner, Faith Stewart, Bill Tanner, Carol Thompson, and Sherry Williams.